Advance Praise for *Casting the Buddha*

'India's many Buddhist monuments remind us that the Buddha was born here, attained enlightenment, and taught here for more than forty years. This book places these monuments in a social, geographical and spiritual context, showing that compassion, non-violence and the pursuit of peace of mind are keys to leading a happy and meaningful life' **His Holiness the Dalai Lama**

'[Shashank Shekhar Sinha's] well-written and carefully researched book offers a fresh, thoughtful look at Buddhism and its monuments in India. The multi-pronged approach enriches our understanding of the historical record, while the focus on a select number of key monuments adds much-needed depth' **Susan L. Huntington, Distinguished University Professor Emerita, Ohio State University**

'Shashank Shekhar Sinha narrates the exciting story of Buddhism in South Asia, including its early history, decline and reinvention in more recent times, with a special focus on monuments, images and material remains. His account is scholarly and at the same time wonderfully engaging and accessible' **Upinder Singh, Professor of History, Ashoka University, and author of** *A History of Ancient and Early Medieval India*

'Shashank Shekhar Sinha's writing breathes life into Buddhist monuments through well-researched narratives across time and space. He explains the philosophies of the communities that built, worshipped and maintained these sites, while also offering a historical context for the development of Buddhism well into the modern period' **Himanshu Prabha Ray, former chairperson, National Monuments Authority, and author of** *Archaeology and Buddhism in South Asia*

'[Shashank Shekhar Sinha] should be congratulated for having successfully collated key case studies and theories within the archaeology of Buddhism for a general audience, and for having distilled the writings of scholars within these fields in an accessible manner' **Julia Shaw, Associate Professor, South Asian Archaeology, University College London, Institute of Archaeology**

Praise for *Delhi, Agra, Fatehpur Sikri*

'The book fuses together heritage conservation and history in a very impressive manner ... It will enrich the understanding of those interested in the history not only about these buildings but also more widely about historical monuments and their preservation' **Rudrangshu Mukherjee, Chancellor and Professor of History, Ashoka University**

'The first real attempt to bring historical sites and buildings of the past within the reach of the masses ... Interestingly, all the "facts" are laid before you without taking a particular position when dealing with controversies surrounding the sites and their afterlife. A must-read for all' **Syed Ali Nadeem Rezavi, Professor of History, Aligarh Muslim University, and author of** *Fathpur Sikri Revisited*

'Monuments are a window into our heritage and past. Given the increasing interest in history and reliance on non-academic sources, it is imperative to locate the monuments in their larger historical contexts. This is where Shashank Shekhar Sinha scores, and authoritatively. From the conception of the monuments to their afterlives, Sinha skilfully connects the dots for the viewers and the readers, in accessible language. His multilayered, multidimensional history of three imperial cities and six World Heritage Sites offers an excellent academic–public interface for the study of monuments, the cities in which they are located, and their extended geocultural connections' **Rana Safvi, author of** *The Forgotten Cities of Delhi*

'A book to be read several times, in different ways – a guide to six UNESCO World Heritage Sites, a work on the history of Sultanate and Mughal architecture and urbanism, and a survey of the important scholarly debates in history and conservation, rendered in an easy-to-read form' **Swapna Liddle, author of** *Connaught Place and the Making of New Delhi*

'Captivating ... rare ... *Delhi, Agra, Fatehpur Sikri* catches you by the collar and takes you around familiar sites once again, leaving you with a brand-new perspective ... One reads the book as one would read a thriller – from start to finish!' *Hindu BusinessLine*

'A tour de force ... serves a three-fold function: as a guidebook with academic heft, a corrective to many misconceptions and myths, and a summation of interesting academic and "public history" questions surrounding six of the most iconic heritage monuments in India ... essential reading for those who plan to visit these iconic monuments as well as for those who would like to have a glance at a textured, multilayered history of medieval India' *Telegraph*

CASTING THE
BUDDHA

Shashank Shekhar Sinha is an independent researcher, publisher and author, known for his expertise in monuments, heritage, Adivasi studies, gender issues and witch hunting. He taught history at undergraduate colleges in the University of Delhi for nearly a decade (1994–2004) and later worked at Oxford University Press (2004–2012) before becoming Publishing Director at Routledge (South Asia), part of the Taylor & Francis Group, in 2012.

Sinha regularly contributes to academic journals and books. He writes a series of articles on UNESCO World Heritage Sites in *Frontline* magazine, and on the politics of heritage for the *Wire*. Sinha has featured on television programmes discussing history and heritage, on channels such as AajTak, Rajya Sabha TV (now Sansad TV), News 18 and NDTV 24x7. He is the author of *Delhi, Agra, Fatehpur Sikri* and *Restless Mothers and Turbulent Daughters*, and co-editor of *Gender in Modern India*.

ALSO BY SHASHANK SHEKHAR SINHA

Delhi, Agra, Fatehpur Sikri

FORTHCOMING IN THE MAGNIFICENT HERITAGE SERIES

Temples of South India

MAGNIFICENT HERITAGE SERIES

CASTING THE BUDDHA

A MONUMENTAL HISTORY OF BUDDHISM IN INDIA

SHASHANK SHEKHAR SINHA

MACMILLAN

First published in India 2024 by Macmillan
an imprint of Pan Macmillan Publishing India Private Limited
707 Kailash Building
26 K. G. Marg, New Delhi 110001
www.panmacmillan.co.in

Pan Macmillan, The Smithson, 6 Briset Street, Farringdon, London EC1M 5NR
Associated companies throughout the world
www.panmacmillan.com

ISBN 978-93-6113-385-5

Copyright © Shashank Shekhar Sinha 2024

The moral rights of the author have been asserted.

The views expressed in this book are the author's own and the facts reported by him have been verified by the publisher to the extent possible. The publisher hereby disclaims any liability to any party for loss, damages or disruptions caused by the same.

All rights reserved. No part of this publication may be reproduced, stored in or introduced into a retrieval system, or transmitted, in any form, or by any means (electronic, mechanical, photocopying, recording or otherwise) without the prior written permission of the publisher. Any person who does any unauthorized act in relation to this publication may be liable to criminal prosecution and civil claims for damages.

Any person who does any unauthorized act in relation to this publication may be liable to criminal prosecution and civil claims for damages.

1 3 5 7 9 8 6 4 2

This book is sold subject to the condition that it shall not, by way of trade or otherwise, be lent, re-sold, hired out, or otherwise circulated without the publisher's prior consent in any form of binding or cover other than that in which it is published and without a similar condition including this condition being imposed on the subsequent purchaser.

Typeset in Dante MT Std by R. Ajith Kumar, New Delhi
Printed and bound in India by Thomson Press India Ltd.

For Babuji, and the conversations we could not have

CONTENTS

A Note on the Series   xiii
Introduction: Framing Buddhist Monuments   1

PART I: MONUMENTS, ARTEFACTS AND CONNECTED HISTORIES

1. The Buddha Comes into Being   19
2. Emergence of Relic Cult, Stupas and Pillars   43
3. The Rise of Images, Monastic Complexes and Popular Cults   60
4. Efflorescence and Spread amidst Brahmanical Revival   93
5. Tantric Infusion, Regionalization and Decline   121

PART II: UNESCO WORLD HERITAGE SITES

6. Bodh Gaya and the Mahabodhi Temple Complex   159
7. Sanchi and the Hilltop Stupa Complex   190
8. Ajanta Caves   218
9. Nalanda Mahavihara   247

PART III: THE RETURN OF THE BUDDHA

10. The Buddha Makes a Comeback   285
11. Buddhism 2.0   299

Author's Note   319
Image Credits   325
Notes   332
Index   358

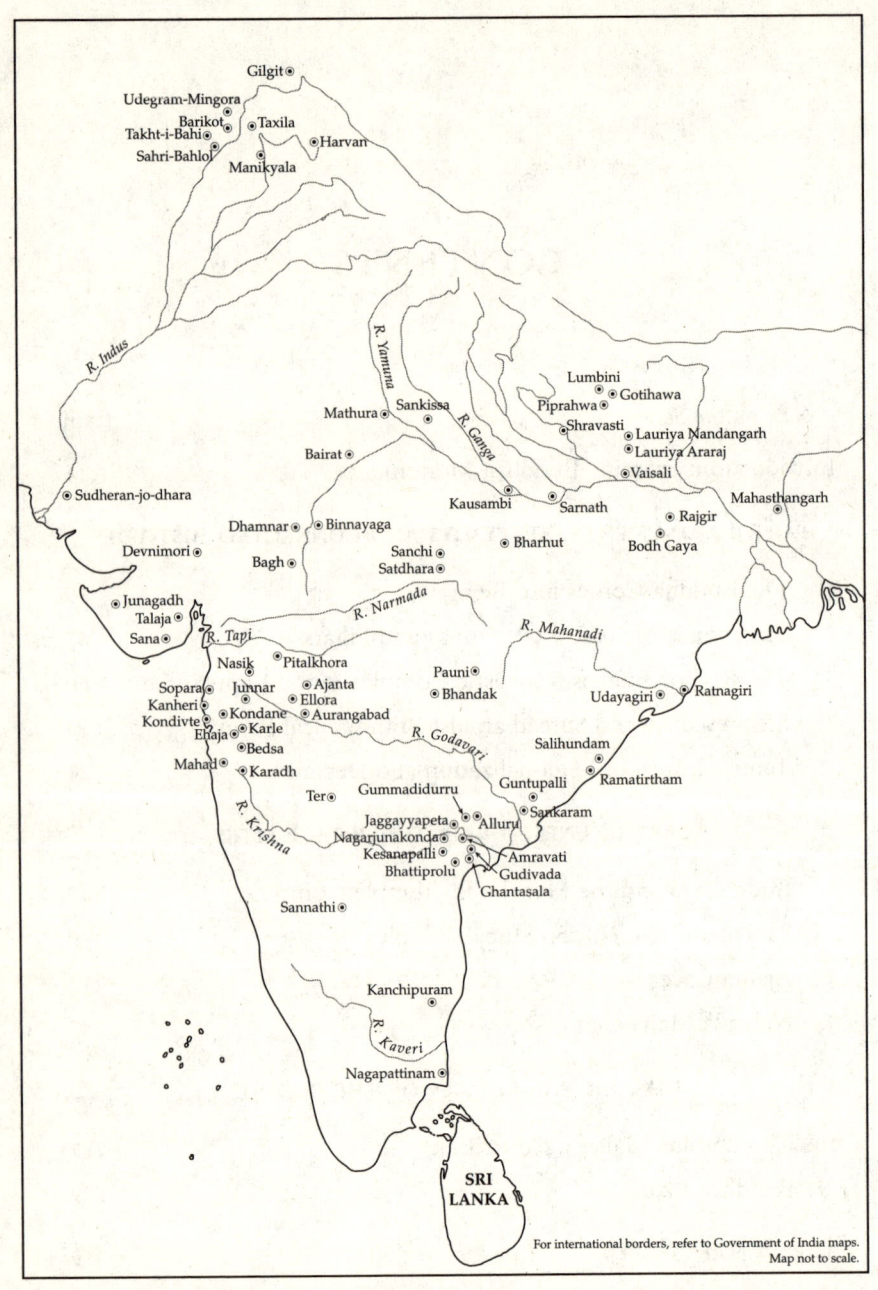

Map depicting the distribution of Buddhist sites in India (after Himanshu Prabha Ray, *Archaeology and Buddhism in South Asia*, 2017)

A NOTE ON THE SERIES

Departing from existing studies on the subject, this series looks at heritage sites and the cities in which they are located in their larger geographical, sociocultural and historical contexts. It brings together latest and complex academic research from across disciplines, including history, archaeology, architecture, art history and heritage studies and presents it in an accessible form. Addressing the gap between the academic and popular understandings of history, the series discusses how stereotypes, assumptions and myths come into being around monuments and their builders, and how they impact our reading of the related historical periods.

Each volume in the series provides a multilayered and multidimensional account of the evolution of monuments, their architectural details, the life and times of those who built them, their afterlives, anecdotes and folklore surrounding them as well as debates and controversies related to the heritage sites. They also contain comprehensive, illustrated and self-sufficient chapters on the UNESCO World Heritage Sites in the respective geocultural region.

The books in the series will form essential reads for teachers, students and scholars of history, archaeology, architecture, art history, heritage studies and tourism and hospitality. Authoritative and accessible, they will be indispensable for tourists, foreign and domestic, and heritage enthusiasts. Finally, architects, conservationists, policymakers, think tanks and organizations working on monuments and heritage cities will also find these volumes very useful.

INTRODUCTION

Framing Buddhist Monuments

Casting the Buddha presents an illustrated history of Buddhist monuments in India, spanning 2,500 years. In doing so, it also outlines the evolution of Buddhism in the region. The term 'monumental history' is derived from the Latin word *monumentum*, meaning a memorial, image, trophy, building, or more broadly, a monument that serves as a reminder of past actors or events. For the purposes of this book, 'monumental history' plays on the word 'monument' and discusses Buddhist edifices, sites and connected histories in this context.

While the major focus of the book is on buildings and structures, it also explores tangible representations of the Buddha and artefacts related to him, such as sculptures, images, votive stupas (also described as burial ad sanctos), paintings, tablets, miniature images, shrines and steles. In a way, it offers an examination of the different material forms – direct, symbolic or extended – in which the 'Enlightened One' was cast.

Does the book document every Buddhist monument in India? No, it does not. Such an exhaustive catalogue would be impossible within the finite scope of this work. Instead, it examines representative monuments to highlight broader trends and patterns. The chapters uncover hidden layers, complexities, intersections and variations across time and space. They reveal how the lives of the monuments closely resonated with those of the people and communities surrounding them – monks, laity, kings, traders, guilds, occupational groups, landlords, agriculturists and villagers. Over time, these structures acquired different meanings and forms, even after their primary builders were long gone and they were no longer in active use.

Another striking feature is the way the book links philosophical and doctrinal developments with architecture. It shows how buildings, along with connected sculptures and artefacts, evolve in relation to changes within the Buddhist faith and its rituals. This evolution is not just limited to developments within the Buddhist faith, but also in Hinduism, Jainism, popular cults and other renunciatory and ascetic traditions. With these layers in mind, the book proposes a new framework for studying such monuments.

HOW THIS BOOK IS DIFFERENT

Books about Buddhist monuments in India are few and far between. Most books expound on the Buddha's life and times, his teachings, Buddhist sects, philosophical schools and metaphysics. They are based almost exclusively on textual sources. Among those connected with monuments, a couple of notable works are Percy Brown's *Indian Architecture: Buddhist and Hindu Periods* (1956) and Sukumar Dutt's *Buddhist Monks and Monasteries of India* (1962),[1] both of which focus on architecture or a category of monuments. In fact, the first book to address the subject directly was Debala Mitra's *Buddhist Monuments* (1971).[2] With an archaeological orientation, it provided a contemporary overview of Buddhist monuments. Now, of course, it has become a bit dated, both in terms of coverage and treatment.

In addition to these broader works, there are guides published on individual Buddhist monuments by the Archaeological Survey of India (ASI). These are quite informative and offer a basic outline of the monuments at a particular site. Unfortunately, most of these guidebooks are not updated periodically, which means the research is quite outdated. Outside of the ASI, there are few good guidebooks available. Most works that help to form our understanding of monuments, be it academic or guidebooks, focus on physicality – the buildings, the structures, the sculptures and the architecture. Sometimes, they also use technical language that can be intimidating to non-specialists.

In the last few decades, the study of monuments has been enriched by the publication of books on art history and architecture, such as Vidya Dehejia's *Discourses in Early Buddhist Art* (1997) and some others.[3] These go beyond the physicality of the monuments to explore the stories surrounding them. Even the books on the archaeology of Buddhist monuments extended their scope to include contemporary social, economic and ritual contexts, besides the networks of relationships between the cities and their hinterlands, the wider historical landscapes and divergences between early precept and practice. In this context, the study of monastic complexes has been significantly enriched by the shift from site-based analysis to studies of the broader landscape setting, as in the case of Sanchi. Another noteworthy development has been the application of remote sensing and GIS, as in the case of Nalanda.[4]

This book presents an accessible macrohistory of Buddhist monuments in India using a more inclusive and holistic framework. Accordingly, the monuments come across as complex ecosystems where buildings, images, sculptures, builders, empires, dynasties, cities, monks, sects, merchants, guilds and communities coexist with beliefs systems, stories, folklore and ritual practices. The book humanizes the monuments, depicting them as sites of social and cultural interactions. My multi-pronged conceptual framework for studying monuments has five overlapping components: the larger geocultural connections, the relationship between the 'part' and the 'whole', the links between the 'tangible' and the 'intangible', the human and extended human connection, and the afterlife. Together, these components offer a multilayered and multidimensional study of Buddhist monumental heritage. This framework not only builds upon updated academic research from disciplines like history, archaeology, art history, architecture, cultural history and heritage studies, but also incorporates popular history and folklore. Let us try and understand these components in some detail, and through examples that are available in plenty.

Let us examine the first component, which is related to a site's larger geocultural connections. These help to understand its less-studied connections with other geographies and cultures, thereby expanding its historical canvas.

Bodh Gaya offers a brilliant example. After its decline, around the 12th to 13th centuries, life-sized replicas of the Mahabodhi temple were built in many countries in East and South Asia, such as Myanmar,

Thailand, China, Sri Lanka and Nepal. Many miniature stone shrines were also circulated, which can now be found in museums across the world. These models served as substitutes for actual physical travel to the site. Viewing the miniature replicas was treated like a virtual pilgrimage, particularly when visiting the actual site of enlightenment of Siddhartha Gautama, the Buddha, was uncertain.

The act of trying to associate with sacred and important Buddhist sites had other manifestations. In the case of Nalanda, kings from faraway lands, such as Harshavardhana of Kannauj (present-day Uttar Pradesh), Bhaskaravarman of Assam and Balaputra of Suvarnadvipa (broadly refers to the region of lower Myanmar, the Malay Peninsula, and Sumatra or a part of it), supported or constructed structures and/or gave substantive endowments for their maintenance.

The second point, about the 'part' and the 'whole', has to do with the relationship between individual or small structures, or artefacts, with the larger monument site in question. The iron pillar in the Qutb Minar complex, for instance, is now a part of the Qutb structure. But the pillar's own journey and life has added to the complex history of the site.

In the Buddhist context, the museumization (removal of many sculptures from temples and monuments by colonial officials and their subsequent placement in museums to showcase Buddhist art) of sculptures can serve as an interesting example. It is important to keep in mind that these sculptures once formed an integral part of the sacred geography of the sites concerned. They need to be studied with other tangible and intangible components. Images recovered from Nalanda, for instance, can now be found in museums in Patna, Kolkata and New Delhi, and around the world in countries like Germany and the United States of America. The votive stupas containing relics or mortuary deposits of monks, at sites like Sanchi, Sarnath, Bodh Gaya, Nalanda, Ratnagiri and Paharpur, are another example. Erected by people belonging to different geographies and backgrounds, they speak of the importance attached to the monastic dead and the larger funerary associations of the monuments concerned.

The third element encompasses the role of various intangible factors in the making of a monument complex. These may include the role of folktales, legends and ritual practices besides unseen factors like trade, migrations, movements, etc.

An interesting part of Buddhism, and some other religious traditions, is how the intangible becomes tangible. Stories, folklore, legends and mythology become part of a sacred core of beliefs, taking the form of sculptures, images or artefacts. For instance, the sculptured panels on the gateways of Sanchi not only depict events from the life of the Buddha but also the Jataka tales and the mythical bodhisattvas. Similarly, mythical deities related to popular cults, like those of serpents (*nagas* and *nagis*) or nature and fertility spirits (*yakshas* and *yakshis*), are also depicted in tangible forms at Sanchi, Nagarjunakonda and Ajanta.

Ritual practices also play a role in this context. *Dharanis* – texts concerned with the problem of death, avoidance of rebirth in hell and other unfortunate destinies – were inscribed on stone slabs and placed inside stupas to grant the structures new ritual meanings. Such stupas can be found at Bodh Gaya, Nalanda, Paharpur and Ratnagiri. Dharanis were also inscribed on images at various monument complexes. Similarly, the fourteenth Dalai Lama's conduct of the *Kalachakra* ('Wheel of Time') ritual is believed to have recharged the monument complexes concerned, such as the one at Amravati (or Amaravati). Broadly speaking, Kalachakra initiation involves teaching of a set of practices aimed at transformation of one's mind and body to lead the person towards Buddhahood. This ritual was also accompanied by physical additions (such as raising the drum of the stupa or installing images of the Buddha and Mahayana philosopher Nagasena around the structure) as seen at Amravati.

The fourth factor, the human and extended human connection, includes the role of individual human beings, mostly influential or powerful; collectivities or networks of people; and human-led or guided entities and agencies. These may include the role of the state, dynasties or empires; kings, monks and merchants; and collectives like guilds, occupational groups and village communities.

In the Buddhist context, these intangibles help us appreciate the contributions of kings and queens such as Ashoka; Kanishka; Jayachandra; Govindachandra and his wife, Kumaradevi; the Ikshvaku queens of Nagarjunakonda and dynasties like the Satavahanas, Guptas and Vakatakas. They played a role in both the construction of monuments and the spread of Buddhism. A subsequent section will highlight the proactive role of the monks and nuns in establishing stupas, monasteries and images.

The fifth part, the afterlife, explores what happened to the monuments after their primary builders passed away. These include constructions or events happening in the aftermath which add new layers or meanings, rekindle memories, and prolong or institutionalize the memory of the site. Sometimes, these later constructions or events even become the dominant prisms through which the site is viewed.

In postcolonial India, for instance, many Asian countries with Buddhist inclinations have built their own temples and monasteries around the Mahabodhi temple complex. This has led to the 'Buddhification' of the surrounding landscape and from the 1960s–70s to the present. These new constructions have become an integral part of the Bodh Gaya experience.

Sanchi has also had interesting afterlives, but in different ways. I will cite just one example here. To institutionalize its memory and cultural value, replicas of the stupa were erected in buildings like the Rashtrapati Bhawan (the office and residence of the President of India) in New Delhi, the M. P. Birla Planetarium in Kolkata, Deekshabhoomi (the site of Ambedkar's conversion to Buddhism) in Nagpur and also in faraway lands like the Luoyang, which is situated in Henan province of China.

Interestingly, monumental histories do not just need to involve more inclusive frameworks but also engage with the text–archaeology dynamic – the two broad source categories for the study of any history. And here, one notices two interesting things: the monuments and artefacts appear earlier than the written texts; second, the archaeological remains sometimes showcase the difference between the precept and the practice.

HOW THE TEXT–ARCHAEOLOGY DYNAMIC WORKS

In Buddhism, a curious situation exists wherein practice (monuments and artefacts) predates theory (texts). Buddhist texts were first written in Pali around the early centuries of the Christian Era. Before this, the

Buddha's teachings were passed down through the oral tradition. It is said that sometime after his death, a general council (also known as the First Buddhist Council) was held in Rajgir (formerly Rajagriha), where some of his close disciples were asked to present his doctrines. For example, Upali was asked to compile the *vinaya* (rules for the monastic order), while Ananda was entrusted with explaining the *dharma* (the doctrine or teachings of the Buddha). Two more councils of this kind were held. The second was held a hundred years after the Buddha's death in Vaishali, while the third was convened by Mauryan emperor Ashoka (c. 268–32 BCE) in Pataliputra, which resulted in the further consolidation of the Buddhist canon. It was during such councils that the idea of the *bhanakas* (reciters who have been mentioned in inscriptions and Buddhist literature) was probably born. The Jataka bhanakas, for instance, specialized in memorizing and repeating the stories of the previous lives of the Buddha, while the *Dhammapada* bhanakas recited the *Dhammapada*, the book of moral maxims. Interestingly, while books and manuscripts are not explicitly mentioned, texts are frequently described as existing in the memory of those who had committed them to rote.[5]

The oral teachings of Buddhism were reportedly written down during the 1st century BCE. While the oral tradition was still in use during the time of Indo-Greek king Menander (also known as Milinda, 140–10 BCE), with the Buddhist text *Milindapanha* recording that the sage Nagasena had memorized the entire Tripitaka (comprising the *sutra/sutta, vinaya,* and *abhidhamma*) in three months. Most scholars agree that the oral canon transitioned to written form in the 1st century BCE. According to Sri Lankan chronicles, the canon was written there during the reign of King Vattagamini (29–17 BCE). It is likely that the texts were also compiled in Pali in India around the same time, during the second half of the century.

How does the Pali canon help us understand monuments and artefacts? It provides valuable insights into the geographical context and socio-economic conditions of the period it describes. Two key aspects stand out in this regard. First, sections of the Pali texts begin with the repeated use of the phrase *evam me sutam* (thus have I heard). This was possibly used to validate the authenticity of the teachings as they were passed down orally. Second, each discourse in the canon opens with a mention of the location where the Buddha was staying at the time, allowing scholars to anchor the teachings in a specific historical and geographical context. By understanding the places associated with the Buddha's teachings, they have been able to use early Buddhist texts to obtain a fairly reliable picture of the Buddha's life and times, corroborating them, wherever possible, from Brahmanical and Jaina scriptures.[6]

Where does this discussion lead us in relation to the earliest monuments? When the first Buddhist monuments were being adorned with stone railings and narrative sculptures, around 100 BCE, the Buddhist canon was yet to be penned down. This implies that the information base for the artists carving relief panels at the Bharhut stupa – which was completed during the reign of the Shungas (the dynasty ended in 72 BCE), according to available inscriptional evidence – was the oral tradition that was traditionally transmitted by the bhanakas. Inscribed sideways along the length of the relief pillars, the contemporary inscriptions of the Bharhut stupa, unlike the basement inscriptions on the 8th-century Borobudur stupa in Java, did not serve as instructions for the sculptors or artists. Instead, they served as inscribed captions to identify the monument or its parts, or as prompts for literate monks taking worshippers around the monument. What is intriguing is that when the Sanchi stupa was constructed half a century later, not even a single identifying label was found. Such inscribed captions were rarely used again in Buddhist art. The disappearance of such captions coincided with the canon coming into being.[7] The later inscriptions are more about donors. The information they provide sometimes significantly differs from the inferences we have drawn from the texts, which were regarded as supreme sources of knowledge.

HOW ARCHAEOLOGICAL REMAINS TELL A DIFFERENT STORY

Despite monuments predating the texts, most studies on Buddhism have historically focused on the textual sources. In chapter 10, we will see that even when the Europeans were discovering Buddhism in the 19th century, heavy emphasis was placed on the texts. Scholars suggested that to understand Buddhism, one should read the Pali texts of Sri Lanka, where they were first committed to writing, and the Sanskrit texts of Nepal, where they were preserved, copied and translated after the decline of Buddhism in India around the 12th–13th centuries.

It was often argued that archaeological and epigraphic remains served as 'handmaidens of literary sources' – meaning they could not act alone as independent evidence. Art, coins and inscriptions were seen as providing valuable information, but their full meaning was thought to be accessible only through the texts. Consequently, it was emphasized that these remains must not only 'support and amplify the literary sources' but also 'be supported and amplified by them'.[8] However, recent studies have begun to challenge the unquestioned supremacy of textual sources, offering compelling arguments that suggest archaeological and material evidence should be viewed as critical, independent witnesses to the past, rather than being secondary to the texts.

First, the textual sources are predominantly scriptural in nature – they are formal literary expressions of the normative doctrine, and they have less of a historical positioning. Second, contrary to the popular assumption that they were widely known, read and practised, a vast majority of the practising Buddhists, monks and laity were unfamiliar with them. Third, there is no actual evidence to suggest that the textual ideal was either fully or partially implemented in practice. Fourth, archaeological and epigraphic sources tell us more about religion as it was practised, as opposed to how it was preached. Fifth, and most importantly, the inscriptions and archaeological remains can and *do* tell us different stories as far as the study of monuments is concerned.[9] They also question certain established stereotypes in the study of Buddhism.

The texts project monks and nuns as renouncers par excellence who were exclusively concerned with spiritual pursuits and meditation. In such constructions, the laity were concerned with ritual practices and institutions termed as 'popular'. These included donations to Buddhist establishments, accumulation of merit, setting up of stupas and monasteries and carrying out rituals for deceased relatives. When the inscriptions are read closely, such monk–laity distinctions appear untenable. In chapters 3 and 4, we shall see how monks and nuns, like the learned ones and teachers, served as active donors and contributed proactively to the setting up of stupas or the production and distribution of images. In the chapter on Sanchi, the monks come across as taking an active part in disposing of the monastic dead. In addition, the findings on irrigation dams and sculptures associated with the popular cults at Sanchi, for instance, tell us how the monks used such methods to spread the teachings of dharma. In the case of Ajanta (chapter 8), the monks appear to have been owners of wealth and sponsors of caves and sculptures. In the inscriptions carved on monuments, they also come across as sons concerned about the well-being of their parents after their death.[10]

There are other interesting cases where the inscriptions either differ from the texts or offer new insights. Epigraphic evidence from the Ajanta caves tells us that the distinctions between the Hinayana and Mahayana schools were not as rigid as they have been made out to be. Inscriptions also provide unique insights into the way we see the afterlife of the Buddha. In chapters 2 and 7, we will explore how the Buddha lived in the form of his relics after his *parinirvana* (the state one enters after death if s/he has attained *nirvana*). His relics are considered 'life forces' signifying his physical presence. Here, again, it was not the laity but the monks who played a significant role in the spread and institutionalization of the relic cult. The Buddha was also believed to live in the medieval monasteries. As we shall learn in chapters 5 and 9, a special chamber called the *gandhakuti* (perfumed chamber) was constructed for the Buddha in the rear wall of the monasteries. He was not only considered a permanent resident, but also, as the inscriptions indicate, the owner of the property.[11]

More examples may come to light with further explorations or a better reading of the excavated material. However, the state of archaeological excavations in India remains patchy. Even prominent sites have not been adequately studied. There are other gaps as well, which impinge on our understanding of Buddhist monuments and Buddhism in India. We do not have much idea of the monuments

INTRODUCTION 11

(mostly wooden structures and artefacts) that existed prior to the 3rd century BCE, or the pre-Ashokan period. Similarly, we don't know how the existence of the eighteen sects of Buddhism – or thirty, according to some – affected the structures and architecture. We only come across scattered references to their existence. Even the evidence regarding the decline of Buddhism in India is deeply fragmented.

HOW THIS BOOK IS ORGANIZED

Casting the Buddha uses a multi-pronged and inclusive conceptual framework, as discussed earlier, to trace the evolution of Buddhist monuments and artefacts in India, across regions and time frames. The book is divided into three sections: 'Monuments, Artefacts and Connected Histories', 'UNESCO World Heritage Sites' and 'The Return of the Buddha'. The first section consists of five chapters mapping the history of Buddhist monuments from the 6th–5th centuries BCE, or the days of the Buddha, to the 12th–13th centuries or the decline of Buddhism in India. These chapters follow a chronological approach, and they overlap too. They discuss the socio-economic and political contexts accompanying the establishment of various monuments, and their modifications and extensions as well.

Chapter 1 explores how the Buddha laid the foundations of his dharma and *sangha* (the monastic order); how he started accepting bamboo and mango groves for the seasonal retreats of his monks; and how the earliest structures consisting of resting or dwelling units, known as *aramas* (gardens or orchards), *avasas* (temporary monk settlements) and the early *viharas* (monasteries), came into being in the Gangetic heartland, which is considered the epicentre of early Buddhism. Chapter 2 discusses the rise of relics in the aftermath of the Buddha's parinirvana, and how Mauryan ruler Ashoka amplified and monumentalized the Buddha's legacy by erecting pillars and stupas, sending missions, and creating what is perhaps the first Buddhist pilgrimage circuit. Chapter 3 explores the post-Mauryan proliferation of Buddhist establishments, focusing on how the stupa became the central element in the development of monastic or stupa–monastery complexes. This growth is examined in the Gandhara region of the north-west (the region comprising present-day Peshawar and

Rawalpindi districts of Pakistan and the Kashmir valley), as well as in central and peninsular India. It breaks down the emergence of Buddhist art centres in Gandhara and Mathura, the caves in the Deccan and the anthropomorphic Buddha images. The chapter also deals with the appearance of the Mahayana tradition and the bodhisattvas, and how deities, motifs and symbols related to popular cults were incorporated into the tradition. This phenomenon was consolidated during the age of the Guptas and the Vakatakas. Chapter 4 highlights the emergence of Buddhist shrines and image worship, proliferation in the cult and images of the bodhisattvas and sculptural efflorescence at Sarnath, alongside sculptures and paintings at Ajanta. It discusses the rise of the *mahavihara* (literally, 'great vihara') in Nalanda; the consolidation and expansion of stupa-monastery complexes in the Gangetic heartland, Gandhara, Gujarat and the Deccan; and the coming into prominence of sacred geographies in Odisha and Tamil Nadu. The chapter also outlines the spread of Buddhist frontiers in East and Southeast Asia. Tantrism and Taras also start acquiring a foothold only to become prominent during the Pala and early medieval times, a development considered in detail in the subsequent chapter. Chapter 5 examines the rise of the Vajrayana ideal and the related mandala architecture; the setting up of mahaviharas in Bihar, Bengal and Gujarat; the coming into prominence of Buddhist establishments in Kashmir, the western Himalayas, Bihar and Bengal; and the spread of Buddhism further south in Tamil Nadu. Analyzing the manifestations and debates related to the decline of the faith during the 12th–13th centuries, the chapter shows how it was prolonged and lingering, as opposed to being sudden, and how the faith continued to exist on the geographical margins of the subcontinent.

The choice of the four chapters in the second section is by default and not design. They discuss the four Buddhist monument complexes in India that have been declared UNESCO World Heritage Sites. Two questions may come up here. Why isn't Ellora featured in this section? That is because Ellora also includes Hindu and Jaina caves, which is why it is discussed in detail in chapter 5. Are these sites exclusively Buddhist? No. The corresponding chapters explore their complexities.

This second section tries to tell a story through the sequence of the chapters. It represents the chronological spread of Buddhist monuments in India. Chapter 6 covers Bodh Gaya, which rose to prominence with the construction of the Vajrasana (diamond throne) under Ashoka (3rd century BCE) and remained the most important site for Buddhists. It also represents the supremacy of the Gangetic heartland in the early phase of Buddhism. Chapter 7 relates to Sanchi, which is in central India. The Sanchi complex, with its structures, sculptures and gateways, peaked in significance during the Shunga (2nd–1st centuries BCE) and Satavahana periods (1st–2nd centuries CE). It exemplifies the spread of Buddhist establishments beyond the Gangetic heartland into the central, peninsular and north-west regions of India. Sanchi represents what we described as a stupa–monastery complex in the first section.

Chapter 8 discusses the Ajanta caves, which are located further south in peninsular India, in the Deccan region. They blossomed during the reign of the Satavahanas and the Vakatakas (mid-3rd century CE to the late 5th and early 6th centuries CE). These caves are representative of an experimentation in the evolution of Buddhist monuments – from constructing structural and independently standing stupas and monasteries, as in Sanchi and Gandhara, to building such structures within rock-cut caves. Here, the chaityas (shrines) and viharas (monasteries) are not only beautifully sculpted but they also have exquisite and elaborate sets of paintings.

Chapter 9 is devoted to Nalanda. It represents the transition from viharas or stupa-viharas to mahaviharas during the Gupta period. The later phase at Nalanda also sees a shift to the Vajrayana tradition, of which the later mahaviharas in Bihar and Bengal became strongholds. It is from these mahaviharas that Buddhist ideas were transmitted to Tibet, Nepal, China, South and East Asia. Nalanda's decline in the period from the 12th to 13th centuries also coincides with the decline of Buddhism in India.

The five overlapping components of our approach to the study of monuments – which include the site's larger geocultural connections, the relationship between the part and the whole, the tangible–intangible dynamics, the human and extended human connection and the afterlife of the site – are strongly evident in the chapters of this section. Each chapter also includes a discussion on interesting debates and anecdotes, such as how Bodh Gaya became a mini Asia, how the Sanchi relics were taken to the United Kingdom and brought back, how the Ajanta caves became known in the West and whether Bakhtiyar Khalji destroyed Nalanda.

Together, these four heritage sites with their different kinds of monuments, sculptural wealth and artefacts, some of which can be found in museums, reflect the complex world of Buddhism. The Mahabodhi temple complex highlights the Buddha's presence at the site through the Bodhi tree, the Vajrasana and the 'monuments of the first seven weeks'. It also showcases the site's links with Shaivism in the form of shrines and sculptures. The Sanchi complex brings to the fore structural stupas and monasteries, the earliest Buddhist temples, sculptures associated with popular cults like nagas and yakshas, pillars and railings, together with the finest sculpted gateways. Like Bodh Gaya and Nalanda, Sanchi also underlines the funerary association of the site through the presence of numerous smaller and votive stupas. The Ajanta caves, likewise, add to the repository some of the most impressive rock-cut shrines and monasteries, as well as iconic Buddhist paintings. Also conspicuously present are the stone images of the Buddhas and bodhisattvas, and those representing Hindu demigods and popular cults. Finally, Nalanda mahavihara presents to us evolved monasteries and temples alongside bronze images. The images found in and around the mahavihara complex show the transition from Mahayana to Vajrayana, as well as Nalanda's links with Shaivism and Vaishnavism. Like Sanchi, the presence of water bodies around Nalanda underlines the role of ecology in architectural development. The four sites also reflect the multiple layers, dimensions, intersections and conflicts within Buddhism and beyond. As do the humans, agents, actors and stakeholders connected to them.

The third section has two chapters that explore the return of the Buddha to the centre stage and its effects on Buddhism. Chapter 10 examines the compositions and translations, debates and discussions, both in Europe and India, along with archaeological excavations in India contributing to the recentering of the Buddha and Buddhism in the 19th and 20th centuries. Chapter 11, titled 'Buddhism 2.0', discusses how Buddhist monuments have gained visibility for reasons beyond religion – soft power diplomacy, identity politics, refugee and diaspora issues, tourism and heritage conservation – and how these factors impart new meanings and forms to both the monuments and Buddhism.

Across three sections and eleven chapters, this book charts the remarkable and monumental journey of a faith that began during the 6th and 5th centuries BCE.

PART I

MONUMENTS, ARTEFACTS AND CONNECTED HISTORIES

1

THE BUDDHA COMES INTO BEING

Lord, I had these sixty dwelling-places built because I need merit, because I need heaven.

This is how the *shresthin* of Rajagriha (present-day Rajgir), an affluent businessman, described his donation of sixty viharas to the Buddha and his monks.[1] These were not monasteries, as we conventionally understand the viharas, but bamboo huts that could act as rain shelters for the monks. Incidentally, there were other related structures in the Buddha's time that served as rain retreats, such as the avasas or the aramas. Donated by kings and affluent citizens, mostly for spiritual merit and fame, such dwellings or resting units represented the earliest Buddhist structures. The bond between *dana* (giving) and *punya* (merit) gave the Buddhists, the Jainas and some other heterodox sects during the 6th and 5th centuries BCE the prototypes of their earliest monuments. It also brought together the seemingly contrasting sentiments of affluence and renunciation, of war and peace, of the material and spiritual. This was the age of the Buddha, regarded as the founder of what later came to be known as Buddhism. It was an age of conflicts and conquests, of opportunities and optimism, of disenchantment and despair. It was an age of ambitious kings and oligarchs, of affluent merchants and bankers, of prosperous landlords and influential renouncers and ascetics.

What made these developments possible? The age of the Buddha was characterized by significant shifts in the socio-economic milieu, sites of action and ideas, and institutions. New actors and stakeholders, who would decide the course of history over the next few centuries or more, were emerging on the scene.

NEW ECONOMIES, NEW POLITIES, NEW ENTITIES

The boundaries of Aryavarta – the land of the Arya – were shifting eastwards, from north-west India and Punjab, which was the heartland of the settlements of the Vedic Age (1600 to 500 BCE), to the Gangetic plains. Forests and wastelands were being cleared for a growing population and to cater to the incipient centres of exchange of goods. The Vedic polities were giving way to kingdoms with defined geographies and dynasties named after the dominant ruling clans. Contemporary texts speak of sixteen powerful states, or proto-states (*solasa mahajanapada*), that were larger and more powerful than the earlier janapadas – which were mostly regions or villages associated with the ruling clans or incipient kingships during the Vedic period.

The mahajanapadas of the 6th and 5th centuries BCE included both *rajya*s (monarchies) and *gana*s, or *gana-sangha*s (oligarchies). These sixteen mahajanapadas lay in the belt extending from Gandhara (with its capital in Taxila) in the north-west to Anga (the region constituting present-day Bhagalpur and Munger districts, with its capital in Champa, present-day Champanagar in Bihar) in eastern India to Avanti (the Malwa region with capitals in Mahishmati, present-day Maheshwar; and Ujjayini, present-day Ujjain) and Ashmaka (also known as Ashvaka, located on the river Godavari, with its capital in Potana or Potali, present-day Bodhan) in peninsular India. The relationships among these states were characterized by warfare, truce and military and marriage alliances.

Among the rajyas, the prominent ones were Magadha (modern-day Patna and Gaya districts of Bihar), Kosala (the south-central region of Uttar Pradesh, which later came to be known as the historical Oudh, or Awadh), Vatsa (based around Kosambi or Kaushambi, which is modern-day Kosam village on the right bank of river Yamuna) and Avanti (in the Malwa region of central India).

The ganas, or gana-sanghas, were closely associated with the Kshatriyas and named after the ruling clans. These included the Vrijjis in eastern India (north of the river Ganga, extending till modern-day

Nepal), the Mallas of Kushinagar (present-day Kasia near Gorakhpur in Uttar Pradesh) and the Shakyas of Kapilavastu (modern-day Piprahwa–Ganwaria region in Uttar Pradesh). The Vrijjis, also known as Vajjis, were said to be a confederacy of eight clans with 7,707 rajas, while the Mallas had 500 rajas. The major rajyas occupied the fertile alluvial tracts of the Gangetic valley, while important ganas and gana-sanghas were situated in and around the Himalayan foothills in eastern India.[2]

HOW THE STATES AND URBANIZATION CAME INTO EXISTENCE

The availability of agricultural surplus is often seen as a precondition for socio-economic diversification. The prospect of multiple crops in a year, greater harvests resulting from rice cultivation and a vast expansion of agricultural settlements in the fertile and alluvial Gangetic plains created the possibility of a food surplus. It also freed a section of the populace to engage in occupations other than agriculture. What specifically made this surplus possible remains a subject of debate among scholars. Earlier, it was held that irrigation was the primary causal factor (see chapter 7 for recent research on this aspect). Provisions for drainage and canals could convert vast tracts of marshland into arable pockets. Control over irrigation networks served as the foundation of the power of the state in such a theory. Later, scholars started putting more emphasis on the role of iron and iron technology in such a transformation.

Low-grade iron was already in use for making weapons around 800 BCE. It was the systematic availability of better-quality iron and a qualitative and quantitative increase in the use of iron artefacts that made the difference.[3] Evidence of iron smelting and production has been found from sites in northern Rajasthan and the western Gangetic plains. A comparatively large number of iron artefacts have been recovered among archaeological finds dating to this period in the Gangetic plains. These include iron axes (which could clear forests for land) and ploughshares (which could plough deeper), besides hoes and sickles.

Scholars argue that iron may have stabilized or enhanced the scope of agricultural production.[4] Buddhist texts also talk about the use of the iron plough in cultivation. Iron technology brought about striking changes in the making of items from wood, bone, glass, ivory, beads, semi-precious stones, shells and stones, and the firing of superior, lustrous and luxurious pottery such as the Northern Black Polished Ware (NBPW) – which is archaeologically associated with a superior level of urbanism. Soon, villages and non-agricultural communities living close to sources of raw materials started specializing in professions like pottery, carpentry, blacksmithery, cloth weaving, basket weaving, etc.

The proliferation of such occupations was accompanied by increasing instances of specialization among artisanal groups, the concentration of artisans and craftsmen close to centres of production or exchange, the organization of professional groups into guilds or corporate bodies known by names like *shrenis*, *nigamas* and *pugas*, and the emergence of money and punch-marked silver coins to facilitate exchanges. These were all interconnected developments that played an important role in the growth of urbanism. Before long, several production and exchange centres developed into towns, which in turn expanded and developed markets and commercial networks. Some capital cities that housed the rulers, courts and bureaucracy also developed into towns. These included Rajagriha in Magadha, Kaushambi in Vatsa, Champa in Anga, Ahichhatra in Panchala (present-day Bareilly) and Shravasti in Kosala (in north-eastern Uttar Pradesh). Other cities, like Vaishali (in present-day Bihar), grew because of their sacred credentials.

The early Buddhist texts speak of a hierarchy of settlements, which includes *grama* (village), *nigama* (local markets or exchange centres), *nagara* (town) and *mahanagara* (bigger, prosperous and politically important towns), such as Kaushambi. Towns like Vaishali, Shravasti, Champa, Rajagriha, Kaushambi and Kashi were of substantial importance to the economy of the Gangetic plains. Others, like Ujjain, Taxila and the port of Bharukaccha (Bharuch), had a wider geographical and economic reach.[5]

The greater availability of material goods for consumption and exchange widened the possibilities of trade, both inland and overseas.[6] Gradually, two major transregional routes emerged: the Uttarapatha, or the northern route, and the Dakshinapatha, or the southern route. The Uttarapatha, a land-cum-river route in north India, stretched from the north-west, ran across the Indo-Gangetic plains and ended at the port of Tamralipti (present-day Tamluk in Midnapore district of West Bengal) on the Bay of Bengal. Several kingdoms were located along this route. The Dakshinapatha stretched from Pataliputra in Magadha to Pratishthana (modern-day Paithan in Maharashtra), the capital of the kingdom of Mulaka, or Alaka, on the river Godavari. It was also connected to ports on the western coast.

The internal trade routes eventually linked with external ones, connecting the subcontinent with Afghanistan, Iran, parts of Central Asia and the Mediterranean. A later connection was facilitated by the establishment of Greek settlements in the north-west, in the aftermath of Alexander's invasion (327–26 BCE). Traders became an important urban group, with wealthy traders, known as *vanijjas*, being highly regarded. Caravans with 1,000 carts moved from one janapada to another, paying tolls and taxes along the way.

The changes in material milieu were also accompanied by transformations in the social fabric and the emergence of new social elites in towns and cities.[7] The term *grihapati* (*gahapati* in Pali), used to describe the quintessential head of the household during the Vedic times, now came to mean a wealthy property owner with land and agriculture. The grihapatis were counted among the seven treasures of a *chakrabarti* king, the ideal and universal ruler of the world. Likewise, *shresthins* (*setthis* in Pali), affluent businessmen connected with trade and moneylending, emerged as prominent members of the urban community, with access to kings. There were several shresthins in Rajagriha and Vaishali. The term 'shresthin-grihapati' ('setthi-gahapati' in Pali) has been used for prosperous people who had both rural and urban bases and owned both lands and businesses.

The economic prosperity of the age was also contrasted by socio-economic disparities and tensions. Contemporary sources describe a Brahman who owned 500 ploughs, hired or wage workers (*vaitanikas*, *karmakaras*), slave labour (*dasas*) and those living extremely poor and miserable lives (*daridra/dalidda*). Pali texts also talk about contrasting categories of the wealthy and the poor or unfortunate, such as the *mahabhoga kula* and dalidda kula, *sadhana* and *adhana*, and *sugata* and *duggata*, respectively. Likewise, families with a higher social status, the *uchha* kulas, were contrasted with families having a low status, the *nichha* kulas. In that age of disparities, the four-fold *varna* hierarchy, like the Vedic times, found itself contending with a new social identity called *jatis* (castes), which were defined by rules of endogamy and commensality. The castes were hierarchical too, and sometimes defined in terms of occupations. They were categorized as high (Brahmans and Kshatriyas) and low (Chandalas, hunters, sweepers and charioteers). However, what makes the social mosaic of the Gangetic valley particularly unique and noteworthy is the presence of several renunciants, known by various names. Some of these were *bhikshus* (those who lived by begging for alms), *shramanas* (those who laboured to know the truth) or *parivrajakas* (wanderers). The shramanas and parivrajakas gave up their homes, cut off kinship and social ties, and lived by collecting alms. They opposed Brahmanical rituals and sacrifices, and wandered from place to place to meet distinguished teachers and philosophers, entering into debates and discussions with them.

What united the renunciants and the affluents, among other factors, was the element of mobility. They were all people on the move. In the early Buddhist texts, such people included renunciants, teachers, students, professionals, kings, soldiers and traders, alongside the Buddha and his disciples. All of them may have travelled along broadly similar routes.[8]

In that age of mobilities, disparities, conflicts and contrasts, a boy named Siddhartha was born to Maya and Sudhodhana of the Shakya ruling clan[9] in Kapilavastu in the Himalayan foothills. Archaeologists have identified Kapilavastu as the villages of Piprahwa and Ganwaria in Basti district of northern Uttar Pradesh. Nepal, however, claims that its archaeological site of Tilaurakot constituted the ancient city of Kapilavastu.

SIDDHARTHA, A RELUCTANT PRINCE, BECOMES THE BUDDHA

One night, sometime around the 6th–5th century BCE, Maya, the wife of Sudhodhana, the Shakya chief of Kapilavastu, dreamt that she was carried away by the four heavenly guardians of the four quarters of the universe to the divine lake Anavatapta in the Himalayas. There, she was bathed, anointed and dressed in white. A great white elephant, holding a lotus flower in its trunk, approached her and entered through her right side. Maya narrated the dream to Sudhodhana. The next day, the wise men in Sudhodhana's court interpreted the dream and prophesied that Maya would conceive a son who would either become a universal emperor or a renowned teacher.

As the legend goes, while on her way to her parents' home, Maya gave birth to a child in a grove of sal trees called Lumbini, near Kapilavastu, the capital of the Shakyas (Fig 1.1).[10] The newborn is said to have stood upright, taken seven steps and proclaimed: 'This is my last birth; henceforth there is no more birth for me.'[11]

Some Brahmans observed the thirty-two marks of a *mahapurusha* (a great man) on the body of the infant. This further lent credence to the prophecy that he would either be a conqueror or a renouncer. The boy was named Siddhartha. His *gotra* (lineage) was Gautama, the name by which he is commonly referred to in Buddhist literature. Other names for him include Shakyamuni (the sage of the Shakyas) and Tathagata ('the one who has thus come', or 'the one who is thus gone'). Tathagata is the name the Buddha uses to refer to himself in the Pali canon.

Mindful of the prophecy, Sudhodhana tried to shield his son from all sorrows. He made him live in beautiful buildings surrounded by all the luxuries possible. Siddhartha learned all the arts a prince was supposed to and excelled as a student. He married his cousin Yashodhara after performing feats of strength and skill at a contest and outperforming all other contenders, including his envious cousin Devadatta. Despite all this, Sudhodhana could not stop his son from seeing the four ominous signs, which were said to have been planted before the prince by the gods.

One day, when he was driving around with Channa, his favourite charioteer, Siddhartha saw an old man. Upon asking Channa, he learnt that all men grow old. That was the first sign. The second sign came in the form of a suffering, sick man covered with boils and shivering because of a fever. The third sign was a corpse being carried to a cremation ground, accompanied by weeping mourners. The fourth sign was a wandering religious beggar who was clad in a simple yellow robe and looked peaceful. Pleased at the sight, Siddhartha's heart was set on becoming a wanderer. Hearing this, Sudhodhana became even more cautious and virtually confined his son in luxury.

Soon, news came that Siddhartha's wife, Yashodhara, had given birth to a son. There were great festivities in the palace. That night, when everyone was asleep, Siddhartha roused Channa and asked him to saddle his favourite horse, Kanthaka. They rode off into the night, surrounded by rejoicing demigods who are believed to have cushioned the horse's hooves so that nobody could hear Siddhartha leaving. After reaching a place far away from the city, the prince stripped himself of his luxurious attire and jewellery, cut off his hair, put on a hermit's robe, and set forth as a wanderer. Buddhist tradition describes this departure as the *mahabhinishkramana* ('Great Going Forth', or the 'Great Departure') (Fig 1.3).

Siddhartha wandered and begged for food before becoming a forest hermit. He met a sage named Alara Kalama near Vaishali, who taught him how to meditate. After perfecting the technique, he left Alara Kalama and joined five ascetics who were practising self-mortification to free themselves of their *karma* (actions or doing) and obtain bliss. Because of his meticulous austerities, Siddhartha soon became the leader of the ascetics. For six years, he practised rigorous asceticism. One day, worn out from penance and hunger, he fainted. When he regained consciousness, he realized fasts and penance were not leading towards his goal. He began to beg for food again to regain strength. At this point, his five disciples abandoned him.

Thirty-five years old by then, Siddhartha sat under a large pipal tree (*Ficus religiosa*) in Uruvela village (present-day Bodh Gaya) on the outskirts of Gaya, which was part of the Magadha kingdom. Sujata, the daughter of a farmer who lived nearby, brought him a large bowl of pudding (rice boiled in milk) (Fig 1.2). It is said that Siddhartha was in such an emaciated state that Sujata mistook him for a tree-spirit who had granted her wish of having a child. After eating the pudding, Siddhartha bathed and sat under the tree again, determined not to leave until he had found a solution to the suffering of the world.

For the next forty-nine days, he sat firm, surrounded by gods and spirits who keenly awaited the moment of his enlightenment. As the story goes, Mara, the spirit of the world and sensual pleasures, or the Buddhist devil, approached Siddhartha and tried to distract him (Fig 1.4). First, Mara told Siddhartha that Devadatta had revolted, captured his wife and dominions, and imprisoned his father. Siddhartha remained unmoved. Mara then summoned demons to attack Siddhartha with a whirlwind, tempest, flood and earthquake. Siddhartha didn't react. Then Mara called on Siddhartha to produce evidence of his goodness and benevolence. Sitting cross-legged under the tree, Siddhartha touched the ground with his right hand and invoked the earth. This gesture became iconic in the Buddhist world as the *bhumisparsha mudra*. 'I am his witness,' the earth spoke in a thunderous voice (Fig 1.5).

Subsequently, Mara called upon his three beautiful daughters – Desire, Pleasure and Passion – to seduce Siddhartha. Mara's distractions did not work; he gave up. On the forty-ninth day, the truth dawned upon Siddhartha. He had found the secret behind sorrow, understood why the world was full of suffering and unhappiness of all kinds, and what a human needed to do to overcome these challenges. He had become the 'Enlightened One'. He was the Buddha.

All episodes connected with the enlightenment – Sujata serving pudding to Siddhartha, Mara's attack, and even the stories and gestures surrounding them, such as the bhumisparsha mudra – became an integral part of Buddhist lore and iconography. They are represented in sculptures and paintings at most Buddhist sites. The pipal tree under which the Buddha meditated became famously known and revered as the Bodhi tree ('wisdom tree' or 'tree of enlightenment') (Fig 1.6). It must be clarified that the Buddha's enlightenment was not a revelation of the divine, but of a set of truths on how to deal with the world's suffering.

For the next seven weeks, the Buddha remained around the Bodhi tree, meditating and consolidating the truths he had discovered. The sites around the tree, came to be known as the 'Monuments of the First Seven Weeks' in the Buddhist tradition.

THE FIRST SERMON OF THE ENLIGHTENED ONE

For some time after his enlightenment, the Buddha thought whether he should proclaim his wisdom to the world or not. At this point, it is believed that Hindu god Brahma descended from the heaven and persuaded him to spread his knowledge.[12] On account of their association with the Buddha, Brahma and Indra (also known as Shakra) became revered figures in Buddhist tradition too.

Following Brahma's advice, Buddha left the Bodhi tree and travelled to Deer Park near Varanasi, now known as Sarnath (formerly known by names like Isipatana, Rishipattana or Mrigadava). Here, he preached for the first time to his five estranged disciples, who became his followers again. In Buddhist phraseology, this sermon is described as the 'Turning of the Wheel of the Law', or the *dharmachakrapravartana*. The dharmachakrapravartana is frequently depicted in Buddhist iconography by two deer (related to Deer Park) and a wheel (signifying the turning of the wheel of law). Sometimes, it is depicted by a wheel itself. Other times, disciples are added to the frame.

The first sermon constituted the core of the Buddha's teachings. These were passed on through the oral tradition and the Buddhist canon that was later written in Pali. The teachings of the Buddha were recited and collected after his death, but they were not committed to writing or canonized as the *Tripitaka* (*Tipitaka* in Pali) until a few centuries later. It, therefore, becomes difficult to separate his original teachings from the later additions. It is also possible that periodic Buddhist councils held after the Buddha's death, such as the ones held in Rajagriha, Vaishali and Pataliputra, introduced their own interpolations.[13] Scholars, however, agree on some fundamental teachings of the Buddha. These were not based on complicated metaphysical thoughts, complex rituals and sacrifices, deity worship and caste distinctions. Instead, they were based on causality and logic, concern and welfare of humanity, and social ethics.[14] Of these, the four Noble Truths and the Eightfold Path lay at the core.

The four Noble Truths were:
- the world is full of suffering (*dukkha*),
- suffering is caused by human desires (*samudaya*),

- the renunciation of desires is the path to salvation or nirvana, which is described as freedom from the cycle of birth and death,
- desires could be removed by following the Eightfold Path.

The Eightfold Path, as taught by the Buddha, advocated a middle line between extreme indulgence and extreme asceticism. Consisting of interrelated activities connected to knowledge, conduct and meditation, it laid emphasis on a balanced and moderate life. The components of the Eightfold Path included the right view, right intention, right speech, right action, right livelihood, right effort, right mindfulness and right meditation or concentration. An important component of the Buddha's teachings was the law of dependent origination (*pratityasamutpada* in Sanskrit, *paticca-samuppada* in Pali). It offered a chain of causation that linked suffering with birth, death and rebirth. The components of this law were presented as a wheel consisting of twelve *nidana*s (links or causes), where one led to the next: ignorance, formations, consciousness, mind and body, the six senses, sense contact, feeling, craving, attachment, becoming, birth, old age and death. In short, the nidanas connected the past, present and future. The goal of the Buddha's teaching was the attainment of nirvana (*nibbana* in Pali) or bliss through enlightenment, an experience that could be attained in this life. Literally speaking, nirvana meant dying out, blowing out or extinction. Metaphorically, it meant the dying out of desire, attachment, greed, hatred, ignorance and the sense of I-ness. Parinirvana (*parinibbana* in Pali) was a term used for the death of an enlightened being like the Buddha.

The link between karma and rebirth was central to the Buddha, though he rejected the idea of the *atman* (soul) as a permanent entity. There were many worlds with different kinds of beings and one could be born as any one of them, depending on karma. However, unlike the Brahmanical tradition, where karma indicated ritual action, according to the Buddha, it meant intentions that led to actions of the mind, body or speech. Rebirth, in turn, was governed by the aggregation of karma in a particular life. Karma, in the Buddha's scheme, could be improved by observing a code of social ethics.

THE BUDDHA'S GEOGRAPHY AND THE SANGHA

What did the Buddha do after his first sermon? Where did he travel to post enlightenment? It is said that a few days after the first sermon, sixty young ascetics became the Buddha's followers, whom he sent in different directions to spread his teachings.[15] He himself was very mobile when it came to widening the reach of his thoughts, travelling throughout the Gangetic valley. In the forty years after enlightenment, we hear about many anecdotes and stories connected with the Buddha. He apparently returned to Kapilavastu and converted his father, wife and son, Rahula, and his cousin Devadatta. At the request of his foster mother and aunt, Mahaprajapati Gautami, he allowed women to become nuns.[16] It seems that the Buddha came back to Uruvela and tamed a fire-spewing serpent, and converted the fire-worshipping Kashyapa brothers and their disciples. He also subdued the child-devouring demoness called Hariti in Rajagriha and converted a notorious bandit called Angulimala.

The Buddha performed some miracles as well, four of which, as we will discuss later, became a part of the 'eight great events' (*astamahapratiharya*) and acquired cult status among Buddhists, particularly after the Gupta period, especially in the 8th century CE. These miracles include the act of levitation in Shravasti; taming the ferocious elephant called Nalagiri, unleashed by Devadatta, in Kapilavastu; accepting honey from a monkey in Vaishali and visiting the Buddhist heaven (*trayastrimsa* in Sanskrit, *tavatimsa* in Pali) where he taught doctrines to his mother before descending to the earth at Sankissa (now identified as Sankisa Basantapura in Farrukhabad district of Uttar Pradesh).

The other four great events are well known: the Buddha's birth in Lumbini, enlightenment in Bodh Gaya, his first sermon in Sarnath and his death in Kushinagar. All these locations are considered sacred in Buddhism.

Later in the book, we will see how these events are represented in sculptural and painted traditions. For now, let us return to the Buddha's territory. According to the Pali canon, the earliest Buddhist literature is associated with the middle Gangetic valley (roughly corresponding to modern-day Bihar and eastern Uttar Pradesh), which constituted the geographical heartland of the Buddha's life and teachings. He travelled and taught extensively in this region, resting only during the rainy season. A fascinating statistical study based on a comprehensive review of early Pali texts provides insights into the places associated with the Buddha. Of the total of 1,009 places listed in the Pali texts, 842 (83.43 per cent) refer to five cities, while the remaining 167 (16.57 per cent) cover seventy-six separate cities, market towns, villages, and the countryside. Moreover, 593 (58.77 per cent) relate to Shravasti (Savatthi in Pali), 140 (13.87 per cent) to Rajagriha/Rajgir (also known as Girivraja), fifty-six (5.55 per cent) to Kapilavastu, thirty-eight (3.76 per cent) to Vaishali and fifteen (1.48 per cent) to Kaushambi.[17] These places, it has been pointed out, formed an irregular triangle with its apex in Champa, the southern side extending up to Ujjain and the northern side to Mathura and further up to Kapilavastu. Some places, like Supparaka and Bharukaccha on the western coast and Pratishthana in the peninsular region, also find mention on this list, but they are associated with disciples such as *thera*s (elderly monks) and *theri*s (elderly nuns).

Shravasti is identified with present-day Saheth–Maheth on the boundaries of Gonda and Bahraich districts in Uttar Pradesh. Located on the banks of the river Rapti, it was the capital of Kosala and a famous commercial centre. Incidentally, the ruler Prasenjit was a patron of the Buddha. Shravasti was the most important centre for the early Buddhists before the rise of imperial Magadha. The Buddha spent twenty-five *versha vasa*s (rain retreats) in monk settlements at Shravasti – nineteen in Jetavana and six in Pubbarama. He is also said to have averted a war between the Kosalas and the Shakyas. The Shakyas had apparently tricked Prasenjit into marrying a slave girl, the daughter of a Shakyan chief from a slave woman, instead of a royal princess. The Buddha is said to have intervened and counselled Prasenjit. As the legend goes, Prasenjit's son, who was born out of this marriage, later massacred the Shakyas. This episode does not have sound historical basis, but it is depicted in relief sculptures on many stupas.[18]

The next in the order of mention is Rajagriha, which was the capital of Magadha janapada before it was shifted to Pataliputra. The ruler of Magadha, Bimbisara (c. 545–493 BCE), and his son and successor, Ajatashatru (c. 493–62 BCE), were among the patrons of the Buddha. Ajatashatru is said to have visited the Buddha with his royal entourage. This scene is depicted on one of the railing pillars of the western gateway of the 2nd–1st century BCE stupa at Bharhut. It carries an inscription, which reads 'Ajatashatru worships the Lord'.[19]

Among the celebrated spots in Rajagriha are the Veluvana or Venuvana (a bamboo forest gifted by Bimbisara), the Tapodanarama on the lake Tapoda, the Jivaka-Ambavana (a mango orchard gifted to the sangha by the royal physician Jivaka) and Nalanda on the outskirts of the city. The Buddha spent his first, third, fourth, seventeenth and twentieth rain retreats in Rajagriha.

The third city was Kapilavastu, the capital of the Shakyas. Situated close to Rummindei in Nepal's Terai region, it was the city of the Buddha's childhood and early adult life. The Shakya territory also produced Upali, a barber who was among the Buddha's foremost disciples.

Vaishali, the fourth city in the order of frequency of occurrence in the early Buddhist texts, is now equated with the ruins near Basarh village in Bihar's Muzaffarpur district. It was the capital of the Lichhavis and the Vrijji confederacy. The Buddha is said to have lived here many times, specifically in the vicinity of the *mahavana* where the *kutagarshala* (hall) stood on the banks of the 'monkey pool' (*markata haradarira*); and at the monastery given to him by the famous courtesan Amrapali (also known as Ambapali), the Ambapali vana.[20] Vaishali was known for its chaityas and local shrines. The Lichhavis had seven such sacred spots on the outskirts of Vaishali, which the Buddha spoke about admiringly.[21]

Kaushambi (also Kosambi), the capital city of the Vatsas or Vamsas, appears fifteen times (1.48 per cent) in the early Pali texts. Ruled by a contemporary of the Buddha, Parantapa is identified with Kosam village on the river Yamuna, near Allahabad (now called Prayagraj). Kaushambi was as important as Shravasti commercially and formed an important staging point connecting Kosala and Magadha. The Pali texts mention several banker families of Kaushambi, and numerous nagas.[22] Interestingly, Kaushambi was known for disputes between monks. Once, two monks fought over the refilling of a water pot

Fig 1.1 A depiction of the Buddha's birth from Bengal, dating to the Pala period (800s)

Fig 1.2 An emaciated Siddhartha being offered pudding by Sujata. A painting from Mulagandhakuti Vihara, Sarnath

Fig 1.3 The mahabhinishkramana: the upper architrave shows 'The Great Departure', while the lower one depicts Ashoka's visit to the Bodhi tree

Fig 1.4 Mara's Attack and Temptation, Kashmir (8th century CE)

Fig 1.5 Buddha calling on the earth to witness (bhumisparsha mudra), 9th century, Tetravan, Bihar

Fig 1.6 A descendant of the Bodhi tree with the enclosure containing the Vajrasana (diamond throne)

Fig 1.7 Gandhakuti in Jetavana Monastery, Shravasti

Fig 1.8 Sculpture depicting the Buddha's mahaparinirvana in the side aisle of Cave 26 at Ajanta

in the toilet, which snowballed into a fight over monastic discipline, involving two groups of monks. The Buddha advised reconciliation. When the monks did not take his advice, he left Kaushambi and stayed in a park on the outskirts of the city, called the eastern bamboo grove. From there, he moved to the Parileyyaka forest. Kaushambi also figures in other disputes between monks. When Yasa Kakandaputta was expelled from Vaishali by the Vajjian monks, he went to Kaushambi and sent messages to orthodox monks in various centres.[23] Later, the city became the site of one of Ashoka's edicts, which is also attributed to an actual or impending division in the sangha.

Champa, which is mentioned six times on the list, was located on a river of the same name – a tributary of the Ganga. Identified with modern-day Champanagar in Bihar's Bhagalpur, it was an important commercial centre and the capital of the Anga kingdom. Merchants from Champa are said to have travelled to the Malay peninsula (Suvarnabhumi) for trade. The city also boasted a considerable number of monks residing in various avasas. The Buddha visited the city several times, as did the monks Sariputra and Vamgisa. Champa lost much of its earlier importance after being annexed by Bimbisara of Magadha.[24]

The Buddha's influence also seems to have grown in peninsular India, beyond the Vindhya mountains, though he never travelled to this region. Ujjayini (present-day Ujjain), the capital of Avanti janapada, appears only four times on the list under discussion. The city was located at a strategic point on the trade route that connected peninsular India with the northern and eastern parts, as well as the ports on the west coast. Though the Buddha never visited the city, Ujjayini was the home of several of his prominent disciples, including Mahakatyayana. The latter was known as one of the ten leading male disciples of the Buddha and was reputed for his skill in expounding the *dhamma* (dharma). A large community of monks eventually grew in Avanti, after Mahakatyayana asked his disciple, Sona Kutikanna, to meet the Buddha at Shravasti and make him aware of the challenges faced by the sangha and the conditions of life in Avanti.[25] Buddhist texts also narrate the story of Bavari, a teacher from Kosala who built a hermitage on the banks of the river Godavari in the kingdom of

Ashmaka or Ashvaka (Assaka in Pali) with its capital in Potana or Potali (modern Bodhan), and sent his disciples on a mission to meet the Buddha. They travelled through Pratishthana, Ujjayini, Vidisha, Kaushambi, Shravasti and Vaishali during their journey.[26]

These territories, which later became a part of the sacred geography of the Buddhists, were held together by the wanderings of the Buddha, the monks and the disciples. The Buddhists had inherited this tradition of wandering from the parivrajakas. Gradually, a monastic order called the sangha evolved. It is argued that the Buddha borrowed the idea of the sangha from the federal organization of the gana-sanghas, particularly the Lichhavis.[27] Initially, the sangha constituted of a wandering body of monks following a common faith. Its members came from different regions and were not rooted to any local habitation. This was the primitive Bhikshu 'sangha of the four quarters'. As the faith spread, this body split into many groups operational in different parts of the country – each with its own life, each locally delimited and functioning on its own. Each of these groups came to be known as a sangha.[28] With the sangha came monastic rules (vinaya), which covered all aspects of the monks' existence, including their relationship with fellow monks and the laity. It was out of the wanderings of the Buddha and the sangha that the earliest Buddhist structures, the resting and dwelling units, emerged.

ORIGINS OF STRUCTURES AND SETTLEMENTS

In the early phase of Buddhism, monks wandered from place to place to spread dharma, the teachings of the Buddha, and to collect food and alms. During the monsoon months, they took shelter. This practice was called versha-vasa (*vassa-vasa* in Pali), again a tradition inherited from the parivrajakas. The places where the monks would retreat were parks or groves, mostly mango or bamboo, where they lived in huts made of bamboo and reed.[29] Donated by kings or wealthy people, such parks and groves were mostly located outside the towns and were called *kutuhalashalas* (literally, 'the place for creating curiosity'), where philosophers could debate or dispute in public. This was different from the Vedic tradition, where teachings or disputations were not held in public.³⁰ In some cases, community halls were also given. The Lichhavis of Vaishali, for instance, are said to have given the *kuthagarashala* (a hut with a pointed roof) to monks.³¹

Gradually, as the early Buddhist texts indicate, two broad kinds of structures emerged out of the rain retreats – the avasas and the aramas. These initial settlements had natural boundaries. While the exact details of these structures are not given, it seems that the avasas were temporary colonies of monks located mostly in the countryside. They were staked out, built and maintained by the monks themselves. The aramas, on the other hand, denoted 'pleasure gardens' and could be orchards, gardens or forests. They were comparatively superior enclosed structures either in or near the towns, or in the suburbs close to houses of wealthy citizens, possibly maintained by the donors. While both structures were used by monks, what set these early Buddhist structures apart from the parivrajakas was the formulation of rules for congregational living and an emphasis on training, manners and etiquettes.³²

Bimbisara, the Magadha king, was the first person to donate property collectively and exclusively to the sangha, in the form of Veluvana arama on the outskirts of Rajagriha. Until then, aramas had been given to individual sects from time to time, for staying and resting.³³ The property gifted to the sangha was also known as *sangharama*, the name by which some monasteries later came to be known. We come across several aramas gifted to the sangha, both by kings and wealthy patrons.³⁴ Shravasti's iconic shresthin-grihapati, Anathapindika, is said to have purchased a bamboo forest, Jetavana, for the sangha from Prince Jeta and constructed a monastery there (Fig 1.7). Amrapali (Ambapali in Pali), the beautiful and celebrated courtesan of Vaishali, is said to have invited the Buddha for a meal and gifted him a grove which became known as the Amrapali/Ambapali vana. Likewise, Jivaka Ambavana was donated to the Buddha by Magadha's royal physician.

Kaushambi had at least four great monasteries – the Kukkutarama, the Ghositarama, the Pavarikambavana and the Badarikarama. The first three were named after three friends and prominent citizens of the city.³⁵ Likewise, the Nigrodharama was a banyan grove in Kudan village near Kapilavastu. It was given to the Buddha when he visited the city for the first time after his enlightenment.

The gifts of aramas were followed by the special sanctioning of the institution of viharas, which were originally huts, or hutments for the monks within the avasas and aramas. The wealthy shresthin of Rajagriha had expressed a desire to build viharas for the sangha. Upon receiving the Buddha's permission, he is said to have built sixty bamboo huts in a day and dedicated them to the 'sangha of the four quarters' (*chatuhdissa* sangha, a term used for a sangha with monks hailing from all quarters, irrespective of the regional provenance), both 'of the present and the future'. Incidentally, this occasion marked the first use of such a formula for the gift of viharas in the texts and inscriptions.³⁶ Gradually, the avasas or aramas gave way to the *layanas* (*lena* in Pali), which meant a private abode or a compact unitary establishment for a settled body of monks, as opposed to the old settlements that were like a shifting or seasonal caravan serai, open to all. The lena was a monastery, as opposed to a settlement of monks, meant specially for a single resident. The later viharas emerged as one of the five different kinds of lenas – they developed as private dwellings for a company of monks.³⁷

There is an interesting debate among scholars about the relationship between these rainy season retreats and the beginnings of a settled life, as far as Buddhist monks are concerned. Some say it was the rain retreats that marked the turning point from 'wandering to settled life'.³⁸ Others argue that the institution of a retreat served to connect the wandering and sedentary lives. Right from the initial days of the sangha, as the early Buddhist texts indicate, the monks lived both itinerant and sedentary lives. The Buddha had started accepting aramas soon after his enlightenment and the founding of the monastic order. Further, while most monks are said to have travelled constantly to spread the Buddha's message, some also stayed in one place for considerable periods of time. Accordingly, the idea of permanent monastic establishments emerged during the life of the Buddha himself.³⁹

Interestingly, textual references to aramas or avasas do not match the archaeological findings. If one were to go by the available archaeological evidence, majority of the structures associated with early Buddhist times are shrines and not residential structures. Further, evidence for residential structures comes mostly from the Mauryan times.[40] So how do we explain this gap between the texts and archaeological evidence? We are not sure. Perhaps the original constructions perished. Perhaps, as they transformed into sacred spots, they were superimposed with more permanent constructions, either at the original site or in the vicinity. Irrespective of such gaps, the aramas and viharas mentioned in Buddhist legends have continued to exist in the collective memory of the followers. And they have acquired tangible forms too, over a period. Structures connected with Buddhist legends and bearing such names adorn many sites today. So, if we were to visit Rajgir (erstwhile Rajagriha) today, the tourist guide would take us to a forested park equipped with modern facilities called Venuvana. Likewise, if one toured modern Shravasti, one would see a site called the Jetavana. And if one were to visit Tilaurakot in Nepal, one would view a structure known as the Nigrodharama. The dates and names of the actual builders of the current structures continue to be debated. However, what remains less debatable is how an entire ecosystem of monks and followers sustained the Buddhist settlements, whenever and in whatever form they existed, both during the time of the Buddha and afterwards.

THE BUDDHA'S FOLLOWERS, THE SANGHA AND THE LAITY

The Buddha's followers had the choice to either join the sangha, a monastic order of monks or nuns, or remain outside it as the laity or lay followers. The monks and nuns were known as *bhikshus* and *bhikshunis*, respectively, while the followers were called *upasakas* and *upasikas*. The sangha played an important role in the dissemination of his teachings. The *Vinaya Pitaka*, one of the three texts constituting the *Tripitaka*, talks about the monastic rules (227 for monks and 311 for nuns), known as the *pratimokha* (*patimokka* in Pali), and was recited by monks in the exclusive fortnightly congregations held on new and full moon days. These were called *upavasatha* (*uposatha* in Pali). People who joined the sangha had to recite the *triratna* (three jewels) formula of seeking refuge in the Buddha, dharma and sangha.

Buddham saranam gacchami
dhammam saranam gacchami
sangham saranam gacchami

(I seek refuge in the Buddha
I seek refuge in dharma
I seek refuge in the sangha.)[41]

They had to shave their heads and wear ochre-coloured robes. They were renouncers but not ascetics – they were expected to renounce family and caste ties, but were required to fulfil the social obligations required by the sangha, which became a new and extended household. Monks and nuns had to take ten vows – they were supposed to strictly avoid the following: destruction of life, taking what is not given (theft), sexual misconduct, false speech, consuming intoxicants, eating after midday, attending entertainments, using perfumes and jewellery, using luxurious beds, and handling gold and silver, including money. Of these, the first five had to be adhered to by the lay followers or the laity.[42]

When the sangha initially came into being, the monks wandered from place to place preaching and seeking alms. Interaction between the monks and the laity took place in several different contexts. They came together on the formal and ceremonial occasion of the upavasatha, the day of observance, when the monks reminded the laity of their vows. But there were informal occasions, too. The monks taught dharma and the principles of righteous living in return for food and alms. Sometimes, the monks were invited by the laity to give discourses and attend important functions. With an increase in the number of followers, the monks were called upon to perform rituals linked to birth, puberty, marriage and death.

There are 105 references in the early Pali texts to monks and nuns whose social backgrounds are known. Of these, Brahmans constitute the largest group (39). This is followed by the Kshatriyas (28), uccha kula (21), niccha kula (8) and grihapati (1). The remaining (8) were parivrajakas before they joined the sangha.[43] Among the Brahmans, we can include some of the Buddha's closest disciples like Sariputra

(Sariputta in Pali), Maudgalyayana (Moggallana in Pali), Mahakasyapa and others, who were householders. Among the Kshatriyas, we may include the Buddha's close associates, like Ananda and Anuradha, his cousin Devadatta, and son Rahula. A significant proportion of Kshatriya representation came from the gana-sanghas (22), which included the Shakyas, Lichhavis, Vrijjis, Mallas and Koliyas. Only five members from the rajyas find mention, of which two came from the Magadha royal family. The uchha kula representation was dominated by the shresthins, while the nichha kula included barbers (like Upali, who was a prominent disciple of the Buddha), potters, fishermen, etc.

The monastic community relied on the laity for food and other forms of support. While lay followers did not take monastic vows, they declared their devotion to the Buddha, dharma and sangha, and adhered to the five precepts of good conduct, like those observed by the monks. As aramas and viharas began to emerge, the concept of dana became more established. The supporters donated lands, constructed viharas and provided robes, medicines and other essentials for the sangha. For the laity, dana was a way to accumulate punya. Among the various forms of dana, providing a vihara was considered the highest form of a gift to the sangha. Followers engaged in dana with the intent of gaining fame, confidence, a place in heaven and rebirth with a higher status. The concepts of dana and punya, as we will explore later in the book, continued to play a crucial role in supporting the construction of Buddhist sites in the following centuries.

Interestingly, even among the lay followers, the majority were Brahmans and Kshatriyas. Grihapatis constituted the next important category. Early Pali texts mention names of 175 followers whose social backgrounds were known. The largest proportion were the Brahmans (76); followed by the grihapatis (33); uccha kulas, or families with higher social status (26); Kshatriyas (22) and the niccha kulas, or families with lower social status (11). The remaining (7) were parivrajakas. Most of these Brahmans were influential teachers with many followers. For example, Sonadanda of Champa region was a teacher of 300 Brahmans. The fact that grihapatis were recognized as the most important component of the laity is evident by how the Pali texts treat the Buddha's first meeting with Anathapindika of

Shravasti. It was described to be as important as his meetings with the kings of Magadha, like Bimbisara or Ajatashatru. Also, when Anathapindika was on his deathbed, Sariputra and Ananda visited him. Prominent among the lay followers from the raja kulas were the kings of Magadha and Kosala, and the royal physician of Magadha, Jivaka. Among the ones belonging to the uchha kulas, we may include vanijjas or traders like Trapusa and Bahalika (known in Pali as Tapussa and Bhallika respectively), who are regarded as the first two disciples of the Buddha, the shresthin of Rajagriha and courtesan Amrapali. The only prominent upasaka of the nichha kula was Chunda, who is said to have given the Buddha his last meal.

When one looks at the followers of the Buddha, whether monks or nuns or lay followers, three constituencies become very important – the Brahmans (who represented religious power), the Kshatriyas (who represented political power) and the grihapatis (who represented economic power). This triumvirate supported the Buddha for different reasons.[44]

For many Brahmans, the focus on the pursuit of salvation, as opposed to rituals and sacrifices, may have been an attraction. For the Kshatriyas, the Buddha hailing from the same varna as them may have mattered. Some scholars even see Buddhism as a Kshatriya reaction to Brahmanical dominance. Besides, most of the Buddha's Kshatriya followers came from the gana-sanghas, which were being crushed by monarchies like those in Magadha and Kosala. For them, the Buddha's teaching that all things were transient may have held a strong appeal. Merchants, traders and bankers, who were accorded a lesser status in the Vedic varna hierarchy, were respected in the Buddhist sangha. The Buddha also laid emphasis on kinship ties. The kinship relations of the Buddha, his disciples, monks and even lay followers, played an important role in the spread of his teachings. Kinship also played an important role in recruitment to the sangha.

The Buddhist faith, as is said, was a haven for social dropouts.[45] It questioned the authority of the Vedas and rejected Brahmanical rituals and animal sacrifice. The Buddha saw the Vedic varna hierarchy as man-made and lacking divine sanction. Members of all four varnas – Brahmans, Kshatriyas, Vaishyas and Shudras – could join the sangha if they fulfilled its requirements. The fact that the monks accepted food from everyone, irrespective of caste or class, made them more acceptable too. However, the Buddha did not disturb the existing social order. He didn't advocate the elimination of caste or call for the reordering of society. Slaves were not allowed to join the order without the permission of their masters and debtors, or without repaying their debts. Likewise, soldiers were not allowed to join without the permission of their political masters. The Buddha did not want to disturb the structure of family and marriage either, which were foundational to contemporary social life. And, it was with great hesitation that the Buddha allowed women to join the sangha. In many other areas, though, his thought and outlook resonated with the times.

The Buddha's teachings, manifesting in the form of the four Noble Truths and the Eightfold Path, suited the urban milieu and popular mood. These ideals appeared to be logical, rational, humane and easier to follow than Brahmanical rituals. He is said to have taught in Prakrit, the language of the masses. Sympathy or support for Buddhist ideas also came from the Buddha's appropriation of popular beliefs and cults, particularly the cult of chaityas (or sacred spots) being regarded as the abode of earth spirits or local deities. These chaityas were often small groves of trees or a single sacred tree, located on the outskirts of villages. Sometimes these included tumuli, or burial mounds (prototypes of later Buddhist stupas), that contained ashes of local chiefs. The mounds at Lauriya Nandangarh in northern Bihar are regarded as an early site of worship. The Buddha also found Vaishali to be 'charming' on account of its local shrines and sacred spots.

By the time of his death, the Buddha's influence was firmly established in the Gangetic plains of Uttar Pradesh and Bihar. His teachings had also taken root in peninsular India, where monasteries had begun to emerge. He spent his last monsoon in the city of Vaishali. After the rains, he and his followers travelled north, to the region where he had spent his youth. In the town of Pava (close to Kushinagar), he was hosted by his disciple Chunda, who offered him a meal of pork (some sources say it was truffle). Shortly after eating, the Buddha was afflicted with severe dysentery, but he insisted on proceeding to Kushinagar. There, on the outskirts of the town, the eighty-year-old Buddha lay beneath a sal tree and prepared his disciples for his death. It is said that the gods gathered to be with him in his final moments, a scene later depicted in many sculptures and paintings. He instructed his disciples not to seek a new leader after his passing, emphasizing that the dharma he had taught them would be their guide. He also told them to rely on themselves and be their own lights. Later that night, he passed away or achieved *mahaparinirvana* (the 'eternal bliss') (Fig 1.8). His last words were: 'All composite things decay. Strive diligently!'[46]

2

EMERGENCE OF RELIC CULT, STUPAS AND PILLARS

When the relics are seen, the Buddha is seen.

This was the response of Mahendra, King Ashoka's son, who is believed to have introduced the Buddha's teachings in Sri Lanka in the 3rd century BCE. As the legend goes, Mahendra (Mahinda in Pali) was impatient to return to India after the end of the first monsoon. He told King Devanampriya Tissa, 'For a long time, O King, we have not seen the Perfect Buddha, the Teacher. We have lived without a Master. There is nothing here for us to worship.'

'But, sir, did you not tell me that the Perfect Buddha has entered nirvana?' the Sri Lankan king asked.

This was when Mahendra explained to the king how seeing the relics meant seeing the Buddha or experiencing his presence.[1] This story, recounted in an episode in *Dipavamsa*, the Pali Sri Lankan chronicle, shows how the spread of Buddhist dispensation in the centuries following the Buddha's death went hand in hand with the movement of the relics. Also, the establishment of the triratna (Buddha, dharma and sangha) not only involved the propagation of the Buddha's teachings and the settlement of monks but also the movement of the holy relics.[2]

EMERGENCE OF RELICS: NAVIGATING THE BUDDHA'S ABSENCE

At the time of the Buddha's death, of the three jewels of the triratna, only two remained to guide the followers – dharma and sangha. The

Buddha had mentioned in clear terms that rather than a successor, dharma should guide the monks and nuns. To preserve dharma, the Buddha's teachings were compiled and passed on to the next generation by way of recitation and copying. Sangha, the third ratna, was to be preserved by the formulation of strict rules for initiation and transmission. The preservation of these two ratnas involved, among other things, the convocation of Buddhist councils. According to the Pali canon, a general council of monks and nuns is said to have been held in Rajagriha, the Magadha capital, soon after the Buddha's death. Upali, one of the Buddha's chief disciples, recited the *Vinaya Pitaka* or the 'Rules of the Order', based on his recall of the Buddha's teachings. Another disciple, Ananda, recited the *Sutta Pitaka*, a collection of the Buddha's sermons on matters related to doctrine and ethics. The Second Buddhist Council is believed to have been held in Vaishali a hundred years after the Buddha's death. Here, differences related to points of monastic discipline and the order led to the emergence of two sects – the orthodox Sthaviravadins (followers of the 'Sect of the Elders') and the Mahasanghikas ('Members of the Great Community'). There is no historical evidence of these two great councils; they only find a mention in Buddhist legends.[3] It may be relevant to briefly add that, in the subsequent centuries, eighteen sects or *nikayas* are said to have emerged from the original two and their subdivisions. Most divisions occurred because of differing perceptions of what constituted the true teachings of the Buddha. Some sects also emerged as regional variants of others. Later, when the Mahayana school (the Great Vehicle) came into being in the early centuries of the Christian era, these earlier sects were collectively bracketed as the Hinayana school (the Lesser Vehicle) to differentiate them from the former.[4]

Coming back to the first two councils, there were also discussions on how to address the absence of the Buddha's physical presence, the first of the triratnas. He had attained nirvana and become free from the fetters of mundane existence. How was this absence or emptiness to be addressed? His images, as we will discuss later in the book, were created much afterwards, around the 1st century BCE, and became common later. It was the relics and the Buddha's remains which filled the gap. His hair and nail clippings, it is held, had already been saved during his lifetime. They had developed their own sacred narratives. The relics came to be seen as 'endowed with life', as constituting the 'living presence' of the Buddha.

After the Buddha's death, his disciples cremated his body. The burnt remains, according to the *Mahaparinirvana Sutra* (*Mahaparinibbana Sutta* in Pali), a scripture that describes the events leading up to the Buddha's death, were divided into eight parts, one for each of the territories in which he lived and taught,[5] and stupas were erected over them. These eight structures came to be known as the 'original eight stupas' among the Buddhists. Known as 'thupa' in Pali, and 'tope' in English, the word 'stupa' is derived from the root 'stup' ('to heap'). As we discussed earlier, the practice of erecting mounds over funerary remains was not unique to the Buddhists. However, the Buddhists developed this practice into a cult and gradually the simple burial mounds gave way to ostentatious structures of great architectural value. In Sri Lanka, the stupa was known as *'dagaba'* derived from the Pali word *'dhatu-gabba'* (*'dhatu-garbha'* in Sanskrit)—a structure containing *dhatu* or corporeal relics within it.[6]

The sacred importance of the relics grew by leaps and bounds as they came to be regarded as equalling the presence of the Buddha himself. Variously described as 'the essence of the Buddha's body' (discussed in detail in the chapter on Sanchi), 'animated and characterized by the same qualities [as that of] the living Buddha', or the 'living energy containing the Buddha's elemental essence', the relics came to be categorized and hierarchized as dhatus, the term by which they became known.[7] On the top of the list were the corporeal relics, the *saririka* dhatu (body parts of the Buddha). Next in importance were the *paribhogika* dhatu (the 'relics of use', which included the objects used or enjoyed by the Buddha). These included his begging bowl, robe and the Bodhi tree under which he attained enlightenment. Even the vessel in which his burnt remains were temporarily stored before being distributed was placed in a stupa of its own. A sapling of the Bodhi tree was carried to Anuradhapura in Ceylon (Sri Lanka) and planted there. As the Buddhist faith spread, Bodhi trees were planted in the monasteries that came up. They were placed in enclosures known as the *bodhighara* (the house for the Bodhi tree). Such monasteries also had a stupa for the relics, in addition to residences for monks and nuns. The third category of relics came into being later, prompted by figural representations of the Buddha. In the mature monasteries of Sri Lanka, there was a hall for images, called the *pratimaghara*. In India, the Buddha came to be worshipped in the form of images around the 1st century BCE. Before that, it is popularly held that he was worshipped in the form of symbols like the Bodhi tree (symbolizing his enlightenment), wheel (symbolizing his first sermon), stupa (symbolizing his death) and footprints or *buddhapada* (symbolizing the 'mark' he left on the world). Some scholars hold that rather than serving as surrogates for his images, these symbols or portraits, depicted on stupas in Bharhut and Sanchi, formed the sacred nuclei of worship at such sites.[8] Whatever may have been the reason behind such symbols or portraits, the figural representations of the Buddha came to be known as the *uddesika* dhatu, the relics of indication.[9]

Given the importance of the relics, they were carefully guarded and preserved by monks and nuns. The Buddha is believed to have said that the relics of Sariputra, one of his close disciples, should be held by monks rather than lay followers.[10] Soon, the relics came to occupy a public character. After the Buddha's cremation, it is held that the Mallas of Kushinagar kept his bones in their council hall, guarded by spears and bows. Seven other armed parties arrived at the site to claim a share, but the Mallas refused. A conflict seemed imminent. At this juncture, a Brahman named Drona stepped in to remind everyone how the Buddha stood for forbearance. He then divided the relics into eight parts. Known as the 'war of relics', this episode is depicted in the oldest surviving Buddhist sculptures at Sanchi (Fig 2.1), Bharhut, Amravati and Gandhara. It shows how public value had come to be placed on the relics.[11]

The Pali canon tells us that the Buddha's relics were interned in structures that came to be known as stupas. The tradition of making stupas dates to pre-Buddhist times. The *Mahaparinirvana Sutra* tells us that eight stupas were built over the cremated remains of the Buddha (also known as Drona stupas) and two over the cremation vessel and embers of the funeral pyre. Later, relics of the Buddha's disciples and other prominent monks were enshrined into the stupas, making them places of veneration and pilgrimage.[12] Interestingly, King Ashoka's pillar inscription at Nigali Sagar, in the Nepalese Terai region, indicates that there was also a tradition of building stupas over the relics of past Buddhas.

These were the conditions in which the famous Ashoka (c. 268–32 BCE) found himself. We don't have much archaeological evidence for the reconstruction of the period between the death of the Buddha and the advent of Ashoka. All sites associated with the historical Buddha, such as Lumbini, Bodh Gaya, Sarnath, Kushinagar, Rajagriha, Shravasti, Kapilavastu and Kaushambi, can be dated to the Mauryan period.[13] Historically, the Ashokan period significantly changes the way we understand Buddhism.

ASHOKA EXTENDS ROYAL PATRONAGE TO THE DHARMA AND THE SANGHA

Ashoka was the second king of the Mauryan empire, which was built on the foundations of the Magadha mahajanapada, represented by kings like Bimbisara and Ajatashatru, among others. The heartland of the Mauryan empire remained the same as that of Magadha, despite political supremacy passing over from the Nanda to the Maurya dynasty. Rajagriha, one of the Buddha's favourite haunts, had given way to Pataliputra (Patna) as the new capital. At the peak of their power, which was under the reign of Ashoka, the Mauryas controlled almost the entire Indian subcontinent from Afghanistan in the northwest to Odisha in the east. This included the whole of peninsular India, except for some parts in the extreme south.

Now known as Ashoka the Great, the Mauryan emperor featured as one of the many kings in the dynastic list of Puranic literature till a little over a hundred years ago. It would not be wrong to say that the nation discovered Ashoka through his Buddhist connections. In 1837, epigraphist James Prinsep, who was also an antiquarian and the first European scholar to decipher the edicts of Ashoka, unearthed an inscription in which Ashoka had referred to himself as *devanampiya piyadassi* (*priyadarsi* in Sanskrit), the 'beloved of gods'. The name did not match any of those mentioned in the dynastic list of kings in the

Puranas, although it was mentioned in the Buddhist chronicles of Sri Lanka. Gradually, the clues were put together. The final confirmation came in 1915 with the discovery of yet another version of edicts in which the Mauryan king called himself Piyadassi Ashoka.[14]

In popular imagery, and in Buddhist tradition, Ashoka is imagined as a king who underwent a sudden and drastic transformation after a war in Kalinga (present-day Odisha), in which there was tremendous loss of human lives. After the war, it is held, the king converted to Buddhism and transformed into *dharma* Ashoka ('righteous') from *chanda* Ashoka ('cruel'). However, it must be clarified that Ashoka did not convert suddenly. He gradually and progressively became attached to the Buddha's teachings. The language and wording of the Ashokan inscriptions also reflect his progressive evolution as a Buddhist upasaka, or a lay follower, the term he uses for himself. It is important to note that while Ashoka patronized the sangha and had close connections with the leading monks of the time, such as Upagupta, he never joined the order.

Let us now see what Ashoka's inscriptions have to say about his association with the Buddhists and the sangha. Located strategically on important trade and pilgrimage routes, these are mostly in the form of rock (major and minor) and pillar edicts. The earliest of his inscriptions comes in the form of minor rock edict I, which, according to one estimate, dates to June 257 BCE. Among other things, it talks about his visit to a sangha, though the details are not given:

> It has been over two and a half years since I have been an upasaka. But for one year, I did not strive vigorously. It was over a year ago, however, that I approached the Sangha and began to strive vigorously ... This promulgation has been promulgated for the following purpose – so that both the lowly and the eminent may strive, that the frontier people also may come to know it, and that this striving may endure for a long time. And this matter will spread and spread immensely – spread at least one and a half times more.[15]

Found in eighteen locations across the subcontinent, including Karnataka and Andhra Pradesh, this is geographically the most widespread of all his edicts. The intended audience of this proclamation included not just the eminent people but also the lowest strata of society and those inhabiting the borderlands. Ashoka, it is held, expected them all to understand technical Buddhist terms and expressions. This emanated from the fact that by the time he became an upasaka, the Buddha's teachings were already popular and there were probably several monastic establishments in the vicinity of the sites hosting the edict. In the Bairat inscription addressed to monks and nuns, Ashoka expresses his 'faith in the Buddha, dharma and sangha', the triratna. This inscription was recovered from a narrow valley surrounded by three concentric ranges of hills, 85 kms from Jaipur, and is now in the care of the Asiatic Society, Kolkata. Here, the king of Magadha praises the Buddha saying that whatever he has said has been 'well spoken' and that 'the true dharma will long endure'. Finally, he prescribes seven sacred compositions, or discourses, on dharma. He wishes that 'a large number of monks and nuns will listen to them repeatedly and reflect on them, as will male upasakas and female upasikas.'[16]

Finally, we come to inscriptions popularly known as the schism edicts, where Ashoka is seen admonishing the sangha. This inscription exists as three versions in pillars found at Sanchi in Raisen district of Madhya Pradesh, Sarnath in Varanasi district of Uttar Pradesh and Allahabad (modern-day Prayagraj) in Uttar Pradesh, but the core message remains intact.

> The unity of the sangha has been instituted. In the sangha, no division is to be tolerated. Whoever divides the sangha, be it a monk or a nun, should be made to put on white clothes and reside in a non-monastic residence.[17]

Here, Ashoka sternly deals with dissensions within the monastic community, or *sanghabheda*, as the disunity of the sangha was known. Any monk who caused disunity, he warns, would be made to wear white clothes instead of the ochre-coloured robes worn by the monks (symbolizing a reduction to lay status) and would be made to reside in *anavasa*, the opposite of avasas.

The Sarnath version of the edict also instructs that 'this decree [royal order] should be communicated in this form both to the sangha of monks and to the sangha of nuns'.

The Sanchi version, on the other hand, adds the clause that the sangha of monks and nuns should last for a long time and should remain united for 'as long as my sons and great-grandsons, as long as the moon and the sun'.

The Allahabad version contains instructions, too. Addressed to the *mahamatras* (senior officials responsible for the propagation of Ashoka's moral philosophy, his version of dharma) of Kaushambi, it states:

> Let one copy of this edict remain with you, deposited in the bureau, and have one copy of it deposited with the upasakas. And let these upasakas go on every Uposatha-day [new or full moon days when the monks gathered and read aloud the monastic rules] so that trust may be developed in this decree; and consistently on every Uposatha-day let [the] respective mahamatras go to the Uposatha-ceremony so that trust may be developed in this decree and attention paid to it.[18]

The Kaushambi edict also directs the mahamatras to send out their subordinates to publicize the edict in their respective regions and beyond, in the border areas. Here, Ashoka is seen using the state apparatus to implement his directives related to the Buddhist sangha.

From minor rock edict 1 to the schism edicts, Ashoka had come a long way as far as his dealings with the sangha and Buddhism are concerned. His association changes, his confidence changes, and so does his tone. From the humble upasaka of minor rock edict 1 to instructing the sangha and prescribing a list of scriptures in the Bairat inscription, to admonishing the sangha, sternly dealing with dissensions and stating punitive actions for those causing disunity, Ashoka had become a more assertive Buddhist trying to regulate matters of the sangha. Was the sangha faced with disunity? Were there dissensions within the monastic order? Very likely, though we do not have any details. In the preceding chapter, we learnt that there were cases of monastic indiscipline in Kaushambi, even during the time of the Buddha. The early Pali works also mention dissensions during the time of Ashoka and how he helped the sangha deal with them. It is held that the emperor convened the Third Buddhist Council in Pataliputra to purge the sangha of deviant doctrines and practices, and to restore the pure and pristine form of the Buddha's teachings, which came to be known as the 'doctrine of the elders' (the Theravada, which struck strong roots in Sri Lanka).[19] Legend has it that Ashoka himself questioned several monks from different monasteries about the teachings of the Buddha, and heretics and dissidents were exposed and expelled from the sangha.[20] Historians have tried to establish a connection between this purge, which is eulogized in the Theravada tradition, and Ashokan schism edicts found in Sanchi, Sarnath and Allahabad. This, however, was not unusual. The exclusion of dissidents was a recognized pattern in sectarian contestations of the time.[21] It was at the Third Buddhist Council that the *Kathavattu*, the book that set out to disprove the wrong opinions and theories of several sects, was composed. Also, the *Abhidhamma Pitaka*, dealing with psychology and metaphysics, was added to the Pali canon as the third pitaka after the *Sutta Pitaka* and *Vinaya Pitaka*.[22]

It was possibly the Pataliputra council that decided to send missionaries to various parts of the subcontinent and beyond. The *Mahavamsa*, a Sri Lankan chronicle, mentions several missionaries being sent out after the conclusion of the Third Buddhist Council – Majjhima, Kassapagota, Dhundibissara, Sahadeva and Mulakadeva were sent to the Himalayan region; Madhyantika was sent to Kashmir and Gandhara; Maharakshita was sent to the Yavana (Greek) country; Mahadeva was sent to Mahishamandala (probably Mysore); Yavana Dharmarakshita was sent to Aparantaka in northern Konkan; Rakshita headed to Vanavasi (in northern Kannara); Mahadharmarakshita went to Maharashtra; Mahendra was sent to Lanka (Sri Lanka); and Sona and Uttara went to Suvarnabhumi (perhaps Myanmar or Southeast Asia).[23] It must be noted that some names of the missionaries sent to the Himalayan region appear in the relic caskets found in Stupa

No. 2 at the Sanchi complex, a point we will discuss in detail later. Island chronicles *Dipavamsa* and *Mahavamsa* talk about Ashoka sending his own son, Mahendra, to Sri Lanka and how the king of the region, Devanampiya Tissa, appears to have modelled himself after the Mauryan emperor. There were frequent exchanges of gifts and missions between the two. Ashoka even gifted a branch of the original Bodhi tree to the island nation that, it is claimed, survived in Sri Lanka though the parent tree in India was cut down in later centuries by anti-Buddhist fanatics.[24] This heightened sense of missionary activity and active proselytization was in some ways more characteristic of Buddhism than of the other religions that evolved in India.[25]

Ashoka was not only spreading the teachings of the Buddha but also monumentalizing the faith by building beliefs into edifices. This was routed through his visits to places that were considered sacred to the Buddhists and had already become sites of pilgrimage. These included sites prescribed by the Buddha at the time of his death. According to the *Mahaparinirvana Sutra*, he also told his disciples that his followers must visit and revere the four places associated with his life: birth (Lumbini), enlightenment (Bodh Gaya), first sermon (Sarnath) and death (Kushinagar). However, Ashoka seems to have visited more than the recommended four, and, in the process, laid down tangible foundations of what is now called the Buddhist circuit.

ASHOKA'S PILGRIMAGES AND PILLARS: MARKING THE BUDDHA'S PATH

In Major rock edict VIII, Ashoka talks about converting his recreational or pleasure tours into religious pilgrimages (dharma *yatra*). This was after he set out to Sambodhi, ten years after his royal consecration. Sambodhi, or Uruvela, has been understood to mean Bodh Gaya. It was the ancient name of the site where the Buddha attained enlightenment. Though Ashokan inscriptions do not record any constructions at the site, archaeological evidence suggests that the slab under the Bodhi tree, which is now known as Vajrasana (Fig 2.2) and is believed to mark the exact spot where the Buddha sat during the process of attaining enlightenment, was constructed by the Mauryan king. It has the characteristic polish and motifs – particularly the

Fig 2.1 War of Relics: Siege of Kushinagar, a relief from the Sanchi gateway

Fig 2.2 Vajrasana and the Bodhi tree on a panel of the Bharhut Stupa

Fig 2.3 Maya Devi temple and the Ashokan pillar at Lumbini

Fig 2.4 Ashokan pillar in the Allahabad Fort by Thomas A. Rust (c. 1870). Capt. Edward Smith surmounted it with a lion capital in 1838, which was later removed.

Fig 2.5 Drum panel depicting a stupa with the Buddha's descent from Trayastrimsa Heaven, Nagarjunakonda (Site 6), late 3rd century CE

Fig 2.6 Vaishali Stupa with the Ashokan pillar.

Fig 2.7 Remains of Dharmarajika Stupa, Taxila (Pakistan)

Fig 2.8 Inscribed panel from Kanaganahalli depicting Ashoka

sculptural band of honeysuckles and geese (*hamsa*) – found on other Ashokan pillars such as those in Rampurva or Sanchi. It is also held that the pillar to the south of the Mahabodhi temple dates to Ashoka's reign, though it is neither inscribed nor does it carry the characteristic Mauryan touch.[26]

Ashoka's constructions, or believed-to-be constructions, in Bodh Gaya have been a subject of several sculptural, inscriptional and textual representations. One of the sculptures associated with the Bharhut stupa, constructed a century after his death, shows a throne alongside the trunk of the Bodhi tree, enclosed by an open-pillared pavilion. *Divyavadana*, a 4th-century Sanskrit anthology of Buddhist stories, also credits Ashoka with the building of temples in Bodh Gaya, Lumbini, Sarnath and Kushinagar; while Xuanzang, the Chinese pilgrim who travelled to India in the 7th century CE, says that Ashoka surrounded the Bodhi tree with a 3 metre high stone wall. A Burmese inscription, which belongs to the 11th century and records repairs to the Mahabodhi temple, mentions that Ashoka built a temple at the spot where the Buddha ate a meal.[27]

Over the next few years, the Mauryan emperor inscribed his presence at several other sites.[28] Four years after his Sambodhi visit, or fourteen years after his consecration, Ashoka's inscriptions talk about his building activity at Nigali Sagar (or Niglihawa). There, he expanded and rebuilt a stupa dedicated to the Buddha Konakamana (or Kanakmuni), believed to be twenty-third on the list of twenty-four past Buddhas. This served as the geographical anchoring of the cult of the previous Buddhas in the 3rd century BCE, and Ashoka's construction there only enhanced its importance. His additions to the site at Nigali Sagar can no longer be seen, but accounts of Chinese pilgrims attest to the presence of the stupa of Konakamana several centuries later. The enlargement of this stupa was recorded six years later, when the emperor made a pilgrimage to the Buddha's birthplace, Lumbini, twenty years after his consecration. During this tour, the emperor visited three sacred sites located close to each other in the Nepalese Terai region – Nigali Sagar, Gotihawa (which is close to Kapilavastu) and Lumbini. The first two sites antedated Gautama Buddha and were associated with the previous Buddhas. Nigali Sagar, as we have already discussed, was connected to Konakamana while Gotihawa was related to his immediate predecessor, Krakuchhanda, the twenty-second Buddha. At Gotihawa, remains of an Ashokan pillar – also known as Phuteshwar Mahadev, possibly because it was worshipped as a *phuta* linga or 'broken phallus' of Mahadev (Lord Shiva) – have been discovered alongside a brick stupa dating to the Mauryan period (not necessarily Ashokan). A pillar was also erected at Nigali Sagar, which talks about Ashoka's presence and his recording of the enlargement of the stupa of Konakamana. The most important of the three sites was, of course, Lumbini.

Lumbini has a Maya Devi temple, which has structures that predate Ashoka. It has a square platform, marked by a point believed to be the exact spot of the Buddha's birth (Fig 2.3). The temple has yielded remains of root features, which have been interpreted as evidence of the first tree shrine, a feature that became very common in the later Buddhist establishments called bodhigharas. At Lumbini, the Mauryan-period construction seems to include a rectangular temple and an enlarged circumambulatory path. No Ashokan epigraph is seen on the extended temple edifice. However, the monolithic pillar erected by Ashoka at the site carries a brief inscription that memorializes his presence. The pillar, only parts of which can be seen now, may have once had an inverted lotus capital and an animal image. Tapering and polished monolithic pillars, crowned with animals and other sacred symbols, were an Ashokan innovation.[29]

The inscription on the pillar says:

King Priyadarsi ... *came in person* [and] worshipped, saying 'Here the Buddha was born, Sakyamuni.' [H]e had a stone wall [fence] made and erected a stone pillar. Saying *'here the Blessed One was born'*, the village of Lummini [Lumbini] was freed from tax and put at one-eighth (emphasis added).[30]

Interestingly, both at the site of the Konakamana stupa and in Lumbini, Ashoka is seen documenting his presence in very direct terms. His inscriptions carry a version of the following expression: 'King Priyadarsi ... came in person [and] worshipped [here].' In

EMERGENCE OF RELIC CULT, STUPAS AND PILLARS   55

Lumbini, he comes across as doing something more. He seems to be using an expression that had become a part of the Buddhist creed and was preserved in different forms in the different versions of the *Mahaparinirvana Sutra*. In one of the versions of this sutra, the Buddha says:

> After I have passed away, monks, those making the pilgrimage to the shrines, honouring the shrines, will come [to these places], they will speak in this way: '*Here the Blessed One was born*', 'here the Blessed One attained the highest most excellent awakening', etc. (emphasis added).[31]

Based on the similarity in the text, it has been suggested that Ashoka was possibly quoting or paraphrasing some version of a text that predated him. In visiting the site, he was doing something that was expected to be done by 'a devout son of a good family'. In an extant version of the old text, the Buddha is quoted as saying: 'Monks, there are these four places which are to be/must be visited by a devout son or daughter of [a] good family during their life.'[32] Ashoka's memorialization of the pillar and the event also had a political overtone. He used the occasion to announce tax relief, which is possibly the earliest documented example of a South Asian king or political patron using a sacred landscape to proclaim revenue concessions.[33]

Some other Ashokan pillars also exhibit a strong Buddhist association, indicating a visit by the emperor or perhaps a royal commissioning. The iconic pillar at Sarnath, adorned by the quadruple lion capital and surmounted by a wheel (representing the Buddha's first sermon), was adopted as the national emblem when India became independent. We have already discussed the schism edicts found on the pillars at Sarnath, Sanchi and Kaushambi. The pillar on which the Kaushambi edict was inscribed now stands inside the Allahabad Fort (Fig 2.4), while the Sanchi edict is in the stupa complex. It has been suggested that before the time of Ashoka, communities of monks had already settled in places like Vidisha and Ujjayini. Ashoka is reported to have erected a stone pillar with an elephant capital at Sankissa, the place where the Buddha is believed to have descended from trayastrimsa (heaven), alongside a stupa and a shrine. Chinese pilgrim Xuanzang reportedly saw 'three ladders' at the site, which marked the spot where the Buddha landed on the earth (Fig 2.5). Finally, the impressive pillar at Vaishali, again topped by a lion capital, does not have an inscription but has been identified as Ashokan because of the remains of a nearby stupa that show it was a contemporary of the emperor's time and bears artefacts (fragments of a stone umbrella and a relic casket) containing the quintessential Mauryan polish.

Many of the sites marked by Ashokan pillars or rock edicts later developed into flourishing Buddhist monastic sites. The emperor set up at least twenty pillars in locations that extended over large parts of Nepal's Terai region and northern India, including Champaran and Muzaffarpur in north Bihar, Sarnath near Varanasi, Kaushambi near Allahabad, Meerut, Hisar and Sanchi in central India. A rich oral tradition developed around these sites, which kept alive the memory of the Mauryan ruler, alongside the development of the legend of *Dharmaraja* ('the righteous king') Ashoka in the Pali canon and other Buddhist writings.[34]

FROM MUD TO BRICK: THE SPREAD OF STUPAS ACROSS THE SUBCONTINENT

Ashoka not only constructed new stupas but also undertook the repair and expansion of the existing ones. As Dharmaraja, his name is associated with the *dharmarajikas*, stupas built to house the relics of the Buddha. The *Ashokavadana*, a 2nd-century CE text, details the story of the eight *drona* stupas built after the Buddha's death. According to this text, Ashoka collected relics from the original stupas and enshrined them in the 84,000 stupas he built across the Jambudvipa – the term used for the Indian subcontinent back then. The *Mahavamsa* reports that 84,000 monasteries, or viharas, were built by the Mauryan king to honour the teachings of the Buddha. It does not mention any destruction of stupas. Both the *Ashokavadana* and the *Mahavamsa* describe a festival of relics marking the completion of the 84,000 stupas. The *Mahavamsa* also provides vivid accounts of

Ashoka's involvement in the festivities, where lavish gifts were given to the sangha, streets were decorated with lamps and flowers, music was played, and sermons were delivered.[35] Buddhist literature describes how the Buddha's cremated remains were divided into eight equal parts, which were distributed between Rajagriha, Vaishali, Kapilavastu, Allakappa, Ramagrama, Vethadipa, Pava and Kushinagar. Mud stupas were built over these remains. It is suggested that the mud stupas at Piprahwa and Vaishali may represent the two of the original eight stupas. During Ashoka's reign, seven of these eight stupas were excavated and the relics were redistributed to other parts of India and beyond. This act of redistribution by the emperor became part of Buddhist legends and is depicted in sculptures. Notably, one of the panels on the southern gateway of the Sanchi stupa illustrates Ashoka's visit to the Ramagrama stupa to retrieve the Buddha's relics.

Even archaeological studies corroborate that the stupas were opened repeatedly.[36] In the case of the Vaishali stupa (Fig 2.6), studies confirm that it was intentionally breached, and approximately three-fourths of the relics removed. The remaining contents of the stupa included ash mixed with earth, a punch-marked coin, a conch, a tiny piece of gold and two glass beads, but there were no bones. Similarly, the term 'one-eighth', or *atha-bhagiye*, mentioned in the Lumbini inscription, is interpreted by some to mean 'one-eighth share of the relics'. Instead of signifying a tax reduction of one-eighth, which would be minimal, this expression is thought to indicate that Lumbini received one-eighth of the Buddha's relics once the eight original stupas were opened.[37]

During Ashoka's time, mud gave way to brick as the construction material for the stupas. The old mud stupas at Vaishali and Piprahwa were either rebuilt or enlarged using bricks. In Rajagriha, Mauryan-age bricks were found in the western part of the mound, marking the site of a stupa. The brick core of the main stupa (Stupa 1) in Sanchi was also constructed during this period. The origins of the Dharmarajika and Dhamekh stupas in Sarnath, the Dharmarajika stupa in Taxila (Fig 2.7) in the north-west and the stupa–monastery complex in Amravati are also attributed to the Mauryan period. In 1982, while looking for Buddhist sites in Tons Valley in Rewa district of Madhya Pradesh, an excavation team discovered a brick stupa (Stupa 1) belonging to the Mauryan period. Nearby, they also found a colossal Mauryan pillar with a polished surface.

Ashoka played an important part in popularizing the cult of the stupa. Under his influence, the stupa quickly became a symbol of Buddhist dhamma and an essential part of monasteries. The focus of veneration shifted to the stupas, whether they contained relics or not.[38]

Recently, some scholars have pointed out that elephants, stupas and the lattice frame on the frieze of the Lomas Rishi cave (in Jehanabad district of Bihar) resembles the design on the Vajrasana throne gifted by Ashoka at Bodh Gaya. This implies that Ashoka was possibly creating dwelling units for the Buddhists, alongside the Ajivikas and other sects. Interestingly, the ancient name of Barabar hills, Khalatika, was also found inscribed on a stupa in Kanaganahalli in Karnataka, which was constructed many centuries later.[39] One of the relief panels of this stupa, in fact, also depicts Ashoka and his queens (Fig 2.8).

The Mauryan period, which marked India's first subcontinental empire, is notable for the transformation of the legacy of the Buddha and the sangha, both horizontally and vertically. Ashoka pulled this legacy out of the confines of the Gangetic heartland and gave it a subcontinental scope, coterminous with his large empire and beyond. He transformed the way the Buddha and his legacy were to be remembered through his initiatives: providing patronage to and, occasionally, instructing and admonishing the sangha; sending missions across the subcontinent; popularizing pilgrimage to sites associated with the Buddha; and monumentalizing the Buddhist faith with pillars, edicts and stupas.

Ashoka was not only demarcating and inscribing but also memorializing the existing Buddhist sacred landscape. Sites that had previously found a brief mention in Buddhist teachings and legends were transformed with new formal structures, facades and symbolism. Through the redistribution of relics from the old stupas and the creation of new ones, Ashoka expanded the spiritual and sacred geography of Buddhist teachings, imbuing it with a new appearance and significance. His monumental achievements influenced the development of future Buddhist establishments. Meanwhile, new sociopolitical changes and shifts in both doctrinal and monastic worlds introduced their own dynamism and geographical dimensions. The early centuries of the Christian era promised exciting prospects for the evolution of Buddhism and Buddhist monuments in India.

3

THE RISE OF IMAGES, MONASTIC COMPLEXES AND POPULAR CULTS

> [O]n this date, an image of the Blessed One Sakyamuni was set up by Monk Buddhavarman for the worship of all Buddhas. Through this religious gift may his Preceptor Sanghadasa attain nirvana, [may it also be] for the cessation of all suffering of his parents ... [and] for the welfare and happiness of all beings.

The above inscription, in some ways, reflects a popular sentiment prevalent in the Buddhist world in the post-Mauryan centuries.[1] Unlike the shresthin of Rajagriha, an affluent businessman who built sixty dwelling places for the monks to earn merit and secure a seat in heaven, this engraving speaks of the transfer of the merit earned by the protagonist to help others – in this case, to end the 'suffering of his parents' as well as the 'welfare and happiness of all beings'. This 'transfer of merit' became a defining feature of the bodhisattvas, compassionate saviours who emerged during this period. Bodhisattvas were believed to use their own spiritual merit to aid others in attaining salvation; they postponed their own nirvana until all beings in the universe had achieved it. Although the idea existed in some form earlier, merit transfer became a central tenet of Mahayana Buddhism and a key motivation behind the establishment of Buddhist structures.

The inscription also mentions the installation of the Buddha's images and the worship of multiple Buddhas – concepts popularized by the Mahayana tradition. In fact, Buddhists continuously reinvented the

THE RISE OF IMAGES, MONASTIC COMPLEXES AND POPULAR CULTS 61

idea of the Buddha, evolving from relics signifying his living presence to stupas representing the Buddha himself to his direct images. In the following centuries, images of the Buddha and the bodhisattvas were installed in monastic complexes that included not only stupas but also viharas and chaityas.

The inscription also highlights the involvement of monks in the installation of these images. Contrary to the popular belief that monks were solely focused on spiritual matters, historical evidence shows that they played an active role in promoting the cult of relics, stupas and images – key elements of the Buddhist landscape, which was further enriched by various factors between c. 200 BCE and 300 CE. These included new political regimes, flourishing maritime commerce and the rise of popular and devotional cults. Out of this complex interplay emerged new patrons, followers and supporters who not only reconceptualized the Buddha, but also the dharma and sangha, leading to a more expansive and vibrant legacy of Buddhism.

MIGRATIONS, NEW EMPIRES AND STATE FORMATIONS

After the disintegration of the first territorial empire under the Mauryas, India witnessed a complex political mosaic. The northern and north-western parts got entangled in political turmoil in Central Asia and the resultant migrations, while the peninsular and southern region saw the emergence of new states and professional groups amidst flourishing inland and maritime trade.

The immediate political successors of the Mauryas were the Shungas, a Brahman family who had served as officials under them. Though Buddhist texts accuse the Shungas (2nd–1st centuries BCE) of persecuting their followers and destroying monasteries, archaeological evidence credits them with the repair and renovation of sites like Sanchi and Kaushambi. Even the stone railing around the Bodhi tree is attributed to the queen of a feudatory of the Shungas. In other parts of northern and north-western India, such as Punjab, Haryana and Rajasthan, there was a reappearance of tribal or clan-based politics; while Kalinga, in modern Odisha, emerged as an independent kingdom in the 1st century BCE under Kharavela. In the north-west, the kingdoms ruled by Alexander's erstwhile generals, such as the

Seleucid empire, gave way to those being controlled by the Hellenistic kings known as Indo-Bactrian Greeks or Indo-Greeks, or *yavanas* in general. The most famous Indo-Greek ruler was Menander (c. 150–135 BCE), who is said to have been converted by famous Buddhist monk-philosopher Nagarjuna, also known as Nagasena. Menander ruled with his capital at Sakala (modern-day Sialkot), then in Punjab.[2] The Indo-Greeks were succeeded by the Parthians and the Scythians, known in Indian sources as the Pahlavas and the Shakas respectively.

The Shakas were divided into several branches and had seats of power in different parts of India and Afghanistan, including Punjab and Mathura. One of these branches was based in western India. Also known as Shaka-Kshatrapas, they were contemporaries of the Kushanas and continued to remain a significant political power till the 4th century CE. Some were also based in the upper Deccan region. The branch of the Shakas based in the north-west were displaced by a nomadic tribe known as Yuezhi (also called Yueh-chih) who hailed from north-western China. Soon, the Yuezhi, ruling from Bactria (in modern-day Afghanistan), were also defeated and the parent tribe broke into five chieftainships. A king called Kujula Kadphises united these five chieftainships and laid the foundation of the Kushana kingdom based out of Bactria.

At its zenith, the Kushana empire spanned Central Asia, Iran, Afghanistan, Pakistan and northern India, reaching as far as Varanasi in present-day Uttar Pradesh. Purushapura, or Peshawar, as we know it, and Mathura constituted two important political centres of the Kushanas under Kanishka (reign held to have started in 78 CE). Regarded as the most famous Kushana ruler, Kanishka is said to have enshrined the Buddha's relics in a huge stupa at Purushapura and also built a major monastery that excited the wonder of foreign travellers.[3] An important Buddhist conclave, popularly known as the Fourth Buddhist Council, was held during his reign, but the location is not very clear. Kanishka is also said to have patronized Buddhist scholars, such as Ashvaghosha and Vasumitra, and sent missionaries to Kashgar and Yunan.

While the Kushanas ruled the north-west and northern parts of India, the Satavahanas established political supremacy in the peninsular region, particularly the western Deccan region. Known as the Andhras in the Puranas, they had transitioned from a chiefdom to a kingdom, with one of their kings gradually assuming the titles of 'Lord of Pratishthana' (present-day Paithan in Maharashtra was their capital) and 'Lord of the Southern Regions'. The Satavahanas were also the early patrons of the Ajanta caves.

While the political map of the time looks like a complex mosaic of fragmented political identities, many of these post-Mauryan polities proactively supported the expanding network of trade, giving the subcontinent a strong commercial vitality. The production, exchange and trade networks discussed in the first chapter on the Buddha's times had become bigger and broader under the Mauryas. Gradually, a strong commercial economy developed around long-distance trade that was supported, among other things, by a growing dispersal of craftsmen and production centres, expansion of mining activities, development of markets and coinage (particularly small-denomination coins by the Kushanas and Satavahanas), linking of land and maritime traffic, the emergence of superior ships, and a supportive network of ports.

TRADE, COMMERCE AND BUDDHIST ESTABLISHMENTS

The Uttarapatha, the land-cum-river northern route; and the Dakshinapatha, the southern route connected to the ports on the western coast, became busier as they were further integrated with numerous other routes along the highways, river valleys and coasts. The caravans, based on what the Jatakas – composed between the 3rd century BCE and the 2nd century CE – indicate, had become bigger. Long-distance routes, such as the north to south-west route from Shravasti to Pratishthana, and those that followed the river valleys of the north were regularly frequented. The political control of the Indo-Greeks, Shakas and Kushanas had brought Central Asia closer to India. The Kushanas also brought the Silk Route and China into the subcontinental trade and exchange network. The Gulf of Cambay continued to receive ships from the Arabian Sea. The period between the 2nd century BCE and 3rd century CE saw trade flourishing between India and the Roman Empire. Peninsular

India expanded trade with Mediterranean Europe, while trade with Southeast Asia, facilitated by the ports on the east coast, also became more profitable. A complex maritime network, involving both coastal and trans-oceanic sailing, and Arabs, Indians, Greeks, Romans and Southeast Asian communities, developed.[4]

The Jatakas tell stories of long-distance journeys over land, river and sea. Indian traders, who owed allegiance to Buddhism, are described as venturing into Suvarnadvipa (Southeast Asia), Ratnadvipa (Sri Lanka) and Baberu (Babylon). There are stories of voyages, difficult journeys and shipwrecks. *Periplus of the Erythraean Sea,* the maritime travellers' handbook of the early centuries, lists goods exported to the Roman empire from the Indian ports on the Indus River delta and the Gujarat coast. Pliny the Elder (23/24–79 centuries CE), the famous author of several encyclopaedic works, complains about the drain of Roman gold into India. There was a southward shift in Roman trade interest. The Sangam poems talk of yavanas (the generic term for foreigners from the West) bringing goods by ship into southern India. They also mention large ships sailing on the river Periyar, bringing in gold and wine, and leaving with cargos of black pepper. Some contemporary accounts also describe Arikamedu, along the Coromandel coast, as a yavana emporia or trading station.[5]

The rise of new political dispensations with different cultural affiliations, the development of overland trade with Central Asia and China, and maritime networks with Europe and Southeast Asia facilitated not just commerce but also the transmission of Buddhist ideas and practices. It encouraged movements of monks and missions as well. The impact of Graeco-Roman ideas could be seen, among other things, in Buddhist art and sculptural traditions, particularly those attributed to the Gandhara school. The Afghanistan–Gandhara region also emerged as an important centre for Buddhist establishments. In the 1st century CE, the first Buddhist missionaries established themselves at the famous White Horse Monastery in Luoyang, China. Later, Yarkand, Kashgar, Khotan, Tashkend, Turfan, Miran, Kucha, Qarashahr and Dunhuang became sites of development of stupas and monasteries. Chinese and Central Asian translations of Buddhist texts, as well as Buddhist scrolls from Gandhara, housed in the British

THE RISE OF IMAGES, MONASTIC COMPLEXES AND POPULAR CULTS

Library in the UK, are good sources of information about this period. It is held that the demand for relics, images and ceremonial objects played an important role in the development of the India–China trade.[6] In the peninsular region, Buddhist caves came to be located along trade routes and heads of important passes, particularly in the western Deccan region.[7]

The post-Mauryan years were not just about changing political–cultural configurations and trade links along the borderlands but also about new consolidations – new states, cities and crafts in the peninsular region. The beneficiaries of these developments, whether kings or traders or professional and occupational groups, extended the scope of religious patronage in their effort to seek social or political validation and to earn spiritual merit. The religious dispensations were in turmoil too, as they were faced with new questions. How were they to accommodate new patrons and followers? How were they to deal with religious affiliations and local devotional cults competing for patronage? How were they to strengthen their own institutional foundations? Questions were also being asked from within – about the legacy of the Buddha, the adequacy of the existing doctrines, liturgy and forms of worship. The Buddha, dharma and sangha were all set for a makeover, perhaps a major one.

THE EMERGENCE OF THE MAHAYANA

One of the major developments in the Buddhist world was the emergence of the Mahayana (the Great Vehicle), which reconceptualized the imagery of the Buddha. Central to this reimagination was the idea of the bodhisattvas, the 'wisdom beings' who were full of compassion, love and charity.

The bodhisattva was a not a new entity in the Buddhist pantheon. The historical Buddha is said to have taught that he was the last in the long succession line of the Buddhas or bodhisattvas. In his previous lives as a bodhisattva, the Buddha had wrought many deeds of kindness and mercy. Gradually, the cult of past Buddhas became widespread and, as we saw in the preceding chapter, was patronized by emperor Ashoka. The orthodox Sthaviravadin ('Sect of the Elders') tradition eventually counted no less than twenty-five Buddhas, besides several *pratyeka* Buddhas who had found the truth without guidance but did not teach it to the world. The orthodox tradition, represented in the Pali canon, never claimed that the Buddha was a supernatural or divine being, though he certainly was a mahapurusha. For them, he was a teacher par excellence who gained supreme insight through ages of striving, spread across different births, and became an *arhat* (*arhant* in Pali), the one who had attained nirvana. The Buddha's death, it is held, broke the chain of his existence – he ceased to be an individual, or to affect the universe in any way. He finally entered the nirvana he had realized at the time of enlightenment.[8] So, what now? In this context, some ideas acquired prominence during the early centuries of the Christian era, which came to be defined as the core of the Mahayana.

If Buddhas and bodhisattvas existed before the historical Buddha, they should also exist in the present universe and in the future – this was one of the critical points of the development of a new mythology. This was how the idea of a future Buddha, the Maitreya, came into being. However, the idea of the bodhisattva that acquired prominence in the early centuries was different from the form in which they existed prior to the historical Buddha. The new bodhisattva was like a suffering saviour, or a Buddha-in-waiting, who went beyond the salvation of the self and willingly delayed the attainment of Buddhahood till the smallest of insects had attained nirvana. In the earlier conceptualizations, the bodhisattva worked with wisdom and love and strove continuously till he attained nirvana or became an arhat. He then freed himself from the cycle of birth and death. The old ideal of arhat began to be looked upon as a selfish goal. People were taught to become bodhisattvas, as opposed to arhats, so that they used their spiritual merit to help others attain salvation.[9]

The idea of transferring merit became one of the key elements of the emerging Mahayana school. It needs to be clarified that this was in circulation even before the advent of the Mahayana tradition in the early centuries of the Christian era. Donative inscriptions from the 2nd and 1st centuries BCE, found at Bharhut, Pauni in Maharashtra and Sri Lanka (from an even earlier period of 210–200 BCE), carried expressions like 'for the benefit of his mother and father' (Bharhut) or 'for the happiness of all beings' (Pauni) and 'for the welfare and happiness of beings in the boundless universe' (Sri Lanka). Mahayana made this idea more popular, ensuring it became widespread in the coming centuries.[10] The followers of new ideas claimed to have found a 'greater vehicle', which could lead several more people to salvation. They started calling themselves Mahayana to distinguish themselves from what they called the 'lesser vehicle', which included the existing orthodox sects.

The Jatakas, which built on the existing folklore and gave them a Buddhist tinge, added another component to the Mahayana tradition. They emphasized, through stories, that the bodhisattvas could be born both as humans and animals, and could even reside as divine beings in the Buddhist heaven. The Mahayana universe had multiple Buddhas and bodhisattvas continuously and compassionately striving for the salvation of sentient beings in their respective fields, or *Buddhakshetras*. These included Avalokiteshvara ('the lord who looks down'); Manjushri (meaning 'gentle, or sweet, glory'), usually depicted with a naked sword in one hand (to destroy error and falsehood) and a book in the other (describing the ten parameters of spiritual perfection to be attained by a bodhisattva); and Vajrapani, who bore a thunderbolt. The Mahayana ideas were set to evolve more in the ensuing centuries and also find expression in Buddhist art and architecture.[11]

The two vehicles – the greater and lesser – like the other Buddhist sects, had their own pitakas. Unlike the texts of the orthodox tradition, which were written in Pali, the Mahayana followers wrote in Sanskrit. In fact, it soon became their preferred language for compositions in India. In other parts of Asia, such compositions tended to be in the local languages. Most of the early Mahayana texts seemingly built on the sermons of the Buddha, but they were greater in length than those in the *Sutta Pitaka*. They, therefore, became known as the expanded sermons, or *vaipulya sutras*.[12] Important Mahayana texts included the *Lalitavistara* (a narrative of the life of Buddha); *Saddharmapundarika* (The Lotus of the Good Law), which was a long series of dialogues of considerable literary merit; the *Vajrachedika* (Diamond-cutter), which was mostly metaphysical writing; the *Sukhavativyuha* (which describes the glories of Amitabha and his paradise); the *Karandavyuha* (which glorifies Avalokiteshvara) and *Astasahasrika Prajnaparamita* (a work describing the spiritual perfections of the bodhisattvas). Of these, the *Lalitavistara*, one of the earliest Sanskrit compositions, was utilized by Sir Edwin Arnold for his famous book *The Light of Asia*, a lengthy poem on the Buddha's life.

Apart from sacred texts, the Mahayana school also produced books on religious poetry and philosophy. It had two chief philosophical schools: the Madhyamika (intermediate), founded by philosopher Nagarjuna in the 2nd century CE; and Yogachara (way of union), apparently founded by a monk named Maitreyanatha.[13] The Madhyamika school builds on the idea of *shunyata* (emptiness or void), which stresses that appearances are misleading and that permanent selves and substances do not exist. Important philosophers of this school included Aryadeva, Buddhapalita, Bhavaviveka, Chandrakirti and Shantideva. The Yogachara school, on the other hand, attaches importance to meditation as a means of attaining the highest goal. Important exponents of Yogachara included Asanga and Vasubandhu (both belonging to the 4th century CE), Sthiramati (6th century) and Dharmakirti (7th century).[14]

The Mahayana school, which was apparently more optimistic and believed in the salvation of even the smallest of the worms, appealed to the mood of the times and soon became popular in different parts of India. It is not clear which part of the subcontinent such ideas first developed in, but they soon became popular in China, Japan, Nepal and Tibet. The orthodox tradition, which began to be called Hinayana, remained strong in Ceylon (Sri Lanka) and later spread to Burma (Myanmar), Siam (Thailand), Cambodia and other Southeast Asian countries. Given their geographical spread, the Hinayana school is sometimes referred to as the 'southern school', while Mahayana is called the 'northern school'. The dichotomy between the Hinayana and Mahayana schools remains one of the dominant frameworks through which the history of Buddhism in the early centuries of the Christian era is understood. Does that mean the Mahayana school represented a schism or split in the sangha? No, not in the sense that 'schism' is understood in Christianity, where it relates to diverse interpretations of the theological dogma. If one were to go by the textual and inscriptional use of the term 'Mahayana', it neither referred to a new sect nor a new monastic community. On the contrary, there were sects within what came to be known as the Hinayana school. Mahayana referred to a new set of ideas and practice within the already existing ones. In short, it presented an alternative vision in response to its imagined other, the 'Hinayana', a term mostly used by the Mahayana followers to refer to non-Mahayana forms of Buddhism. It did not cause any split in the sangha. Travel accounts by Chinese pilgrims and travellers Faxian (4th–5th centuries) and Xuanzang confirm that the Mahayana and non-Mahayana monks continued to live together in the same monasteries.[15]

The most direct implication of Mahayana ideas at the level of popular practice was the worship of the Buddha and the bodhisattvas in the form of human images in shrines. This brings us to another perceived difference between the Hinayana and Mahayana schools. It is popularly held that the Mahayanists worshipped images, while the Hinayanists mostly venerated the stupas and relics. It is said that the Hinayanists deliberately avoided the worship of images. How can a person who has ceased to exist in a physical form be represented? How can the Buddha's nirvana, which is inconceivable in visual form or human shape, be represented? Some scholars have contradicted this idea outright. Basing their views on textual, archaeological and inscriptional evidence, they have pointed out that almost all of Hinayana sects were receptive to and actively interested in the cult of images. Also, the followers of both Mahayana and Hinayana schools revered and worshipped the Buddha's images.[16] This brings us to another important question: how did the first images of the Buddha come into being?

THE ANTHROPOMORPHIC BUDDHA AND SCHOOLS OF ART

The Buddha's images start appearing commonly, both in relief and free-standing sculpture, in the 2nd and 3rd centuries. It is popularly held that the first images were created during the Kushana period, around the 2nd century CE. In the early 20th century, Alfred Foucher propounded a theory. Buddha images, he said, originated in the

Gandhara region in the early centuries of the Christian era. It was the Western influence, particularly Graeco-Roman, in the Gandhara region that stimulated the creation of an anthropomorphic image of the Buddha. Representing the Buddha without his bodily images was a 'monstrous abstention'. 'If they did not do it,' Foucher argued, 'it was because it was not the custom to do it.'[17] Interestingly, around the same time, Japanese scholar Okakura Kakuzo argued that the anthropomorphic Buddha emerged under Chinese influence. He argued that the Kushanas, who introduced such an image in India, had Mongolian origins.[18]

Foucher was criticized by Ananda Coomaraswamy, who held that the creation of the impetus for the Buddha's image was rooted in indigenous beliefs and sculptural tradition. He asserted that the first anthropomorphic Buddha originated in the indigenous Mathura school of art.[19] More recently, some scholars have cited the case of some pre-Kushana images of the Buddha. A gold reliquary found at Bimaran in the Kapisa (Begram) region of Afghanistan, which carries a standing Buddha flanked by Hindu gods Indra and Brahma, dates to the late 1st century BCE. Another one – a seated hallowed figure, again flanked by Brahma and Indra – found in Pakistan's Swat Valley belongs to the early 1st century CE. Based on the occurrence of these stone images of the Buddha, scholars have argued that such visual representational norms were already in place in the pre-Kushana times. The production of the Buddha's images gained wider currency under the Kushanas (late 1st century to 3rd century CE). It needs to be clarified that the emergence of anthropomorphic images did not mean an end to the aniconic representations of the Buddha. Both traditions continued to coexist,[20] sometimes at the same site. At Gandhara and Nagarjunakonda, for instance, Buddha images are found in sculptural relief alongside aniconic or non-human or symbolic representations.[21] The tradition of making images was popularized by art centres based in the Afghanistan–Gandhara and Mathura regions. These centres are often referred to as the two schools of Buddhist art.

Constituting territories in north-western India and parts of modern-day Pakistan and Afghanistan, the Gandhara region was one of the sixteen mahajanapadas. It experienced the development of a cosmopolitan and syncretic culture as political control passed through the hands of the Macedonians, the Mauryas, the Graeco-Bactrians (Hellenistic), the Shakas, the Indo-Parthians and the Kushanas. Buddhist traditions had largely been introduced in the region by the Mauryas. The sculptural art of Gandhara is known for combining stylistic influences of the Hellenistic, Persian and Kushana cultures. Buddhist sculpture in Gandhara is particularly noteworthy for introducing anthropomorphic depictions of the Buddha, bodhisattvas and associated figures.

The Gandhara school of art flourished mostly between the 1st and 5th centuries CE, though it continued in parts of Kashmir and Rajasthan till the 7th century CE. Most Gandhara sculptures were made of stone, primarily blue schists and green phyllite, in the initial years. From the 1st century CE, stucco or lime plaster began to be used, replacing stone as the sculptural material by the 3rd century CE.[22]

While the themes of the Gandhara school were indigenous, the style and execution were Graeco-Roman. In fact, the Graeco-Roman influence strongly manifests in the facial features of the Buddha, his curly or wavy hair usually ending in a top knot called *ushnisha*, elongated earlobes, a muscular body, finely delineated robes and a halo around his head (Fig 3.1). Standing Buddha images, mostly in the protection-granting *abhay* mudra, are very common. One also comes across some seated buddhas, mostly in the *dharmachakra* mudra (teaching pose) or *dhyana* mudra (the meditative pose). Some Buddha figures also have a moustache. Unlike the Buddha figures, the bodhisattva figures found in Gandhara are often heavily ornamented, have elaborate hairdos and/or turbans and wear sandals. Many of them too, have moustaches. These include Maitreya (with a vase in his left hand) and Avalokiteshvara (Padmapani, with a lotus in his hand). Gandhara artists also sculpted scenes from the life of Gautama, alongside Jataka stories, like their counterparts in central India and Andhra.

Unlike the 'foreign-influenced' Gandhara school, the Mathura school was regarded as a predominantly indigenous one that produced sculptures across religious traditions – Brahmanical, Buddhist and Jaina – and included images of popular deities like yakshas and yakshis, nagas and nagis, alongside those of Buddhas and bodhisattvas, Jaina *tirthankaras* and Hindu deities. The headless statue of Kanishka is also attributed to this school. Centred around the southern capital of the Kushanas, this school mostly produced works in the locally available red sandstone.[23] In the early phase, the school produced images in a heavy masculine form reflecting super abundant physical energy but devoid of spiritual expression. Later, influenced by the ideology of Yogachara – which laid emphasis on the study of perception, cognition, and consciousness through the prism of meditation and philosophical reasoning – the images lost their physical weight and heaviness and acquired graceful and luminous forms. The Mathura school is also known for producing the seated Buddhas in abhay mudra. As opposed to their Gandharan counterparts – with their inward-looking meditative expressions – Buddhas produced contemporaneously in Mathura look directly at the viewer. They have round, smiling faces, broad shoulders and mostly sit on a lion throne as opposed to the one in lotus pose. Their heads are smooth, mostly shaven or with curly hair, and topped with tiered or coiled ushnisha, unlike the stylized hair of the Buddhas of Gandhara. They are most often depicted wearing monastic robes or *sangati*, which looks like a translucent Indian dhoti, with one shoulder left bare. Their heads are surrounded by a halo with scalloped edges, above which is a pipal tree. The Buddhas are flanked either by two small attendants or by gods Indra and Brahma. Among the bodhisattvas, there are specimens of Maitreya, Vajrapani and Avalokiteshvara. The Mathura artists also carved scenes from the Buddha's life. A colossal Buddha image standing along a shaft, carrying a parasol (*chhatra*), now found in the museum at Sarnath, is typical of the mature Mathura style. Another mature Mathura-style image of the Buddha can be seen in Rashtrapati Bhawan (Fig 3.2), New Delhi. The Buddha's images were also produced in art centres in peninsular India, like in Amravati and Nagarjunakonda. Other centres in Andhra, such as Goli (in Palnadu district) and Gummadidurru (Krishna district), also produced Buddha images on limestone slabs and some free-standing figures for enshrinement in temples.[24]

It was not just the images and Mahayana Buddhism that changed the way the Buddha and his legacy were understood, but also the

THE RISE OF IMAGES, MONASTIC COMPLEXES AND POPULAR CULTS 73

new monastic complexes, which were developed around a stupa. Also known as stupa-monasteries, these complexes had a shrine where the Buddha was worshipped. Even the idea of the stupa was changing as it became more ritualized and came to represent the Buddha himself.

STUPA-MONASTERY COMPLEXES BEYOND THE GANGETIC HEARTLAND

From earthen mounds to mud stupas enshrining the relics of the Buddha, to relic towers encasing relics of other Buddhist monks, and brick stupas under Ashoka, the cult of the stupa underwent a significant evolution under the Mauryas. In the post-Mauryan period, while relics continued to remain sacred, there was a shift in the focus of veneration – from the relics to the stupas, with or without the relics. The practice of enshrining relics of the local monastic dead in stupas also became popular.

The cult of the stupa became more formalized and ritualized in the early centuries of the Christian era. These structures then came to represent the Buddhist dharma and the Buddha himself. Gradually, grand festivals were held upon the completion of stupas and enshrinement of relics, where all sections of society participated. Sculptural relief panels at Bharhut and Sanchi show festivals related to the consecration of relics, with devotees, floral offerings and musicians (Fig 3.3). A bas-relief from Bharhut, dating to the 1st century BCE, depicts festivities around the installation of the Buddha's crest jewel, *cudamani*. It shows an assembly of people with folded hands showering flowers, alongside dancers and musicians. Bharhut also depicts relic processions headed by dancers and musicians.[25]

Texts like *Apadana*, *Buddhavamsa* and *Cariyapitaka*, Pali biographies of the Buddha written in the post-Ashokan period (in the 2nd century BCE) talk about the stupa cult and all the paraphernalia such as *danam* (gift) and the merit-making associated with it, stupa worship rituals and special stupa festivals that also required the presence of divine beings. All these were being put into architectural practice at the monastic sites. The intangible textual references surrounding the stupa cult were finding tangible manifestations in the donative inscriptions (which talk about the profile of the donors and the nature of donations), relief panels (particularly those related to stupa worship and festivals) and images or sculptural depictions of mythical beings like yakshas, nagas and other divine beings within the stupa complex. These texts were being translated into stone at Sanchi, Bharhut and Amravati, particularly in the portions built by the Shungas and Satavahanas. The stupa festivals, it is argued, constituted the continuation of the biography of the Buddha in that time and space. It also marked the congregation of a universal society where the emperor, donors and divine beings came under one complex agency to sponsor and organize such festivals, which were also characterized by the recitation and performance of the texts being discussed.[26]

One of the most direct manifestations of the growing cult of the stupas was the proliferation of such structures as free-standing and within caves. In western Deccan, rock-cut stupas were found inside Buddhist *chaitya* caves (Fig 3.5 shows various forms of stupas). The stupas also became the nuclei for the growth of monastic complexes in the early centuries. These complexes included dwellings for monks (viharas), stupas and shrines (chaityas). Scholars also point to a phenomenal spatial expansion in Buddhist monastic sites from the 2nd–1st centuries BCE. Broadly speaking, four geographical concentrations of monastic complexes developed as the Buddha's legacy spread out of the Gangetic heartland into north-west and peninsular India – central India, Gandhara, eastern Deccan and western Deccan. Most of them were located close to urban centres or along major trade and pilgrimage routes. These sites were neither visited by the historical Buddha in his lifetime, nor were they connected to any important event in his life. Also, most of these complexes were built over many centuries and show a gradual evolution of sculpture and architectural style, as well as religious thought and practice. While most such complexes shared architectural and sculptural features, there were distinct regional variations.[27]

How did this major geographical spread become possible? Scholars have assigned a variety of reasons. Some attribute it to the key processes of urbanization, state formation and innovations in irrigation and agriculture,[28] while others say it was because of maritime trade, especially in the case of monastic sites located along

THE RISE OF IMAGES, MONASTIC COMPLEXES AND POPULAR CULTS 75

the Deccan coast.²⁹ Most, however, hold that the sangha and the community of monks and nuns played an important role.³⁰ Regional dynamics were not only a major factor in the development of the monastic complexes, but they also showed how the sangha adapted to local contexts to gain greater legitimacy. Let us now look at the geographies and the distinct and regional features of the monastic complexes that emerged during the period under consideration.

Gandhara

The Gandhara region in the north-west rides on the fame of the Gandhara school of art, which produced numerous images of the Buddha and the bodhisattvas, and was based out of the Peshawar valley. A new term, the 'Greater Gandhara', has been gaining currency in academic circles in the recent years. This includes the neighbouring Swat and other river valleys, the Taxila region located 35 kms north-west of the modern city of Rawalpindi in Pakistan and eastern Afghanistan.³¹ Ashoka had served as the governor of the Taxila region before becoming the Mauryan emperor. His presence in the region is attested to by his edicts in Kharosthi script. Most stupa-monastery complexes in the Gandhara region, including Takht-i-Bahi in Pakistan and Guldara in Afghanistan, are currently in ruins. In the majority of Gandharan stupa-monasteries in the Peshawar valley, images of the Buddha are placed in a series of multiple chapels surrounding the court or sacred complex of the main stupa. The main stupa also had clusters of monasteries and smaller stupas around.³²

An examination of the Buddha images found in the valley reveals the interesting practice of relics being installed in the Buddha statues through a hole in the head, through the ushnisa.³³ This was possibly done to make the image ritually more alive, powerful and communicative. But perhaps the most famous Buddhist structures of the region have been found at Taxila, which was located at the junction of trade routes coming from eastern India, West Asia, Kashmir and Central Asia. Currently a UNESCO World Heritage Site, Taxila is known for the remains of three cities described as the Bhir mound, Sirkap and Sirsukh. Buddhist structures have been located both inside and outside the settlement area. Excavations here have revealed the presence of a sacred Buddhist landscape consisting of stupas, monasteries, apsidal temples, miniature shrines, tanks and wells. Taxila's most iconic landmark is the imposing Dharmarajika stupa (Fig 2.7, Chapter 2), so named as it is believed to contain the relics of the Buddha who was also known as Dharmaraja. The structural remains of the stupa complex, locally known as Chir Tope, belong to the Mauryan period and early centuries of the Christian era.

The circular or wheel-shaped base of the Dharmarajika stupa possibly came into being in the 1st century CE, when the structure was rebuilt after an earthquake. Around the same time, a ring of smaller stupas was built around the main structure, which later gave way to miniature shrines. The small stupas have been found to contain bone relics, relic caskets, beads, coins, etc. Here, a 1st-century CE silver scroll inscription in Kharosthi refers to the enshrinement of the Buddha's relics in a stupa inside the complex by a Bactrian called Urasaka, for the 'bestowal of health' on a Kushana king. A small gold casket in the stupa contains the said relics. The presence of a strong relic cult comes across as an important feature of the Gandharan monastic complexes. The distribution of relics is a theme that also finds representation in the Gandharan sculptural panels.[34] Another distinguishing feature of the stupas of the north-west, at least in comparison to those in central India, is that they had a tower-like appearance with sculptural decorations (like pilasters, niches, chaitya arches and stucco images) on the dome and the base.[35]

The discovery of a wheel-shaped stupa containing relic caskets at Sanghol, near Chandigarh, along with remains of monastery, carved stone slabs, pillars, crossbars, and red sandstone sculptures also puts Punjab on the Buddhist map of the Kushana period. The artefacts found here are associated with the Mathura school. Coming back to Taxila, the other famous structure here is the Pippala monastery. It consists of an open quadrilateral court with a stupa in the centre and cells on all four sides. This plan comes across as standard in northern India in the early centuries of the Christian era. It can be seen in many places, including Sanchi. In the later monasteries, a roofed and pillared hall appears in place of the open quadrangular courtyard and the central stupa/Buddha image gets shifted to a sanctuary with a path around it for circumambulation.[36]

Fig 3.1 Schist image of the Buddha from Gandhara (Pakistan), dating to 3rd century CE

Fig 3.2 Image of the Mathura Buddha from 5th century CE, currently housed at Rashtrapati Bhawan, New Delhi

Fig 3.3 Relief from the Satavahana period showing stupa worship by followers, including foreigners, at Sanchi (99–1 BCE)

Fig 3.4 Drum slab from Amravati Stupa (100–299 CE)

Fig 3.5 Various forms of stupas (after Percy Brown, *Indian Architecture*, 1956)

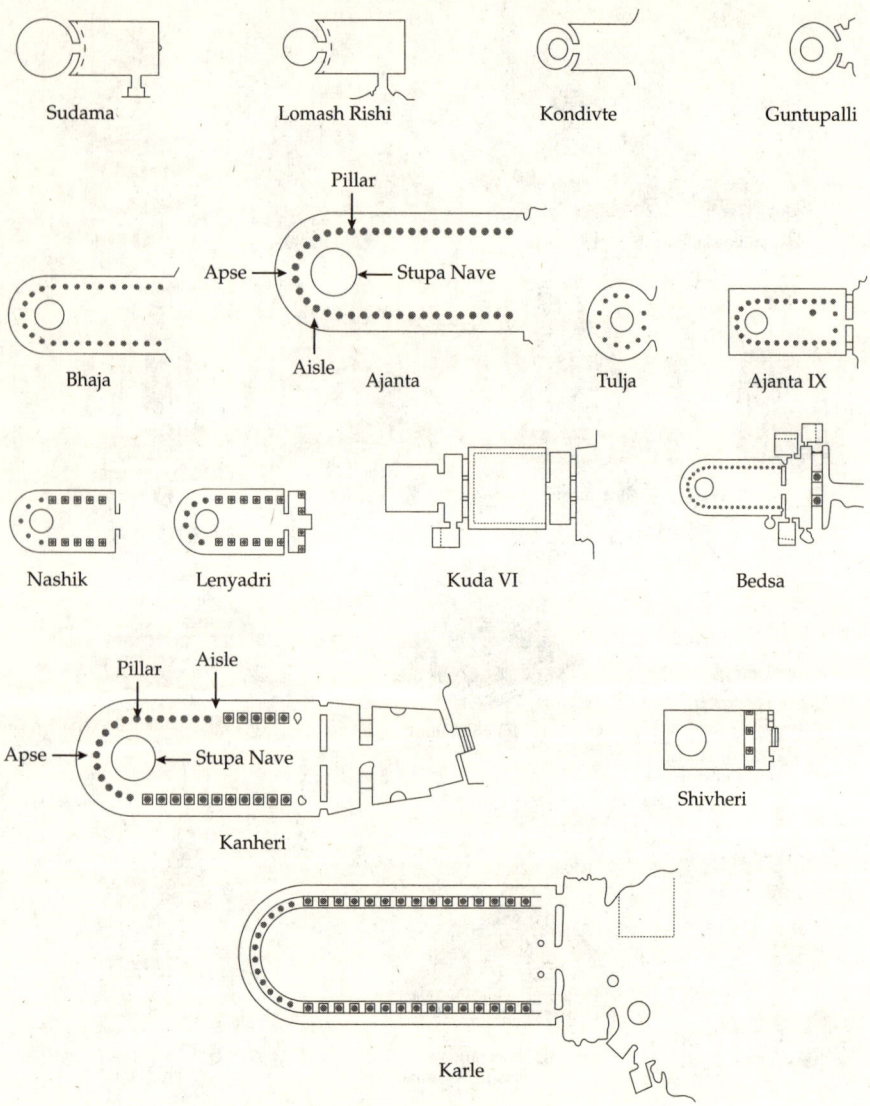

Fig 3.6 Evolution of rock-cut chaityagriha or shrine architecture (after Upinder Singh, *A History of Ancient and Early Medieval India*, 2009)

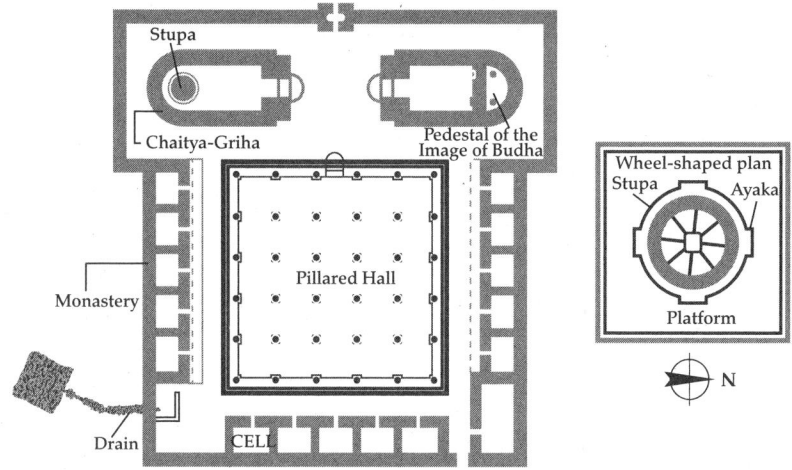

Fig 3.7 Plan of a typical monastic complex, Nagarjunakonda (after Debala Mitra, *Buddhist Monuments*, 1971)

Fig 3.8 Naga Muchalinda guarding the Buddha's throne, Pauni (railing pillar, Jagannath Tekri), 2nd–1st century BCE, National Museum

Central India

Complexes in central India were marked by sites like Sanchi – with its associated monastic sites like Sonari, Satdhara, Bhojpur and Andher – and Bharhut. The sculptures at Bharhut, located in present-day Satna district of Madhya Pradesh, range from the 3rd century BCE to the end of the 2nd century BCE. The stupa does not exist now, but its scattered parts can be found in various museums, including the Indian Museum in Kolkata (which houses a major collection) and the Allahabad Museum. Intricately carved sandstone railings and gateways once adorned the Bharhut stupa. Their sculptural relief offers one of the earliest examples of narrative Buddhist art. The prominent themes include representation of events from the Buddha's life and the Jataka stories. Geologically, the Bharhut monastic complex was located within the Rewa-Panna plateau, bordered on all sides by the Vindhya mountains. Seen against the backdrop of a wider archaeological landscape, there seems to be a direct connection between the consolidation and expansion of the Buddhist monastic community in the Bharhut area in the later centuries of the Christian era, and the wider routes of transport and communication that probably ran along the river Tons, connecting the monastic complex with urbanized areas of the Mauryan empire both in the north and south. This allowed the stupa site to evolve. Manifestations of this trend could be seen in the increased monumentality (such as the construction of the stupa railing), donations recorded on the stupa railing, pilgrim traffic, the emergence of additional sites such as Kunti Har and Potaniha (on river Tons), alongside the increased presence of coins, intensification of agricultural practices and the emergence of villages in the later centuries.[37]

Unlike Bharhut, the Sanchi complex in present-day Raisen district of Madhya Pradesh is very well-preserved. Made famous through Alexander Cunningham's *The Bhilsa Topes* (1854), Sanchi is 10 kms away from Vidisha, a prominent urban and art centre in the early historic period. It was located on the river Betwa, along an important trade route connecting the urban centres of the Gangetic plains with those across the Vindhya mountains in the south. According to legend, it was the birthplace of Devi, the daughter of a merchant of Vidisha and one of Ashoka's wives. The stupa-monastery complex is built on top of a hill and forms a part of a cluster of monastic sites that were constructed 2nd–1st centuries BCE onwards.

The mud and brick core of Stupa 1, also known as the Mahastupa or the Great Stupa, at Sanchi was built in the 3rd century BCE, along with the Ashokan pillar that carries the schism edict. The Shunga period saw the stone encasing and enlargement of the stupa built by Ashoka and the construction of Stupa 2 (on the western slope) and Stupa 3 (on the hilltop). The elaborately carved gateways were added to Stupa 1 and Stupa 3 by the Satavahanas in the 1st century CE. Unlike the stupas of Gandhara, the stupa surface in central India was not decorated – sculptural decoration featured only on the railings and gateways adorning the stupas. Sanchi, however, offers more insights into the way Buddhist sites were emerging.

Landscape surveys and excavations in the Sanchi region have revealed the presence of sixteen ancient irrigational dams – the earliest ones were constructed around the 3rd and 2nd centuries BCE – that were managed by the monks and supplied water to the surrounding agricultural communities. Sculptures associated with popular cults, such as the nagas and yakshas, were also installed in the monastic complex. Both these practices were used by the monks to gain local following.[38] The region's association with the cult of the monastic dead is also very striking and manifests in several ways. First, the relic caskets of the Buddha's close disciples, like Sariputra and Maudgalyayana, have been found at Sanchi and Satdhara, alongside the remains of the local monastic dead from Stupa 2.[39] Second, excavations in Bhojpur, Sonari and Andher have revealed the existence of cemeteries and the worship of the monastic dead. Third, there is a presence of several small votive stupas/burial ad sanctos containing urns and pieces of bones around the main stupa at Sanchi. Relics and reliquary inscriptions from Sanchi, Sonari and Andher also point to the establishment of the Hemavata school, after 'Hemavata' or the Himalayas, where, as discussed earlier, monks were sent during Ashoka's time.[40]

Eastern Deccan

Monastic complexes in the eastern Deccan were mostly concentrated in Amravati and Nagarjunakonda, which were also regarded as art centres. Remains of some old stupas have also been found at Jaggayyapeta (also spelt as Jaggaiahpet), located 70 kms northwest of Amravati, while a monastery complex has been discovered in Thotlakonda near Vishakhapatnam. Here, the monuments are predominantly structural with only a few rock-cut excavations and with the sites concentrated in coastal Andhra and Telangana regions. A settlement has also been discovered in Sannati near Gulbarga district of northern Karnataka.

The Amravati site is in ruins, like the complex at Jaggayyapeta. The discovery of an Ashokan inscription here connects Amravati to the Mauryans. Founded around 3rd-2nd centuries BCE, near Dhanyakataka, the capital of the Satavahanas, the Amravati stupa lies on an old commercial route that connected Dhanyakataka (also called Dharanikota) and Vijayawada. Like in Sanchi, Bhaja, Bedsa, Kanheri and Mathura, funerary remains – primarily of the local monastic dead – have been recovered from Amravati, too.[41] Constituting one of the largest Buddhist monuments in ancient India, and the largest in the Andhra region, it was known as the *mahachaitya* (great shrine). But thanks to several indiscriminate excavations from the 1790s to the late 19th century, Amravati sculptures made several journeys (including being used to build Robertson's Mound at Masulipatnam) before reaching the Government Museum, Chennai, and the British Museum, London. Later, some sculptures also reached the Indian Museum in Kolkata and the National Museum in New Delhi.[42] The only parts of the shrine surviving now are the drum of the brick stupa (Fig 3.4), the circumambulatory path and a few railing pillars. There is not much information available about the physical characteristics of the complex.

The sculptures, which are kept in the British Museum, are known as the Amravati Marbles. They consist of external, decorative carved relief panels that show narrative scenes from the life of the Buddha, as well as other Buddhist symbols and emblems.[43] Drawings made by Walter Elliot around the mid-19th century also give us an idea about the shrine complex. Together, these sources show us how the dome, railings and gateways of the Amravati stupa were decorated with beautiful relief carvings (Fig 3.4).

Located on the banks of the river Krishna, in Andhra Pradesh's Guntur district, Nagarjunakonda was once a 15-sq km valley rich in historical remains. When the construction of the gigantic Nagarjuna Sagar dam was initiated in 1955, many structures were transplanted and rebuilt on top of Nagarjunakonda hill, which stood out as an island in the midst of the lake created by the dam. Also, replicas of some structures were set up on the banks of the reservoir. Nagarjunakonda is primarily known for Buddhist remains (though Brahmanical shrines have also been found) of the ancient Ikshvaku capital of Vijayapuri, which was located here.[44] This was also where Nagarjuna, the famous philosopher of the Mahayana school, is believed to have lectured once. According to the inscriptions found at the site, at least four different sects – the Mahaviharavasin, Mahishasaka, Bahushrutiya and Aparamahavinaseliya – were based here.

The mahachaitya at Nagarjunakonda is said to have housed the corporeal remains of the Buddha. A gold relic casket, reportedly containing the fragment of a bone, was discovered here. The monastic complex at Nagarjunakonda has around thirty Buddhist establishments dating to the 3rd–4th centuries. These, however, differ in architecture and layout. Some of them had a stupa and a monastery; others had a stupa, monastery and chaitya; and some others had monasteries and chaityas. Isolated stupas and small votive stupas also dot the sacred landscape (Fig 3.7). The base and a part of the dome of some of the great stupas of the Andhra region are faced with sculptured limestone slabs. Relief structures also depict the stupas with railings, though very few of them (mostly plain and uninscribed) have been found. Nagarjunakonda had emerged as a pilgrimage site by the 3rd century CE, and a special *chaityagriha* was constructed at the site for the teachers of Ceylon (Sri Lanka) who preached Buddhist teachings in far-off places like Kashmir, China, Odisha, Tamil Nadu, Gandhara, northern Konkan, etc.[45]

A cluster of early historical Buddhist monastic sites has been found in the northern coastal part of Andhra Pradesh. These include Thotlakonda, Bavikonda, Pavurallakonda, Sankaram and Dharapalem. The Thotlakonda monastery complex, located 16 kms north of modern Vishakhapatnam, has yielded remains of several viharas, chaityas, stupas and cairns. The occupation of this site has been dated between the 3rd to 2nd centuries BCE and 2nd to 3rd centuries CE.

In recent times, the hilltop stupa complex at Phanigarhi (based on its shape of a serpent's hood) has been much talked about. Located 45 kms from Suryapet district in Telangana, the site has revealed remains of a huge stupa, two apsidal halls containing chaityas, two large buddhapadas, three viharas, carved architraves of a stone gateway and several limestone sculptural panels depicting events from the life of the Buddha, Jataka tales, buddhapada slabs, and images of the Buddha and bodhisattvas. In recent excavations, a life-sized stucco image of a bodhisattva, a rare octagonal shrine and an octagonal pillar surmounted by a profusely embellished dharmachakra have come to light.[46]

The monuments in the Andhra region, mostly constructed out of solid brick or stone, exhibit striking features in their construction plans. While the Amravati stupa has a solid brick core as the base, most stupas at Nagarjunakonda follow a spoked-wheel plan made of bricks, with the spaces in between filled with mud. The spoked-wheel plan, translated in architecture, is a key Buddhist symbol – the chakra that endowed the structure with great strength. The wheel-shaped plan also occurs in some stupas located outside the Andhra region, such as the Dharmarajika stupa in Taxila, Shahji-ki-Dheri near Peshawar and in Mathura. Another striking feature of many Andhra stupas is the presence of five tall free-standing pillars at four cardinal points on the platform. Known as Ayaka pillars, these structures apparently represented the five important events in the Buddha's life – birth, redemption, enlightenment, first sermon and death. Ayaka platforms have also been found at Vaishali in Bihar. A rich yield of relic caskets and the presence of congregation halls are also noticeable in the Andhra monuments. The congregation halls indicate the site's status as a centre of pilgrimage. Some scholars say that, in the absence of multiple urban centres along coastal Andhra, pilgrimage may have served as an alternate medium for mobilization of resources.[47]

The location of the monastic complexes – outside the city, or fortified area, but not too far from the settlement – in Amravati and Nagarjunakonda also offers important insights into the sangha–laity relationships. At Amravati, the site of the stupa overlapped with a local burial site and many urns were found near the Buddhist remains. At Nagarjunakonda, megalithic burials and memorial pillars – donated by royal women to commemorate the deaths of Ikshvaku kings – are found close to the cluster of Buddhist structures. Memorial pillars are also found close to a demolished stupa in Sannati. It is said that Buddhist monks not only preferred to live near the burial sites but also performed some role in the death rites of the laity. It is argued that the fringe, or 'outside' area, of the city constituted a special space and allowed for the accommodation of Buddhist monks as well as outcastes. Further, the exceptionally well-organized institution of Buddhist monasteries, which were based in the fringe, participated in the crucial functions of cremations and trade. The site of the monasteries in Amravati and Nagarjunakonda was also very close to, or overlapped with, centres of trade and exchange. Merchants and craftsmen were important donors, too, apart from royal women. The monasteries and the cities, thus, were crucially interlinked, which created an ambience for the positive reception of monks (and a 'new religion from north India') in the Deccan region and gave them ('outsiders') a comparative advantage over the conservative and hierarchical Brahmanical presence ('insiders').[48]

Western Deccan

The Buddhist monasteries in western Deccan were mostly rock-cut caves excavated between c. 100 BCE and 200 CE. Moving from the west to the east, the western Deccan consisted of the Konkan coastal strip adjoining the Arabian Sea, the Western Ghats and the elevated Deccan plateau. More than eighty sites have been discovered here, with around 1,200 rock-cut monastic centres. The largest concentration, of more than 100 sites, is at Kanheri (in the fertile river basin of the river Ulhas, in the vicinity of Bombay on the west coast) and Junnar (on the river Kukdi, 90 kms north-west of Pune).[49]

The excavation of early Buddhist caves in the slopes of the Western Ghats was contemporaneous with the advent of long-distance maritime trade with Rome. The location of these monastic sites on land routes, particularly at the heads of important passes connecting the inland centres with the ports, indicates a causal link between trading enterprises and the new monasteries.[50] The caves at Shelarwadi, Bhaja, Bedsa and Karle, for instance, were located close to the Bhor Ghat pass and the descent to the coast near Bombay and Thane.

Some historians have even suggested that monastic establishments may have actively participated in trading ventures by advancing money to merchants, or by selling them surplus produce from their fields. Inscriptions from Nashik and Karle – both located strategically for control over regional trading routes from the interior to the west coast – record the donation of entire villages, which may have come with large agricultural tracts producing more than what was required by the monasteries. Interestingly, some inscriptions found in the caves of the western Deccan also describe gifts from yavanas, which meant foreigners in general, and not just the Greeks.[51]

The monastic complexes in the western Deccan consisted of several hundred caves that were often decorated with sculptures and adorned with carvings, depending on the stage of their evolution. These complexes contained two kinds of monuments – chaityas containing an internal stupa, and viharas. It is said that the idea of excavating rock-cut caves came from natural caves such as that of Indrashala, near Rajgir. In Buddhist mythology, Indrashala cave is regarded as the site where the Buddha was visited by the king of the gods, Indra, also known as Sakra.[52] The excavation of caves was not a Buddhist innovation. Excavated chaityas had already made their beginnings during the Mauryan period, with the Lomas Rishi and Sudama caves in Barabar hills, at Jehanabad, near Gaya. These followed a simple apsidal plan – a rectangular hall in the front, called a nave, leading to a curved or circular chamber in the rear, known as an apse. In western Deccan, the first phase of rock-cut chaityas consisted of a rectangular hall ending in a circular or curved stupa chamber, with a circumambulatory passage around the stupa.

The internal stupa was an object of veneration. This plan was also seen in caves excavated in Kondivite, Bhaja, Tulja, Pitalkhora, Kondana, Nashik, Bedse and Ajanta.[53] In the second phase, which was more developed, rows of pillars were introduced along the side walls, extending into the curved chamber at the end (Fig 3.6

shows the evolution of cave shrines). This created a defined path for circumambulation. This plan can be seen at caves in Nashik and Junagarh, and particularly those in Karle, Karad, Kanheri, Kuda, Mahad and Shelarwadi. Sometimes, as in the case of Kanheri, in place of the stupa, one sees a small chamber cut into the rear wall. The rectangular halls in these caves carried a vaulted or arched ceiling (as opposed to a flat one) with wooden ribs. The entrances to some of the caves were through a horseshoe-shaped window, also called a chaitya arch. The vaulted ceiling of the hall of the Karle caves still retains its 2,000-year-old original wooden ribs.

In some cases, the entrances were preceded by verandas that were flanked by architectural compositions in relief, such as the elephant torsos at Karle. During the Satavahana and the Shaka–Kshatrapa phase (2nd and 3rd centuries), such chaityas grew both in size and ornamentation. The verandas and the entrances in the later-phase caves became more ornate with relief carvings and sculptures, while the pillars inside carried carved sculptures and the walls of the hall were adorned with paintings or narrative reliefs, particularly from the Jataka tales.

The viharas in the Western Ghats followed a simple plan – a square or rectangular hall with small cells in the rear, side walls and a fourth frontal side. Of more than 500 Buddhist caves in the Western Ghats, more than 80 per cent are viharas. Some examples of these are found at Pandavleni, Kondane and Junnar. The cells cut into the walls had raised rock-cut beds and pillows and niches for lamps. These were fronted by an open veranda. During the later period, a shrine was introduced in the rear wall with a sculpture of the Buddha or bodhisattvas, preceded by a connecting chamber, like a vestibule. Such vihara-shrines can be seen at Kanheri. Large viharas were preceded by doorways and verandas. Also, most viharas had rock-cut water cisterns to hold rainwater.[54]

The most ornate parts of the rock-cut monasteries were the pillars or columns of the halls and the rectangular hall of the chaityas. These had pot-like bases, octagonal shafts (long, narrow parts) with inverted pot or lotus-petalled capitals, over which lay the flat tops or abacuses with stone disks (*amalaka*) and pyramidal motifs. These columns carried brackets, mostly animals with human riders, which connected them with the ceiling. Some lofty columns can be seen at Karle and Kanheri. The horseshoe-shaped chaitya arches were another distinctive feature of some caves in the monastery complexes.

The sculptural themes of some of the caves were also very striking. We have already talked about the brackets on the columns, which depicted human couples riding on crouching elephants, lions, horses, bulls or winged beasts. Also common were the auspicious *mithuna* figures, or men and women in affectionate poses, the mythical yakshas and yakshis, and nagas with serpentine hoods. In contrast to the art of the structural stupas at Sanchi, Amravati or Nagarjunakonda, one can see narrative figures in some caves at Pandavleni and Bhaja.[55] Some scholars have suggested that the early caves were not painted, and that it was only after the 2nd century CE that the practice of simply smoothening the cave walls gave way to plastering and painting.[56] The evidence of painting in the earlier Deccan caves could be seen at a cave in Kanheri.

The monastic complexes under discussion not only give us insights into the nature of the emerging Buddhist establishments but also into the contemporary Buddhist relief art. The sculptures associated with the stupas – whether on the dome and the base, as in Gandhara; or in the railings and gateways, as in Sanchi; or the caves, as in the Deccan, constitute some early examples of Buddhist art in India.

MONASTIC COMPLEXES AND EARLY RELIEF ART

Examples of early Buddhist relief art can be seen in Sanchi, Bharhut, Amravati, Nagarjunakonda, etc. Although there is a difference in the medium or stone used by the artists, the sculptural relief at these sites follows a broad similarity in terms of the theme, vocabulary and even style of composition.

What were the constituting elements of this relief art? First, the sculptures adorned the surface and were executed on it. Based on the intricate and elaborate surface decoration, and the shallowness of relief carvings at Bharhut, Sanchi and Amravati, scholars have suggested that these represented a translation of the wood carvers' art into stone. Second, the sculptures had a frontal and not rounded orientation. The viewer could appreciate the sculpture from the front alone, unlike the sculptural depictions of the preceding Mauryan period that could be appreciated from all directions. Third, unlike the largely imperial character of Mauryan art, the sculptural reliefs of this period reflected popular tastes and patronage. Fourth, the theme in Buddhist relief art was largely narrative in character, with human beings forming an important part. Some scholars have elaborated that the reliefs at these monastic sites represent two kinds of narration: monoscene and continuous. Monoscene narration depicts a single major episode, which reminds the viewer of the entire story. In continuous narration, one scene merges into the next without a break – different scenes of a story are depicted in sequence.[57]

There are certain themes and symbols that are repeated in sculptural relief at many sites, and over centuries, not just during this period. These include what have been popularly understood as scenes connected with the Buddha's life. His birth, for instance, is depicted by a lady (Maya) seated on a lotus or flanked by an elephant or elephants. Prince Siddhartha's 'Great Departure', or mahabhinishkramana, is depicted by a bridled horse and a groom holding an umbrella over the head of an invisible rider. Likewise, there are scenes that are believed to represent the Jataka stories. It is easier to identify such scenes at Bharhut, Pauni and Amravati because they are labelled. Then there are symbols that find more occurrences than others. These include a tree, a wheel and a stupa. It has been traditionally believed, both by academia and the public, that these constitute important episodes in the Buddha's life without showing him in a bodily, anthropomorphic form. In such a scheme, the tree is said to represent the Buddha's enlightenment, more particularly the Bodhi tree, under which he attained enlightenment. The wheel is supposed to depict his first sermon at Sarnath, known as the dharmachakrapravartana. Likewise, the stupa is believed to represent the Buddha's death, known as mahaparinirvana. The stupa was popularly believed to be built over the relics of the Buddha. The relics, as we discussed in the preceding chapter, were of different kinds – those connected to his body, those related to the items he used, the places he visited and rested, and those that indicated his presence, like images.

In recent decades, some scholars have questioned this long-held wisdom about the symbols representing important events in the

Buddha's life and acting as substitutes for his images, a practice known as aniconism. It has been argued that objects like sacred trees, wheels, stupas, pillars and others did not *depict* but *commemorated* special events and places associated with the Buddha. In such a scheme, objects or symbols, mostly accompanied by lay worshippers in sculptural reliefs, depicted sacred sites or traces, viewing which brought merit to the laity. And these were worthy of devotion in their own right. Viewed in this context, the trees at Bharhut depict the sacred trees at sacred sites, rather than the enlightenment event. Such objects and symbols constituted strong emblems of popular Buddhist devotion – they neither required anthropomorphic representations, nor did they act as substitutes for the Buddha.[58] Besides commemorating and depicting stories from the life of the Buddha, and the sacred motifs and sites, the early Buddhist relief art of the monastic complexes also showcases deities associated with popular cults, such as the nagas and the yakshas.

POPULAR CULTS AND BUDDHIST ART

Nagas and nagis, snake-like demigods associated with water, fertility and health, were among the popular devotional cults of the period. Alongside yakshas and yakshis, these cults were widely revered across different religious traditions and worshipped in dedicated shrines. Evidence indicates that these deities were among the first Indian gods to be represented as free-standing, anthropomorphic stone sculptures. Consequently, Buddhist, Jaina and Brahmanical traditions competed to appropriate, absorb or subordinate them.

Buddhist interactions with these popular cults were complex and possibly region-specific. Two main models explain the Buddhist relationship with these cults. The conversion model, based on textual accounts and 2nd-century BCE bas-relief depictions, suggests that the Buddha's subordination and conversion of the yakshas and nagas led to their representation at Buddhist sites. Conversely, the localization model proposes that these deities were incorporated into Buddhist rituals to legitimize the sangha's presence in new regions.[59]

Images and shrines of yakshas and yakshis have been found in Mathura, Besnagar and Pawaya in Madhya Pradesh. They appear in the sculptural reliefs of both Bharhut and Sanchi, and they appear together with the nagas and nagis in depictions related to stupa festivals. The *shalabhanjikas* (women holding the branches of a tree), which are prominent in Sanchi, Sanghol and elsewhere, are considered part of the yakshi motif group.[60] Approximately 1,000 fragments of sculptures depicting these popular deities (across sects) have been recovered from the Sanchi area, dating from the 3rd century BCE to the 12th century CE. Scholars suggest that these deities facilitated the integration of an 'external' Buddhist tradition into 'internal' or local roots. Over time, they were incorporated into a broader Buddhist iconographic programme in the region.[61]

Evidence of the naga cult has been found in various regions, including Mathura, Rajagriha, central India, the Deccan and even southern India. The nagas are depicted either as humans with multiple cobra hoods, or as multi-hooded serpents. Several traditions link the nagas with Buddhism. For instance, Muchilinda, the naga king, is believed to have protected the Buddha from a thunderstorm at Bodh Gaya, while he meditated after attaining enlightenment (Fig 3.8). Nagarjuna, the renowned Mahayana philosopher, is said to have discovered the *Prajnaparamita Sutra* in the naga realm. According to Buddhist text *Divyavadana*, Ashoka visited the land of the nagas to retrieve relics from the Ramagrama stupa. It is also believed that Buddhist relics were handled by the nagas before being enshrined in stupas.[62]

Free-standing naga sculptures began to appear by the 2nd century BCE, notably in the Sanchi region, but their association with the Buddha emerged later. Images of Muchilinda protecting the Buddha were first seen around the 2nd century CE. The earliest evidence of this pairing comes from Amravati in the Andhra region, which flourished during the 2nd–3rd centuries CE. In Amravati, nagas are depicted near the Buddha's footprint, his headdress, relic caskets and stupas. However, it is important to note that in Amravati, the relationship between the Buddha and Muchilinda, or between the Buddha and nagas, was never on an equal footing. It remained hierarchical. The nagas were consistently portrayed as servants, devotees and guardians.[63]

The presence of the nagas in textual, epigraphic and sculptural settings not only gave Buddhist ideas and institutions wider and popular legitimacy but also helped them acquire local roots. Their representation also had a regional dimension. In Sanchi, they appear mostly in the proximity of the dams or irrigation facilities managed by the monks, which indicates their links with water and agrarian production. Faxian, for instance, mentions that the nagas were propitiated within monastic compounds in Nalanda on account of their ability to ensure rainfall and agricultural success. It has also been suggested that nagas are commonly found on the entrances of early monasteries at Ajanta and Pitalkhora because they were believed to carry purifying properties that could help get rid of negative influences.[64]

BEYOND ROYALTY: MONKS, NUNS, TRADERS AND COMMONERS AS PATRONS

The expanding and evolving religious and architectural landscape of the Buddhists also required a supportive and sustainable set of patrons. During the Buddha's time, it was kings like Bimbisara, Ajatashatru and Prasenjit, or traders and agricultural and landed elites like Anathapindika, or an occasional affluent courtesan like Amrapali, who donated to the sangha. Later, as discussed earlier, Ashoka played an important role in the consolidation and expansion of the Buddhist faith and monastic establishments. Apart from demarcating the pilgrimage sites with pillars, he also built stupas across the subcontinent. Given his contribution to the cause, he has been appropriated in Buddhist legends and texts, and his imagery has even been monumentalized in stone. The discovery of a relief sculpture from Kanaganahalli stupa at Sannati, in the Gulbarga district of Karnataka, shows the Mauryan king flanked by his queen and female attendants. Historians believe a similar sculptural panel from Sanchi also depicts Ashoka, but the Kanaganahalli sculpture (Fig 2.8, Chapter 2) is accompanied with a confirmatory Brahmi inscription that mentions the term 'Ranyo Ashoka' (King Ashoka).

After Ashoka, Kanishka stands out as the most important Indian king in the Buddhist tradition. While Ashoka is celebrated as a key figure in the southern Theravada tradition that has roots in Sri Lanka, Kanishka is revered in the northern tradition that began in China.

Kanishka is also associated with the Gandhara and Mathura schools of art. His headless statue remains a prominent exhibit at the Mathura Museum. Kanishka's reign is noted for the expansion of Mahayana Buddhist ideas into China and along the Silk Route. Some of his gold coins feature his image on one side and a standing Buddha on the other. However, most of his coins depict deities from other religious traditions patronized by the Kushanas, such as Brahmanical, Greek and west Asian, particularly Persian deities.

The 'Kanishka casket', believed to contain bone relics of the Buddha, was discovered in the Shahji-ki-Dheri stupa near Peshawar, which was built by Kanishka. Dating to 127 CE, it is housed in the Peshawar Museum (with a copy in the British Museum) and features images of the Buddha accompanied by Brahma and Indra, as well as a king commonly identified as Kanishka himself.

Apart from Ashoka and, to a lesser extent, Kanishka, details of other royal patrons are more commonly found in donative inscriptions. Notably, inscriptions from the Satavahanas and the Shaka-Kshatrapas, despite their Brahmanical affiliations, highlight their patronage of Buddhist establishments. Royal women from the Satavahanas and Ikshvakus were known to donate to Buddhist sites, while their male counterparts primarily supported Brahmanical institutions.

However, what is not adequately highlighted in the Buddhist texts and legends is that the non-royals constituted a significant category of donors during this period. And here the donative inscriptions, which predate the Pali canonical texts, offer crucial insights. The earliest donative inscriptions found on the railings of Bharhut and Sanchi, dating from c. 120 to 80 BCE, indicate that a substantive proportion of the donors were monks and nuns. These included those who were actively involved with establishing and embellishing sacred objects and sites, and those concerned with the cult of the stupas and donative, merit-making activities.[65] If we take the example of Bharhut, around 40 per cent of the donors were either monks or nuns. Of these, a considerable proportion were doctrinal specialists, teachers or transmitters of canonical knowledge, such as reciters or performers, and not just regular monks. If we look further within this segment, 40 per cent of the donors connected with the stupa cult, or the cult of images, were monks, mostly doctrinal specialists, while the rest were followers of different categories. Over time, the proportion of monastic donors increased significantly. In Mathura, for example, Buddhist inscriptions reveal that monks and nuns comprised over 50 per cent of the donors. Similar findings emerge from other regions as well. In the context of donations associated with relics, chaityas and images related to Buddhist cave temples in western India (excluding endowments for material support like cells, caves and cisterns), monks and nuns contributed more than 65 per cent, with the remainder coming from lay followers.

These donative inscriptions challenge the rigid distinctions we often make between the religious activities of monks and nuns versus lay followers. Contrary to the notion that cult and religious giving were predominantly concerns of the lay people, the earliest donative inscriptions show that monks and nuns played an important role in merit-making activities related to the stupa and images. The inscriptions suggest that the monks and nuns were not only active in developing the stupa-relic cult but also played a dominant role in it. During the early Kushana period, contemporary inscriptions indicate that the cult of images was almost entirely, if not exclusively, supported by the monastic community, with their influence growing over time.[66]

After the monks and nuns, the donor space was occupied by the lay followers, which becomes particularly apparent in the inscriptions of Bharhut and Sanchi. Bharhut attracted pilgrims and donors not only from central India but also from Pataliputra in the east and Nashik in the west. In the case of Sanchi, while most donors, came from the neighbouring territories of central India, some also came from Rajasthan and Maharashtra. This indicates that both Bharhut and Sanchi had become places of pilgrimage even before the onset of the Christian era. The carvings and embellishments of Sanchi were not funded by royals but by commoners that included family groups, village associations, merchants and bankers of both Buddhist and Hindu leanings. Interestingly, Sanchi inscriptions record an equal proportion of male and female donors; in fact, there was a higher incidence of female patronage. Of particular interest here is the practice of collective gifts made by kinship groups or lay followers and villages.[67] In the case of western Deccan, the donors included lay followers like traders, merchants, weavers and oilpressers, ironmongers, jewellers, gardeners, fishermen, guilds of bamboo workers and yavanas).[68] The yavanas figure in the list of donors at many sites, including Sanchi, Nashik, Junnar and Karle.

The post-Mauryan phase brought significant changes to Buddhism, including new ideas (Mahayana and the transference of merit), mythologies (bodhisattvas and Buddhist heavens), appropriations (Jataka folk tales), inclusions (popular and devotional cults) and establishments (new and extended monastic complexes). This occurred as the subcontinent became more integrated with the global economy through long-distance trade, new political powers emerged in northern and peninsular India and the patron base expanded. Buddhist monuments redefined themselves as monastic establishments and spread from the Gangetic heartland to new regions, acquiring extended structures and regional characteristics in Gandhara, central India and the Deccan region. New artefacts, such as images, shrines and sculptural panels, were created. The monastic community held these diverse elements together, with monks and nuns playing proactive roles in spreading dharma and sangha and establishing stupa-monastery complexes. These ideas, practices and buildings evolved as the Buddhists navigated new sociopolitical landscapes, interacted with other religious traditions and devotional cults, and explored new geographies during the Gupta–Vakataka Age (c. 300–600 CE).

4

EFFLORESCENCE AND SPREAD AMIDST BRAHMANICAL REVIVAL

The kings of these countries [madhyadesha], the chief men and householders, have raised viharas for the priests [monks] and provided for their support by bestowing on them fields [agricultural lands], houses and gardens with men and oxen. Engraved title deeds were prepared and handed down from one reign to another.

This was how Chinese traveller Faxian described the monasteries flourishing in the region south of Mathura in north India, noting their substantial property and assets. He also pointed out that the monks were well-settled in the viharas and did not have to bother about arranging day-to-day requirements.[1] This description also broadly applies to other regions of the subcontinent during the period c. 300–600 CE, known as the Gupta–Vakataka age. This era, celebrated for its artistic achievements, saw a revival of sites associated with the Buddha's life, alongside the geography of old Magadha. Kings and empires returned as patrons, with Nalanda and Sarnath emerging as prominent centres of Buddhist learning, while Ajanta rose to significance in peninsular India.

Interestingly, the Gupta–Vakataka period also witnessed a 'Brahmanical revival', characterized by the ascendancy of the Sanskrit language, Puranas and temple-based sectarian cults centred around deities like Shiva and Vishnu, along with the worship of goddesses (mainly Shakti) and the rise of tantrism. The religious landscape of the time was marked by the continued influence of popular devotional cults and the emergence of Bhakti (devotion to a personal God) and tantra worship. How did these developments impact Buddhism and its practitioners? How did these changes manifest across different regions? The two factors that played a crucial role in shaping Buddhism during this period were regional political dynamics and trade.

THE RETURN OF THE ROYAL PATRONS: THE GUPTAS AND THE VAKATAKAS

As India became more integrated with trading nations across Asia, Africa and Europe, monks and merchants ventured into new frontiers. Ports on the western coast and in southern India maintained trade connections with Arabia, Persia and Byzantium, while enhancing commerce with Sri Lanka, China and Southeast Asia. The expanding Silk Route facilitated the movement of monks between India, China and Central Asia. Concurrently, itinerant merchant communities from Central Asia extended their trading networks into eastern and Southeast Asia, significantly contributing to the introduction of Buddhist teachings and images in China.[2] The spread of Buddhist ideas in Southeast Asia had an interesting trade connection. It was the demands of trade with the eastern Mediterranean, particularly of spices and semi-precious stones, which led Indian traders of Buddhist and Hindu affiliations to venture into Southeast Asian waters. Monks and missions followed soon after.

The post-Kushana and Satavahana era saw significant changes in India's political and social landscape. With state formations and new hierarchies emerging, kings and rulers granted lands and villages to officials, individuals and religious institutions – including Buddhists – to consolidate and legitimize their power. Genealogies were elaborated and rulers adopted grand titles. In a period characterized by fluid political boundaries, the region constituting the core of the old Magadha and Mauryan empires emerged as the new Gupta empire. In the Deccan, the Vakatakas inherited the legacy of the Satavahanas.

The Guptas ruled over most of north India from 300 to 600 CE, with their empire encompassing modern Bihar, Uttar Pradesh and Bengal (the highlands of central India and parts of the eastern coast).

Their control extended through military conquests and a network of tributary states. While the Gupta kings are primarily known for their patronage of Brahmanical cults, some also supported Buddhism. Some Buddhist sources suggest that Gupta king Vikramaditya sent his queen and son, Baladitya, to study under renowned Buddhist scholar Vasubandhu in Nalanda. Another Gupta king, Narasimhagupta, is said to have become a Buddhist monk and devoted his life to meditation. Seals and inscriptions of the Gupta kings indicate that some of them built monasteries in Nalanda and supported them through land and village grants.

In eastern Deccan, the decline of the Ikshvakus and the Nagarjunakonda complex did not diminish the significance of the Amravati mahachaitya, which continued to attract pilgrims and patrons. The Vakatakas, ruling as a major political power in the Deccan from around the mid-3rd century CE to the late 5th or early 6th centuries CE, had matrimonial ties with influential imperial dynasties, including the Guptas. Although their inscriptions describe them as Brahmans, the Vakatakas patronized Buddhist establishments like those at Ajanta. The period between 300 and 600 CE also saw the spread of Buddhist monastic establishments in the Tamil country, in the deep south, along with the proliferation of the Mahayana school.

COUNTLESS BODHISATTVAS AND COUNTLESS HEAVENS: THE EXPANDING MYTHOLOGY OF MAHAYANA

Although the Mahayana school and the cult of the bodhisattvas began to take root in the early centuries of the Christian era, it was between the 4th and 6th/7th centuries that they acquired firm grounding. During this period, inscriptions related to the Mahayana school emerged at sites such as Mathura, Sarnath, Ajanta, Bodh Gaya and Nagarjunakonda. It was also when images and/or paintings of the bodhisattvas made their appearance in the Buddhist caves at Kanheri, Ajanta and Aurangabad in the Deccan. Additionally, this era saw the composition of Mahayana texts like *Manjushri-mulakalpa*. During this period, prominent Yogachara thinkers, such as Asanga and Vasubandhu, and Madhyamaka philosophers like Buddhapalita, Bhavaviveka and Chandrakirti, were active and influential as well.

The Buddhist pantheon expanded to include not only countless bodhisattvas but also several heavens and Buddhas' lands, which served as abodes for the Buddhas and the bodhisattvas, and as rest stations for lay worshippers on their way to salvation. While the Pali canon, associated with the conservative tradition, talks mostly about the provisions of food and lodging for the Buddha and the sangha, the Mahayana Sanskrit texts indicate that objects of donation now included monumental stupas, monastery buildings and luxury goods that had come to include items like coral, glass objects, pearls and precious stones exported from India to China, and Chinese silk imported into India.

The progressive use of these new luxury items in Buddhist ritual practices and ceremonies standardized the concept of *sapta ratna* (seven treasures), a term traditionally used for a group of prized offerings made to the Buddha, mostly precious metals and stones. This new dynamic also stimulated the demand for luxury goods and strengthened the relationship between the monasteries and the commercial laity, who could count on the bodhisattva's transferable merit to seek higher spiritual attainments.[3] The expanding materialism and mythology of the Mahayana school offered infinite possibilities. One of the ways this was made possible was through the doctrine of the *trikaya*, the three bodies.

Some scholars believe the trikaya doctrine, which was probably developed from an old Mahasanghika ideal, says that Gautama Buddha was not merely a human but also the earthly manifestation of a powerful spiritual being. According to this doctrine, the Buddha had three bodies: the body of essence (*dharmakaya*), the body of bliss (*sambhogakaya*) and the created body (*nirmanakaya*). Of these, only the created body was visible on earth. The body of essence eternally pervaded the universe as the ultimate Buddha, with the other two bodies serving as its emanations. The body of bliss existed in the heavens, while the created body referred to different forms assumed by the Buddha on the earth. The Buddha's body of bliss was the presiding deity of the chief Mahayana heaven – the Sukhavati (happy land) – where the blessed were reborn in lotus buds arising from a lovely lake in front of the Buddha's throne. This divine Buddha was usually called

Amitabha ('of immeasurable glory'), or Amitayus ('of immeasurable age'). Amitabha came to occupy the position of the Father in heaven. He, the historical Gautama Buddha, and bodhisattva Avalokiteshvara were closely associated and played a big part in the Mahayana scheme as they were chiefly concerned with this region of the universe and this period of cosmic time. However, there were many other heavenly Buddhas presiding over other heavens and universes.[4]

The religious atmosphere of the time was also characterized by cross-cultural borrowings and contestations. There were intense philosophical debates between Buddhist and Brahmanical traditions. The rivalry and competition between the Buddhists and the Shaivites (followers of the Shiva pantheon) was very conspicuous and involved disputes around doctrinal matters and patronage. However, it will be safe to say that there were enough instances of assimilations and intersections, as shall become evident in the following section.

THE RISE OF BHAKTI AND SHAKTI: APPROPRIATION OF POPULAR CULTS

All three dominant religious traditions – Brahmanical, Buddhist and Jaina – borrowed from/assimilated/appropriated, in varying degrees, the ascendant popular cults or traditions of the time. These included the Bhakti ideal, which involved devotion to a personal God (in contrast to the priest- and sacrifice-dominated Vedic Brahmanism); popular and devotional worship of yakshas and yakshis, nagas and nagis, and other celestial beings like *apsaras* (heavenly dancers and singers), *gandharvas* (divine musicians), *kinnars* (half-humans, half-birds) and *vidyadharas* (pair of males brandishing swords); Shakti, which centred around the worship of the female consorts of male deities; and Tantrism, which built on the cult of Shakti but went beyond and included initiation rituals, secret rites, magical formulae and sexual union. Other similarities and intersections seen among the dominant religious traditions of the time included image worship in shrines and the emergence of pantheons of gods. These pantheons involved the worship of presiding deities accompanied by a host of subsidiary deities. The pantheon phenomenon was particularly strong in Shaivism (centred around Lord Shiva) and Vaishnavism (centred around Lord Vishnu), but it also manifested in the growing Mahayana deities in Buddhism and the cult of tirthankaras in Jaina tradition. In Buddhism, the Bhakti ideal manifested in the growing cult of the bodhisattvas (the Buddhas-in-waiting) and in the worship of Buddhist deities in shrines. The apsidal- and circular-shaped chaityagrihas of the preceding centuries gave way to full-fledged temples with different architectural styles. Unfortunately, Gupta-period temples have not survived, but we can form an idea of their architecture from archaeological remains and contemporary textual accounts. Examples include Temple 17 of Sanchi (Fig 4.1), Mahabodhi temple at Bodh Gaya, Mulagandhakuti at Sarnath and Baladitya temple at Nalanda.[5] Sometimes, the shrines or temples were shared among multiple religious traditions. Ellora, for instance, has caves dedicated to Brahmanical, Buddhist and Jaina deities. The incorporation of popular regional cults like yakshas, yakshis, nagas, nagis and other celestial beings in the Brahmanical, Buddhist and Jaina traditions had already begun in the early centuries of the Christian era. This continued during the Gupta–Vakataka age. Images of Yakshi Hariti and her consort, Panchika, could be seen in a subsidiary shrine in the Buddhist caves at Ajanta (Fig 4.2). Legend has it that Hariti, a demoness who devoured children in Rajagriha, was tamed by the Buddha and assured food in every monastery. This was how the custom of installing her images began in the Buddhist monasteries.[6] In the last chapter, we came across stories of nagas being tamed by the Buddha in Amravati and Bodh Gaya. The Ajanta caves and other Buddhist shrines of the time also have images of yakshas, nagas and other demigods, but they appear more as dwarfs, palace guards or subordinate figures at subsidiary places like entrances, facades, door jambs, pillars and pillar brackets (Fig 4.3). This phenomenon, scholars say, reflects an attempt on the part of the dominant religious traditions to appropriate popular cults to expand their base and then subordinate them. One no longer comes across independent worship of such popular deities in dedicated shrines.[7]

Tantrism, which centred around the practice of tantra, was another phenomenon that became common in the Brahmanical traditions, particularly the Shaiva and Shakti cults, and the Buddhists. It did not, however, hold great appeal among the Jainas.

TANTRISM ENTERS THE FAITH, TARAS APPEAR ON THE SCENE

Among the Buddhists, a tantric tradition called the Vajrayana (the 'cycle of the thunderbolt') became important from the 7th–8th centuries, particularly in eastern India. The exact origins of Tantrism are difficult to point out, but it is agreed that the cult started acquiring form around the 5th century CE. It conceptualized the godhead as a union of the masculine and feminine energies. Over a period, some attributes came to be associated with Tantrism. These included energy (Shakti), initiation (*diksha/deeksha*), prayers and magical formulae (mantras), meditation (dhyana), postures and yogic practices, sexual rites and terrifying deities. Tantra practices were broadly aimed at awakening the *kundalini* – energy coiled up in the body like a serpent – and pulling it upwards to unite with the supreme. The notion of puja, or worship, in Tantra often involved the transformation of the worshipper into the deity. Gradually, the idea of the five elements, the *panchatattva*, became popular. The elements came to be identified as the five Ms – *mamsa* (meat), *matsya* (fish), *madya* (alcohol), *maithuna* (sexual intercourse) and *mudra* (parched grain). In tantric rituals, diagrams known as yantras, mandalas or chakras played an important role.[8]

In some cases, Tantrism was linked to the idea of Shakti, particularly among the Shaivites. However, the Shakti cult also grew outside of Tantrism. The union of Shiva and his wife, Uma (in various forms), became one of the dominant ways of defining the cult. Gradually, many Brahmanical goddesses, and personifications of different facets of their personalities, found their way into the Shakti fold. One of the starting points of such a belief was that the gods were mostly transcendent and aloof, that it was the goddesses or female consorts who played an active role in the world. The gods were, therefore, best approached through their wives and consorts, who constituted the force or potency (shakti) of their husbands. One of the manifestations of this belief was the introduction of wives in the Buddhist world.

The Buddhas and bodhisattvas were gradually endowed with wives, popularly known as Taras.[9] The first confirmed textual evidence of Tara worship comes from the 5th century CE, in *Manjushri-mulakalpa*. However, some scholars feel that the first feminine divinity who found her way into the Buddhist pantheon was Prajnaparamita ('the perfection of wisdom or insight'), who personified the qualities of the bodhisattva. There are debates on the origins of Tara as well.[10] Some scholars trace her origins to the tradition of Vedic Brahmanism and say she is mentioned in the Rig Veda. Others see her as the second of the ten mahavidyas, avatars of the great Mother Goddess Mahadevi, or Adi Parashakti, who in turn manifests in the trinity of Parvati, Lakshmi and Saraswati. Mahayana legends, however, situate Tara within the expanding Buddhist pantheon. She is believed to have emerged either from the teardrops of Avalokiteshvara (who cried looking at the suffering in the world and the thought of liberating so many souls) or from a lotus that grew from his tears. Tara, therefore, becomes a personification of compassion and is regarded as a saviour who liberates souls from suffering. She could also assume forms to help and protect her devotees. Tara was gradually assimilated in the Mahayana tradition as a bodhisattva, and later as a Buddha and the mother of Buddhas in Esoteric Buddhism, the Vajrayana Buddhism of the Tibetan tradition.

The expanding world of Buddhism had interesting regional manifestations, which we will explore now.

PAINTED CAVES, MAHAVIHARAS AND NEW COMPLEXES: REGIONAL ARCHITECTURAL MANIFESTATIONS

The Gupta–Vakataka Age saw a growth in size and/or architectural enhancement of the existing sites in the Gangetic heartland, besides the addition of new sites in the clusters that emerged in Gandhara, Gujarat and the Deccan. Some sites became architecturally noticeable too, such as those in Odisha, Nalanda and Tamil Nadu.

In the Gangetic heartland, sites like Sarnath, Bodh Gaya, Kushinagar, Kaushambi, etc., remained important. Bodh Gaya, the site of the Buddha's enlightenment, had already acquired a seat (the diamond throne) and a pillar during Ashoka's time, and a stone railing around the Bodhi tree during the Shunga period (1st century BCE). This original railing, as we shall discuss in Chapter 6, was expanded around 5th–6th centuries CE, during the reign of the Guptas, who held sway over the region. The Gupta period's railing pillars are made of granite as opposed to the earlier ones that were constructed in sandstone and carried medallions adorned with lotus flowers and narrative episodes from the life of the Buddha. One male figure bearing a trident, featuring on the expansion, has popularly been identified as Lord Shiva. The brick predecessor of the current Mahabodhi temple also emerged in the 5th–6th centuries CE, during the time of the Guptas. Xuanzang also saw great monasteries around the temple, which were not older than the Gupta Age.[11]

Sarnath

The erection of Buddhist monuments in Sarnath possibly began during the pre-Ashokan period. Like the Buddha's site of enlightenment, the site of his first sermon also acquired much of its current shape during the Gupta period.

The main shrine, the Mulagandhakuti Vihara, is believed to be the sacred place where the Buddha stayed during his first rainy retreat. Also known as the Mulagandhakuti, or the chamber of the Buddha, the structure is made of brick and plaster, and is overlaid with carved stones.

It went through several modifications.[12] The pre-Ashokan constructions seem to have been done with wood. The Mauryan king erected a pillar with the lion capital, crowned by a wheel with thirty-two spokes (the dharmachakra) in front of the Mulagandhakuti. Ashoka possibly also created other monuments at the place, including the Dharmarajika stupa that was crowned by a monolithic railing. The cylindrical stupa, called the Dhamekh stupa, is also attributed to Ashoka.

During the Shunga period (2nd–1st centuries BCE), Sanchi-style stone railings replaced the original wooden ones around the Mulagandhakuti. Monasteries were added around the sacred site during the time of the Kushanas (1st century CE) and the Guptas. Kushana and Gupta inscriptions at the site indicate the existence of three sects of monks – Vastiputrika, Sammatiya and Sarvastivadin, along with the Mahayanists. Xuanzang even indicates the existence of a mahavihara, housing 1,500 Sammatiya monks, possibly built during the reign of the Guptas. The mahavihara, a Gupta-period architectural innovation, consisted of a group of monasteries within an enclosure and carried a rich artistic decoration.

After the Guptas, the Mulagandhakuti Vihara was enlarged and acquired the status of the main shrine, or a temple with a Buddha image in the sanctuary. The shrine had a lofty Gupta-style tower, as Xuanzang would have us believe. It was originally surrounded by chapels and a Gupta-style standing Buddha was discovered in one of the surviving chapels,[13] besides an Ashokan monolithic Chunar sandstone railing, which once crowned the Dharmarajika stupa located nearby. The large courtyard on the eastern side of the shrine contains the remains of many stupas. On its west stands, in situ, the inscribed stump that once carried the famous lion capital (now housed in a museum). This pillar bears the famous schism edict of Ashoka.

The Dharmarajika stupa, as excavations reveal, was enlarged six times – the first time was under the Kushana period, the second during the Guptas, the third during the 7th century, the fourth and fifth between the 9th and 11th centuries, and the last during the 12th century, when the monastery of Kumaradevi, the Buddhist queen of the king of Kannauj, who ruled from Banaras, was built. During the Gupta period, the circumambulatory path, the *pradakshinapatha*, was added and the stupa was encompassed with a solid outer wall that had four doorways in the four cardinal directions. Interestingly, this stupa was pulled down by one Jagat Singh in 1794, as he wanted to use it as building material for some construction in Banaras.[14]

The Dhamekh stupa is a cylindrical stone tower, which lies on top of a circular stone drum. The drum has niches that may have once housed Buddhist statues (Fig 4.4). Below that lies a band of elaborate carvings with geometrical and floral patterns, and human and bird figures. The carvings repeat the ornamental design that once adorned the original cloth covering and reflects the Gupta craftsmanship in creating scroll patterns. Faxian, who visited Sarnath during the Gupta period, found four stupas and two monasteries here. This period is also known as the golden age of art at Sarnath. Some of the Buddha's best-known images were made during this time.[15]

Kushinagar

Like the places related to the Buddha's enlightenment and first sermon, Kushinagar (the site of his death, or mahaparinirvana) was paid attention to during the Gupta period. The town was practically in ruins when Faxian visited between 399 and 410 CE and found it inhabited mostly by the families of the societies of monks.[16] He records seeing several stupas and monasteries built over holy spots connected to the life of the Buddha. Xuanzang, who visited more than a century later (620–644 CE), reiterates seeing the stupas on the holy spots where Subhadra, the last monk to be ordained by Shakyamuni and become an arhat, died; where the Buddha was cremated by Mahakasyapa, his close disciple. He also mentions the stupa was built by Ashoka. During the Gupta period, a devout Buddhist, Haribala, installed a colossal nirvana statue, a reclining image of the Buddha made in Mathura, near the main stupa attributed to Ashoka. The stupa possibly contained human relics of the Buddha. This reclining statue is now in the Mahaparinirvana temple at the site (Fig 4.5). Apparently, Haribala also restored or renovated the main stupa. Clay seals, with legends in Gupta characters, found near the image shrine, also point to the existence of a Mahaparinirvana Mahavihara.

Like the Gangetic plains, a land closely associated with the Buddha's travels and teaching, the sites of his relics – such as Gandhara or Gujarat – also underwent architectural enhancement. New sites and monastic complexes were added to the clusters that had emerged in the early centuries of the Christian era.

Gandhara Region

The period between the 3rd and the middle of the 5th centuries experienced a remarkable growth in the patronage of Buddhist sacred sites and monastic institutions in the Gandhara region. This was the mature phase of what we understand as Gandharan architecture today. Buddhist sites of the time included Taxila and monastic establishments like Takht-i-Bahi, Sahri-Bahlol, Jamal Garhi, Ranigat and Thareli.

Buddhist remains in these places can be seen in the Indian Museum at Kolkata. Jaulian, a famous centre of Buddhist learning, art and architecture in Taxila, was developed largely between the 2nd and 4th centuries CE. It once consisted of a main stupa surrounded by twenty-seven subsidiary stupas. The site also had sixty shrines adorned with scenes from the life of the Buddha. Jaulian played an important role in the spread of Buddhism along the Silk Road.

This period at Gandhara saw a systematic transition from schist to stucco as the building material for sculptures. This shift made it possible to rapidly execute, embellish and paint sculptures or images. The period from the 4th to the mid-5th centuries also saw the production of giant images of the Buddha and, to a lesser extent, bodhisattvas. Given the brittle nature of schist, most such monumental images, including those up to forty feet tall, were executed in clay, with stucco being used for the hands, feet and heads. Around the 5th–6th centuries, the Gandhara region was conquered by the Huns, which led to a decline in Buddhist patronage. However, Buddhist communities continued to thrive in the adjacent Swat Valley, Kashmir and Afghanistan. The sculptures seen in Kabul valley of Afghanistan follow the Gandhara artistic tradition, which is partly seen in the sculptures found at Afghan sites like Hadda, including the head of a bodhisattva.[17] One of the brilliant achievements of the period were the two giant Buddhas (one was 175 feet tall and the other was 120 feet tall) of Bamiyan, nestled in the Hindu Kush mountains. Carved into the sandstone cliffs during the 6th–7th centuries, these formed the largest Buddha statues in the world before the Taliban destroyed them in 2001 (Fig 4.6). Decorated with flowing robes and wavy curls of hair, these images reflected the coming together of the Gupta, Graeco-Roman and Central Asian styles. The Bamiyan valley was located close to one of the important branches of the famous Silk Route, which connected China with West Asia and Europe. The presence of fertile plains amidst a harsh terrain made this valley an ideal site for missionaries and merchants. Buddhism was introduced here during the Kushana period and, gradually, numerous monasteries, shrines and sanctuaries came up in the caves along the foothills. This area remained a site of Buddhist activities from the 2nd century to around the 9th century CE, when Islam became the dominant religion in the region. When Xuanzang crossed the Bamiyan valley around 643 CE, he found more than ten monasteries and 1,000 monks at the site. Further, the giant statues were adorned with metal, colour and gems.[18]

In addition to these regions, one can see development, or enhancement, of existing sites and clusters in Sanchi in central India, the Junagarh–Devni Mori–Vadnagar region of Gujarat and the Deccan, where the Ajanta caves present a beautiful example.

Sanchi

The Gupta conquest of the Malwa region around the early 5th century gave a fresh lease of life to the Sanchi monastic landscape. This was manifested in the construction of more stupas, installation of Buddha images from Mathura to the entrances of the main stupa (Stupa 1, or the mahastupa) and other stupas, and the erection of squarish Buddhist temples. The construction of, or additions to, Temples 17 and 18 happened during the Gupta period. Both these temples have images of Hindu goddesses Ganga and Yamuna at the door jambs, a clear Gupta addition. During the Gupta period, many monasteries were added to the stupa complex as well. These lie in two complexes south and east of the mahastupa. Inscriptions on the railing of the mahastupa also point to the existence of the Mahavihara of Kakanadabhota, the name by which Sanchi was known during the reign of the Guptas. It received donations in cash and the revenues of a village.[19]

Gujarat

The earliest archaeological evidence of Buddhist presence in Gujarat dates to Mauryan king Ashoka's time. His rock edict in the Girnar hills has a fragmentary inscription that refers to a white elephant, which brings happiness to the whole world. Given Ashoka's Buddhist inclinations, some scholars say this symbolized the Buddha-to-be, or the Buddha entering his mother's womb as a white elephant.[20] However, Buddhism acquired deeper roots in Gujarat between the 1st and 4th centuries CE, during the reign of the Western Saka Kshatrapas, when rock shelters, chaitya caves and cisterns were excavated in the Girnar hills–Junagarh area. The monastery at Intwa, known as Maharaja Rudrasena Vihara, is attributed to the Saka Kshatrapa Rudrasena (199–222 CE).[21] Interestingly, Junagarh in the Girnar hills was not only a pilgrimage site for the Buddhists, but also for the Hindus and Jainas. The excavation of Buddhist sites continued under the Maitrakas, too, who ruled between the 5th and 8th centuries. Among the prominent caves of the Girnar hills–Junagarh area, one may include those at Khapra Kodiya, Bava Pyara and the ones in Uparkot Fort. Rock shelters, chaitya caves and water cisterns were also excavated in the Vankia hills in the Gir–Somnath district, which was recently carved out of Junagadh district. Between the 2nd and 6th centuries CE, the focus of Buddhist excavations shifts to the coastal region of Gujarat, where rock-cut caves have been found in Koteshwar and north-western parts of the Kutch region. Bronze images of the Buddha, dated to the 4th and 7th centuries CE, have also been found around this area. Other coastal Buddhist sites in south Gujarat include Talaja in Bhavnagar district, which has revealed thirty rock-cut caves, and Kadia Dungar near Bharuch.[22]

Among the prominent monastic complexes in Gujarat, Junagarh, Devni Mori and Vadnagar are known as the 'three jewels of Buddhism'. Located in the Aravalli district, in the proximity of trade routes in western India, Devni Mori emerged as a prominent Buddhist site during the Gupta–Vakataka period. Since the archaeological site was submerged under a dam, the history of Devni Mori is constructed largely through the excavation report of 1966, and sculptures and artefacts housed in the Shamlaji Museum and the Baroda Museum and Picture Gallery. These indicate the existence of a stupa and a vihara. A casket containing a relic of the Buddha was recovered from the stupa, suggesting it must have been a pilgrimage site. The inscription on the casket and coins found at the site indicates that the stupa was built in the late 4th century CE, under the patronage of King Rudrasena III of the Western Kshatrapas. Also, two Buddhist monks – Agnivarma and Sudarshana – played a prominent role in the planning and construction of the stupa. One of the striking features of Devni Mori is the presence of four-inch and six-inch tall images of the seated Buddha. Made of terracotta, these sculptures reflect the influence of both the Gandhara and Mathura schools of art.[23]

Fig 4.1 Temple 17, an early standalone Buddhist structure from the Gupta period, Sanchi

Fig 4.2 Subsidiary shrine with Yakshi Hariti and her consort, Cave 2, Ajanta

Fig 4.3 Serpent King Nagaraja and his queen in the external courtyard of Cave 19, Ajanta

Fig 4.4 Dhamekh Stupa in Sarnath

Fig 4.5 Mahaparinirvana stupa temple at Kushinagar

Fig 4.6 A photograph of the Big Buddha in Bamiyan, Afghanistan, taken in 1939/40 by Annemarie Schwarzenbach (1908–42)

Fig 4.7 A statue of the Buddha in the 'Wheel of Dharma' position, made from chunar sandstone, dating to the Gupta period (5th century CE), Sarnath

Fig 4.8 Tara flanked by female figures and dwarfs in Cave 7 of the Aurangabad Caves

Fig 4.9 Cave 7, Aurangabad. Left: Bodhisattva as the saviour from Eight Great Dangers. Right: Female Buddhist deities with attendants and celestial beings

Vadnagar in Mehsana district, located on the edge of lake Sharmistha, was a fortified ancient settlement. It was an important centre of trade, connecting northern Gujarat to Rajasthan, Malwa, Saurashtra and the Deccan. Archaeological finds from here indicate that Vadnagar was an important Buddhist site between the 1st and 7th centuries CE.[24] The earliest find from this site included a red sandstone image of a bodhisattva brought from Mathura. According to an inscription found on the pedestal, it was brought for the chaitya of the Sammatiya monks at the site. Recent readings of the inscription also suggest that the image was a gift by a nun from the Sastha Bhikkhuni Sangha. Subsequent excavations at Vadnagar revealed the existence of a Buddhist monastery belonging to the 2nd–7th centuries CE. Located within the fortified settlement, this monastery had two small stupas – one square and another circular on plan – and an open central courtyard around which nine cells were constructed. The arrangement of cells around the courtyard created a swastika-like pattern. This plan could also be seen in monasteries at Sanchi and Sirpur in central India, and Taxila in Pakistan, all belonging to the same period (1st–7th centuries CE). Xuanzang, who visited Vadnagar around 640–41 CE, refers to the site as Anandapur. He mentions that 1,000 Sammatiya monks were in residence at ten *sangharamas*, or monasteries, here.

Ajanta

Like Gujarat, Buddhist caves were also excavated in Ajanta, in the Deccan region, and perhaps earlier. The Ajanta caves (discussed in detail in Chapter 8), seen as masterpieces of Buddhist religious art, represent a unique amalgamation of sculpture, architecture and painting. They were excavated in a horseshoe-shaped structure (Fig 8.1, Chapter 8) along the river Waghora, a little over 100 km from the city of Aurangabad, now known as Chhatrapati Sambhaji Nagar. These caves, mostly chaityas (containing a stupa) or viharas (with cells around a central hall), were carved out in two broad phases spread over a period of 600–700 years, from the 2nd century BCE to the 6th century CE. The first, or earlier, set of caves was excavated under the patronage of the Satavahana dynasty (c. 2nd century BCE to the 3rd century CE). The second, or later, phase of excavations was carried out several centuries later, under the patronage of the Vakataka dynasty that ruled between the mid-3rd century CE to the late 5th–early 6th century CE. Walter M. Spink, one of the foremost experts on Ajanta, argues that the caves belonging to the second phase were executed around the mid-5th century, over a brief period of only twenty years, during the reign of King Harishena.

The caves associated with the earlier period are popularly described as the 'Hinayana' caves, and they are known for aniconic or symbolic representations of Buddha in the sculptures and paintings. The caves of the later period, on the other hand, are widely known as the 'Mahayana' caves. The sculptures and paintings in the later period caves mostly represent the Buddha and the bodhisattvas in an anthropomorphic form. The chaityas belonging to the earlier Satavahana phase at Ajanta were based on the usual architectural plan that included a nave and an apse.

Aisles or passages for circumambulation were created by two rows of pillars, which met at the rounded back (Fig 3.6, Chapter 3). The hall had a vaulted ceiling adorned by a gallery of arches and cross beams running along the arches, quite like their earlier wooden prototypes. These were approached by a porch, or a pillared veranda, with one to three doors. The entrance to the cave was surmounted by a tall, horseshoe-shaped window called the chaitya window. In the later Vakataka caves, a courtyard appears in front of the facade with mini shrines. The facade becomes more ornate and the chaitya window larger, flanked by sculptures, balconies and arcades (Fig 8.5, Chapter 8). The walls inside are decorated with figures of the Buddha and celestial beings, and the stupa acquires an image of the Buddha and a multi-tiered parasol supported by gods, angels and dwarfs (Fig 8.4, Chapter 8).

Like the chaityas or prayer halls, the monasteries at Ajanta also underwent an architectural transformation from the earlier Satavahana to the later Vakataka phase. The basic plan earlier consisted of an oblong-pillared veranda, a hall with no decorative columns or pilasters and cells on three sides for dwelling purposes. The later monastery caves contained decorative pillars, were more spacious, had sculptural and painted decorations and narrative paintings, and more residential cells. They housed a shrine chamber at the back (Fig 8.6, Chapter 8), a structure we will return to in the following section on Nalanda, and subsidiary shrines in the back and side walls and the veranda. They could be approached by a courtyard and a porch.

While the existing Buddhist clusters were becoming bigger, many new monastic sites were becoming visible as well. These, or their neighbourhoods, might have had some Buddhist antecedents, but architecturally, they became noticeable or distinctive only during the Gupta–Vakataka period. These included monastic complexes at Nalanda, Odisha and Tamil Nadu.

Nalanda

The monument complex popularly known as 'Nalanda' lies within a fenced enclosure located just 12 km away from Rajagriha, the old capital of Magadha, one of the Buddha's favourite haunts. We will discuss Nalanda, which is now a UNESCO World Heritage Site, in detail in Chapter 9.

Though Nalanda is known as the world's oldest university, contemporary sources describe the site as a mahavihara, a great monastery. Yet, Nalanda was more than a vihara, a monastic dwelling, in the traditional sense – it functioned as a premier monastic-cum-scholastic establishment in ancient and early medieval India.

The excavated complex of Nalanda has unearthed remains of temples, monastic dwellings, votive structures/burial ad sanctos, as well as art works in stucco, bronze and stone, dating from the 5th to the 12th centuries CE. Though this complex evolved over a long period of 700–800 years, its systematic beginnings can be traced to the Gupta times. Both Xuanzang's account, which remains a major source for our reconstruction of Nalanda's history, and seals and inscriptions found in the mahavihara point to the role of the Gupta kings in building the complex. The Guptas, as already discussed, patronized Buddhist establishments despite their Brahmanical leanings. By the time of the Guptas, the idea of the vihara had evolved and become elaborate. The traditional viharas, whether independent structures (as in Bodh Gaya or Sanchi), erected within caves (as in Ajanta), or a part of a larger monastic complex (as in

Gandhara) were meant for the residence of monks. They also acted as centres for the spread of the Buddhist faith. Under the Guptas, a new kind of monastic organization (the mahavihara) emerged. It was an aggregation or confederation of several individual monasteries. In these mahaviharas, old and traditional monastic learning outgrew its inbred religious character and became progressively liberalized. It was made available to not only the monks but also to all seekers of knowledge.[25]

There was also standardization in the design of individual monasteries. From the 5th century onwards, several monastic structures – including those at Ajanta, Bagh and Nalanda – had a special cell created in the centre of the back wall, facing the main entrance, that housed an image of the Buddha. These special cells, also known as shrine chambers or gandhakutis (the 'perfumed chambers') were meant to serve as the residence of the Buddha himself (Fig 9.4, Chapter 9). The Buddha was believed to be a resident of such monasteries between the 5th and the 14th centuries. He is said to have lived in these quarters, owned property and gifts, and been involved with business from there through a special group of monks called the gandhakuti *varikas*.[26]

The Gupta period also saw the establishment of a new design in monastic and temple architecture. The monasteries, which were now richer in artistic decoration, both inside and outside, were topped by Gupta-style *shikharas* or towers. Xuanzang, too, saw several monasteries with towers on top. Another Gupta period feature was the *panchayatana* plan, which consisted of a principal shrine with four subsidiary shrines in the four corners, a design also seen in Vishnu temples. The panchayatana plan was observed at the brick and plastered construction at Site 3/Stupa 3/Temple 3 in Nalanda, which is the most iconic of all the monuments in the excavated and enclosed zone. In fact, the original Mahabodhi temple at Bodh Gaya, built in brick during the time of the Guptas, also follows the panchayatana plan. Temple 3 at Nalanda is also known for the highest concentration of miniature stupas, both votive and commemorative, alongside Temple 12/Site 12 (Fig 9.2 and Fig 9.7, Chapter 9). Built on a square base with a cylindrical drum, these stupas are principally of two types

– those built of brick, mostly between the 5th and 8th centuries CE (belonging to the Gupta and early Pala period), and those constructed in stone between the 8th and 12th centuries CE (belonging to the mature and late Pala period). The brick stupas were covered with stucco, painted or gilded, and adorned with stucco images.[27]

Finally, the mahavihara also functioned as an educational establishment. Xuanzang mentions 10,000 residents staying on the campus, while Yijing (also known as I-tsing) puts the corresponding figure at 3,000. How could the current enclosed and excavated site sustain such a large population? This question has led scholars to look for extended boundaries and wider links. Recent satellite imageries and surveys (by M. B. Rajani and others) have shown that Buddhist Nalanda was much larger than the excavated and enclosed area, and that it included the carefully planned, human-made tanks surrounding the complex. So, like other Buddhist sites including Sanchi in Madhya Pradesh, Thotlakonda in Andhra Pradesh or Anuradhapura in Sri Lanka, Nalanda also had multiple water bodies, tanks, reservoirs, etc., to support agriculture and sustain habitations. Further, the extended boundary also included some more temples and monasteries, which are currently located outside the monument complex.[28] Historians have also suggested that Nalanda enjoyed a dynamic relationship with the agricultural villages and the habitations surrounding it, as well as the network of monasteries found in the vicinity (such as Odantapura, Yashovarmapura monastery at Ghosrawan and Telhara located 33 km north-west). Interestingly, these surroundings have yielded a variety of artefacts and antiquities connected not just with the Buddhists but also with the Hindus and Jainas.[29]

Odisha

Like Nalanda, the sites at Odisha became architecturally prominent during the Gupta times, though they had pre-Gupta connections. The Pali canon talks about two merchants, Tapusa and Bhallika (or Trapusa and Bahalika) from Ukkala (which has been identified by some as Utkala, the ancient name of Odisha), who offered the Buddha rice cakes and honey when he was meditating after attaining enlightenment. The Buddha apparently gave them strands of his hair and his nails, which the two merchants are said to have enshrined in a stupa upon their return to their homeland, Asitanjana. Some people have identified Asitanjana with the Radhanagar hills in Odisha's Jajpur district, but others differ. Odisha's connection with the Buddha has also been routed through Ashoka. The Mauryan king started patronizing the Buddha's teachings in a big way after the violent Kalinga War. Edicts at Dhauli and Jaguada, along with the rock-cut elephant at Dhauli, attest to his presence in the region.

However, according to archaeological evidence, Odisha experienced the growth of Buddhist dhamma and monuments in the period between the 5th and 13th–14th centuries, when more than a hundred sites become known. A 3rd-century inscription found in Nagarjunakonda refers to communities of monks at places like Tosali, Palur and Pushpagiri. Around this time, we also see Buddhist establishments in coastal Odisha, around the Langudi hills located in the delta plains of river Mahanadi, about 90 km from modern-day Bhubaneswar and Lalitagiri. Excavations at Langudi hills reveal the existence of thirty-four rock-cut stupas dating around the 2nd–3rd centuries CE, though its sculptures date to the 7th and 9th centuries CE. Excavations at Lalitagiri, on the other hand, have brought to light remains of a 2nd–1st century stupa, an apsidal shrine that contained a seat set up by a nun and some lay followers, and relics wrapped in gold foil alongside Kushana- and Gupta-period inscriptions.[30]

Tamil Nadu

Unlike Odisha and Nalanda, Buddhist ideas and institutions had to cover a lot of ground to strike roots in the deep south, in the Tamil country. According to legends, Buddhist ideas reached the Tamil region around the 3rd century BCE, during Ashoka's time, when missions were sent out to Sri Lanka. Most scholars, however, argue that Buddhism acquired an institutional footing in the Tamil country around the middle of the first millennium CE, a period also characterized by the rise of the Pallava dynasty in the north, the Pandyas in the south and the Cholas in the central part of the Tamil country. Buddhist presence in the Tamil region is attested to by the literature and also archaeological and epigraphic evidence. Two Tamil epics, *Silappadikaram* and *Manimekalai*, particularly the latter that dates to c. 550 CE,³¹ shed important light on the growth of Buddhist establishments in the region.

According to information available in the epics, cities like Vanji, Puhar and Madurai had a Buddhist following among the merchants and artisans. Unlike other regions, the Buddhists in Tamil country had to compete intensely, and sometimes acrimoniously, with other faiths common in northern India, including Vedic Brahmanism and Jainism, for royal patronage and followers. The epics give references to many Buddhas and bodhisattvas, and the concept of trikaya that was discussed earlier in the chapter. They also talk about the 'chain of dependent origination' prevalent in the conservative Theravada tradition. *Manimekalai* also speaks of expositions of philosophers like Dignaga, Buddhaghosa and Dharmapala, all of whom belong to the 5th–6th centuries CE. Of particular interest to us is the story of Manimekalai, the protagonist of the same name as the epic. Manimekalai was introduced to the Buddhist world by a renowned teacher called Aravana Adigal, who was based in Kanchipuram. Illankilli, the brother of Ouhar's Chola king Killivalavan, is said to have built a stupa, a vihara and a chaitya at Kanchipuram. Manimekalai is associated with the upkeep of the buddhapada. Under her influence, Killivalavan is said to have gifted a prison house to the Buddhists who used it as both a charity house and a monastery. During a famine at Kanchipuram, Manimekalai provided relief to the people by distributing food from her divine alms bowl, *amutacurapi*. Some scholars have argued that the *Manimekalai* both embodied and envisioned a Buddhist community that was explicitly local or 'Tamil'.³² By the time Xuanzang visited Kanchipuram in the 7th century, the city had perhaps passed its Buddhist prime. The pilgrim talks about dilapidated viharas without monks. He also mentions a giant stupa built by Ashoka.³³ A seven-foot Buddha image, stylistically dated to the 4th–6th centuries CE, found in the Kamakshi Amman temple in Kanchipuram, speaks of the Buddhist influence in the region during this period. This image is now housed in Government Museum, Chennai.

Another town on the east coast of Tamil Nadu, Kaveripoompattinam (Puhar), emerged as an important Buddhist centre. Tamil literary works describe the city as being a Buddhist centre of learning that had a monastery during the rule of the Kalabhras (4th–6th centuries CE), who are said to have obscure origins and were defeated by the Pandyas, Pallavas and Chalukyas. Archaeological excavations in Kaveripoompattinam have revealed the remains of a monastery, a temple and a buddhapada dated to the 4th–7th centuries CE. A small bronze image of the Buddha was also found in one of its cells in the monastery.[34]

SCULPTURAL EFFLORESCENCE: THE ASCENDANCY OF SARNATH AND AJANTA

In the early centuries of the Christian era, narrative reliefs showing events, episodes and places connected with the Buddha figured as decorative sculptures on or around the stupas. Human representations of the Buddha and bodhisattvas, as seen in the preceding chapter, had also started emerging under the aegis of the Gandhara and Mathura schools of art. Both centres continued to function during this period, but with some changes in sculptural styles. Buddhist narrative sculptures also continued to appear in the old and new stupas in Gujarat, and in the caves of Deccan, alongside images that were becoming more prominent. But the Gupta Age was when Sarnath and eastern Bihar emerged as new centres of Buddhist art.

If one were to look at the Buddhist art scene in general during this period, one would notice that images of the Buddha started becoming more ornate and sophisticated, and bigger. They depicted more postures and mudras than before, the plain halo became ornamented and the robes became transparent. Independent giant statues of the Buddha from this period can be seen at Mathura and Sarnath, and later, on a much bigger scale, in Bamiyan. Paintings of the Buddha and events from his life came to be depicted in places like Ajanta and a few other caves in the Deccan. The bodhisattvas, too, started becoming visible in the sculptural representations. Tara made a cameo appearance at this stage, only to become more pronounced sculpturally in the next couple of centuries, as her cult matured.

The Mathura school continued to play an important role in the production and supply of red sandstone images to different Buddhist sites in northern, central and eastern India including Sarnath, Shravasti Kaushambi, Berachampa (West Bengal), Lumbini, and Shaikan Dheri (West Pakistan).[35] The monks, too, continued to aid in the supply and installation of such images. The face of the Buddha in the Mathura images from the Gupta period did not look out at the world, like the earlier times. Instead, it looked within, as if in contemplation and reflecting a calm inner bliss. The Buddha wore a translucent robe with folds marked by string-like ridges and his hair was depicted by rows of small curls that concealed the tapering protuberance. The Gupta period saw Mathura producing a series of magnificent and large Buddha images, which are now scattered in museums throughout the world. The great specimens of the Mathura school can be seen in the statues of the standing Buddha at the Rashtrapati Bhawan in New Delhi and the Government Museum, Mathura.

Mathura also produced Sarnath's earliest Buddhist images – an early Kushana period large Buddha with a parasol now found at the Sarnath Museum. They were brought to Sarnath by a monk named Bala. Two huge bodhisattvas belonging to the Kushana period, also in the Sarnath Museum but made of the local chunar sandstone, perhaps set the tone for the Sarnath school of art that was characterized by the face and body features of the images becoming more refined and the drapery transparent. The Gupta-period Buddhas at Sarnath, both seated and standing, carry a more ornamental halo with a lotus pattern, have short and curly hair covering the head, show serene meditative expressions, adorn transparent drapery covering both shoulders with no folds and exhibit an elegant bearing of the body.[36] They also have bulging lips, half-closed eyes and a sensuous modelling of the face and head, some visible Gupta-period features.[37]

The cross-legged, seated image of the Buddha in dharmachakra mudra, seen at the Sarnath Museum, is regarded as one of the most exquisite examples of the art of the Gupta period, and even ancient India. Its halo is carved with the characteristic floral scroll work and carries two celestial figures. Under his throne are seven figures worshipping a wheel – the dharmachakra and two deer. This figure has a site-specific connotation and reminds us of the Buddha's first sermon, the dharmachakrapravartana delivered at the Deer Park (Mrigadaya) in Rishipattana (Place of the Sages) in Sarnath (Fig 4.7). Sarnath has also yielded over a hundred images of the standing Buddha in abhay mudra (the protection-giving gesture) with his webbed right hand (one of the thirty-two major marks of the Buddha) and holding the hem of his robe with the left. These belong to the Gupta period and were made during the 5th and early 6th centuries. Some scholars point out that the right-hand gesture was also used to show the Buddha in a teaching posture in the earlier Gandhara depictions (c. 1st or 2nd centuries CE). However, these images from the Gupta period reflect a dual gesture called *vyakarna* mudra (a symbolic gesture of predicting someone's future enlightenment), a subject popular in the Mahayana sutras. The standing images of the Sarnath Buddha are usually accompanied by the parasol, which was a Kushana period iconographic convention.[38]

Images of the Buddha, though not so huge, also began to proliferate caves like Ajanta, Karle, Kanheri and Kuda in western Deccan. Mostly in a preaching or blessing posture, they appear almost everywhere – in shrines and antechambers, on the walls of the veranda and halls, on the pillars and their brackets. Episodes from the life of Gautama Buddha are also depicted and some, like the 'Assault and Temptation of Mara' or the 'Miracle at Shravasti', are very conspicuous. Of particular interest at Ajanta are the depictions of the Buddha as the spiritual sovereign, the *chakravartin*, in palace-like settings. An inscription found in Cave 17 describes the Buddha as a 'king among ascetics'. Images of the Buddha are also shown seated on a lion/royal throne (Caves 15, 16, 22), in some cases with royal insignia such as the parasols and fly-whisk bearers. Finally, in Cave 23, the Naga doorkeepers wield axes (instead of flowers, as seen in the earlier caves) symbolizing royal doorkeepers guarding a palace. Even the bodhisattvas are shown as royal attendants to the Buddha.[39]

The bodhisattvas appear in several caves at Ajanta, in both sculptural and painted forms. These include the iconic paintings of Padmapani Avalokiteshvara and Vajrapani in Cave 1, or the images of bodhisattvas attending to the Buddha in Caves 2, 7 and 16. Bodhisattva Avalokiteshvara is also depicted in some cases as the saviour of humankind against the 'eight great perils', which included shipwreck. This depiction had a special appeal among the merchants and traders. The saviour version of the bodhisattvas also appears in sculptures and/ or paintings in caves in Kanheri, Pitalkhora and Aurangabad (Fig 4.9),[40] especially among the ones excavated during the 5th–6th centuries, and later at Ellora. Some of the Aurangabad caves also depict female attendants accompanying the bodhisattvas, which some scholars feel reflects the tantric or Vajrayana influence. For example, Cave 7 at Aurangabad depicts Tara flanked by two female figures and dwarfs (Fig 4.8). Tara's images have also been found in other Buddhist caves in the Deccan, such as Ajanta, Karle, Kanheri and, later, in Ellora.

An interesting characteristic of the period is representations of the Buddha and the bodhisattvas in metal and terracotta. These include copper or bronze images found in Sultanganj in Bihar, Gandhara, coastal Gujarat, Amravati and coastal Tamil Nadu, besides some sites in the Gangetic heartland. We have also seen how terracotta Buddhas were being made in Devni Mori in Gujarat.

THE FAITH ACQUIRES NEW FRONTIERS, SPREADS IN EAST AND SOUTHEAST ASIA

One of the first countries that Buddhist ideas struck roots in was Ceylon (Sri Lanka). The history of interaction with Sri Lanka had started during Ashoka's time, when Buddhist missions were received by King Tissa at Anuradhapura and a branch of the original Bodhi tree was planted there. Anuradhapura soon developed as a prominent Buddhist centre with stupas and viharas. It is now a UNESCO World Heritage Site. The interactions with Sri Lanka continued in the subsequent centuries. An inscription at Bodh Gaya also attests to the presence of Sri Lankan monks at the site of the Buddha's enlightenment, as early as the 6th century CE. In the 5th century, Buddhist monk Buddhaghosa travelled to Sri Lanka, translated several scriptural commentaries into Pali and wrote a book called *Visuddhimagga* (the Path of Purification), which soon acquired the status of a classic on Theravada doctrine and meditation. Sri Lanka later became a launch pad for Buddhism into Southeast Asia and China. It must, however, be clarified that the movement of monks and ideas from India to other countries was not a linear process. It was a complex one that involved a lot of to-and-fro engagements.

The other region with which Buddhist links opened during the Mauryan times was Central Asia, routed as it was through the Gandhara region. The Dharmarajika stupa laid the foundation for many subsequent Buddhist establishments in the region. The Kushana period widened the international trade networks by connecting the oasis states of Central Asia with the maritime world of the Bay of Bengal. Taxila also emerged as a leading site of Buddhist learning, drawing students from many places. The merchant communities from Central Asia, particularly the Sogdians, played a leading role in introducing Buddhist teachings and images to Han-ruled China, which was going through a period of urbanization and commercial expansion.[41] Many Indian monks, particularly from Kashmir, also visited China during the Gupta times. Most carried with them Buddhist texts and were involved with important compositions and translations. These included Sanghabhuti, the author of a commentary on the *Sarvastivada Vinaya* (381 to 384 CE); Punyatrata who stayed in China between 424 and 453 CE; Buddhayashas, who travelled to Kashgar and from there to Kucha in the 5th century; and Kashmiri prince Gunavarman, who first travelled to Sri Lanka and Java, from where he headed to Nanking in 431 CE.[42] Between the 5th and 6th centuries, many Indian monks from outside of Kashmir also visited China and became associated with some major translations, particularly those like Kumarajiva, Paramartha and Bodhidharma. Paramartha, who went to China with several Buddhist texts as part of a return mission by a Gupta king to the Chinese court, stayed there for twenty-three years. Bodhidharma's disciple Dazu Huike founded what came to be known as the Chan (Zen in Japanese) school of Buddhism.[43]

Buddhist ideas received royal patronage under the Northern Wei dynasty (386–534 CE) in northern China and the Liang dynasty (502–557 CE) in southern China. Such dynasties used Buddhist ideas to legitimize their political authority and create a distinct identity for themselves, a phenomenon later experienced in Japan and Korea. The demand for Buddhist artefacts and texts, the intensification of long-distance commercial activity and the emergence of

Nalanda as a premier centre of Buddhist learning deepened the presence of Buddhism in China during the 5th and 6th centuries. This expanding relationship between India and China also brought Japan, Korea and Sumatra within the Buddhist realm during the Gupta period. Gradually, diverse and local forms of Buddhist teachings, schools and structures developed not just in East Asia but also in Southeast Asia.

Myanmar and Thailand had already been exposed to Buddhist doctrines in the early centuries of the Christian era. The discovery of Pali inscriptions associated with Theravada Buddhism in Myanmar and Thailand, the finding of Sanskrit inscriptions of the Bengal-based monk Buddhagupta from Malayasia and the recovery of Buddhist statues, votive tablets and stupas from the Malay peninsula attest to the presence of Buddhism in this region between the 5th and 7th/8th centuries CE. As discussed earlier in the chapter, Indian traders of Buddhist and Hindu affiliations played an important role in the trade in spices and semi-precious stones with Southeast Asia. The monks weren't far behind. Ships sailed from Tamralipti and Amravati to Myanmar and Indonesia. Likewise, the ports of south India sent ships to Tenasserim (Malaysia), Trang (Thailand), the Straits of Malacca and Java. The ports on the west coast of India were also connected with Southeast Asian trade. Soon, there was a strong cultural connect with Thailand, Cambodia and Java. An interesting manifestation of this was the intertwining of Buddhist and Puranic norms with the local cults in Cambodia and Java. This manifested in interesting iconographic expressions like the Angkor Wat and Bayon temples in Cambodia, the stupa at Borobudur and the Prambanan temple in Indonesia.[44] The emergence of the powerful Srivijaya empire in Sumatra in the 7th century also contributed to the spread of Buddhist ideas in Southeast Asia.

The development of Buddhism in Tibet was almost contemporaneous with its spread in Southeast Asia. In the 7th century CE, King Songtsen Gampo (who ruled from c. 614–650 CE) used Buddhism as a tool to consolidate his hold among the powerful clans in the region.[45] By the time of King Tri Songdetsen (who reigned from 754 to 797), the faith had acquired firmer footing on Tibetan soil.

Buddhist monks from Nalanda, like Padmasambhava, Shantarakshita and Dipankara (popularly known as Atisha), visited Tibet between the 8th and 11th centuries. They are credited with the introduction of the Vajrayana school there.

The Gupta–Vakataka age was an interesting one for Buddhism in India. On the one hand, the Buddhist pantheon was growing bigger, the Buddha's images were becoming larger, viharas were giving way to mahaviharas, sites associated with the Buddha's life were becoming more elaborate, new art centres and establishments were blossoming and the Buddha's legacy was acquiring roots in East and Southeast Asia. On the other hand, there was a blurring of religious boundaries between Buddhism, Jainism and Brahmanical Hinduism, which was experiencing a revival. Features like the worship of images in shrines, the emergence of a pantheon of deities and the incorporation and architectural subordination of deities associated with the popular cults were becoming common to most dominant religions of the time, alongside the prevalence of the idea of bhakti, worship of Shakti and Tantrism. The stage was set for complex negotiations in India, between a settled Buddhism and a reviving Brahmanism. The old geography of Magadha and its surroundings were set to play an important role in these negotiations.

5

TANTRIC INFUSION, REGIONALIZATION AND DECLINE

> The [Turks] destroyed Odantapura and Vikramashila, and killed many Bhiksus. At that time Sakya Sribhadra [a learned monk from Kashmir] fled towards Orissa [probably mistaken for Jagaddala monastery in northern Bengal]. Within three years after that, he reached Tibet and gave initiation to many Bhiksus. Others fled to other places. Thus Buddhism came to end in Magadha.

This is how the last few years of Buddhism in eastern India, primarily Magadha, are described in *Pag sam jon zang*, which was written by the 18th-century Tibetan historian Sumpa Khan-po Yeçe Pal Jor (1702–75).[1] During the 12th and 13th centuries, the Turks and Afghans attacked Buddhist establishments, causing the monks to flee to Tibet, Burma, Cambodia, Arakan (modern-day Rakhine in Myanmar), etc. This era was also marked by scholar-monks who travelled to prominent seats of Buddhist learning to meet teachers, collect manuscripts and delve into translation projects.

Most of these monks visited Tibet, Nepal or countries in East and Southeast Asia to transmit Buddhist ideas and translate seminal works. In many ways, the narrative of Turkish destruction of Buddhist sites often dominates the imagery of early medieval Buddhism. But this attack primarily occurred towards the end of Buddhism's last public run in the subcontinent, roughly between 600 and 1300 CE.

This early medieval period saw significant developments: the revival of Brahmanical ideas, backed by a more encompassing Puranic ideology; the establishment of regional Buddhist enclaves, some of which exist to this day; the emergence of Vajrayana, a tantric form of Buddhism, or a more ritualized form of Mahayana; and the flourishing of mahaviharas, alongside fragmented polities and realignments of trade.

REGIONAL IDENTITIES, RELIGIOUS MUTATIONS, REALIGNMENTS IN TRADE

The reign of the Guptas and the Vakatakas was followed by a more fragmented political landscape. This continued in large parts of north and peninsular India till the Turks came and established the Delhi Sultanate. The period between 600 and 1200 CE is mostly seen as one when states, regions and regional identities became ascendant.

The vacuum left by the Guptas in northern India was temporarily filled by the Pushyabhutis in the 7th century. They extended control over north, north-west and parts of eastern India. The most famous Pushyabhuti king, Harshavardhana (popularly known as Harsha), ruled from Kannauj, which had replaced Pataliputra as the political-urban hub of the Gangetic plains. Harsha is regarded as an important ruler in Buddhist writings. He is credited with some constructions at Nalanda and the convening of a religious assembly at Kannauj, where Chinese pilgrim Xuanzang spoke about Mahayana doctrines. In eastern India, the death of Shashanka, the ruler of Gauda (also known as Gaur) who is said to have destroyed Buddhist establishments in Bengal and cut down the Mahabodhi tree, in the 7th century was followed by political chaos. Finally, the Palas established control over Bengal and Bihar, and ruled between the 8th and 12th centuries. They were patrons of Buddhism, and their rule is associated with some well-known mahaviharas. The Pala period is also famous for Buddhist art and sculptures.

Odisha continued to remain in a fragmented state from the 8th to 12th centuries. Several kingdoms and dynasties arose during this time. Of these, the kings of the Bhaumakara dynasty, who patronized the Buddhists, took on titles like *paramaoupasaka*, 'the most devout lay follower'. In the north-east, Assam emerged stronger under Bhaskaravarman who is known to have supported monastic establishments at Nalanda.

Meanwhile, the post-Vakataka Deccan was marked by rivalries between the Chalukyas of Badami (also known as the Western Chalukyas), the Pallavas who ruled from Kanchi and the Pandyas based in Madurai. The Chalukyas gave way to the Rashtrakutas in the 8th century. The latter are associated with the construction of structures at Ellora. The far south was dominated by the Pallavas who ruled from Kanchipuram, the Pandyas, the Cholas who were based around Uraiyur (now part of Tiruchirapalli city) and Tanjore, and the Cheras who controlled the Kerala coast.

Meanwhile, the north-west region was witnessing a transition, too. Kashmir was successively ruled by the Karkota (who patronized the Buddhists), Utpala, Turkish Shahiya (which had its base in Kabul valley in Afghanistan) and Shahi dynasties between the 7th and 12th centuries, a period that saw the gradual yet progressive decline of Buddhism. The mountainous Himachal tract was torn between the rivalries of ruling houses like Trigarta, Chamba, Kullu and Kashmir, and the growing Tibetan influence. The Arabs, who had been thwarted in the west, captured Sind and Multan. Finally, north and central India also experienced changes with the establishment of the Rajput states in the 12th century.

The proliferation of states and regional entities was also accompanied by the Brahmanization of royal courts across the subcontinent, which partly cost Buddhists their royal patronage. The Brahmans legitimized the political power of the new kings and lords by constructing genealogies and the performance of sacrifices and rituals. In return, they got permanent land grants in both habited and inhabited rural or fringe areas, where they introduced or intensified Brahmanical learning, caste norms, the use of Sanskrit and the worship of gods in temples. The Brahmans, who had so far championed the Vedas, also became carriers of Puranic religion. How did these developments impact the Buddhists or the Jainas? With focus on a slightly different set of religious ethos – including personal devotion (bhakti), reduction of the role of priests and Vedic sacrificial rituals, individualized rites of worship, prominence of image worship – the Puranic religion appealed to the popular mood of the time. In doing so, it challenged the space occupied by Buddhism, and even Vedic

Brahmanism. In addition, by dividing large groups of population into castes and religious sects, the assimilation of numerous cults and deities, constructing mythologies connected with gods and making them available in regional languages and oral traditions, the Puranic ideology was substantially eroding the ideological base of the Buddhists. An attempt was also made to assimilate the Buddha into Vaishnavism, as the ninth of Lord Vishnu's ten incarnations. Finally, the Puranas shaped the formation of sects and sectarian tendencies. Founders of new sects like Shankaracharya, Madhvacharya and Ramanujacharya and Basavanna gained prominence. With formal organization and defined philosophies, these sects got into strong contestations with the Buddhists and the Jainas as they tried to extend their reach across north India. Occasionally, they also branded the latter as heretics. Some, like Shankaracharya, also used philosophical forms, institutional organization (network of *mathas*) and debate and discussion formats that imitated or paralleled those of the Buddhists.[2]

The changing political and religious configurations were also accompanied by a realignment of trade and urbanism. So, while urban centres with Buddhist connections like Shravasti, Kaushambi, Kapilavastu and Vaishali were on a decline, others like Kannauj and Varanasi became very powerful. Like the urban centres, there was a reorientation of long-distance trade. Trade with the Eastern Roman empire declined even though spices and jewels remained popular in Europe. The Arabs brought northern Africa, the Mediterranean region and East Asia together. Soon, they emerged as the leaders of overland and maritime routes that connected Europe and East Asia, and also the Indian Ocean trade. By the 11th century, there emerged three connecting segments of the Indian Ocean trade – from the Persian Gulf and Red Sea to Gujarat and Malabar, from the Indian coast to the south-east or Indonesian archipelago, and from Southeast to East Asia (primarily China). There was an eastward shift in India's maritime trade, towards China and East Asia, with Sri Lanka being an important hub.[3] India's trade with Southeast Asia and China also grew during this period, as did the importance of ports along the east coast. Bengal, with the Ganga delta and the trans-Meghna region up to the south-eastern parts of Bangladesh, offered a maritime route while

Harikela's (Chittagong) proximity to Arakan provided an overland corridor to Southeast Asian mainland.[4] The Buddhist connection was apparent in the growing trade links and circuits. The Palas benefitted both from the Arab trade circuit with Southeast Asia and the Chinese trade route on the way to East Africa, as both used ports on the Bay of Bengal. They used Buddhism to control trade and form diplomatic relations with Southeast Asia and Tibet.[5] We hear of a Pala king helping Balaputra, a ruler of Suvarnadipa, build a monastery at Nalanda and maintain it. Another king, from the Srivijaya dynasty, built a monastery at Nagapattinam in southern India. On the other hand, the Buddhist component in India–China trade was declining with the Sinification of Buddhism and the development of local schools and practices in China. So, while the movement of monks and the translations of texts continued, there was a decline in the demand for Buddhist ritual items.[6]

RITUALIZATION AND EXPANSION IN MAHAYANA, AND VAJRAYANA BUDDHISM

The Mahayana form of worship, which had emerged in the earlier centuries, became enriched by the prevalence of images and devotional worship in the subsequent years. It was now getting more ritualized. Shantideva's *Bodhicharyavatara*, an 8th-century text, describes the Mahayana rites of worship, which were practically the same as Brahmanical image worship – bathing of the image with perfumed water, offering flowers, food and clothes, swinging censers, burning incense and the performance of vocal and instrumental music.[7] Interestingly, the descriptions in the donative inscriptions of the Maitrakas at Vallabhi also talk about provisions for flowers, oil, lamps, incense, etc.[8]

The Buddhist pantheon was expanding to include Buddhas, bodhisattvas and goddesses. The group of *dhyani* buddhas was a fresh addition. The dhyani buddhas were a group of five 'self-born' celestial buddhas who have existed since the beginning of time. They have earthly forms and their own distinctive attributes. Such buddhas, particularly known in the later Mahayana and Vajrayana traditions, are usually identified as Vairochana, Akshobhya, Ratnasambhava,

Amitabha and Amoghasiddhi.[9] Though the expression 'dhyani buddhas' is not found in key Buddhist texts, the nomenclature is used to describe groups of images consisting of five meditating buddhas in the mandala designs, which constituted a new pattern of arrangement of the images at various monastic sites. Mandala literally means a circle and, by extension, a circular diagram. Broadly speaking, it represents – by way of a painting, a diagram, an iconographic arrangement, an architectural plan or a 3D model – a Buddhist universe or palace showing deities and their surroundings. At the centre of this symbolic representation is a Buddhist deity (male or female, or a couple) surrounded by protective barriers or deities, sometimes ferocious in appearance. Such representations were, and are, used as meditation tools in the tantric form of Buddhism. Mandala art and architectural formations can be seen at sites with Vajrayana affiliations.

In the iconographic mandala designs, the Buddha's image continued to remain the focal point of worship, but it was surrounded by attendant figures. In short, it showed new conceptual groupings of the buddhas and the bodhisattvas. Such an arrangement could be seen in the Buddhist caves of Ellora, which were excavated between the 7th and 8th centuries, particularly the three-storeyed Cave 12 that was excavated later (Fig 5.1), and also in some caves (Caves 6 and 7) at Aurangabad. The new arrangement of images, in mandalas, shows the emergence of a new Buddhist circuit around the middle of the 1st millennium CE, which went beyond Ellora and Aurangabad to include monastic sites in eastern India, central India, and the western Himalayas.[10]

However, the most conspicuous feature of the Buddhist pantheon during this period was the ascendancy of tantric Buddhism, in part through the introduction of feminine divinities. The most important of these were the Taras, who were mostly spouses and consorts of the buddhas and bodhisattvas. The Hinayana school had been concerned with arhatship – obtaining right knowledge through self-discipline and meditation. Mahayana had introduced the concept of bodhisattvas – buddhas-in-waiting who delayed nirvana and helped other sentinel beings obtain salvation. The new school, also known as Mantrayana or Vajrayana (the 'vehicle of mantras'), was based on the detailed incantation of magical formulae. Vajrayana or tantric Buddhism believed in acquiring the magical power called the diamond, or *vajra* (thunderbolt). It became very popular in eastern India, especially in Bengal and Bihar, and was patronized by the Pala kings. When Xuanzang visited India in the 7th century, he saw many monasteries practising the Vajrayana form of Buddhism. The chief divinities of the new sect were the Taras. In tantric Buddhism, Tara came to be considered as the shakti of the Buddha. Sometimes, she was also seen as an emanation of the Buddha. The Taras, associated with the bodhisattvas in the earlier centuries, became very powerful during the early medieval period. *Manjushri-mulakalpa* lists Taras under various names, including Mamaki, Bhrikuti, Lochana, Pandaravasini, Shveta and Sutara. Later texts also speak of the various forms of Tara, of which Green Tara (associated with peacefulness and enlightened activity) and White Tara (compassion, long life, and healing) became very popular. The graceful-looking Shyama Tara or Khadiravani Tara was considered an emanation of Amoghasiddhi, the Dhyani Buddha, while the terrifying four-armed Mahachina Tara or Ugra Tara, originated from Akshobhya.[11] Interestingly, Tara also got reconfigured within the tantric, Shaiva and Shakti traditions in the early medieval times to produce a set of *piths*, pilgrimage sites, in Bengal, Bihar and Odisha. This includes the famous Tarapith temple on the banks of the river Dwarka in Birbhum district of West Bengal, where she is seen as an incarnation of Goddess Kali.

Alongside Tara, some lesser deities, mostly demon-like or ferocious figures, also became a part of the Vajrayana pantheon. These included the *matangi*s (outcast women), *pisachi*s (demonesses), yoginis (sorceresses) and *dakini*s (she-ghouls). It was believed that these figures needed to be compelled, rather than persuaded, to bestow magical powers on the worshipper. This could be done by reciting the right magical formula (mantra) or by drawing the correct magical symbol (yantra). The most prominent of all the Vajrayana mantras is the six-syllable *shadakshara* – Om mani padme hum (Praise to the jewel in the lotus). The shadakshara is still written and repeated thousands of times in Tibet and several parts of India such as Sikkim and Ladakh daily. Apart from the spiritual importance, it was believed to have sexual symbolism. The shadakshara was a reference to the divine coitus of the heavenly buddhas and the prajnaparamitas, of the Avalokiteshvaras and their Taras.[12]

The emergence of a new set of deities in the Buddhist pantheon and new ways of worshipping them was accompanied by a further strengthening of the cult of stupa worship, which continued well into the 12th and 13th centuries. New ritual texts prescribing details of stupa worship also came into being. References in *Mahavastu* indicate how stupa worship rites in the early centuries of the Christian era included circumambulation, paying obeisance, offerings of flowers, cotton and silk clothes, incense, placing of lamps and playing of instrumental worship.[13] By the 5th and 6th centuries, stupa worship had also begun to include sandal paste, oblations and other offerings. By the 8th and 9th centuries, new tantra classifications, such as *kriya* and *charya* tantras, had come into being in Tibetan Buddhism, which stressed the worship and maintenance of the stupas. Kriya tantras dealt with the making and establishment of images, while the charya tantras discussed rites and rituals for daily worship. There are many written manuals in the Tibetan-Buddhist tradition that relate to the selection of sites and consecration of the stupa. These continue to be followed in Ladakh and the regions in the western Himalayas. The Tibetan texts also talk about gandhakutis. Texts such as *Vimalosnisa* and *Rasmivimala*, originally written in Sanskrit and now surviving in Tibetan translations, are architectural manuals that discuss in detail rituals and processes related to the construction of stupas. The worship of stupas was not only getting ritualized but, under the impact of tantrism, the structural stupas also started acquiring a mandala form. With the addition of varied and many deities in the Buddhist pantheon, an elaborate liturgical literature the *Sadhanamala* came into being. It consisted of a collection of texts (*sadhanas*) which contained details of ritual practices as well as the iconography of the images.[14]

One aspect of the early medieval period, which goes relatively unnoticed, is the growing cult of the eight sites associated with the life events of the Buddha. We are familiar with the four principal events – birth (Lumbini), enlightenment (Bodh Gaya), first sermon (Sarnath) and death (Kushinagar). Visits to these sites had been advised by the

Buddha himself. Gradually, these became a part of the established pilgrimage circuit. Before long, four other cities, where the Buddha performed miracles, also became a part of the circuit. These included Shravasti (where the Buddha emitted fire and water from his body and multiplied his form a thousand-fold), Sankissa (where the Buddha descended from heaven), Vaishali (where a monkey famously offered him a bowl filled with honey) and Kapilavastu (where the Buddha tamed Nalagiri the elephant). It is not widely known that images carrying the 'Eight Sacred Locations' (*astamahachaitya*s) formed a part of a sub-cult known as the *Astamahapratiharya*, common among the laity. The cult developed a series of images throughout the Shunga and Kushana periods, but none of the sculptural representations showed all eight events in one single frame. Perhaps the first depiction of all eight scenes in one frame appears in a 5th-century stele discovered in Sarnath and now kept at the Sarnath Museum.[15] This integrated image became seminal to the Astamahapratiharya cult in north India for the next 600–700 years. Depictions of a seated Buddha surrounded by the eight events of his life, both in stone and clay, became a popular image in eastern India from the 8th century (Fig 5.2). It comes up in several images of the Buddha, which date to Pala-period Nalanda. With this image, a monk or a lay person could pay homage to the Astamahapratiharya without even stepping out of his home. This image perhaps also made it possible to receive an initiation into the tradition related to the primary Mahayana text *Astasahasrika Prajnaparamita Sutra*.[16]

NEW SACRED GEOGRAPHIES AND REGIONAL ARCHITECTURAL MANIFESTATIONS

The new rituals, cults, tantric practices and expanding Buddhist pantheon also manifested in the architectural landscape of the existing sites, through fresh excavations and building activities, especially in the Deccan, Tamil country, Gujarat, Kashmir and the new sacred cores becoming prominent in eastern India and the western Himalayas. Most of these sites reflected the influence of the Vajrayana school, but some showed traces of ritualized Mahayana. Vallabhi in Gujarat, meanwhile, showed a lingering Hinayana link.

130   CASTING THE BUDDHA

Deccan

In the Deccan, the Ellora caves represented the last phase of excavations. It was also a centre of art activity for nearly four centuries, from around 550 CE to 950 CE. One of the unique features of Ellora is the existence of Buddhist, Brahmanical and Jaina caves, side by side. While Ellora inherited the tradition of cave excavation that began in the western Deccan in the early centuries of the Christian era, some of its features represent the hallmark of Buddhist art and architecture in the early medieval times, including the mandala depiction – groupings of images of the Buddha and bodhisattvas, representations of Tara and the expanding pantheon of Buddhist divinities.

Contrary to the popular opinion, rock-cutting activity first began here with the Hindu caves (and not Buddhist) in the middle of the 6th century. Buddhist caves were mainly excavated during the 7th century, alongside some Brahmanical ones. The 8th century was a period of intense excavation of Hindu caves, which was when the famous Kailashnath temple was also carved. Work on the Jaina caves started in the 8th century and continued in full swing during the 9th and 10th centuries. Caves 1 to 12 are the Buddhist caves.[17] Among them, one can see both shrines (chaityas) and monasteries (viharas), though most are in ruins. The most common architectural plan of the monasteries is that of a large hall with pillars having square bases and cushion capitals, cells and mini shrines containing images and galleries. The cells are found on the side and rear walls of the hall, and also on the veranda. The shrines have a circumambulatory passage. Some caves (such as 10, 11 and 12) are rich in sculptures (Fig 5.3).

The most common motifs in the sculptures of Ellora are images of buddhas and bodhisattvas. The Buddha is mostly shown seated on a lion throne (*simhasana*) wearing a robe. His images carry the characteristic marks of great men (mahapurusha *lakshanas*), such as a protrusion between the eyebrows (*urna*), webbed fingers and curly or wavy hair usually ending in a top knot (ushnishas). He is shown mostly in three mudras – preaching (*vyakhyana* mudra), meditating (dhyan mudra) and touching the ground with the index finger of his right hand (bhumisparsha mudra). In most cases, the Buddha is accompanied by the bodhisattvas – Padmapani holding a lotus (padma) and Vajrapani carrying a thunderbolt (vajra) – along with a host of other attendants, male and female, including flying celestial beings (such as the *vidyadharas*) who hold garlands. Unlike the Buddha, the bodhisattvas and other attendants are shown wearing a lot of jewellery. Sometimes, the bodhisattvas also appear independently with female deities, or attendants, representing the Mahayana and Vajrayana influences. Tara, the Buddhist saviour, is sculpted in more than one cave. Of particular interest here are the depictions called the 'bodhisattva's litany' (Cave 3) and 'Tara's litany' (Cave 9, which is regarded as the only litany of Tara in western India). In such depictions, Avalokiteshvara, or Tara, is shown surrounded by the eight great perils (*astamahabhayas*) – fire, dacoits, false imprisonment, shipwrecks, lions, snakes, elephants and ghosts. We have already discussed how, in their roles as protectors against shipwrecks and dacoits, the bodhisattvas and Taras had a strong following among merchants and traders, particularly those travelling overseas. Other sculptural representations include deities like Jambhala, the Buddhist god of wealth; Mahamayuri, the goddess with a peacock to her right; the four-armed Bhrikuti; demigods like the nagas; and figures like guardians, or gatekeepers (*dvarapalas*), and dwarfs on the pillar capitals, or fly-whisk bearers around the Buddhas and bodhisattvas.

Cave 5 at Ellora has three bays separated by rock-cut platforms, very similar to those found at the Darbar Hall in Kanheri (Cave 11). Popularly known as the 'dining hall', the exact function of the cave is still not established (Fig 5.4). Locally known as *sutar ka jhopda* (carpenter's hut) or 'vishvakarma', Cave 10 is modelled like the apsidal-shaped chaitya halls of Ajanta (such as Caves 19 and 26) with a central nave and side aisles separated from it by octagonal pillars. The hall, which has exquisite sculptures, has a vaulted ceiling with wooden rib-shaped rock patterns. The triforium, or the area above the pillars, has niches carrying small images of the Buddha. The chaitya has a stupa with a recessed arch and carries a colossal statue of the Buddha. A distinctive part of the cave are the vase-and-foliage capitals in the corridor, which are characteristic of the Gupta period. It is held that Cave 10 represents the last of the rock-cut chaityas in western India. Cave 11, known as the *Do Thal* (double-storeyed) is actually triple-storeyed and also has images of Durga and Ganesha alongside a host of Buddhist deities like the Buddha, Padmapani, Vajrapani, Avalokiteshvara, Tara and Chunda.

Cave 12, known as the *Teen Thal* (triple-storeyed), is located at a slightly high level and heavily decorated with sculptures, particularly those of Buddhist goddesses. It has a cistern in an extended area. The rear wall of the ground floor has the Buddha mandala – a sculpture with eight bodhisattvas around the seated Buddha. This three-dimensional mandala representation is also seen in Caves 6 and 7 at Aurangabad. Mentioned in various texts like *Manjushri-mulakalpa* and *Sadhanamala*, these groupings of the buddhas and bodhisattvas were considered sacred and helped the devotees achieve desired goals.

This mandala formation puts Ellora in a new circuit of Buddhist sites that had emerged around the middle of the 1st millennium and can be seen in Cave 70 at Kanheri, Sanchi and Sirpur in central India, Bodh Gaya in Bihar, Ratnagiri in Odisha, and Lahaul and Spiti in the western Himalayas.[18] Coming back to Cave 12, the sanctum on the second floor has a big image of Tara. In the rear wall of the top floor, one can see the seven *manushi* (human) buddhas (also seen in a painted panel in Cave 22 of Ajanta) in a meditating position, each with a distinguishing tree and halo. It is said that these represent the last seven Buddhas. Of particular importance here is the presence of a cluster of twelve goddesses in the side and rear walls of the antechamber (Fig 5.5). These been identified as Vajradhatu-ishvari, holding a Chintamani jewel; Chunda holding a lotus and a book; Khadiravani Tara seated on a lotus and holding a lotus stalk; Janguli with a crown of cobras; Mahamayuri holding a peacock feather; Usnisavijaya holding a water vessel; and Bhrikuti, Pandara and Tara. These goddesses are generally regarded as representations of Tara[19] and depict the growing influence of tantric Buddhism.

While Ellora represents new excavations, it isn't as if the old caves of the Deccan did not flourish or remain relevant. In Kanheri, in western Deccan, images of a seated Buddha (sometimes flanked by bodhisattvas) and Avalokiteshvara continue to remain prominent. A 9th-century inscription from Cave 11, also known as the Darbar Hall, records donations for books and repairs. There are similar examples from eastern Deccan as well. Amravati, for instance, continued to exist till the 14th century. While bronze images of standing Buddha from Nagapattinam, belonging to the period between the 4th and 6th centuries, are kept in the Government Museum, Chennai; limestone statues of bodhisattvas like Avalokiteshvara, Manjushri, Vajrapani and Cunda (belonging to the 8th and 9th centuries) are now housed in the British Museum. Inscriptional evidence from Sankaram, 50 kms from Visakhapatnam, indicates that the Buddhist monastic establishment at the site continued to receive donations in the 9th century, and that a series of rock-cut or brick-built stupas also appeared on its eastern mound called Bojjannakonda. Finally, Salihundam, 8 kms from Kalingapatnam, the ancient port city, has reported images of Tara, Marichi, Bhrikuti and Manjushri.[20]

Further south, along the east coast, Kaveripoompattinam, which had been a centre of Buddhism in the Tamil country from the 2nd century BCE to the 6th century CE, was giving way to Nagapattinam, a sea town located another 50 kms south.

Tamil Nadu

From the 8th and 9th centuries, Nagapattinam became the centre of Buddhist activity in Tamil Nadu.[21] According to some inscriptions, a Srivijaya king had erected a monastery called Cudamanivihara here, in the 11th century, in the name of his father. This happened during the reign of Chola kings Rajaraja I (985–1016) and his son and successor, Rajendra I (1012–44). Rajaraja also gifted a village as an endowment for the lofty shrine of the Buddha at the monastery. Interestingly, a Kalyani inscription of Burmese king Dhammaceti, dated 1479, mentions how some shipwrecked Burmese monks visited a pagoda built by a Chinese king and worshipped the statue of the Buddha there. Nagapattinam, however, became more famous for the Kayarohanaswami temple dedicated to Lord Shiva. The inscriptions on the walls of the temple, dating to the 11th–12th centuries, indicate that the Srivijaya king also presented ornaments for the silver image of Nakaiyalakar, the lord of Nagapattinam. Subsequently, there were also donations of lamps and images related to other forms of Shiva. This gave the site a multireligious context and landscape. In 1867, when the Jesuits were demolishing the Chinese pagoda at Nagapattinam, to build what is now known as St Joseph's College, more than 350 bronze images of the Buddha were discovered around the site, which can be now seen in several museums, including the Government Museum in Chennai. Interestingly, these bronze images also reflect the changing nature of the deposits in the stupas. In the early centuries of the Christian era, such deposits included bone, ashes, reliquaries, coins, jewellery and precious stones. By the 5th and 6th centuries, we see *dharanis* (inscribed texts) being placed inside the stupas at Bodh Gaya, Nalanda and Paharpur. The dharanis were also inscribed on images. Around the 8th and 9th centuries, we see bronze images being deposited in the stupas. Examples of this can be seen in several places, including Sopara, Kanheri, Ratnagiri, Devni Mori, Sanchi and Sarnath.

The bronze images found in Nagapattinam add another layer to our understanding of Buddhism. The epithets found in the inscriptions of these images show that notions of divinity associated with Shaiva and Vaishnava (related to Shiva and Vishnu) traditions, particularly the former, were also being applied to the Buddha. The relationship between these three traditions was a complicated one in the Tamil country, with debates being common between the ascendant Shaiva and Vaishnava saints and the Buddhist monks in the 11th century. This was also evident in the imagery and paintings of the time at the Brihadeeswara temple at Tanjore. Images of the Buddha seated under the Bodhi tree are sculpted on some of the outer walls of the temple. The seated Buddha can also be seen in the Tripurantaka ('destroyer of three cities') painted panel in chamber 11 of the ambulatory gallery. In the painting, an angry Shiva (the Tripurantaka) is seen fighting the asuras while a seated Buddha, shown as an avatar of Vishnu, is trying to delude the asuras and wean them away from the path of Shiva worship.[22] The tale of Buddhism in early medieval Tamil Nadu does not end here. More than a hundred 11th-century colossal stone images of the Buddha, found along the coast of Tamil Nadu, tell another story.[23]

While the Tamil country and the Deccan were seeing new excavations and building activities, the Buddhist sites in the west and north-west, particularly Sindh and Gujarat, were experiencing their last interactions with the faith.

Gujarat

The Maitraka kingdom in the Saurashtra region of Gujarat inherited the Gupta tradition of granting royal patronage to monasteries despite their Shaivite inclinations. Its capital, Vallabhi, rose to fame as the 'Nalanda of the West'.[24] Although physical remains of the monasteries did not survive, it is possible to learn about them through royal charters and inscriptions, and the eyewitness account of Xuanzang. When the Chinese pilgrim visited Vallabhi in 640 CE, he discovered a large monastery near the city, which was named after its arhat, Acala. Locally known as the Bappapadiya Vihara (Monastery of the Father), it became the seat of Mahayana learning. There were a hundred monasteries and 6,000 priests of the Hinayana school in the region. Under a royal lady named Dudda, Vallabhi turned into a central monastic establishment in the 6th century and was maintained by the state. This establishment became known in the royal charters as Dudda-vihara mandala, or simply mahavihara, which is an aggregation of monasteries. A grant made to this monastery complex in 565 CE lists, among other things, the acquisition of books on Buddhism. It also mentions the resident monk community as the Bhikshu sangha of eighteen schools, possibly a reference to the eighteen nikayas of the Hinayana school. Image worship at Vallabhi monasteries was accompanied by rites and rituals. When the Rashtrakutas replaced the Maitrakas in the 8th century, they moved focus away from Vallabhi and found another monastery at Kampilya, near Surat, where 500 monks once stayed. This was the last Buddhist stronghold in ancient Saurashtra.

Sindh

Buddhist establishments in the Sindh region were in good condition till the 8th century. Xuanzang apparently found 'innumerable stupas' and 'several hundred Sangharamas' inhabited by around 10,000 monks during his visit there.[25] The Arabs, after their conquest of Sindh in 711 CE, focused on the subordination of the inhabitants. They were a rapidly expanding trade empire with a long history of relationships with Central Asia and China. The urban mercantile Buddhists seemingly felt that a collaboration with the Arabs would not only reopen interregional trade routes, maritime and overland, but also provide commercial opportunities in the East and help the cause of their religion. The Arab merchants, however, soon displaced the Buddhists as the dominant urban mercantile class in Sindh and marginalized them from international trade. The decline in the Buddhists' share of the mercantile surpluses was accompanied by a reduction of the credit and transport facilities of the viharas and the stoppage of tax-free lands. The viharas therefore fell into decay. Except Mirpur Khas (where Arab coins of an undetermined date have been found), none of the surviving Buddhist structures in Sindh were built after the Arab conquest. The absence of Arab-period Buddhist artefacts and the lack of any reference to Buddhists in Arabic or Persian literature testify to a decline of Buddhism in Sindh. Even Al-Biruni (973–1048), an Iranian scholar who visited Sind in 1030, was unable to locate either any Buddhist monks or books in Sindh for his encyclopaedic work on India, the *Kitab-ul-Hind* or *Tarikh-ul-Hind*.

Unlike Sindh and Gujarat, where Buddhism started fading in the 8th century, things lingered on for a little longer in Kashmir, which also became a centre of transmission of Buddhist teachings to China and the regions in the western Himalayas.

Kashmir

There are two broad traditions regarding the introduction of Buddhism in Kashmir. The first is attributed to King Surendra, who is said to have introduced the Buddha's teachings immediately after his death. The second tradition credits Mauryan king Ashoka with not only sending Madhyantika (Majjhantika) as a Buddhist missionary to Kashmir and Gandhara but also with the construction of some stupas and viharas. Stupas at Hukalitar and Vethavutur in Budgam and Anantnag are associated with Ashoka, as is the monastery at Pandrethan, located very close to Srinagar. More systematic and archaeological evidence is, however, available from the Kushana period onwards. The Fourth Buddhist Council is said to have been held in Kashmir under the Kushana king Kaniskha, when some famous commentaries in Sanskrit were composed. Buddhist structures at Harwan (Indo-Parthian style) and Uskara (Gandhara style) are assigned to the Kushana and post-Kushana periods.

Fig 5.1 The three-storeyed Cave 12 at Ellora

Fig 5.2 Eight scenes from the Buddha's life, depicted on a black schist stele from Bihar, dating to the Pala period (10th century)

Fig 5.3 Carvings on the facade of Cave 10 at Ellora

Fig 5.4 Cave 5 at Ellora, commonly known as the 'Dining Hall'

Fig 5.5 Cluster of Buddhist goddesses in Cave 12 at Ellora

Fig 5.6 Monastery 1 at Ratnagiri (Odisha)

Fig 5.7 Tara as the saviour from Eight Great Dangers, from Ratnagiri (Odisha)

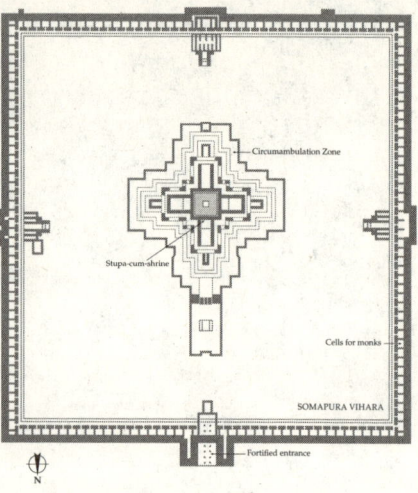

Fig 5.8 The Somapura and Vikramashila monasteries share a similar layout, featuring a cruciform stupa–shrine at the centre and rectangular cells arranged along the square boundary.

Fig 5.9 Remains of Somapura Monastery (Bangladesh)

Fig 5.10 Remains of Kesariya Stupa, Kesariya (Bihar)

Fig 5.11 Bronze statue of Akshobhya, the Buddha of the East, from the Pala period (late 800s), Kurkihar, Bihar

Fig 5.12 Tabo monastery complex

Huna attacks, particularly those under Mihirakula, destroyed many Buddhist structures in Kashmir, Gandhara and western Uttar Pradesh. Stupas and monasteries continued to be built at Pandrethan around the 7th and 8th centuries, and many of its sculptures are currently housed in the SPS Museum, Srinagar. Xuanzang, who visited India in the 7th century CE, spent some time at Jayendra Vihara that had a colossal image of Buddha made by Jayendra, the maternal uncle of Pravarasena II (who ruled Kashmir in the 6th century CE). According to his account, there were more than a hundred Buddhist monasteries and around 5,000 monks in the region. Also, some stupas carried bodily relics of the Buddha.[26] Buddhism experienced some revival under the Karkota dynasty in the 8th century, particularly under King Lalitaditya. Excavations at Parihaspur, which is close to Srinagar, have revealed the remains of a stupa, a vihara, a chaitya and a few Buddhist images.

The decline of Buddhism coincided with the rise of Shaivism in Kashmir in the 8th and 9th centuries CE. The later Turkish attacks also contributed to the process. However, Kalhana's *Rajatarangini* and some inscriptional evidence indicate that Buddhism continued to receive some patronage in Kashmir; viharas, shrines and statues continued to be erected, though in a much smaller way, till the 13th century.[27] Some of the monasteries, like Jayendra Vihara in Srinagar and the Raja monastery in Parihaspur, declined by the 11th century. However, others like the Ratnagupta monastery and Ratnarashmi monastery at Anupamapura continued to flourish in the 11th and 12th centuries.[28]

Kashmir had become a principal seat of Buddhist learning, particularly the Sarvastivada tradition, one of the early sects that had reportedly separated from the Sthaviravadins during the Third Buddhist Council held under Ashoka. The region also sent monks to propagate Buddhist ideas in surrounding regions like Central Asia, China, Tibet and Ladakh. According to Xuanzang, Sarvastivada Buddhism of Kashmir travelled till Khotan (modern-day Hotan in north-western China). In its heyday, Khotan had around 4,000 Buddhist establishments, including monasteries, temples and chapels.[29] Interestingly, the number of Buddhist scholars who went to China from Kashmir was more than that from the other parts of India. But perhaps a more enduring and tangible legacy of the Kashmir region comes from the neighbouring Lahaul-Spiti valley where Buddhist establishments were set up around the Tabo monastery, 9th century onwards, and still survive. While Kashmir was entering its last phase of Buddhism, eastern India was becoming the new hotspot. Between the 8th and 12th centuries, sites in Bihar, Bengal and Odisha represented the sacred nucleus of Buddhism in India.

Odisha

In Odisha, the Diamond Triangle consisting of Udayagiri, Ratnagiri and Lalitagiri came into the limelight during the early medieval period. The same was the case with artefacts, practices and rituals associated with their sacred complexes, including extended stupa complexes (mahastupas), enshrinement of the text of the *Pratityasamutpada Sutra* or dharanis in the stupas, mandala images, colossal Buddha heads and representations of dhyani buddhas and Tara. We will discuss these in more detail as we go along.

Udayagiri and Ratnagiri are located in Jajpur district, while Lalitagiri is in Cuttack. Prominent between the 6th and 13th–14th centuries, these three sites also document a shift from the Mahayana to the Mantrayana, or Vajrayana (esoteric), form of Buddhism. From the 8th century, we also notice the emergence of mahastupas at the three sites alongside some more monasteries.

The sites of Lalitagiri and Udayagiri, which had developed around old stupas containing relics, are dated to the early centuries of the Christian era.[30] The old stupa at Udayagiri evolved into into a circular chaityagriha, or shrine in the first phase of constructions. The shrine and the area around it continued to see additions and expansions right up to the 12th–13th centuries. Gradually, the early circular chaityagriha gave way to an apsidal shrine between the 4th and 7th centuries. Soon, stupas, monasteries, small shrines, platforms, circumambulatory pathways, images of the Buddha and bodhisattvas, and enclosures, came up around the apsidal shrine as the sacred core evolved into chaityagriha complexes.

In Udayagiri, the structures are broadly concentrated in two parts – the south and eastern parts and the north-western part. In the south and eastern parts, we come across a massive water reservoir, the chaityagriha complex and Monastery 2 (containing a shrine chamber and some votive stupas), all of which developed between the 1st and 12th centuries CE. In the north-western part, we find a mahastupa and a monastery built in the 8th century CE.

The chaityagriha complex has a lion on a pedestal with a huge image of the Buddha, shrines of Buddhist deities like Bhrikuti and Avalokiteshvara, and several small stupas (some of which contain bones and reliquaries and/or inscribed texts called dharanis, to which we will return soon). Several Mahayana sutras, including *Guhyadhatu*, *Vimalosnisa* and *Rasmivimala*, prescribe depositing the dharanis inside the stupas. Stone slab inscriptions carrying dharanis for enshrinement in stupas have been found not only in the three sites at Odisha (from the 7th century CE) but also in Nalanda, Paharapur, Bodh Gaya and the Abhayagiri monastery in Sri Lanka. The dharani stupas were considered highly meritorious and contained protective spells, besides bestowing merit on the donors.[31]

In the north-western part of Udayagiri, the most unique structure is the mahastupa, which is a mandala stupa on a high platform. It has images of four dhyani buddhas in the four cardinal directions – Akshobhya on the east, Amitabha on the west, Amoghasiddhi on the north and Ratnasambhava on the south.

In Udayagiri and Ratnagiri, such mandala stupas also marked the physical manifestation of the *charya* and yoga tantra-based architecture and landscaping plan associated with Mantrayana. It first appeared in the 7th century in Lalitagiri but later became widespread across the Bay of Bengal.[32] Located next to the Udayagiri Mahastupa is Monastery 1, which has a giant statue of the Buddha in the sanctum. The structure is surrounded by water channels. Like Udayagiri, in Lalitagiri, too, the chaityagriha complex has the greatest concentration of smaller brick and masonry stupas and monolithic votive stupas.

In Ratnagiri, however, the largest concentration of smaller stone stupas can be seen around the large stupa, or the mahastupa. Built between the 9th and 13th centuries, these small stupas have sockets to enshrine relics such as charred bones or reliquaries like plain earthen vases. Dharanis have also been enshrined in the core of some stupas, and they have a clear funerary association. Ratnagiri has two monasteries built between the 8th and 12th centuries. Monastery 1 is a two-storeyed brick structure with a beautifully carved doorway in stone (Fig 5.6). The entrance leads to a large open courtyard with big cells, a veranda and a shrine with a colossal statue of the Buddha. On the left of the entrance is a huge Buddha head that is followed by other colossal heads of the Buddha in various sizes. At the extreme end of the courtyard is a twelve-foot giant Buddha statue, in bhumisparsha mudra, flanked by images of Mahayana deities like Vajrapani and Padmapani. Some scholars hold that Monastery 1 was the mahavihara of Pushpagiri, as recorded by Xuanzang. According to the Tibetan tradition, Ratnagiri was known for famous tantric teachers, who got their education here and taught other students. Also, Ratnagiri played an important role in the emergence of Kalachakra tantra. Scholars also hold that many images found at Ratnagiri indicate a Vajrayana influence.[33]

We notice some interesting developments related to the stupa cult, rituals and practices in Odisha, which also have manifestations in the larger Buddhist world. Of these, we have already talked about the dharanis and mandala stupas. There are a few more.

The first is the enshrinement of the *ye dharma* verse (*ye dhamma* in Pali), or the text of the *Pratityasamutpada Sutra*, inside the stupas. This text from the sutra appears on stone slabs and terracotta plaques inside the stupas at Lalitagiri, Udayagiri and Ratnagiri from the 5th century. According to Buddhist textual tradition, the *Pratityasamutpada Sutra* is a doctrine connected with the Buddha and his theory of dependent origination. The essence is summarized in a short sentence explained by Assaji, one of the Buddha's first five disciples, to monks Sariputra and Maudgalyayana: 'He who sees the *Pratityasamutpada Sutra* sees dharma; he who sees dharma sees the Buddha.' By the 4th–5th centuries CE, this sutra had become the hallmark of Buddhist ideas as they expanded to other parts of Asia. In addition to being enshrined in the stupas, this text featured on stone images, clay tablets, metal plaques, and on palm leaves, paper and cloth. Terracotta plaques featuring *Pratityasamutpada Sutra* became widespread in the Indian Ocean region, from the Malay peninsula to the Buddhist sites in Odisha and Bodh Gaya. Likewise, clay tablets containing the text of this sutra have been found in Bodh Gaya, Sarnath, Kasia (Kushinagar), Lauriya Nandangarh, Vallabhi, Nalanda, Mainamati and Odisha. In the three sites of the Diamond Triangle, the *Pratityasamutpada Sutra* appears on the back and pedestals of the Buddha and Buddhist images from the 8th century. Buddha images, flanked by two bodhisattvas and inscribed with the *Pratityasamutpada Sutra* on terracotta plaques, in Lalitagiri are believed to represent his body of essence (dharmakaya) according to the Mahayana doctrine of trikaya.[34]

The second is the mandala grouping of images. Five types of mandalas have been found in Buddhist sites in Odisha – stupa mandala with four dhyani buddhas, each flanked by two bodhisattvas; sculptural mandalas of eight bodhisattvas around a central Buddha; four by four bodhisattvas surrounding four dhyani buddhas, with a fifth one in the centre; free-standing bodhisattvas forming a mandala pattern; and a mandala diagram on the back of an image. Of these, the mandala of the eight bodhisattvas around a central Buddha is unique to Udayagiri. The third is the presence of tantric deity Tara, which constitutes another striking feature of Buddhist sites in Odisha. She is found sculpted on ninety-nine niches in monolithic stupas in Ratnagiri. Tara is represented in both a seated form as well as other forms described in *Sadhanamala*, a tantric Buddhist text composed between the 5th and 11th centuries. From the 7th to the 12th centuries, Tara is depicted both in sculptures and epigraphs as a saviour, who, like Avalokiteshvara, protects her worshippers from the eight great perils (Fig 5.7).[35]

While Odisha was experiencing Buddhist efflorescence, its neighbours Bihar and Bengal were becoming the nuclei of the Buddhist world under the Palas, who like their predecessors, the Gaudas of Bengal, ruled over a large empire that included the present states of Bihar and West Bengal in India and parts of Bangladesh.

Bihar and Bengal

The Pala period represents one of India's most brilliant phases in terms of intellectual and artistic activities in the history of Buddhism. During their reign, the eastern Gangetic region had prominent

Buddhist centres that attracted monks, devotees and pilgrims from all parts of Asia. Till the 10th century, the focus of Pala art and architecture remained the old Magadha region associated with the historical Buddha. After that, it shifted to Bengal.[36] The Palas are known to have supported or established grand monasteries, or mahaviharas, which included Nalanda (which had already come into being under the Guptas), Somapura (better known as Paharpur, now in Bangladesh), Vikramashila (identified with Antichak in Bhagalpur, Bihar) and Odantapura near Nalanda (whose exact location has not been found).

Of these, Nalanda had been in existence for almost two centuries when the Palas came to power. When Xuanzang visited India, Nalanda was at its intellectual and architectural prime. He mentions the lofty spires or towers of Nalanda, a Gupta-style architectural feature, alongside those of Sarnath, which were 'mingling with the clouds'. The pilgrim also mentions how only three old monasteries had retained their magnificence in the Magadha region. These included those at Telhara, Mahabodhi and Nalanda. In Bodh Gaya, Ceylonese monk Mahanaman had sought permission from the Gupta kings to build a monastery for monks from Ceylon in the Mahabodhi temple complex. This was the beginning of the Mahabodhi monastery.[37]

The Palas are also known to have made donations to Nalanda. The post-Gupta history of Nalanda has two phases.[38] The first phase, lasting from the 6th to the 9th centuries, saw the continuation of the liberal cultural traditions inherited from the Guptas. The second, from the 9th to the 13th centuries, saw Nalanda transitioning from a vibrant intellectual centre of Mahayana traditions to a stronghold of Vajrayana, the tantric form of Buddhism. All images of tantric deities found in the mahavihara complex belong to the Pala period. Monk and scholar Taranatha, who wrote in the 16th–17th centuries, talks about the lives of several eminent *siddhas* or tantra gurus from Nalanda, who spearheaded the Vajrayana tradition. One of them, Abhyakaragupta, became the abbot of the Mahabodhi monastery and the mahaviharas of Nalanda and Vikramashila. Nalanda's contact with East and Southeast Asia also continued, routed through China. Subhakarasimha, a tantric monk and scholar from Nalanda, along with others like Vajrabodhi and his student Amoghavajra, are believed to have introduced tantric Buddhism in China in the 8th century. By the middle of the 8th century, Tibet was replacing China as far as to-and-fro movements of Buddhist monks were concerned. Tibet had strong connections with the mahaviharas in eastern India, and most of our knowledge regarding their functioning comes from Tibetan accounts. Indian monks also exercised great influence in Tibet. It may be relevant to mention here that the mission of Padmasambhava, the scholar from Uddiyana (now in Swat Valley, Pakistan), to Tibet in the 8th century was assisted by two scholar-monks from Nalanda – Shantarakshita and Kamalasila. Together, they helped establish the lama system in Tibet and the region's first Buddhist monastery at Samye (Bsam-Yas). However, it was only during the 11th century that tantric Buddhism acquired firm roots in Tibet, thanks mainly to the missionary work of monk–scholar Dipankara, and sidelined the native Bon cults.

Tibet also had a strong association with Odantapura mahavihara, whose archaeological remains have not been found. The only thing scholars concur on is that it was located somewhere in Bihar Sharif district of Bihar. Perhaps Gopala, the Pala ruler credited with its establishment in the 8th century, wanted to set up a parallel, if not a rival, centre of Buddhist learning at the newly established city of Odantapura. According to Tibetan legends, the mahavihara was built on a lake that had miraculously dried up. Also, the Samye monastery was built on the same model in 749 CE. Unfortunately, only the ruins of Samye survive now. By 1234, when Tibetan monk Dharmakirti visited India, Odantapura had become a garrison of Turkish soldiers who raided monasteries and other Buddhist establishments in eastern India.[39]

Unlike Odantapura, the archaeological coordinates of Somapura mahavihara have been identified.[40] It is also known as the Paharpur monastery, on account of its proximity to Paharpur village in Naogaon district of Bangladesh. Somapura is now a UNESCO World Heritage Site (Fig 5.9). The clay seals found in the mahavihara describe it as 'Dharmapala Vihara', so the monastery had some association with Pala king Dharmapala (c. 770–810 CE). Built on the foundations of a

Jaina temple, the monastery follows a large quadrangular plan with a fortified entrance on the north. It consists of a cruciform, or cross-shaped, stupa-cum-shrine at the centre with four projections in the four cardinal directions. This shape perhaps represented a mandala. The central pyramidal stupa (and shrine) has a three-level terraced structure and is surrounded by a circumambulatory path that follows the cruciform shape. The four walls of the mahavihara contain cells where the monks lived. At its peak, the monastery had 177 rectangular cells, which possibly housed around 600 to 800 monks. Between each arm of the central stupa–shrine, there are rectangular projections adorned by a frieze of decorative bricks, terracotta plaques and stone bas-reliefs that depict humans, animals and Brahmanical and Buddhist mythological figures. Unlike other stupas, the Jatakas are conspicuous by their absence at Somapura. Rather, scenes from contemporary social life are depicted in the decorative panels. Interestingly, the plan of the mahavihara – cruciform basement, terraced and pyramid-shaped central shrine – is common to the Buddhist temples of Java, Cambodia and Burma, which has led some to conclude that the Somapura mahavihara influenced the architecture of these regions. Other buildings in the mahavihara complex included a kitchen and dining hall.

Like Somapura, the mahavihara at Vikramashila has a huge square-shaped structure with cells on four sides and a cruciform brick stupa at the centre (Fig 5.8). Located on a hillock around the confluence of rivers Kosi and Ganga, Vikramashila mahavihara was located at a popular tantric and pilgrim site, where the river Ganga flowed northwards.[41] Built during the reign of King Dharmapala in the late 8th or early 9th century, the mahavihara employed many tantric preceptors. The two-terraced, cross-shaped brick stupa–shrine in the centre has pillared chambers, one on each side, which housed colossal images of a seated Buddha. At its peak, the monastery had a total of 208 cells, fifty-two on each side, all of which opened into a common courtyard. Buildings found in the complex include a library, some temples and votive stupas. A unique feature of the Vikramashila monastery is the presence of underground chambers, possibly meant for meditation, beneath the main cells. According to some estimates, the monastery housed around 1,000 scholars in the 12th century.

Unlike Somapura and Vikramashila, Jagaddala vihara was a mid-sized monastery founded during the later period of the Pala rule. As a tantric centre of Buddhist learning, it was at its prime during the 11th and 12th centuries. Like Somapura and Vikramashila, it had an open courtyard surrounded by monastic cells on each of its four arms, though their number was comparatively small, only thirty-four. However, Jagaddala did not have a main stupa or shrine in the centre. Towards the end of the Pala period, when many other mahaviharas had declined, Jagaddala became a refuge for many prominent Buddhist monks, many of whom translated Buddhist works from Sanskrit to Tibetan. This mahavihara was located close to Paharpur and both monasteries were closely connected in terms of movements of monks, learning traditions and intellectual debates.[42] Unlike Nalanda, which was patronized by royals of all categories, elites, monastic communities and lay followers, mahaviharas in south Bihar and north Bengal (such as Vikramashila, Somapura and Jagaddala) received their donations mostly from rulers, subordinate rulers, monks and perhaps elites. In south-eastern Bengal, too, local rulers patronized the monasteries till the 9th century CE.[43]

Most of these mahaviharas acted as separate corporations with their own official terracotta seals, which have been recovered from Somapura and Nalanda. Most also received rent-free land grants, with Nalanda being a prime example. Was there any connection between these mahaviharas? Yes, of course. There was a constant movement of scholars and ideas. We have already discussed how, according to Tibetan histories, some monk–scholars headed multiple mahaviharas. According to a 12th-century inscription found in Nalanda, one Vipulashrimitra, a resident of Somapura, seems to have built a monastery in Nalanda and constructed a temple of Tara in Somapura.

The monk Dipankara is said to have studied and been ordained at Nalanda, pursued further studies at Odantapura and then became the head of Vikramashila monastery, from where he left for Tibet. In addition, there was a continuous movement of monks and scholars between Tibet and monasteries in eastern India. This resulted in several significant Tibetan translations, some of which have found a place in Tibetan canonical tradition. Some Tibetan monks were also appointed as officials at these monasteries and held in great esteem. These mahaviharas were also a part of a network of higher institutions supervised by the state. They were interlinked with a system of coordination among them, which allowed good scholars to move easily from one position to another among these mahaviharas.[44]

In addition to these mahaviharas in north Bengal, there were some in Murshidabad and western Medinipur, too. Among the comparatively lesser-known, small monasteries in Bengal, one may include Devikota Vihara, Bhasu Vihara, Nandadirghi Vihara and Traikutaka Vihara. Image inscriptions also attest to the presence of the Apanaka mahavihara in Kurkihar, Bihar, which functioned from the 9th to the 12th centuries.[45] Recent excavations have brought to light remains of some other monasteries that belong to the Pala period, though the royal links have not been adequately established. These include a Mahayana monastery in Lal Pahari, in Lakhisarai district of Bihar, that was functional during the 8th–9th centuries; and a small one near Juljul Hill in Hazaribag district of Jharkhand, which belongs to the 10th century CE and shows Vajrayana influence. The monastery in Lakhisarai is described as 'Srimaddharma Vihara' in the clay seals found at the site. It was perhaps the first hilltop Buddhist monastery in the Gangetic valley.[46] On the other hand, images of the Buddha in bhumisparsha mudra and tantric deity Tara have been recovered from the Hazaribag monastery.[47]

The Pala period is not just known for monasteries. The current structure of the Kesariya stupa, known as 'devalaya' (house of gods) among the locals of east Champaran, also belongs to the Pala period (Fig 5.10). However, the stupa complex has a long history. Some believe that the Buddha stayed here before proceeding to Kushinagar, his final destination. Remains of the capital of an Ashokan pillar, belonging to the 3rd century BCE, have been found here. Also, bricks belonging to the Gupta and post-Gupta periods have been found, suggesting an expansion, possibly during Harsha's times. Interestingly, the Kesariya stupa looks much different from the earlier hemispherical stupas of

Sanchi, Bharhut and Amravati. It is similar in design and architecture to the Borobodur stupa in Indonesia, hinting at a possible link between the Palas and the Srivijaya dynasty. Both stupas are located on a hill, both follow a mandala design (Kesariya follows a circular mandala; Borobodur contains squared terraces), both appear flat horizontally and both have intermittent rows of chambers on each terrace, housing statues of the Buddha.[48]

Southeast Asian links of Buddhism have been evidenced in the case of sites in south-eastern Bangladesh, particularly Harikela (Chittagong) and Samatata (Comilla–Noakhali area) that lies across the river Meghna.[49] Connected to Southeast Asia via land and water, these sites contributed immensely to the transmission of Buddhist ideas, practices and artefacts from the 7th century. Studies of clay tablets, miniature Buddhist images and stupas, and other artefacts found on both sides of the Bay of Bengal, show remarkable similarities in terms of ritual practices and iconography. But they also suggest the existence of strong sculptural and metal casting traditions in Buddhist sites like Chittagong and Comilla. In fact, some art historians have even suggested that there was a parallel school of sculpture in the trans-Meghna region, which corresponded with the Pala period but produced sculptures stylistically different from the dominant Pala-Sena style. Salban vihara in Mainamati (an important monastic site in Comilla) has revealed several miniature or portable images of the Buddha and the bodhisattvas, which not only constituted ritual objects but also served as souvenirs and objects of donation across South and Southeast Asia. A hoard of sixty-six bronze images of the Buddha and the bodhisattvas, belonging to the 9th and 10th centuries CE, were recovered from Jhewari (or Jhiuri) near Chittagong in 1927. Likewise, bronze images of Tara and Manjushri have also been excavated from Mainamati. These two finds bear a strong resemblance with the bronze images found in Java around the 8th and 9th centuries CE. There are also strong similarities in the miniature stupas found at Salban vihara and those found at Wat Khuhaphimuk in Yala, Thailand. Small clay tablets containing images and inscribed with the quintessential 'ye dharma' verse have been found throughout eastern India and countries in Southeast Asia. Of particular interest is the strong similarity in the clay tablets, containing images of the eight bodhisattvas in a mandala formation, in Nalanda and Salban vihara and sites in Thailand and Malayasia. The eight bodhisattvas were worshipped in these regions around the 8th and 9th centuries CE. Other motifs in the clay tablets, which experienced multiple replications in Bihar, Bengal and some countries of Southeast Asia, include the Buddha in a Mahabodhi temple-like structure and the eight-armed Tara, as a saviour of followers from the eight great dangers or perils.

The Pala times are associated with the widespread production of sculptures and images, both Buddhist and Brahmanical, many of which have been found in museums in India and abroad. The typical stone sculptures of the time were made of greyish to grey-black stones, mostly schist and phyllite. Images of the Buddha were very common in Pala sculptural art, especially those connected with the eight events of his life. Another noticeable feature of the Pala sculptures is the influence of tantric Buddhism, where several deities are depicted as fierce. The Palas are also known for metal images, especially bronze. In 1930, a set of 226 bronze sculptures, mostly Buddhist and belonging to the Pala times, were found in Kurkihar, near Bodh Gaya. Kurkihar was certainly an important centre for production of such images in this period (Fig 5.11). Some of Pala bronze sculptures can be seen in the Nalanda and Patna museums, and palm-leaf paintings, centred around the Buddha and including Brahmanical divinities. They represent a diverse body of materials, styles and flourishing artistic workshops.[50] While a few pieces are in silver and gold, most sculptures were made of alloys, with copper as the dominant element. As far as the palm-leaf paintings are concerned, only fragments of murals at Nalanda and manuscripts on palm leaves have survived by way of tangible evidence. Literary sources, however, mention a cloth-painting tradition in Nalanda. Paintings resembling the Pala period have been found in Myanmar, Nepal and Tibet. In fact, the Pala-era cloth paintings may have been the forerunners of the *patas* of Nepal and *thangkas* of Tibet. The art and architectural styles of the Pala period were later transmitted to Nepal, Tibet, Myanmar, China and Indonesia. By the 12th and 13th centuries, the Pala reign ended abruptly, as did the mahaviharas and Buddhist art and culture that had taken root in these countries.

The only region where Buddhist activities outlasted the Pala period was the western Himalayas, where the Tabo monastery continued to see core construction activities right up to the 20th century.

Western Himalayas

Lahaul-Spiti and Kinnaur were situated between two significant trade routes – the Silk Route, which connected China and Central Asia with the Arab, Persian and Mediterranean regions; and the Grand Trunk Road, which linked Pataliputra with Tamralipti in the east to Taxila in the north-west. In addition, there were several link routes that helped sustain the trade traffic on these main routes.[51]

One can see two distinct phases of Buddhist expansion in Himachal Pradesh. The first phase was confined to Kangra, Kullu, Sirmour and other areas. It was only when Buddhism was declining in these regions that Lahaul-Spiti and Kinnaur became the centre of activities, reaching their climax during the late 10th to the 12th centuries. That is when the entire trans-Himalayan region became a cradle of Buddhism. It seems that the Kanihara, Chetru and Pathiar-Lakhamandal triangle was a core area of Buddhist structures in Kangra. Several structures and artefacts – including stupa, the Buddha's footprints, stone and brass statues of Buddhist deities – belonging to the mid-6th and 7th centuries have been discovered from this region.

The establishment of Buddhism in Tibet around the mid-8th century, known as the period of first diffusion, prepared the foundation for the growth of Buddhist activities in the trans-Himalayan zone. The earliest archaeological evidence for this comes in the form of rock carvings of the three bodhisattvas – Avalokiteshvara, Maitreya and Vajrapani – from Gondala (near Keylong in Lahaul and Spiti district) and Kardang (later became the site of the famous Drukpa Lineage monastery). Several Mahayana monasteries existed in the kingdom of Trigarta (in Kangra), Kuluta (in Kullu Valley) and Satadru (around present Sanghol near Sirhind) when Xuanzang visited these areas in the 7th century. It was the prevalence of Buddhism in the Lahaul-Spiti valley during the period of first diffusion of Buddhism that prepared the grounds for the second diffusion during the 10th and 11th centuries. By then, Buddhism had declined in central and southern Himachal. By then, Tabo monastery was set to occupy centre stage (Fig 5.12).[52]

The Tabo monastery complex is bound by Ladakh in the north, Lahaul in the West, Kullu in the south east and Tibet and Kinnaur in the east. Located in the Spiti valley of Himachal Pradesh, very close to the Tibetan/Chinese border, the complex presents evidence of construction from the 10th to the 20th centuries, making it one of the oldest Buddhist sites still in use. The complex includes nine temples and twenty-three stupas, built between 996 and 1908 CE. In addition, there are cave shrines located along the hill slopes. The walls and the circumambulatory passages of the temples are decorated with beautiful murals, which depict the history of Buddhist interactions between the Tibetan and Indian traditions. The walls of the cave shrines have beautiful 15th-century murals depicting the Taras and the bodhisattvas. Given its murals, the Tabo monastery complex is also known as the 'Ajanta of the Himalayas'. The monastery complex has also wielded an abundance of manuscripts, coins and inscriptions.

The Tabo monastery was built in the 10th century,[53] during the rule of the Purang-Guge kingdom that had ancestral links with the Tibetan monarchy. It is held that territories including upper Kinnaur, Spiti, Lahaul, Zanskar and Ladakh came under the control of this dynasty in the mid-10th century, especially under its first two kings. The third king, popularly known by his religious initiation name Yeshe Od, started an intensive missionary campaign throughout his territory to reverse the setbacks Tibetan Buddhism had suffered in the 9th century CE. He wanted to purge the resident Buddhist practice of its local cult traditions, such as the Bon, and folk influences. This drive saw him enlisting the support of monk–scholar Rinchen Zangpo (958–1055 CE), who had been trained in Kashmir. Together, they established the Tabo monastery. This period is also known as the era of 'second diffusion of Buddhism' in Tibet.

The kings of the Purang-Guge established many trade routes from Ladakh to Mustang and constructed temples along these routes. The temples were built over four phases. The main temple was built in 996 CE, while Maitreya's temple, Brom-ston temple and Mandala temple belong to the second phase (1042–1100 CE). Within the Tabo Monastery complex, the Golden Temple was constructed between 1450 and 1550 CE and others, like the Brom-ston Temple, Temple of the Master, the Protector's Chapel and the White Temple (Nuns' Temple), are attributed to the last phase (1600–1900). The main temple, the Tsuglakhang, has an entrance hall, an assembly hall that leads to the shrine and an ambulatory passage. The architectural plan of the assembly hall is very striking and is based on the mandala groupings of images and the presence of dhyani buddhas. The walls are covered in beautiful, detailed murals and thirty-two clay sculptures representing the families and realms of Akshobhya, Ratnasambhava, Amitabha and Amogasiddhi, with Vairocana (the main deity) seated on a lotus throne in the centre. While the construction happened over several phases, the temples retained the original iconographic shapes and the mandala pattern of the sculptures.

Other features of the Tabo Monastery complex include the presence of burial sites, cairns and memorial slabs around the stupas. These possibly reflect the influence of the pre-Buddhist Bon cult and regional folk traditions. Many of the deities associated with the local Bon cult were eventually assimilated into the Buddhist fold. The widespread presence of monasteries, belonging to various schools and sub-schools of Buddhism, in the Lahaul-Spiti region is also noteworthy. Today, only a large corpus of images of gods and goddesses of the Mahayana and Vajrayana traditions have survived.[54]

The Tabo Monastery was the last, and perhaps the only, surviving bastion of Buddhism in India. By the 10th–11th centuries, three distinct centres of Buddhism had emerged – Tibet, connected to the Bihar-Bengal region, had emerged as the hotspot of Vajrayana tradition; Sri Lanka, from where a revitalized Theravada/Pali Buddhist network spread to Southeast Asian countries like Burma and Thailand; and China, which had become the focal point of the Mahayana–Vajrayana Buddhism in East Asia, with centres in Japan and Korea.[55] By the 12th–13th centuries, eastern India had also lost its prominence. Most Buddhist centres in the Gangetic plains and the peninsular region saw no further constructions. Around eighteen centuries after the Buddha propounded his dharma, the faith had outrun most of its public course in its bastions. The Buddha's legacy was now to survive only in the geocultural margins, or in the form of languishing structures or ruins, sometimes occupied by other religious traditions or sects, an aspect that offers several interesting afterlife stories. We will discuss some of these in the section on World Heritage Sites, but for now let us get back to *how* and *why* Buddhism experienced a downfall.

DECLINE, DEMISE OR DOWNFALL

Most authors argue that Buddhism declined and disappeared from the Indian subcontinent around the 12th–13th centuries. Some even say it became extinct in the country of its origin. Others say it experienced a downfall, or a downward slope. Interestingly, there are several apocalyptic prophecies of decline within the larger Buddhist tradition itself. Most of these come in multiple versions, and with timelines. Even the Buddha is said to have predicted that the sangha would decline in 500, instead of the expected 1,000, years if women were allowed to join. Most such prophecies are based on internal human failings like the admission of women, divisions within the sangha, or corruption in traditional monastic practices and behaviours, etc. There is only one prophecy, known as the Kaushambi story, which talks about both internal failures and external attacks. Found in both Mahayana and non-Mahayana literature, and available in multiple versions, this story attributes the demise of the dharma to invasions from northwest India, led by a combined force of Greeks, Shakas and Parthians who destroyed temples and stupas. As the story goes, this coalition is eventually defeated by the Buddhist king of Kaushambi, who then convenes a great religious assembly of monks from different regions. At this assembly, the monks fight over ideological issues. This conflict escalates into open warfare where all the monks and the last remaining arhat are killed.[56] Historical evidence does not obviously tally with this story, for many of the invading kings turned out to be champions and patrons of Buddhism. However, it does talk about external invasions, which later manifested in the depredations of the Hunas, Turks and Afghans. Also, different versions of this story were prevalent at various points of time, including the early medieval period.

Historians normally attribute the decline or demise of Buddhism to four factors – the failure of the faith to maintain a distinct identity vis-à-vis the Hindu traditions and sects; an aggressive Brahmanical revival, backed by the reach of Puranic Hinduism and thinkers like Shankaracharya who deployed the same philosophical norms and mobilizations methods like the Buddhists; the excessive permeation of tantric practices, which submerged its original ethical thinking and led to its degeneration; and finally, the Turkish or Afghan attacks and depredations, which destroyed the identifiable Buddhist establishments, particularly in eastern India.[57]

A combination of these factors, it is argued, contributed to the decline or downfall of Buddhism in India. However, these factors do not present the complete picture. They do not explain the reasons behind the dwindling support and patronage for Buddhists. Neither do they factor in the role of the monks who once provided irrigation services to the laity, as in Sanchi, performed death rites and lived with the outcastes, as in Nagarjunakonda, or helped with day-to-day rites and ceremonies for the lay followers to help spread the dharma. Did the monks – who had been extremely mobile in the past, who had been proactively setting up stupas, images and Buddhist establishments, who had been majorly concerned with the spread of the dharma – become more sedentary, more concerned with philosophical and scholarly pursuits, and more confined to the mahaviharas, thereby losing their connection with the laity? Some scholars feel that the withdrawal of monks from day-to-day interactions was responsible for the decline of Buddhism in the middle of the 2nd millennium CE.[58]

Perhaps the reasons for the decline or downfall are more complex and lying deeper between the structural issues confronting Buddhism and regional complexities. We need extensive studies of these macro–micro dynamics to arrive at a better understanding. That being said, some trends were fairly apparent.

First, the process of the decline was more gradual than sudden. Buddhism had already started weakening in the Gupta–Vakataka period. The Huna invasions in the 5th–6th centuries had sapped many Buddhist establishments in Gandhara, Kashmir and western Uttar Pradesh. Also, as discussed in the preceding chapters, Buddhism was already on the decline in the Gangetic heartland and peninsular India, much before the Turks attacked northern, north-western and eastern regions in the 12th–13th centuries. Xuanzang, who travelled to important Buddhist sites in the 7th century, says many of them were either deserted or had passed their prime. After the Gupta–

Vakataka period, Buddhism had started acquiring a more regional character, flourishing or surviving in pockets in north-western and eastern India, patronized more by provincial kings than commercial classes and the common folk. When these patrons became weak or disappeared, either through political displacement or external attacks; or they changed their patronage preferences, thanks largely due to the massive Brahmanization of royal courts in the early medieval times, Buddhism was bound to languish. It needed an Ashoka or a Kaniskha to resuscitate it, but they were nowhere on the scene. Further, whatever potential patronage could have come by way of land grants and related agricultural expansion was cornered by the Brahmans who incorporated the new castes and groups into Puranic Hinduism. Finally, the zeal and mobility of the monks and the backing of traders and merchants that, along with supportive royals, had taken the faith outside the confines of the Gangetic valley, were now driving it offshore – towards Nepal, Tibet, East and Southeast Asia, which would become the next geographical axis of Buddhism.

Second, despite the perilous state of Buddhism in the 12th–13th centuries, efforts were continuously being made to revive it. While the Turks were descending into the Gangetic plains, Queen Kumaradevi was building a monastery in Sarnath, which was expected to last 'as long as the moon or sun'. Likewise, Jayachandra, a king of the Gahadavala dynasty, was constructing a monastery near Bodh Gaya. Even the old establishments were being re-endowed. King Govindachandra of Kannauj, Queen Kumaradevi's husband, recorded a gift of six villages to the Jetavana monastery in Shravasti to keep the sangha alive. Even after the Turkish depredations in the region, a nonagenarian monk and teacher, Rahul Sri Bhadra, was still trying to hold a class at Nalanda in the 13th century with seventy students.[59]

Third, Buddhism did not suddenly disappear from the subcontinent. It first got relegated to the geographical, political and cultural margins, and continued to survive in many pockets like Amravati and Ratnagiri till the 13th–14th centuries.[60] Some sites held on for longer, albeit in changed forms. Bodh Gaya and Nalanda, for instance, continued to be visited by Tibetan monks and Newar Buddhists from the Kathmandu valley. Pilgrims from Thailand and Myanmar also visited Bodh Gaya till as late as the 15th century. Burmese kings are known to have sent missions to repair the Mahabodhi temple since the late 18th and 19th centuries, much before the British established formal political control over India. Some monks and scholars from the Mahayana and Vajrayana traditions, including Sariputra (1335–1426), Vanaratna (1348–1468), Buddhagupta (1514–1610) and Krishnacharya (who died in 1640), continued to travel to Buddhist sites in India in search of Sanskrit manuscripts till as late as the 16th–17th centuries, though most scholar-monks were travelling to China, Nepal, Tibet and other countries in Southeast Asia. We also come across the incident of Sariputra being appointed as the priest of Bodh Gaya around 1400. An illustrated Buddhist tantric text, titled *Kalachakra tantra*, was compiled in Bihar during the 15th century. Written in Bengali script on palm leaves, it is now housed at the Cambridge University Library. Some pockets in the south also continued to get occasional visibility. A late 15th-century inscription of Burmese king Dhammaceti, which we discussed in the section on Tamil Nadu, mentions how some shipwrecked Burmese monks arrived at Nagapattinam and worshipped the Buddha in a pagoda constructed by a Chinese king. Later, when the pagoda was broken by the Jesuits in the 19th century, a large corpus of bronze images of the Buddha was found. There are also some accounts of crypto-Buddhists. Odia language chronicles mention the persecution of several hundred people believed to be Buddhists in the Prachi valley near Bhubaneswar by Gajapati king Prataparudra Deva (r. 1497–1540) in the 16th century. Some scholars, in fact, argue that Buddhism continued to survive in the form of the Mahima cult in Odisha.

As opposed to these sites, which figure occasionally and in fragmented ways, Buddhism continued to thrive in Lahaul and Spiti, Bengal, Tibet and Nepal. Bengal continued to see some new constructions. Around 1776, an image of Tara was installed inside a temple complex situated on the banks of the river Ganga near Howrah. This temple also had a Shaiva association and housed multiple Shiva lingas (phallic representations). But the site that remained most vibrant and active was the coastal and hilly region of Chittagong. We have already discussed how it was an important sculptural centre known for miniature images of the Buddha and the bodhisattvas, bronze-casted images of Tara, Manjushri and other deities, clay tablets featuring the eight bodhisattvas and the eight-armed Tara, etc. Along with Comilla, Chittagong also served as a site of transmission for Buddhist ritual practices and artefacts in Southeast Asia in the medieval times. Later, in modern times, Chittagong appeared as a fulcrum for Buddhist tantric practices and a centre for dissemination of Buddhist poetry in Bengali, Persian and Arabic, till the Chittagong Buddhists were converted by the Arakanese monks to 'pure' Pali tradition in the 19th century. Today, Chittagong lies in Bangladesh. Scholars, bringing into the frame present-day borders and national boundaries, have pointed out that these notions did not exist then, that Indic Buddhism (mostly the Mahayana and Vajrayana traditions) continued to flourish among Newar Buddhists of the Kathmandu valley since the Gupta–Vakataka period. Even if we consider these scattered instances, Buddhism survived in a fragmented state in India till the 16th–17th centuries. After this, it experienced a decline that was neither drastic nor dramatic but more of a downward slope with periodic resurgences.[61]

The lamps lit by generations of devout and zealous Buddhists were running out of oil and finding it hard to survive the onslaught of the winds blowing in the north and peninsular India during the early medieval times. Some lingered for a while, few lit other lamps in the neighbouring countries, others (especially those burning on the margins of the winds) managed to keep the flames alive. However, most were extinguished or buried in the sands of time, only to be recovered by Brahman pandits, Indian intelligentsia, colonial officials, archaeologists, adventurers and enthusiasts in the 19th century. These lamps were reignited, but their flames were different, as was the oil used.

PART II
UNESCO WORLD HERITAGE SITES

6

BODH GAYA AND THE MAHABODHI TEMPLE COMPLEX

There I saw a delightful stretch of land and a lovely woodland grove, and a clear flowing river with a delightful ford, and a village for support nearby.

This is how *Majjhima Nikaya*, a collection of middle-length discourses related to the *Sutta Pitaka* of the Pali canon, describes Siddhartha Gautama's arrival at Bodh Gaya before his enlightenment.[1]

This once-quiet land has now become a bustling town with tourists, pilgrims, monasteries, temples, hotels and shops. Today, visitors to the Mahabodhi temple complex will be struck by the presence of monks donning colourful robes – those in red are typically from Tibet, Nepal, Bhutan, Mongolia and China; those wearing orange generally hail from Sri Lanka, Thailand, Myanmar and Vietnam; and those attired in black and grey are mostly from Japan, Korea and Taiwan. These colourful robes and the mushrooming of multiple foreign monasteries and temples around the complex indicate how Bodh Gaya has, once again, become the centre of the Buddhist universe and a global pilgrimage destination. Those not familiar with the history of the place will be confronted with several questions on seeing the temple complex. Why are so many monuments and artefacts, of different shapes and sizes, crowding the space around the Mahabodhi temple? Why have so many foreign monasteries and temples, in different architectural styles, sprung up around the temple? Why do most images of the

Buddha show him sitting cross-legged, with the right hand touching the ground? Why does one see both Buddhist and Hindu temples in the complex? Why, unlike other World Heritage Sites, is the Mahabodhi temple complex not controlled and managed by the Archaeological Survey of India (ASI)? These questions underscore how we need to deploy multiple frames to understand the layers of this site. They also point to the continuous transformation of the physical and sociocultural landscape of Bodh Gaya over time.

The Mahabodhi temple complex is located on the banks of river Phalgu, a tributary of river Ganga, 10 kms from Gaya, a town known prominently for Hindu funerary rituals. Regarded as the most sacred site in the world for Buddhists, it is described as the 'navel of the earth'. The area around the temple complex is known as Bodh Gaya. Siddhartha Gautama, the prince of the Shakya kingdom, attained enlightenment here sitting under a pipal tree in the 6th–5th century BCE. He then became the Buddha, the 'Enlightened One'. The tree under which Siddhartha sat in meditation is popularly known as the Bodhi tree, or the 'tree of knowledge', and the site of enlightenment is known as the Bodhi *manda* (area of enlightenment). After attaining enlightenment, he put forth a set of teachings (*sasana*) that later acquired the form of a religion called Buddhism, which has followers across the world.

Incidentally, Bodh Gaya was earlier known as Uruvela, Sambodhi and Buddhagaya.

EPISODES SURROUNDING PRINCE SIDDHARTHA'S ENLIGHTENMENT

To understand the structures and artefacts at the Mahabodhi temple complex and its surroundings, it is important to know how the Buddhist literary tradition, the Pali canon or the Sanskrit biographies, reconstruct the Buddha's activities here. After leaving his home and kingdom behind, Prince Siddhartha Gautama became an ascetic and begged for food as a wanderer. He learnt the technique of meditation from a sage named Alara Kalama. He also joined a group of five ascetics, and like them, started practising self-mortification and rigorous fasts and austerities. One day, he fainted. When he regained consciousness, he gave up on fasts and penance and went back to begging for food. At this point, the five ascetics who had become his disciples abandoned him. Siddhartha's wanderings took him to Gaya, which the Buddhist texts describe as a place known for the presence of ascetics (including the fire-worshipping Kasyapa brothers) and purificatory baths, besides being a haunt of the yakshas and other spirits regarded as deities.

It seems that Siddhartha left the relative hustle-bustle of Gaya and went to a quieter place called Uruvela on the outskirts, which was a *senanigama* or a camp village located on the banks of the river Phalgu (also called Niranjana).[2] Here, he was seated under a pipal tree when Sujata, the daughter of a farmer who lived nearby, brought him a bowl of food. There are different versions to this story, including one where she mistakes the Buddha for a deity associated with the tree. Worshipping trees was part of an established popular tradition in ancient India, as was the practice of meditating under trees. Interestingly, Sujata's legend is also corroborated by archaeological findings in the area. A two-level terraced stupa discovered close to the Mahabodhi temple, on the other side of the river Phalgu, in a village known as Bakror, carries an inscription that describes the structure as the 'house of Sujata'. This stupa was built by Pala ruler Devapala in the 9th century, though the initial phase of construction is dated to the 2nd–1st century BCE. Sujata's story is also seen in the beautiful frescoes painted on the walls of the Nichigai Suzan Horinji temple (also known as Japanese temple) at Sarnath.

Coming back to Siddhartha's story, after consuming the food Sujata gave him, he bathed and sat beneath the pipal tree again. A host of gods and spirits surrounded a meditating Siddhartha, a scene often depicted in Buddhist iconography, waiting to witness the moment of his enlightenment. Mara, the Buddhist devil, tried to distract Siddhartha, the details of which we have discussed in Chapter 1. He also asked Siddhartha to produce evidence of his goodness. At that point, Siddhartha reportedly touched the ground with his hand and the earth itself said: 'I am his witness.' This gesture, known as the bhumisparsha mudra, became a dominant theme in the Buddhist iconographic and sculptural programme and became increasingly common between the

6th and 13th centuries. It conveyed the miraculous power of the site that was connected to many ritual practices.[3]

After Siddhartha attained enlightenment, Hindu god Brahma persuaded him to teach the truths to the world. The Buddha then left Uruvela and preached his first sermon to his estranged disciples at Sarnath. It seems the Buddha came back, tamed a fire-spewing serpent and converted the fire-worshipping Kasyapa brothers and their disciples. The taming of this serpent is depicted in a sculptural panel on the eastern gateway in Sanchi. It is also said that the Buddha preached the 'fire sermon' to 1,000 former fire-worshipping ascetics on the Brahmayoni hill, now a major tourist attraction in Gaya.

INTERSECTION OF BUDDHIST, SHAIVITE AND VAISHNAVA PASTS

Bodh Gaya, or Gaya, has an ancient Hindu connection. On the basis of Brahmanical and Buddhist texts, some scholars have argued that Gaya emerged as a pilgrimage site (*tirtha*) associated with *shraddha* (rituals associated with deceased ancestors) only around the beginning of the Christian era, though it was known as a place for purificatory baths and as an ascetics' haunt before that.[4] Others, however, argue that ancient Gaya, including what is now called Bodh Gaya, was a sacred centre associated with deities and the dead, and that shraddha rites were held here even before the Buddha's enlightenment. They hold that Sujata's offering of food to Siddhartha reflected a practice associated with the funerary shraddha ritual.[5] While this continues to be debated, there is no doubt that, at some point, the Bodhi tree of Uruvela became a part of the Brahmanical shraddha circuit. The Mahabodhi *taru* (Great Bodhi tree) is prescribed as a site for shraddha in several texts, including *Gaya Mahatmya* (probably dated to the 8th or 9th centuries) and *Tirtha Chintamani* (dated to the 13th century). Within the larger Hindu tradition, Bodh Gaya has a long-standing relevance for both Shaivites and Vaishnavites.[6]

The Shaivite connection, as we will discuss in this chapter, with the temple complex comes out through the presence of a 5th-century CE male figure bearing a trident (popularly identified as Lord Shiva) on the railing; the 'Kesava Prasasti', an 8th-century inscription recording the installation of a four-faced Shiva linga engraved on a pre-existing lintel consisting of the icons of Vishnu–Surya–Lakulisa, now housed in the Indian Museum, Kolkata;[7] and the statues of Uma–Maheshwara (Shiva and Parvati) and Ganesha, dated to the period between the 8th and 12th centuries CE. The Shaiva connection was further strengthened in the late 16th century when Bodh Gaya became the base of Shiva worshippers, known as the mahants. Bodh Gaya's Vaishnava connection manifests, among other things, in the presence of Vishnu sculptures in the temple complex from the 8th century CE. The Buddha had also come to be worshipped as one of the incarnations of Vishnu around the 6th–7th centuries. Also, Gaya – with the famous banyan tree Akshayavata – enjoyed a long association with the Vaishnava and shraddha traditions.

In addition, Gaya (and Bodh Gaya region) was known for the presence of popular devotional cults. We have already discussed how the region was known to be a haunt of the ascetics and the yakshas. Archaeological excavations at the Taradih mound, located 20 m west of the Mahabodhi temple, have revealed fire pits (associated with the fire worshippers) and figurines of nagas (associated with the Naga cult). Plaques of yakshas and yakshis have also been reportedly found in the region.[8] Even the railing around the Mahabodhi tree, among other things, has depictions of tree, spirits, yakshas and yakshis, Vedic gods, nagas and other mythical creatures.[9] The shaping of Bodh Gaya, therefore, took place in a larger socio-religious context, going beyond just the Buddhist faith.

THE TEMPLE COMPLEX

The Mahabodhi temple complex (Fig 6.1) broadly consists of the Bodhi tree, which is believed to be the fifth incarnation of the tree under which the Buddha attained enlightenment (Fig 1.6, Chapter 1); the Vajrasana, or the 'diamond throne', which demarcates the site of Buddha's enlightenment (dated to the 3rd century BCE with additions made later); a stone railing circumambulating the Bodhi tree and the Mahabodhi temple; the brick Mahabodhi temple dated to the 5th–6th centuries CE (renovated several times before being reconstructed in its

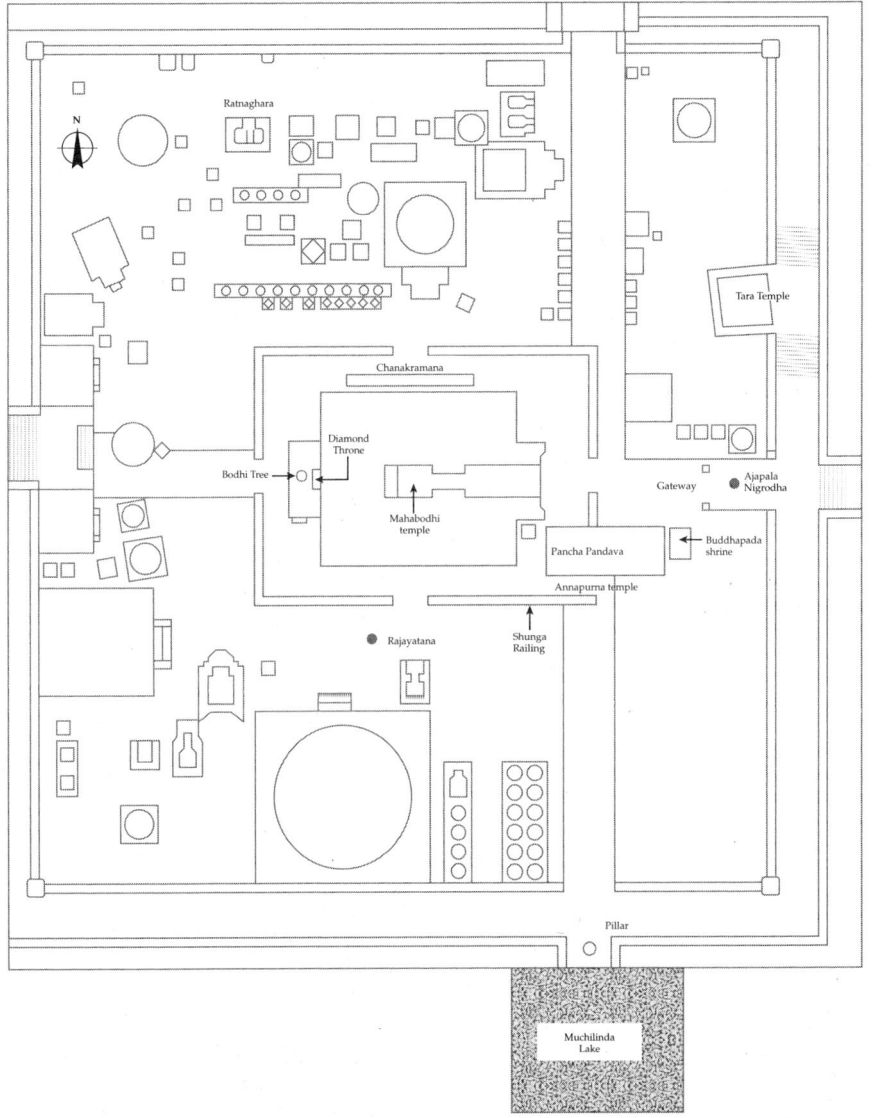

Site map of the Mahabodhi temple complex (after Fredrick Asher, *Bodh Gaya*, 2008)

present form in the 19th century) and sacred sites associated with the seven weeks after the Buddha's enlightenment (see site map).[10]

While the Bodhi tree may have been venerated even before Mauryan king Ashoka arrived on the scene, historical evidence suggests that the first structures to be built in the temple complex are attributed to him. Ashoka is credited with building a slab beneath the Bodhi tree, called the Vajrasana or Diamond Seat (also known as the 'Adamantine Seat' and the 'Thunderbolt Throne'), a red sandstone platform with a polished surface that apparently marks the specific spot where the Buddha meditated. The Vajrasana currently lies within an enclosed structure, away from the reach of visitors. This seat was enlarged at least twice: first, around the 2nd century CE when a new layer was added with two gold impressions of the Kushana king Huvishka; and second, around the 6th century CE, when the northern, southern and eastern sides of the Vajrasana were enlarged to merge it with the image carrying the platform of the sanctum sanctorum of the main brick temple being built then. It is possible that a pillar also stood near this seat or slab in its early phase and the whole structure gave the semblance of a tree shrine known as the bodhighara. The pillared tree shrine appears in a relief on the railing at the Bharhut Stupa (constructed in the 2nd century BCE, during the Shunga period), where it appears crowned by an elephant capital (Fig 2.2, Chapter 2). Representation of the tree shrine are also seen on a carved panel on the eastern gateway of the Great Stupa at Sanchi (1st century BCE), where an object symbolizing the triratna (Buddha, dharma and sangha) adorns the seat of the bodhighara. Notably, neither the Buddha nor Brahmanical deities were worshipped in anthropomorphic forms before the 1st century BCE. Some scholars also suggest that an uninscribed pillar shaft, now standing south of the Bodhi tree, may have been a part of the pillar depicted at Bharhut. It is popularly held that this pillar was erected by Ashoka, though it neither has the characteristic Mauryan polish nor any supporting inscriptional evidence (Fig 6.2).[11]

Perhaps the next stage in the evolution of the temple complex was the stone railing surrounding the Bodhi tree and the Mahabodhi temple. The relief style of the Bodh Gaya railing is similar to those at the Bharhut Stupa and Sanchi (built around the 1st century BCE, during the reign of the Shungas). This railing has an interesting history. The present structure is a replica of the original, which is displayed at the site museum established by the ASI in 1956.

Archaeological evidence suggests that the original railing was built around the 1st century BCE and expanded around the 5th or 6th centuries CE. The repeat occurrence of an inscription recording a donation by Kurangi, the queen of Indragnimitra, regarded as a feudatory of the Shungas, indicates that the stone railing was erected around the pillared tree shrine towards the beginning of the 1st century BCE. With this installation, the elementary tree shrine acquired an open-pillared enclosure and a path of circumambulation. Considering the difference in the style of carving and the construction material used, archaeologists and historians point out that the original railing was expanded around the 5th or 6th centuries CE, during the time of the Gupta dynasty (c. 300–600 CE) that held sway over the region then. The original railing pillars are constructed in sandstone and carry medallions adorned with lotus flowers and narrative episodes from the life of the Buddha. The pillars belonging to the later period, on the other hand, are made of granite. The later additions also include a few anthropomorphic representations of what are believed to be figures of Vedic deities like Indra and Surya (both respected in the Buddhist tradition) or mythological creatures like the yakshas and yakshis. One male figure, bearing a trident and featuring in the later expansion, has been identified as Hindu god Shiva.

The scattered pillars and coping stones of the railing were recovered from both the Shiva-worshipping mahant's compound, located a little distance from the Mahabodhi temple, and other parts of the temple complex in the 19th century, when a comprehensive restoration exercise was under way. These were first reassembled around the Bodhi tree. Later, the original railing was shifted to the site museum and a replica was installed around the tree.

The discovery of a replica of the Mahabodhi temple on one of the relief plaques found in Kumrahar, a Kushana-period site on the outskirts of Patna, has led some scholars to conclude that the tree shrine and the open-pillared enclosure gave way to a brick tower-like structure under the Kushanas. Most experts, however, hold that the brick predecessor of the current temple emerged later, during the 5th or 6th centuries CE, during the reign of the Guptas. The shift from a pillared shrine to an enclosed pyramidal temple also involved a change in the object of veneration – the Bodhi tree gave way to the Buddha's seat, or throne. This shift may have resulted from political events involving the desecration or destruction of the Bodhi tree rather than any ideological changes. There are several accounts describing the destruction and regeneration of the tree, which had emerged as the central icon of the Buddhist faith. Xuanzang mentions the Bodhi tree being destroyed by Ashoka before his conversion to Buddhism. Later, Ashoka's queen is said to have destroyed it. Upon seeing the tree's miraculous properties, the Mauryan king is said to have replanted it after bathing its roots in milk. In the 7th century CE, Shashanka, the ruler of Gauda, destroyed the tree again.[12]

In any case, the present Mahabodhi temple and some related structures seemed to have emerged in some form by the 5th or 6th centuries CE. Other structures had also come up or were coming up. Chinese pilgrim Faxian, who visited Bodh Gaya in the early 5th century CE, reports several pagodas (temples) and images around the Bodhi tree, as well as three monasteries. By the 6th century CE, a community of Sinhalese monks had settled at the site. An inscription of a Sri Lankan monk, Mahanaman, dated 588–89 CE, records the establishment of a beautiful mansion for the 'teacher' (Buddha) in the *Bodhimanda*, the site of his enlightenment. The existence of a large temple is also affirmed by a 6th–7th century CE inscription that records the gift of plaster and paint to a building known as the Vajrasana gandhakuti, the 'perfumed temple' enshrining the 'diamond throne'. Xuanzang speaks of a huge ornamented vihara east of the Bodhi tree (where the main brick temple stands now), painted in white lime and carrying golden figures in all the niches on different storeys. He also mentions several other structures in the complex and some stupas, too.

The next milestone in the development of the Mahabodhi temple complex was during the Pala period. This was a phase of sculptural efflorescence, a phenomenon that does not get adequate notice in studies done on Bodh Gaya. The Palas were Buddhists who ruled between the 8th and 12th centuries. Like the Gaudas, their predecessors, they controlled a large empire that included modern-day Bihar and West Bengal in India and parts of Bangladesh. The Palas are known for the establishment of great monasteries like Vikramashila and Somapura Mahavihara (also known as Paharpur). During their reign, Bihar and Bengal also became prominent Buddhist centres and attracted monks, devotees and pilgrims from all parts of Asia.[13] What is striking in the archaeological finds of the pre-Pala period is the absence of Buddhist statues at the site of Buddha's enlightenment – not even those imported from Mathura, which supplied images to many monastic sites. Only a few statues belonging to pre-Pala times have been found. The earliest statues found at Bodh Gaya belong to the late 4th and early 5th centuries (Gupta period). These include red sandstone images of a seated Buddha, now found in Indian Museum, Kolkata; and a standing figure of the Buddha in abhay mudra, now found in the Mahant's compound. Also, only two images that could be dated with certainty have been found for the period between the Guptas and the Palas. One is now in the Indian Museum and the other is in the Mahant's compound. These are small black stone images of the Buddha, seated in meditation with both hands folded in his lap, a gesture known as dhyana mudra. In these images, he is protected by the serpent Muchilinda – a reference to an incident that unfolded at Bodh Gaya, which we will discuss in the section 'Monuments of the Seven Weeks'. How does one explain this striking absence of the Buddha's images in the pre-Pala period? Looking at the architectural tradition of eastern India around this time, one notices a marked preference for brick buildings (such as the Mahabodhi temple) with stucco images and ornamentation. This could also be seen in another prominent Buddhist site, Nalanda, which is around 70 kms away. Even photographs from the 19th century show the site with stucco images.[14] So, what happened to them? Most perished over time, and many were removed during the late 19th-century restoration of the temple.

In marked contrast to the preceding period, Bodh Gaya is known to have produced many stone images of Buddhist deities, and some Brahmanical ones, during the reign of the Palas.[15] There is no direct evidence of royal support to Bodh Gaya under the Palas, but political stability and congenial conditions for religious patronage and pilgrimage account for this phase of impressive sculptural programme. Stone images produced during this period can be seen in the niches of the Mahabodhi temple tower, elsewhere in the temple complex and in the Mahant's compound. Others could also be seen at the Bodh Gaya site museum, at the Indian Museum in Kolkata, Patna Museum and some overseas museums like the British Museum (London) and the Museum of Fine Arts in Boston. Most such images are carved in black stone, which was obtained either from local basalt or phyllite quarried from Jamalpur in the Munger district of Bihar. Almost all Pala-period images of the Buddha show him in the bhumisparsha mudra, clearly attesting to the enduring importance of the event of enlightenment. Some such images also show the Buddha wearing a crown, possibly indicating his status as a chakravartin, or universal monarch, in the spiritual realm. The 'crowned Buddha', incidentally, happens to be a widely depicted sculptural motif in eastern India during the 10th and 12th centuries CE.[16] Besides the Buddha, Bodh Gaya is known for numerous images of Buddhist deities such as Avalokiteshvara, Padmapani, Vajrapani, Tara, Marichi, Yamantaka and Vajra Varahi – all stylistically belonging to the Pala period. Viewed in a larger context, these images underline the influence of the Mahayana and Vajrayana traditions at the Mahabodhi temple complex between the 8th and 12th centuries CE. The Mahayana presence at the site is also confirmed by the discovery of two local inscriptions carrying an important formula popularly related to the tradition – the first belongs to the Sri Lankan monk Mahanaman, and the second is found on an image donated by a monk named Viryendra from Somapura (now in Bangladesh), dated 10th century CE. The Mahayana formula reads: *'yad atra punyam tad bhavatu sarvvasattvanam anuttara jnanavaptaye stu'*. This broadly translates as 'whatever religious merit [there is] in this [act], let it be for the acquisition of supreme knowledge of all sentient beings.' Even, Dharmasvamin, the Tibetan monk who visited the temple complex in the 13th century, talks about the presence of a Tara temple and forty Mahayana monks.[17] Besides Buddhist sculptures, the Pala period images of Brahmanical deities like Uma–Maheshwara and Ganesha have been found in the Mahabodhi temple complex, the Mahanta's compound and the site museum, indicating the prevalence of a complex religious–cultural mosaic at Bodh Gaya.[18]

Bodh Gaya, like Nalanda, or Buddhism in general, declined after the 12th–13th centuries CE. The popular explanation offered for this decline is the invasion by Bakhtiyar Khalji, the Afghan commander of Turkish rulers Muhammad Ghuri and Qutbuddin Aibak, who laid the foundations of the Delhi Sultanate.[19] We will explore this 'invasion' in detail in the chapter on Nalanda. For now, it is sufficient to say that there is no conclusive evidence of any direct attack on Bodh Gaya, or for that matter, on Nalanda. Some scholars connect the repair of the temple by a Burmese delegation, as recorded in an inscription of 1305 CE found at the site, with the idea of a Muslim invasion. It is, however, difficult to establish if such repairs were necessitated because of destruction caused by an invasion or the absence of maintenance over a long period. But yes, Afghan and Turkish depredations in eastern India did hasten the decline of the Palas and unestablished the royal patronage Buddhist establishments enjoyed under them. The consequent political instability also affected trade and economic networks, and related mercantile support. Pilgrimage to the site was impacted as well. Tibetan monk Dharmasvamin, who visited the Mahabodhi temple in 1234, described that the site was dilapidated and that there were only four monks residing in the monastery inside the temple complex (as opposed to 1,000 reported by Xuanzang, who visited in the 7th century). The resident monks, Dharmasvamin recorded, had protected the temple by drawing an image of Maheshwara (Shiva) on the plastered entranceway. Some monks, he also said, had fled out of fear of the 'Turushka' (Muslim/ Turk soldiers). Some monks may have converted to Islam, while others fled to Nepal and Tibet.

What happened to the Mahabodhi temple complex after the 12th and 13th centuries? Perhaps the physical site continued to disintegrate. Metaphorically, the Mahabodhi temple was being recreated in other countries in East, South and Southeast Asia as replicas and miniatures in different mediums. We will discuss this in a separate section in this chapter but, for now, let us return to the evolution of the buildings and artefacts and explore the monuments along the central walkway and those associated with the Buddha's seven-week stay at the site after attaining enlightenment.

The Central Walkway and the Mahabodhi Temple

The Mahabodhi temple complex is approached from the east through a flight of steps. A long, central walkway leads to the main brick temple and its surrounding sites. The temple is preceded by a small forecourt, with niches on either side containing statues of the Buddha, and a gateway built around the 5th or 6th century CE. The doorway to the temple, like some other Buddhist shrines in Ajanta, is flanked by figures of the standing Buddha belonging to the Pala period – the one to the right dates to around the 8th century and shows him in abhay mudra, while the one on the left dates to the 10th century and depicts him in varada mudra (with his hands facing downwards). The low basement of the 50 m high temple is decorated with mouldings and geese and honeysuckle designs.

The doorway of the temple opens into a small hall, beyond which lies the sanctum. The sanctum contains a large seated, gilded and painted statue of the Buddha, with his right hand touching the earth in bhumisparsha mudra (Fig 6.3). Made of black stone, this statue dates to the Pala period. Above the sanctum is the main hall with a shrine containing another statue of the Buddha, where senior monks gathered to meditate. The truncated pyramidal superstructure (distinct from the curvilinear shikhara over north Indian Hindu temples) over the temple's sanctum creates an elevated terrace. This contains niches housing stone images, mostly of seated Buddhas, belonging to the Pala period. Further above these niches are mouldings and niche-shaped chaityas. At the top of the truncated pyramidal tower rests the amalaka or a stone disk. The parapet of the temple contains shrines in four corners, each of which has a statue of a standing Buddha belonging to the Pala period, and each is topped by a small tower identical to the main one. This plan of a central shrine surrounded by four subsidiary shrines was called the panchayatana, or five-fold, plan. It became common during the Gupta period and can also be seen at Nalanda.[20]

Back on the central walkway, to the south of the gateway to the main temple, lies a hemispherical black stone block carrying a representation of the buddhapada (Fig 6.4). The footprints lie in front of a small shrine, which looks similar to the Mahabodhi temple and dates to the 19th century. Moving further towards the main temple, next to the buddhapada, lies the Panchapandava Annapurna temple, which has a long structure with an arched portico. The first three of the sanctums have Pala period images of the Buddha and bodhisattvas, and the next two contain Shiva lingas that again reminds one of the multiple religious associations.

The most important artefacts and monuments of the site – the Bodhi tree, the Vajrasana and the railing – lie on the rear, or west, side of the Mahabodhi temple, while the votive or small stupas and shrines surround the temple on most sides. A major attraction is the 'Monuments of the First Seven Weeks' – while those belonging to the first six weeks are located within the inner, middle and outer circular boundaries; the seventh one, the Muchilinda Lake (also known as the Lotus Pond), is located outside the enclosure, to the south of the main temple.

Monuments of the First Seven Weeks and the 1989 Re-inscription

It is believed that the Buddha spent the first seven weeks after enlightenment in and around the Bodhimanda, or Bodhi *Pallanka*, the site of his enlightenment, consolidating the knowledge he had gained. The central path going around the Mahabodhi temple is marked with the six sites that are supposed to indicate the Buddha's first six weeks after enlightenment. The seventh is located a little outside the temple enclosure in the south, but forms a part of the larger temple complex. The current layout of these seven sacred monuments, now marked by marble and stone signboards, follows a plan finalized only in 1989.[21] There is an interesting story behind this recent re-inscription, discussed later in this section, which tells us why we should read about the monument complexes and their parts carefully. At this stage, it needs to be clarified that the idea of the seven sacred sites is a very old one, that their exact location and orderly sequence have always been a subject of debate. This idea was very popular in Burmese Theravada accounts written much earlier. In the 19th century, the seven sites were also identified by Alexander Cunningham (1814–93), who is regarded as the founding father of the ASI and known for his excavation and restoration of the Mahabodhi temple. Cunningham's identification scheme was based on his reading of Chinese pilgrim Xuanzang's travel accounts. His plan did not have the same orderly sequence as the 1989 scheme. Except the Bodhi tree and the "Cankamana" (currently identified as the monument of the third week), he placed the other sites in locations different from those in the present scheme, including some outside the temple compound. It is worth noting that even Xuanzang did not offer very specific locations for some of these sites. The monuments of seven weeks also appear in several writings of the Maha Bodhi Society (MBS), including in an 1891 article titled 'Buddha Gaya and Its Surroundings' by Dharmapala Anagarika, the founder of the MBS, as well as several subsequent scholarly accounts and popular guidebooks written throughout the 20th century. However, all pre-1989 accounts of the MBS are ambiguous about the exact location of the sites associated with the Buddha's last three weeks. They are listed as 'yet to be found', or located outside the Mahabodhi temple yard.

What does the 1989 inscription and scheme say about the time the Buddha spent after his enlightenment? According to the text inscribed on these signboards, the Buddha spent the first week in bliss seated under the Bodhi tree. This is called the Bodhi Pallanka.

He spent the second week gazing unblinkingly at the Bodhi tree (*animesha lochana*). The site of this gaze is marked with a platform under a tree, on a raised area to the north of the central path, outside a temple popularly known as the Tara temple. The platform carries Pala-period images of Brahmanical deities like Uma–Maheshwara and Ganesha, alongside Bodhisattva Avalokiteshvara. The Tara temple, which was probably built around the 6th century CE and restored in the 19th century, looks like the Mahabodhi temple in design. It appears whitewashed and carries a gilded image of Bodhisattva Manjushri in the sanctum.

The Buddha spent the third week (some say the second week) walking back and forth in meditation in an area called Chanakramana, or Ratnachankrama ('jewel walk'). This site is identified as the space within the railing of the north wall of the Mahabodhi temple. It is said that flowers or lotuses sprang miraculously under the Buddha's foot as he walked east and west for ten paces. Ratnachankrama currently has a raised platform (about 1 m high and 16 m in length) carrying footprints that are symbolic of the Buddha's steps (Fig 6.5).

Ratnaghar chaitya, or the 'jewel house', is the place where the Buddha is supposed to have spent his fourth week, meditating on the 'Law of Dependent Organization' (*patthana*). This is now identified with the remains of a small shrine located to the north-west of the main temple, outside the inner railing.

Along the central path, at the bottom of the stairs leading up to the Mahabodhi temple, is a pillar that marks the site of the Ajapala Nigrodha tree, the banyan tree under which the Buddha meditated during the fifth week after enlightenment, answering the queries of Brahmans. Here, he is supposed to have famously said that people become Brahmans only by their deeds, not by birth.

The Buddha is believed to have spent his sixth week meditating in front of the Lotus Pond, to the south of the Mahabodhi temple, outside the enclosure walls. Here, he sat in perfect composure as the mythical serpent king Muchilinda protected him from violent rains and strong winds. Currently, there is a lake at the site, from the centre of which emerges a modern image of the Buddha being shielded by Muchilinda (Fig 6.6). Donated by a group of Burmese visitors, this statue was made by famous sculptor U Han Tin. The Buddha's relics brought from Burma were enshrined just under the hands of his image.

The Buddha's seventh and final week at Bodh Gaya was apparently spent under the Rajayatana tree, where he is believed to have sat in contemplation and finally aroused himself to receive rice cakes and honey from two merchants, Trapusa and Bahalika from Utkala (possibly present-day Odisha). Some say these merchants were from Myanmar and that the Buddha offered locks of his hair to them, which now lie enshrined in Shwedagon Pagoda, Yangon (Myanmar). In 1989, a group of Burmese visitors brought a Rajayatana tree from Myanmar (where it is known as Linlun), and planted it south of the Mahabodhi temple, just outside the Shunga-period railing.

Let us now come to the story behind the 1989 inscription of the 'Monuments of the First Seven Weeks'. The trigger for the installation of a new set of signboards, mentioning specific locations of the seven sacred monuments, was a hunger strike by Indian monk Bhante

Aniruddh in 1988. This strike was precipitated by an attempt on the part of the superintendent of the Mahabodhi temple to remove a historical pillar from a site believed to mark the Buddha's fifth week after enlightenment (the Ajapala Nigrodha tree). The hunger strike soon snowballed into a campaign led by prominent Burmese Theravada monks living in Bodh Gaya and was joined by members of other Buddhist temples and establishments. Letters were written to the media and to the Bodhgaya Temple Management Committee (BTMC) and the Advisory Board, which guides BTMC on matters related to the Mahabodhi temple, about the incident. Finally, in 1989, the BTMC decided to install the seven signboards based on their identification from the text *Jinattha Pakasani* ('Exposition of the Story of the Victor [Buddha]'). Written in 1920 by Kyithe Layhtap Sayadaw, this text was widely read in Burmese monasteries. This re-inscription was done despite opposition from Thai and Sinhalese monks who argued that the Buddha spent his last three weeks at a little distance from the Bodhi tree.[22]

What does the re-inscription of the seven sites signify in this case? Blurring the boundaries between faith and academic knowledge, these seven signboards present Mahabodhi temple's officially sanctioned, literally carved-in-stone, master narrative. The stories they tell have been institutionalized as the history of the seven sites, bypassing all earlier narratives in the Buddhist tradition. They also ignore Bodh Gaya's complex past. Later interviews with the decision makers connected to the re-inscription scheme revealed that they were all aware that the seven sites were approximate, that no one was aware of the Buddha's exact movements. However, most felt that it would cause unnecessary confusion if there were any further corrections to the 1989 inscription, demarcating the specific locations of the seven sites. Besides, it was easier for the pilgrims and visitors to see all the sites within one defined complex.[23] Interestingly, the 1989 scheme was not the only occasion to bring about changes to the place of the Buddha's enlightenment. The physical–cultural landscape of the site has continued to undergo change since its ancient past and the days of early pilgrimage to Bodh Gaya.

MONKS, TRAVELLERS AND PILGRIMAGE

Bodh Gaya became a pilgrimage centre soon after the Buddha's death. According to the Pali canon, the Buddha is said to have mentioned to his close disciples that all Buddhists should visit the four places closely connected with his life – Lumbini, Bodh Gaya, Sarnath and Kushinagar. Later, in the 3rd century BCE, Mauryan ruler Ashoka visited the places connected with the life of the Buddha and marked them for future pilgrims. Bodh Gaya was one of them. Later, pilgrims to the site, whether monks or lay Buddhists, donated images, which was both a manifestation of patronage and a corollary to the rites of pilgrimage. Many such images have been removed from the Mahabodhi temple complex and been kept in museums in Kolkata and elsewhere. Some pilgrims also erected stone steles, donated terracotta tablets or even constructed small shrines. Information related to such donations could be had from the inscriptions recorded on such images, though some did not mention the donors. These inscriptions have not been studied adequately. Most of such inscriptions, especially those related to the Bengal–Bihar region carry the 'ye dharma' verse without mentioning the names of the donors. As discussed earlier, 'ye dharma', in a single verse (*gatha*), sums up the core tents of the nuanced law of dependent origination (pratityasamutpada in Sanskrit, or *paticca-samuppada* in Pali) and was first realized by the Buddha at Bodh Gaya.[24] Used in both Pali and Sanskrit, the law of dependent origination forms one of the fundamental concepts of Buddhism and explains the cause of suffering, connecting it with rebirth, old age and death.[25] Frequently deployed after the 5th–6th century CE, this verse was first used in the stupas (as dharanis) and later in images, tablets, seals and other mediums as a sacred formula, or hymn, with talismanic properties.

An inscription found in the complex, dated to the 4th century CE, mentions the donation of a stone image of the Buddha by a group of monks belonging to the Theravada order, who were also teachers of the vinaya (rules for the monastic order).[26] Likewise, donative inscriptions belonging to the later Pala period, specifically during the reign of Gopala III and Mahipala I of the 10th and 11th centuries, reveal that monks from faraway regions, like Somapura Mahavihara (Paharpur in Bangladesh) or the north-western part of the

Fig 6.1 The Mahabodhi temple complex, viewed from the southeast corner. The Tara temple is to the far right

Fig 6.2 Uninscribed pillar shaft, believed to have been erected by Mauryan king Ashoka

Fig 6.3 A gilded black stone statue of the Buddha in bhumisparsha mudra from the Pala period, located in the sanctum of the Mahabodhi temple

Fig 6.4 Buddhapada: Representation of the Buddha's footprints.

Fig 6.5 The Jewel Walk, where the Buddha is believed to have spent his third week after enlightenment. The raised flowers on the left represent his paces

Fig 6.6 Muchilinda Lake, where the Buddha is believed to have spent his sixth week, protected from a rainstorm by a mythical serpent

Fig 6.7 Smaller votive stupas are found throughout the temple complex

Fig 6.8 A section of a collage stupa at the Mahabodhi temple complex, Bodh Gaya

Fig 6.9 Model (miniature replica) of the Mahabodhi temple, Bihar (12th century)

Fig 6.10 The Royal Thai Monastery, Wat Thai, Bodh Gaya

country (Sindhu territory), donated images of the standing Buddha or the eighteen-armed Buddhist goddess Cunda. Some inscriptions also record the contributions of such images by scribes or artisans, including a unique instance of a donation of a four-faced Shiva linga in the 7th–8th century for the welfare of the Buddhist and resident monks of the Mahabodhi temple.

From the late Gupta period, pilgrims from all over Asia started visiting the place associated with the 'awakening of the Buddhas'. We have already discussed the inscription of Mahanaman earlier, which indicates the presence of a community of Sri Lankan/Sinhalese monks in a monastery at the site in the 6th century CE. They seemed to have settled at Bodh Gaya and exercised considerable authority over the site.[27] Interestingly, Mahanaman had also donated a shrine and an image at the Mahabodhi temple. Between the 5th and 13th centuries, many monks, pilgrims and travellers from China, Tibet and Myanmar visited Bodh Gaya. In the absence of wider archaeological excavations around the Mahabodhi temple complex, accounts (mainly Chinese and Tibetan) and inscriptions (Chinese, Burmese and Sinhalese) left behind by such monks and pilgrims help us reconstruct the history of the place and the faith. These visitors also became important conduits for the spread of the Buddhist faith in their respective countries.

As far as Chinese travellers to Bodh Gaya are concerned, there are two broad phases – 5th to the 8th century CE, and mid-9th to 13th centuries CE.[28] The gap in between was possibly related to the political instability resulting from the decline of the Tang dynasty. Faxian and Xuanzang, the two famous Chinese pilgrims, have, among other things, described the monuments found in the Mahabodhi temple complex. Yijing, who visited Bodh Gaya briefly during the 7th–8th centuries CE, informs that many Chinese monks had stayed at Bodh Gaya for longer periods; some had even died there. Wang Xuance, an envoy of the Tang dynasty who had visited India three times (and Bodh Gaya multiple times) between 646 CE and 662 CE, mentions the practice of erecting inscribed stone steles by pilgrims, and how spiritual merit could be gained through veneration and offerings made at the site of the Buddha's enlightenment. These accounts offer crucial insights into a period for which we have limited inscriptional evidence.

A marked feature of the second phase of Chinese travels to Bodh Gaya, and India, roughly between the mid-9th century and the 13th century CE, is the presence of a sizeable number of monks among the visitors. These monks brought back Buddhist scriptures for Chinese translation projects supported by the imperial courts. Many pilgrims were also sent by the Song dynasty (960–1279) to generate merit for the emperors, or their ancestors, through offerings at the sacred sites. They brought back sacred objects such as relics of the Buddha, chintamani pearls (wish-fulfilling pearls), or leaves from the Bodhi tree. Many such visitors erected stone steles in the Mahabodhi temple complex. A good number of inscribed stone steles, belonging to the period between the mid-9th century to 1033, were excavated from Bodh Gaya. Collected by Alexander Cunningham and edited by French scholar Édouard Chavannes, they constitute an important source of information on Bodh Gaya for these crucial centuries. They also record Chinese activities and engagements at the sacred site.

In addition to the Chinese, there were pilgrims and travellers from Burma, Tibet, Japan and Korea, too. A much-invoked inscription from the year 1295 records repairs to the Mahabodhi temple by a Burmese delegation. The Burmese royals took active interest in repairs at the temple. We will discuss later in the chapter how a repair mission led by a Burmese delegation in the 1870s precipitated a conflict between the Shaiva mahants and the colonial state.

Bodh Gaya also figured prominently on the Tibetan Buddhist pilgrimage map. The account of Tibetan monk Dharmasvamin, who visited Bodh Gaya in 1234, is also considered a dominant source for understanding the decline of Bodh Gaya.

Any pilgrimage to Bodh Gaya had a funerary association as well. A Chinese inscription records the construction of a stupa, by a monk named Hui Wen, in the memory of deceased Song dynasty emperor Taizong. Likewise, King Tilokarat, the patron of the 15th-century replica of the Mahabodhi temple at Wat Chet Yot in Chiang Mai (Thailand), had his ashes placed in a shrine in the Bodh Gaya temple complex.[29] It is this funerary association that partly explains the presence of several small stupas of various sizes around the Bodhi tree and the Mahabodhi temple. And, if we go by what Cunningham said, the ones we see now at the site only represent the lowest strata. There were at least four tiers of similar stupas built in stone above this stratum. The later ones were built on top of the earlier ones. Cunningham said: '[S]o great was the number of these successive monuments [small stupas], and so rapid was the accumulation of stones and earth, that the general level of the courtyard was raised about 20 feet above the floor of the Great Temple.'[30] While these stupas have popularly been described as votive stupas (Fig 6.7), a considerable number contain anonymous funerary deposits like bones and ashes and are also known as 'mortuary stupas' or *kulas*. Most of these date to the 8th century CE or later.[31] According to a Buddhist literary tradition, the Buddha was believed to actually have been present at the sites with which he had had direct physical contact during his lifetime. Further, a death in the presence of the Buddha – symbolized by the presence of small stupas containing funerary deposits around the Bodhimanda – meant rebirth in heaven.[32] This brings us to another related point. Most of these surrounding small stupas, particularly those erected in the early medieval period, don't have defined tops (or finials or cupolas). Further, many of them have dharanis enshrined in their core – a feature Bodh Gaya shares with other sites like Ratnagiri in Odisha, Nalanda in Bihar and Paharpur in Bangladesh. It is important to understand that these group of texts, which have only recently begun to receive the attention of researchers, were dominantly concerned with the problem of death, avoidance of rebirth in hell, unfortunate destinies and the release of those already born. The strong funerary associations of the dharanis can be seen in the fact that they are found in exactly the same archaeological context as anonymous funerary deposits of ashes and bones.[33]

Even if we keep the mortuary stupas and funerary connections aside, the presence of an extraordinarily large number of votive stupas/burial ad sanctos around the site of Buddha's enlightenment attests to the importance of Bodh Gaya in the Buddhist pilgrimage circuit. Interestingly, fragments of votive and mortuary stupas, and old images of Buddha and bodhisattvas, have been reassembled to form mounds and are known as collage stupas (also called *sahasrabuddha* stupas and 'Thousand Buddha stupas') (Fig 6.8). Located on either side of the central pathway leading up to the main temple are very recent creations, but they relate deeply to the site's metamorphic characteristic as an active pilgrimage site.[34] Coming back to the past, Bodh Gaya's supreme location on the Buddhist pilgrimage map is also borne out in the numerous replicas and representations of the Mahabodhi temple constructed after the 11th century.

REPLICAS, REPRESENTATIONS AND THE IDEA OF A VIRTUAL PILGRIMAGE

The Buddha and his dharma had started acquiring roots in other parts of Asia during the Gupta and post-Gupta periods. Between the 11th and 15th centuries CE, replicas or representations of the Mahabodhi temple in stone, terracotta, wood and cloth paintings were taken to, or produced in, Burma, China, Nepal, Tibet, Bangladesh and some Southeast Asian countries. Some scholars think that these were souvenirs, like the modern-day versions found in the shops around the Mahabodhi temple.[35] Most, however, feel that the replicas served a larger and more profound purpose. These imageries probably served as substitutes for seeing and experiencing the site – which played host to the most important event of the Buddha's life – without visiting the faraway temple in person. It was like a virtual pilgrimage. Since cameras did not exist then (and photographs were not possible), this could only be realized through sculptures or representations.

One can discern some trends in the way the Mahabodhi temple was represented in the replicas composed in different mediums. First, most sculptures or representations showed only the main temple with an image of the Buddha. However, some 11th–12th century compositions in stone and wood, found from Burma and Tibet, not only show the Mahabodhi temple but also the walled temple enclosure. Some sculptural representations from south-east Bangladesh, belonging to the 12th century, and Tibetan cloth paintings from the 12th–14th centuries only show the tower of the Mahabodhi temple with an image of the Buddha.[36] In the latter two cases, the representations also depict the eight scenes from the life of the Buddha, a theme that had started appearing from the Gupta/post-Gupta periods and became common by the 8th century. Second, almost all Buddha images in such replicas and representations depict him in the iconic bhumisparsha mudra, the significance of which has been discussed earlier. Third – and this is particularly true for the terracotta sealings and stone steles depicting the Buddha enshrined in the Mahabodhi temple, either produced at the site or elsewhere – they also carry the 'ye dharma' verse discussed earlier in the chapter.[37]

Several three-dimensional, miniature replicas of the Mahabodhi temple in stone, belonging to the 11th–12th centuries CE, can be seen in museums across the world (Fig 6.9). These include the Metropolitan Museum of Art and Rubin Museum of Art in New York, the Museum of Fine Arts in Boston; the Los Angeles County Museum of Art, Victoria and Albert Museum in London, and Asian Civilizations Museum in Singapore, alongside private collections from Burma and Tibet. Seen in conjunction with depictions on sealings and other sculptural representations, they underline the importance of the idea of 'seeing', 'visualizing' or 'imagining' the Buddha and/or the place of his enlightenment – a concept strongly prevalent in the Tibetan Buddhist tradition – and of the merit produced in carrying such replicas across regions.[38] Interestingly, representations of the Buddha in bhumisparsha mudra within the Mahabodhi temple have also been found in metal. A unique find in this regard has been the 12th–13th centuries CE model excavated from Jaipurgarh in 1976, which is now housed in the Gaya Museum.

In addition to the smaller representations, full-scale replicas of the Mahabodhi temple were also built in Burma (at Shwegugyi and Mahabodhi temples in Bagan), Thailand (Wat Jed Yod temple at Chiang Mai and Chiang Rai), China (Five-Pagoda Temple in Beijing, which in turn inspired the 18th-century Diamond Throne Pagoda in the same city) and Nepal (Mahabuddha temple at Patan) between the 13th and 16th centuries. Another such replica was erected in Mongolia in the 18th century. In many cases, the miniature models carried by Indian monks, or those returning from pilgrimage to the Mahabodhi temple, became the prototypes for the construction of this first set of full-size replicas. It has been suggested that such surrogate constructions sought 'to replicate the experience at Bodh Gaya' or 'provide a localized metaphoric pilgrimage' when access to the actual site became very difficult after the 12th–13th centuries, on account of political uncertainties, but the desire and need to visit the site remained unabated. Visiting one of these large-sized replicas, or viewing the miniature models, was tantamount to undertaking the pilgrimage to the original, physical site in Bodh Gaya.[39] But the full-sized replicas served an important political purpose, too. The symbolic relocation of the holiest Buddhist site bolstered the political prestige of the rulers and emperors in whose dominions the replicas of such sacred centres were reconstructed. By the 20th century, numerous copies of the Mahabodhi temple had been built in China, Burma and Thailand. As late as 2014, another copy of the temple and the compound was constructed in the form of Thatta Thattaha Maha Bawdi Pagoda in Myanmar.[40]

FROM HINDU MAHANTS TO COLONIAL RESTORATION: REMAKING THE SITE

While the idea of the Mahabodhi temple was being taken to other countries, the site of the Buddha's enlightenment was fast disintegrating. An abandoned and dilapidated Bodh Gaya was visited by a wandering ascetic and a follower of Lord Shiva, Gossain Ghamanda Giri, in the late 16th century. Possibly impressed by the sanctity of the site, he established a monastery there and became the first mahant (chief priest) of Bodh Gaya. It needs to be clarified that the mahants, who trace their lineage to the teachings of 8th-century philosopher Shankaracharya, did not forcibly take over the site.[41] Gradually, a succession of Shiva-worshipping mahants strengthened their control over Bodh Gaya. By the late 18th to the early 19th century, the mahants were claiming ownership of the land and the status of zamindars by citing *firmans* (royal order) obtained from Mughal emperor Shah Alam II (r. 1759–1806), which granted them rights to the village of Taradih, including the physical site of the Mahabodhi temple complex. Meanwhile, the temple complex continued to disintegrate, only to be rediscovered by enthusiasts from Europe in the 18th and 19th centuries. Later, the Mahabodhi temple was restored by colonial administrators and archaeologists.[42]

The first phase of rediscovery of the Mahabodhi temple, in the 19th century, was largely driven by the popularity of the Romanticism movement in Europe and the connected fascination for landscapes and ruins. In the case of Bodh Gaya, this manifested in paintings/drawings/sketches of William and Thomas Daniell, who visited in 1790, James Crockatt in 1800, Charles D' Oyly in 1824 and Markham Kittoe in 1847. Francis Buchanan-Hamilton, after arriving in India in 1811, not only produced drawings of the site but also described how it had been ruined. All verbal and visual depictions of Bodh Gaya effectively fed into the 'British sense of India as a land of ruin and decadence requiring rescue by a European colonizer'.[43] The emergence of archaeology as a modern discipline around the mid-19th century added a new dimension to this framework. European and British scholars claimed to conduct a scientific study of India's past in which Buddhism, Buddhist monuments and the Buddha played an important part. This exercise was carefully projected as a part of the 'civilizing mission', as part of which the Europeans were trying to help India restore its past.[44]

The claims and interests of the colonial administration and the Hindu mahants came to a point of collision when a Burmese delegation tried to repair the Mahabodhi temple in 1870. The Burmese king sponsoring the repair was motivated by the Theravada Buddhist ideal of dharmarajas, who saw the restoration of the temple as a way to earn merit and an act that would bolster his political prestige.[45] Also, Burmese delegations had repaired the Mahabodhi temple in the past. The 1870 repair delegation asked for the mahant's permission, which irked the colonial administrators who contested the mahant's claim as the owner of the Mahabodhi temple complex. They blamed the mahant for the ruined state of the complex and asserted their right to preserve and restore India's historic sites. At first, the colonial administration issued guidelines for the repairs to be conducted by the Burmese delegation. It appointed Raja Rajendralal Mitra, an Indian philologist, and a member of the ASI, to inspect the repairs. Later, it ended up restoring the temple itself through a massive rebuilding exercise under the leadership of Alexander Cunningham, who had retired as a soldier and become the director general of the ASI, and J. D. Beglar, his assistant engineer.

Much of the current physical appearance of the Mahabodhi temple – including the elevation of the terrace, the construction of upper storeys over the sanctum, the four corner towers on the terrace, the re-fashioning of the facade and the re-arrangement of the sculptures in the complex – stems from this large-scale restoration carried out by the British from 1879 to 1884, at a cost of Rs 200,000. Interestingly, stucco images of the seated and standing Buddha in different mudras, which proliferated the complex, were completely obliterated. Free-standing stone images were put in the niches of the building and the original iconographic program was also sidelined.[46] In 1876, Cunningham even had a sapling planted from the seed of the older Bodhi tree, which had died around the time of the restoration.[47]

The restoration, however, faced two major problems. First, it was premised on a modern historical and archaeological view, which was at odds with the renovation of a sacred monument and the traditional religious practices associated with it.[48] Second, it privileged a seemingly original and monolithic Buddhist image in contrast to a multivocal or multireligious orientation of the site, which had undergone multiple renovations in the past. Very few visitors to the temple complex know that it preserves only the barest of traces of the earlier structures, most of which were swept away by the 19th-century restoration.[49]

DHARMAPALA, MAHA BODHI SOCIETY AND PAN-ASIAN BUDDHIST REVIVAL

Despite the colonial restoration, the Mahabodhi temple complex continued to disintegrate towards the end of the 19th century. There were even reports of encroachments and visitors taking away sculptures and carved stones. When Sri Lankan monk Dharmapala Anagarika visited Bodh Gaya in 1891, he was shocked to see the site in ruins and started demanding Buddhist control of the Mahabodhi temple.[50] His campaign 'Buddha Gaya for the Buddhists' gave birth to the Buddha Gaya Maha Bodhi Society (now called the Maha Bodhi Society) in Colombo on 31 May 1891. The primary objectives of this society were to rescue, restore and re-establish Bodh Gaya as a Buddhist religious centre through an international campaign, and to revive Buddhism as a pan-Asian force.[51] Dharmapala's speeches and the activities of the MBS, including scholarly publications and international conferences, did a lot to popularize Bodh Gaya as the 'Buddhist Jerusalem'. A pan-Asian Buddhist solidarity began to emerge around the site. Soon, the MBS got involved in a protracted legal battle with the Hindu mahants over control of the temple. This case attracted the attention of poet and journalist Sir Edwin Arnold, author of *The Light of Asia* (1879). Sir Arnold's writings reinforced the idea of reclaiming Bodh Gaya for the Buddhists. He lobbied with the secretary of state for India to transfer the control of the Mahabodhi temple to the Buddhists and told him that '400 millions of Eastern peoples' would bless his name 'night and day'.[52] The Buddhist campaign also drew support from Mahatma Gandhi, other nationalist leaders and the Indian National Congress (INC). Subsequent political negotiations saw the mooting of a compromise draft bill called the Buddha Gaya Temple Act, 1935, which was finally passed as an act by the Bihar Legislative Assembly after India became independent. It is currently known as Bodh Gaya Temple Act (Bihar Act XVII of 1949). Overturning the colonial position on the Mahabodhi temple during the late 19th-century restoration, this Act 'shifted Bodh Gaya's position from that of an archaeological and art historical object under the control of a local zamindar [mahant] to a religious monument'[53] managed by a committee. The mahant was, however, able to retain control over the Panchapandava shrine inside the temple complex. In the 1950s, the management of the Mahabodhi temple was passed on to the government-administered Bodhgaya Temple Management Committee (BTMC). The committee consisted of a chairperson and eight members – four Hindu (including the mahant) and four Buddhist members. The district magistrate served as the ex-officio chairperson of the committee, if s/he was a Hindu. This provision kept the balance of the committee in favour of the Hindus. In 2013, the act was amended to make provision for a 'non-Hindu' to head the temple committee. Despite legislations and settlements, the Mahabodhi temple complex continues to remain a contested site – between those asking for Hindu control and those advocating complete Buddhist control. The latter includes the Ambedkarite Buddhists (followers of Navayana, a new interpretation of Buddhism developed by iconic

Dalit leader B. R. Ambedkar) who have actively campaigned around Bodh Gaya since the 1990s.

HOW BODH GAYA BECAME A MINI ASIA

The Buddha and Bodh Gaya figured prominently in independent India's relationship with other Asian countries that had Buddhist populations. Its first prime minister, Jawaharlal Nehru, saw in Bodh Gaya an important cultural and symbolic resource for strengthening a nation-state and projecting India as a culture superpower among the other newly independent Asian nations. The Bihar government was a happy ally in this scheme, as it ushered in tourism and economic development for the state. In the preceding section, we discussed how the Maha Bodhi Society played an important role in kindling a pan-Asian Buddhist revivalism around Bodh Gaya. Developments in independent India further gravitated towards making Mahabodhi Temple the navel of the earth and the centre of the Buddhist world once again.[54]

The Indian government decided to celebrate the 2,500th anniversary of parinirvana of 'one of the greatest sons of India' (the Buddha) in a grand way. The year-long event in 1956, particularly the three-day Buddha Jayanti celebrations, was attended by thousands of Buddhists from outside India and delegations from Asian countries. This landmark occasion served to revive Buddhism in Bodh Gaya and revitalize its key Asian connections. The central government also constituted the Bodh Gaya Temple Advisory Board in the same year. With the help of representatives from various nations, this board was handed the task of allotting land for the construction of Buddhist monasteries, temples and resthouses. Following the Chinese occupation of Tibet in 1959, Bodh Gaya (alongside Dharamshala) became an integral part of the exile geography of Tibetan Buddhists led by the Dalai Lama.

The subsequent decades saw the establishment of temples and monasteries by Asian countries with large Buddhist populations, including Burma, Thailand, Tibet, China, Vietnam, Korea, Japan, Sri Lanka and Bangladesh (Fig 6.10). This process picked up further momentum after the 1980s. Most such structures, particularly those built after the 1980s, represented the unique aesthetic and architectural styles of different Buddhist traditions prevalent among different nations. The emergence of such monasteries, temples and guest houses also brought diasporic communities that followed their respective forms of worship and veneration. Visually, the structures with different architectural styles and the varied forms of worship give us a sense of the diverse forms of Buddhism prevalent across Asia and beyond. These brought about a dramatic transformation in Bodh Gaya's physical and cultural landscape.

The proliferation of new monastic establishments and diasporic communities, together with a global dissemination and exchange of Buddhist ideas, practices, institutions and teachers, invested this sacred site with a pan-Asian Buddhist identity. The sponsoring of Buddha-centred activities by these international establishments and communities, with the support of prominent Buddhist leaders and the central and Bihar governments, led to further 'Buddhification' of the sacred space at Bodh Gaya. These include the construction of the Buddha's images (such as the giant statue provided by the Daijokyo sect of Nagoya, Japan, which was unveiled in 1989) and the celebration of public rituals such as the famous Tibetan Kalachakra ceremonies. The Dalai Lama has conducted five Kalachakra initiations in Bodh Gaya (1974, 1985, 2003, 2012, and 2017) and the one held in 1985 attracted a quarter of a million participants from thirty-one countries.[55] The post-liberalization phase in India accelerated the growth of Buddhist monasteries and religious shrines, along with upscaling tourist infrastructure like roads, meditation centres, hotels, restaurants and cafes at Bodh Gaya. Currently, Bodh Gaya has more than 100 monasteries or establishments sponsored by different countries.[56] Post the year 2000, new dynamics contributed significantly to the site's global identity and its universal appeal as a supreme pilgrimage site. These include Bodh Gaya being designated as a UNESCO World Heritage Site status (2002), the inauguration of Gaya International Airport (2002) and the celebration of the 2,550th anniversary of the Buddha's parinirvana in 2006. These developments tremendously enhanced the site's tourism potential. In 2009, Bodh Gaya attracted 420,000 foreign tourists, overtaking Goa as the most popular destination. By 2011, the figures for overseas tourists had doubled to 972,487.⁵⁷ Domestic tourism has grown, too. The surge in tourism has led to the area around the Mahabodhi temple complex being dotted with resthouses, restaurants, souvenir shops, internet cafes, handicraft shops, travel agencies, book shops and daily provision shops, besides trained and untrained guides, hawkers, informal sellers, casual workers and beggars.

Rapid changes to Bodh Gaya's physical and cultural landscapes, and the status of a World Heritage Site, have also set into motion new problems and contestations. The UNESCO advisers, for instance, have suggested a comprehensive redevelopment of the town to facilitate international tourist traffic. In 2006, the Bihar Government in collaboration with Housing and Urban Development Corporation (HUDCO) published the City Development Plan (CDP) for Bodh Gaya which proposes a creation of a restricted buffer zone around the Mahabodhi temple. The central and state governments' attempts at formulating plans to enhance the site's tourism potential have met with strong resistance from locals who have socio-economic interests in the area surrounding the Mahabodhi temple.

Bodh Gaya, which has historically remained a site of contestations between the Buddhists and Hindus, is faced with a new problem – those who see it chiefly as a lucrative tourist destination versus those who see it as a pilgrimage site. The latter has brought about the coming together of some unlikely allies, including the Maha Bodhi Society, the Hindu mahant, foreign Buddhist temples and the local businesspeople.⁵⁸ Meanwhile, considering the growing Asian identity of the site, the Bihar government, in July 2023, constituted a new advisory board that will direct the Bodhgaya Temple Management Committee on all matters related to the protection and management of the site. The new committee includes ambassadors of Myanmar, Bhutan, Thailand, Japan, Cambodia, Mongolia, South Korea, Vietnam, Laos and the high commissioner of Sri Lanka, besides government officials, legislators and a representative of the Dalai Lama.⁵⁹ While deliberations and contestations continue to surround Bodh Gaya, its sacred landscape continues to change like never before. In 2023, India's largest reclining statue of the Buddha was inaugurated at the site where he attained enlightenment.

Two other recent developments are particularly relevant here. A geo-spatial study of the Mahabodhi temple complex conducted in 2023 revealed the presence of architectural structures beneath the temple and its surroundings. The study was conducted by Bihar Heritage Development Society (BHDS) and Cardiff University (United Kingdom) using ground surveys and satellite images. While excavations are awaited, this could potentially mean that the temple complex extended beyond its current boundaries. And, in 2024, the National Democratic Alliance (NDA) government announced a plan in its budget to develop a Kashi-Vishwanath temple-style corridor in Vishnupad temple at Gaya, and Mahabodhi temple at Bodh Gaya. Perhaps a remaking of the World heritage Site is in the offing. The future of Bodh Gaya depends on how these plans pan out.

7

SANCHI AND THE HILLTOP STUPA COMPLEX

He who dismantles, or causes to be dismantled, the stone work from this Kakanava [the Stupa at Sanchi], or causes it to be transferred to another house of the teacher [the Buddha], he shall go to the [same terrible] state as those who commit the five sins that have immediate retribution.

This is what a 1st-century BCE inscription on the western gateway of Stupa 1, or the Great Stupa, reads like. There are two other inscriptions on the same stupa, which convey the same message. Some Mahayana texts, composed much later, also mention how taking property belonging to the stupa or reliquary came under the category of 'five acts with immediate retribution'. These five sins, or five acts, constituted the most serious of offenses as per the Indian Buddhist tradition. These included taking the life of one's mother, father, or an arhat; wounding or causing physical harm to a Buddha; and causing a division within the sangha. So, what was so special about this stupa? As discussed in Chapter 2, by the Mauryan period, the relics had given way to the stupa (which housed the Buddha's relics) as the primary objects of devotion. The stupas containing such relics were considered to signify the very presence of the Buddha.[1] Circumambulating such a stupa meant experiencing his presence.

Welcome to Sanchi, the earliest surviving Buddhist stupa in the Indian subcontinent. The stupa complex here presents a history of Buddhism in stone, spanning some fifteen centuries – from the 3rd century BCE to around the 12th century CE.

For a curious visitor, Sanchi raises multiple questions. Why is it so important for the Buddhists despite sharing no connection with any event in the Buddha's life? Why was the stupa constructed on a remote hilltop? Why is there a cluster of several smaller stupas and other structures around the main stupa? What are images of yakshas or nagas doing in a Buddhist complex? Was the Mauryan emperor Ashoka responsible for such a massive architectural exercise? Do the water bodies in the hilltop complex, or in the surroundings, have any connection with the building of the site?

Part of the answer lies in the presence of the relics. But answers to other questions need to be located in the structures, sculptures and artefacts found not just in the Great Stupa complex but also in the surrounding Buddhist sites such as Sonari, Satdhara, Morel Khurd and Andher – all located within 10 kms of Sanchi.

Located in Madhya Pradesh's Raisen district, around 50 kms from the capital city of Bhopal and 10 kms from the ancient trading, religious and art hub of Vidisa (modern-day Vidisha), the Sanchi hilltop complex is famous for its stupas, pillars, temples, monasteries and sculptures. Declared a World Heritage Site in 1989, it remains a unique place to see the beginnings, efflorescence and decay of Buddhist art and architecture. In a way, it covers the entire span of Buddhism in the Gangetic plains and peninsular India.

Around the 6th–5th centuries BCE, or during the Buddha's time, Sanchi was part of the Akara mahajanapada in the western Malwa region. According to early votive inscriptions found at the site, Sanchi was known as Kakanava or Kakanaya in ancient times. A 5th-century CE inscription, belonging to the Gupta dynasty (c. 300–600 CE) and found on the main stupa, indicates the site was known as Kakanadabota. Inscriptional records from the late 7th century CE refer to Sanchi as Bota-Sriparvata.[2]

The Sanchi hilltop stupa complex remains one of India's best-preserved architectural sites. The current appearance owes a lot to the restoration efforts of John Marshall, the director-general of the ASI from 1912 to 1918. He also instituted one of the country's earliest site museums at Sanchi. Following a nomenclature practice set up by Marshall, most of the monuments are known by their numbers (1 to 50), rather than independent names. The main centre of attraction at Sanchi is Stupa 1, also known as the Great Stupa or the mahastupa. All other monuments are clustered around this structure, which also represents the earliest construction at the hilltop complex.

MONKS, DAMS AND POPULAR CULTS

Sanchi helps, but also complicates, our understanding of the spread of Buddhism outside the Gangetic valley. The presence of Ashokan structures means that by the 3rd century BCE Buddhist faith had moved out of its Gangetic heartland and spread into central India. This could have been possible because of the westward expansion of the Mauryan empire and the commensurate movements of monks from the middle Gangetic plains. The Buddhist faith in the middle of the plains, as discussed in Chapter 1, had strong links with flourishing urban centres and royal households like those of Kosala, Magadha and others. Later, under the patronage of Ashoka, it acquired roots in other parts of the Indian subcontinent.

Sanchi presents a slightly different story. It was neither a site actively patronized by royal households nor was it an urban centre. It was a rural hinterland of urban Vidisha. Now, Vidisha was located at the confluence of two rivers, Betwa and Bes, on the flourishing transregional highway linking Mathura (northern route) and Pataliputra (eastern route) to western and southern India. It comes across as a sprawling urban centre around the middle of the 1st millennium BCE. Vidisha was also known for the prevalence of the Bhagavata cult, an early form of Vaishnavism. Greek ambassador Heliodorus, a bhagavata and worshipper of Hindu god Vasudeva-Krishna, erected a pillar in the town in the 2nd century BCE. The pillar is now known as *Khamba Baba*, the 'Pillar Saint'. Later, Vidisha became an important centre of art, producing some of the finest art works.

Sanchi did not experience proactive or sustained Mauryan patronage. Even the inscriptions found in the stupa complex do not support the idea of any direct or proactive imperial patronage, either of the Mauryas or of the dynasties that controlled the region later, like the Shungas or the Satavahanas. How did such an elaborate architectural exercise then become possible on the hilltop? Was Sanchi a part of a wider rural ecosystem, which offered sustained economic support to other Buddhist establishments in the region? Did Sanchi develop a network with other ritual and habitational settlements in the surrounding landscape? Some recent archaeological surveys and excavations (by Julia Shaw and others) have made it possible for us to answer such questions. Going beyond the hilltop stupa and the complex, which is how Sanchi has dominantly been understood, such surveys throw significant light on the surrounding socio-economic and ritual landscapes. Shaw and others study the wider archaeological landscape around the Sanchi hilltop complex, which consists of multiple Buddhist sites and settlements across an area of approximately 750 sq kms. And they do it with the help of modern scientific techniques like remote sensing, hydraulic studies, pollen analysis and geological dating. These surveys have revealed the existence of seventeen dams spread throughout the excavated area, which help us understand the urban sequence at Vidisha and the spread of Buddhist settlements at Sanchi and neighbouring sites.

The earliest of these dams were constructed around the 3rd and 2nd centuries BCE. Their construction coincided with the establishment of the earliest Buddhist monuments in Sanchi and its surrounding areas. The survey shows that the dams, and the reservoirs they created, helped agricultural and crop production, particularly rice, for the growing population in Vidisha's hinterlands. The dams built on slopes, such as those at Sanchi, acted as inundation tanks for upstream irrigation; those built in the deeper valleys facilitated downstream irrigation. These irrigation facilities were managed by the monks and the sangha. At Sanchi, and in the surroundings, the monks were engaged in an exchange network with the agricultural communities. The sangha provided 'practical services' like water for domestic use and agricultural improvement, which was considered crucial for the patronage of the non-monastic population. Such a situation finds a close parallel in the practice of monastic landlordism reported from Buddhist sites in Sri Lanka around the 2nd century BCE. The provision of such practical services also reflected an engagement with the faith's philosophical concern for human suffering and identifying means of its alleviation.[3] Such occurrences contradict the stereotypical view of the Buddhist monks as being exclusively involved in spiritual pursuits.

Sanchi and Bharhut (constructed around the same time) also question the wisdom on the role of monks in other aspects, for example, in the spread of the stupa cult. The Pali *Vinaya*, which is considered a book on the laws to be followed by monks, contains no section regarding their behaviour vis-à-vis the stupas. It was, therefore, assumed that the construction and worship of the stupas was the concern of the lay followers, not the monks or the sangha. In contrast, the donative inscriptions from Sanchi show that the monks and nuns were not only actively involved in setting up the stupas but also controlled and dominated the related cultic practice. Both at Sanchi and Bharhut, monks and nuns accounted for more than 40 per cent of the active donors. For example, of the ninety-three clear donative records found at Stupa 2 in Sanchi, forty-four are gifts of monks and nuns. These inscriptions record gifts of objects used for construction or embellishment of the stupas, such as coping stones, pavement slabs, railing pillars, crossbars, berm and stairway, and balustrades.[4] Likewise, as we shall see later, the monks also played an important role in the development of the relic cult – contrary again to the popular belief that relics were meant to be venerated by the lay followers.

The monks were not only involved with the relic cult and the setting-up of stupas (and images in the later centuries), but they also established connections with pre-existing popular local cults like those of the yakshas and yakshis, and nagas. These popular deities, connected with fertility and water, enjoyed a large following in the wider Sanchi area even before the arrival of Buddhist monks. Assimilating or appropriating them helped an 'external' Buddhist tradition strike 'internal' or local roots. Such deities became part of a wider Buddhist iconographic programme in the Sanchi area. The first anthropomorphic images of yakshas and nagas began to appear soon after the arrival of the monks. Around 1,000 fragments of sculptures of these popular deities (across sects) have been recovered from the area between the 3rd century BCE and 12th century CE.[5] The propitiation of the nagas served an additional purpose. The nagas were popularly known for their ability to cause environmental havoc, either by withholding monsoons or by causing excessive deluges. So, appeasing them played an important role in the monks' networking with the local agricultural communities. A good number of naga sculptures have been found across the wider Sanchi area, dating to the 1st century BCE and the 5th century CE. In most cases, these images are found close to, or on, top of dams or irrigation facilities managed by the monks, reiterating their links with water and agrarian production. These findings also tally with a later account of Chinese pilgrim Faxian, regarding the propitiation of nagas in the Gupta period. Faxian also suggested that the nagas were appeased within monastic compounds on account of their ability to ensure rainfall and agricultural success.[6]

THE ASHOKAN CONNECTION, ARTEFACTS AND LEGENDS

The earliest monuments in the Sanchi hilltop complex are the ones built by Mauryan emperor Ashoka in the 3rd century BCE. These include the core of Stupa 1, which was originally built in mud and brick, and a pillar found nearby. The stupa's floor occupies the same level as the quintessential finely polished sandstone pillar. The discovery of fragments of a chunar sandstone umbrella, bearing the characteristic mirror-like polish seen on Ashokan pillars also reiterates the Mauryan connection (Fig 7.1). This umbrella possibly stood on top of the original stupa. The Ashokan pillar at Sanchi originally consisted of a tapering monolithic shaft adorned by four lions. While the stump of the monolithic pillar still lies in situ (Fig 7.6), its lion capital is now exhibited in the site museum. The pillar carries an Ashokan edict identical to the one found at Sarnath, warning monks and nuns against schisms in the Buddhist community. The pillar was later broken into several pieces by a local zamindar who thought the structure could be used for pressing sugarcane.

Why did Ashoka choose Sanchi? We discussed in Chapter 2 that the Mauryan emperor had earmarked sites associated with the Buddha for the benefit of future pilgrims. The Pali canon credits him with the erection of stupas in different parts of his empire. In his zeal to spread Buddhism, Ashoka is said to have opened seven out of the eight original mud stupas containing the bodily relics of the Buddha and got them redistributed and enshrined in the stupas he built. According to a legend, he constructed around 84,000 stupas all over northern India and parts of what is now Nepal, Pakistan, Bangladesh and Afghanistan. In the process, Ashoka also laid the foundations for Stupa 1 at Sanchi. The presence of the 'schism edict' on the Ashokan pillar points to the possible existence of a monastic establishment in the region, even before the pillar was set up. The finding of seventeen dams and related irrigational structures in and around Sanchi indicates that these monastic establishments had an active network with the surrounding agricultural communities. The Pali canon also attributes Ashoka with sending out Buddhist missions to different parts of his empire and neighbouring Sri Lanka after the conclusion of the Third Buddhist Council. While the credentials of the said council are yet to be established historically, relic inscriptions found in other stupas in the wider Sanchi region confirm the presence of the Hemavata group of Buddhist monks. Interestingly, relics found in Stupa 2 in Sanchi include those of Hemavata teachers like Kassapagota and Majjhima. These two teachers are also mentioned in the Pali text *Dipavamsa*, as part of a Buddhist mission to the Himalayan (Hemavata) region after the conclusion of the third council.[7] These Hemavata monks seem to have arrived in Vidisha in the 2nd century BCE. The inscriptions indicate that they soon took control of the existing Buddhist sites, like Sanchi and Satdhara, and renovated them. They also built new establishments at Sonari, Morel Khurd and Andher.[8]

Ashoka's connection with Sanchi is popularly known through the legend of Devi, the daughter of a wealthy merchant from Vidisha. He is said to have married Devi while serving as the governor of Ujjayini (modern-day Ujjain). Sri Lankan Pali chronicles, *Mahavamsa* and *Dipavamsa*, the only early Buddhist texts which refer to Sanchi, mention that Mahendra, the son of emperor Ashoka and Devi, while heading to Sri Lanka as a missionary, halted in Vidisha to pay a visit to his mother. Devi is believed to have taken him to the beautiful monastery of Vedisagiri, which she had built.[9] Scholars believe this monastery could have been one of the structures in the Sanchi hilltop complex. Interestingly, one of the monasteries on the western slope, called Monastery 51, is popularly attributed to Devi. The guides taking tourists around the site talk about this story in detail.

RELICS AS A LIFE FORCE AND THE HILLTOP STUPAS

Why was the Great Stupa located on a hilltop? A short answer to this question is that the location enabled people in the surrounding areas to continuously experience the presence of the Buddha and 'see' him as well. In the post-Buddha period, the stupas were no longer seen as simple burial mounds. It came to be believed that the enshrining of the relics of the Buddha and prominent monks inside such structures 'charged' and magnified their ritual significance. And the Great Stupa is believed to contain the relics of the Buddha. The development of the relic cult contributed to the process of the ritualization of the stupas – seeing them was considered equivalent to 'seeing' and 'worshipping' the Buddha, or the monks whose relics were enshrined inside them. The relic was thought to be impregnated with the characteristics that defined and animated the living Buddha.[10] Even the monasteries, which emerged later around these stupas, were laid out in a way that they did not hamper the monks' view of the latter. The visual prominence of the stupa, therefore, projected the living presence of the Buddha, the dharma and the sangha into the surrounding areas, contributing to the process of proselytization of the faith. This was not just true of the Sanchi main stupa but other stupas in the region as well. Intervisibility of the stupas was also important, so it was possible to see other stupas in the neighbouring areas – such as those at Morel Khurd, Andher, Sonari and Satdhara – from the Great Stupa at Sanchi.

The growing importance of the relic cult manifested in the architecture of Sanchi in other ways as well. One of the sculptural panels on the Great Stupa depicts the 'war of relics', which followed the death of the Buddha (Fig 2.1, Chapter 2). We have already discussed this story in Chapter 2, but let us briefly recollect. After the Buddha's death, the Mallas of Kushinagar guarded his cremated remains that were kept in their council hall. Soon, seven other competing political entities came to ask for their share of the relics. They were refused. A conflict seemed imminent when a Brahman mediated and pacified the parties. The 'war of relics' scene is also depicted in sculptural panels at Bharhut, Amravati and Gandhara. The relics made the stupas special, sacred structures. As discussed in the opening paragraph of this chapter, taking away the property of the stupa amounted to committing 'five sins' that had immediate retribution. Four of these five sins dealt with harming living persons of rank. The stupa was, by association, understood and classified as a 'living person of rank'.[11] The ritual and political efficacy of the relics meant that they had to be guarded or protected against theft, especially during times of turmoil. Many stupa sites started having fortifications – boundary walls with bastions and towers. Examples of these include the eastern edge of the Sanchi hill and Building 43, both belonging to the 10th–11th centuries CE.[12]

STUPAS 1, 2 AND 3, AND THE MAKING OF THE COMPLEX

The monuments at Sanchi can be divided into two broad groups: those located on the hilltop and those on the western slope. The hilltop monuments can be further divided into those located on the main terrace and those in the eastern or southern areas, all bound by a stone circuit wall (see site map).[13]

The main terrace contains several monuments around Stupa 1, which have evolved over a long period of time. The latter, representing the earliest known phase of construction at the Sanchi hilltop complex, remains the principal attraction. The Great Stupa measures 36.8 m (120.7 ft) in diameter and 71 ft (21.64 m) in height from the ground level to the stone umbrellas on top. Currently, the restored structure consists of a hemispherical mound or dome, called *anda*, built over a relic chamber believed to contain the cremated remains of the Buddha. Interestingly, the neighbouring Stupa 3 was found to contain bodily remains of the Buddha's immediate disciples Sariputra and Maudgalyayana. The dome of the Great Stupa has a truncated and flattened top that supports a square chamber, the *harmika*. This chamber contains a central pillar, *yasthi*, crowned by a parasol or three-stone umbrella formation, the *chattravali*. The parasol marks the specific spot where the relics rested in the heart of the stupa (Fig 7.2). It was supposed to mark the relics or indicate the presence of the Buddha, the 'spiritual sovereign', the same way that parasols signify the presence of a monarch or deity. The stupa has two circumambulatory passages. The first passage is an elevated

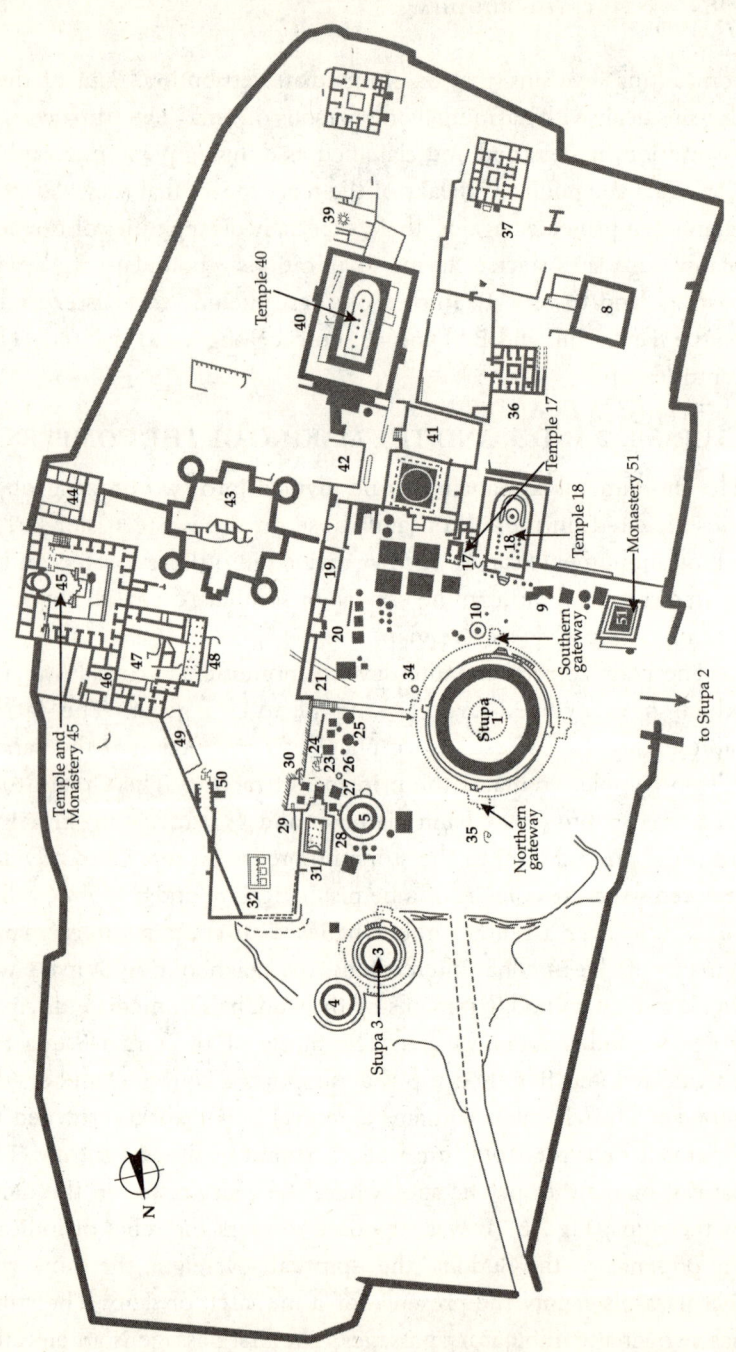

Site map of Sanchi Hilltop Complex (after Debala Mitra, *Sanchi*, 2003)

terrace (*medhi*) enclosing the dome. It has a massive three-bar railing or balustrade (*vedika*) and is accessed by a flight of stairs on either side of the southern gateway. The second circumambulatory passage is on the ground and surrounds the dome; it is the pradakshinapatha. The stupa lies within a stone enclosure with a three-bar railing having four carved gateways (*toranas*) in the four cardinal directions. The ground balustrade, or vedika, in turn consists of stone uprights (*stambha* or *thaba*), horizontal crossbars (*suchi*) and copings (ushnisha), most of which have inscriptions mentioning the name of the donors. The three umbrella-like formations on the central pillar symbolize the 'three jewels', the triratna of Buddhism – the Buddha, dharma and the sangha.

Like the other structures surrounding it, the Great Stupa evolved and was embellished over centuries, between the 3rd century BCE and the 6th–7th centuries CE. During the Mauryan period, around the 3rd century BCE, the core of the stupa was built with mud and fired bricks. It was probably surrounded by a wooden fence with gateways at the four cardinal points. The next major construction or renovations happened in the post-Mauryan period, under the Shunga dynasty. The Shungas were the immediate successors of the Mauryas, who held sway over this region during the 2nd–1st centuries BCE. Literary evidence credits them with reviving Brahmanical sacrifices and building Hindu temples. The Shungas are also believed to have persecuted the Buddhists and destroyed their sites. One popular tradition holds that Pushyamitra, the founder of the Shunga dynasty, destroyed the main stupa at Sanchi. On the other hand, another legend credits his son, Agnimitra, with giving it a facelift. It must be clarified that there is no direct evidence of any attack on the stupas by the Shungas. It is also important to bear in mind that the Bharhut stupa, regarded as a magnificent example of Buddhist art and architectural heritage, was erected in central India during the Shunga period. In fact, the monastery at Kaushambi also came into existence at this time.[14] So, while literary evidence may project the Shungas as pro-Hindus and anti-Buddhists, archaeological findings from Sanchi, Bharhut and Kaushambi contest this assumption. For Sanchi, the Shunga period brought the stone encasing and enlargement of the stupa built by

Ashoka. Shunga constructions at the site include a stone terrace with stairways, a stone pavement and the square-shaped harmika with the triple umbrella-like formation on the top. Balustrades were also erected around the terrace, the berm or rim of the stupa and the circumambulatory passage on the ground. Fine-quality sandstone from the Nagori hills was used for the railings and crowning umbrellas. Finally, new stupas like Stupa 2 (on the western slope) and Stupa 3 (on the hilltop) were also constructed.

Stupa 3, located just 45 m from Stupa 1, is much smaller (8.23 m in height and 15 m in diameter) and more hemispherical. It has a stairway, a rim railing (also known as berm), a harmika railing and a single umbrella on the top – all built during the 2nd century BCE (Fig 7.3). The ground railing is in ruins, with only the uprights surviving. It has only one carved gateway, which was built later. Stupa 2, located on the base of the western slope, is like Stupa 3 but does not have a berm, a stairway balustrade, a surmounting umbrella, or even a gateway. Its ground balustrade is richly decorated with plant and animal motifs, both real and mythological. These include stags with elephant heads, lions with human faces, women with horse heads, besides birds, fish, human figures and demigods such as nagas, yakshas, yakshis, and kinnars. It is from this stupa that relics of some monks belonging to the Hemavata group, of the Third Buddhist Council fame, were recovered. However, the relics found in Stupa 2 go beyond those of the monks associated with this council. They contain relics of at least three generations of teachers or monks. This means that, by the 2nd century BCE, relics of not just the Buddha and his immediate disciples but also those of other monks were worshipped.[15] The inscriptions at Stupa 3 also indicate that donations for the stupas of the local monastic dead had also become prevalent. Seen in the larger context, inscriptional evidence from Buddhist sites like Sanchi, Sonari, Andher, Mathura, Amravati, Bedsa, Bhaja and Kanheri indicates that the relics of the local monastic dead were permanently housed in a significant number of monastic sites in the early centuries of the Christian era. Further, the remains of the local monastic dead were treated and enshrined in the same way as the relics of the Buddha.[16]

The next prominent architectural phase at Sanchi was during the 1st century CE, when the Satavahana dynasty, which had extended its sway over eastern Malwa, constructed the elaborately carved gateways to Stupa 1 and Stupa 3. The Satavahanas claimed Brahmanical status and controlled a large empire in central and western India, and the Deccan, with the capital at Pratisthan (present-day Paithan near Aurangabad). They also developed trade and commerce networks. Unlike Stupa 3, which has only one gateway, Stupa 1 has four gateways in the four cardinal directions. These are identical in conception and design – each gateway has two square pillars connected by three curved architraves or moulded beams. The pillars are topped by capitals, while the architraves have spiral scrolls at the end. An inscription on the top architrave of the southern gateway of Stupa 1 records that it was a gift from Ananda, the royal architect of King Satakarni, identified as Satakarni II of the Satavahana dynasty. The king's coins have been found in the Malwa region, or the western part of Madhya Pradesh. It may be relevant to add here that the early group of Ajanta caves were also carved during the reign of the Satavahanas.

Around 150 CE, the Satavahanas were displaced by the Shaka-Kshatrapas, who started as governors of the Kushanas, ruling from Mathura, but later assumed independence and ruled from Ujjain. The Shaka-Kshatrapas were displaced by the Gupta rulers around the late 4th or early 5th century CE, when Chandragupta II established control over Malwa. One of the inscriptions dated 412–13 CE on the balustrade of Stupa 1 mentions this.

The Gupta period saw some architectural additions at Sanchi, including temples, monasteries and smaller stupas, besides images. Sanchi's demand for Buddha images was largely met by Mathura, made evident by the discovery of some Mathura sandstone images in the complex executed in the early Gupta style. This indicates that, even in the 4th century CE, Mathura continued to cater to such demands. Some of the pedestals, which once carried images and are now displayed in Sanchi Archaeological Museum, also attest to the practice of Buddhist images being imported from Mathura in the Kushana period. The Gupta period saw the installation of four Buddha images against the rim/berm of Stupa 1 at the four entrances (Fig 7.4).

An inscription on the ground balustrade of the Great Stupa tells us that this happened before 450–51 CE, made possible by an endowment of a female lay worshipper named Harisvamini for the Buddhist community of Kakanadabota (as Sanchi was known then).[17]

Buildings continued to be constructed around the Great Stupa on the main terrace and other parts of the larger stupa complex. In the next section on gateways and sculptures, we will see how temples and monasteries continued to be constructed during the 7th–8th centuries. There is also evidence of images and artefacts belonging to the 10th–12th centuries. But for now, we let us turn our attention to one of the grandest art and architectural achievements of Sanchi – the carved gateways.

SCULPTED GATEWAYS AND ARCHITRAVES: MOTIFS AND NARRATIVE PANELS

The four gateways (toranas), installed in the four cardinal directions around the Great Stupa, constitute the most impressive artistic creation of its class in ancient India. All four gateways are identical in design and consist of two square pillars crowned by capitals. On top of the pillar capitals are three sculpted architraves with spiral, scroll-shaped ends (Fig 7.5). Although all four were built around the same time, the southern gateway was the first to be erected and formed the original entrance to the stupa. This is indicated by the location of the Ashokan pillar at this entrance, as also the landing of the stairway on that side (Fig 7.6).

The gateways are intricately carved both on the front and back, and even on the sides of the pillars.[18] The use of fine-quality whitish sandstone obtained from the nearby Udayagiri hills facilitated the process of carving and ornamentation. There are traces of red paint on the eastern gateway and on the balustrade, which indicate that they were painted at some point in the past. The carvings on the gateways stylistically resemble the ivory carvings belonging to the Satavahana period, which were excavated at Begram (ancient Kapisa) in Afghanistan. In fact, an inscription on the southern gateway at Sanchi mentions that it was executed by the ivory workers of Vidisha. It may not be unlikely that the original carvings were executed in wood and later translated in stone.

The carvings on the gateways, pillars and architraves show a variety of motifs and narrative panels, including the Bodhi tree, triratna, stupas, representations of the Buddha in various forms, the eight auspicious symbols (*ashtamangalakas*), the wish-fulfilling creeper (*kalpalata*) or wish-fulfilling tree (*kalpavriksha*), besides figures of animals, humans and mythical creatures. They depict episodes and miracles from the Buddha's life and stories of his previous lives, as told in the Jataka tales. In the Jatakas, the Buddha was often born as an animal or bird who ended up teaching lessons of compassion and morality. Among the human or mythical figures, a mention may be made of horse riders, yakshas, yakshis or nymphs.

Yakshas and yakshis, as discussed earlier, reflected the accommodation of pre-Buddhist devotional cults. The figures of women holding branches of a fruit-laden tree (shalabhanjikas), which appear as decorative brackets between the pillars and the lowest architraves, also reflect the Buddhists' engagement with a popular fertility cult. Likewise, nagas have been depicted on several railings of Stupa 2. Even the popular Buddhist story of the subordination of the serpents of the fire temple of the Kasyapa brothers is depicted on one of the gateway panels of Stupa 1. Some reliefs also show devotees in Greek attire (Greek clothing and musical instruments) celebrating the stupa. This indicates that the practice of stupa worship had come into vogue. The scenes depicted on the single carved gateway of Stupa 3 are mostly those found on the four gateways of Stupa 1, except 'Indra's Paradise', which is a unique contribution of the former.[19]

The gateway carvings and embellishments were funded not by any royal enterprise but by common people, including men and women, family groups, village associations, and merchants and bankers of both Buddhist and Hindu leanings. Such donations (dana) were connected to the idea of earning spiritual and religious merit and gaining a fortunate birth in the next life – virtues sought by both Hindus and the Buddhists. An interesting feature of donations at Sanchi is the practice of collective gifts made by kin groups or lay followers and villages. The donative inscriptions also reflect an equal proportion of male and female donors.[20] Also striking is the fact that monks and nuns accounted for almost half the donations. The donors may have

Fig 7.1 Remains of the Ashokan Pillar

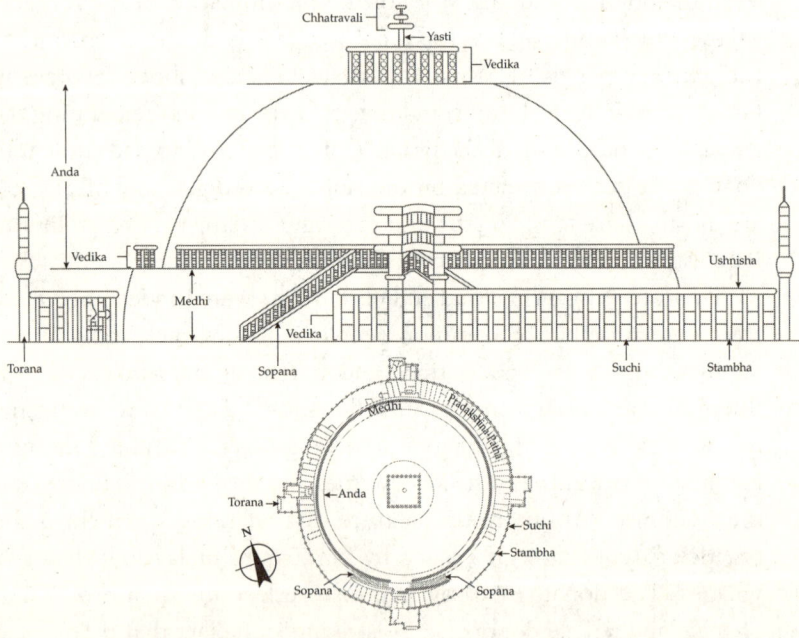

Fig 7.2 Plan of Stupa 1 at Sanchi (after Debala Mitra, *Buddhist Monuments*, 1971)

Fig 7.3 Stupa 3, which contained the relics of Sariputra and Maudgalyayana.

Fig 7.4 Buddha statue in dhyanmudra, on the berm facing eastern entrance.

Fig 7.5 Eastern Gateway, one of the four toranas located at the cardinal directions

Fig 7.6 The Southern Gateway, featuring a staircase leading to the terrace for circumambulation. The in-situ remains of the Ashokan Pillar can be seen to the right of the gateway.

Fig 7.7 Temple 18, built on an apsidal plan

Fig 7.8 Remains of Temple and Monastery 45

Fig 7.9 Remains of Monastery 51 in the background

Fig 7.10 Birla Planetarium in Kolkata, with a dome inspired by the Sanchi Stupa

requested their favourite stories to be carved on the panels and then have their names inscribed on them. This may explain why certain stories (such as the Buddha's 'Enlightenment', 'the Great Departure', 'Great Monkey Jataka') are repeated on the gateways.[21] Donative inscriptions at Sanchi also indicate that the donors not only came from neighbouring territories but also from regions like Rajasthan, Maharashtra and parts of north India. Like Bharhut, Sanchi had become an important place of pilgrimage even before the onset of the Christian era.

The architects of Sanchi used visual storytelling as a way of popularizing the Buddhist faith. This gave a historical dimension to the events in the Buddha's life. The artists at Sanchi used the technique of narrative reliefs to tell different stories; and these reliefs were filled with details of everyday life. In making them, the artists broke down the story into a series of episodes or scenes. Such stories could then be depicted through the monoscenic mode, where the focus is on a single identifiable episode or scene of a larger story.[22] These scenes appear both in the rectangular panels of the pillars and the architraves. The Chaddanta Jataka, depicted on the top architrave of the northern gateway, for instance, represents twenty elephants and a lotus-filled lake to tell the story. In the continuous narrative mode, such as the one employed in the depiction of the 'Great Departure' on the architrave of the eastern gateway (Fig 1.3, Chapter 1), the artists did not use frames to demarcate individual scenes. Instead, the story flows seamlessly across the available space. In addition to these two techniques, some rectangular gateway panels, such as the 'Great Monkey Jataka' depicted on the western gateway pillar, tell the story in five (or multiple) episodes without indicating a sequence or chronology. In the story-telling technique at Sanchi, the artists gave primacy to legibility – background reliefs were as large and clear as the ones on the front – than perspective. The absence of emotion on the faces of the sculptures is another artistic convention deployed here.

There is a debate among scholars on how the Buddha was represented in the sculptures in early Buddhist art, including those at Sanchi and Bharhut. Some hold that the Buddha was depicted in emblems or symbols, or aniconic forms such as footprints, wheels, empty thrones and a canopy under the Bodhi tree, rather than in a human or anthropomorphic form. They say that there was an artistic or unwritten convention around the 1st century BCE to depict the presence of the Buddha symbolically instead of a bodily form. But how could one depict the transforming radiance of the Buddha? It was also held that after more than 550 births, the Buddha had freed himself from the bond of the physical body.[23] Other scholars argue that aniconic emblems, including the empty throne, the wheel, the Bodhi tree or the stupa were not intended to serve as surrogates of the Buddha's images. Rather, they were intended to serve as sacred locations of the faith, visited by the lay followers sometime after the death of the Buddha. They represented practices of pilgrimage (tirtha) and devotion associated with the sites concerned. Several aniconic scenes at Sanchi – such as devout worshipers venerating a wheel – indicated the prevalence of such a practice that had emerged in Buddhism, rather than a substitution for the prohibited practice of creating a human Buddha. Further, it is relevant to understand here that the Buddha images were being produced at the same time as the so-called aniconic representations.[24]

SMALLER STUPAS, PILLARS, TEMPLES AND MONASTERIES

There are numerous stupas, pillars, monasteries and temples located around the main terrace, housing the Stupa 1, and in the surroundings.[25] Several free-standing pillars have been found at Sanchi, most of which now exist in fragments. The earliest of them, of course, is the chunar sandstone Pillar 10, which was erected by Ashoka and lies near the southern gateway. Pillar 35, near the northern gateway, belongs to the 5th century CE and had a figure of Vajrapani with a halo on the top. This pillar capital now lies in the site museum.

Many small stupas are still found across the main terrace around the north-east, south-east and south-west corners of the Great Stupa. Such stupas, in the vicinity of the main stupa, are also found in various Buddhist sites including Bodh Gaya, at the Dharmarajika stupa in Taxila, Mirpur Khas in Sindh, Nalanda, Paharpur and Ratnagiri in Odisha. Some of these smaller stupas show regional specifications, but most of them were commonly found to contain relic deposits such as bones and ashes of devout lay followers and indicate a strong funerary connection. Even the sites around Sanchi had a similar association. Excavations at Bhojpur, Sonari and Andher have revealed evidence of cemeteries as well as elaborate housing and worship of the monastic dead.[26]

In the past, there was a multitude of small stupas of varying sizes and shapes at Sanchi. Many of these were cleared in the operations that took place around 1881–83, when the ground around the main stupa was cleared up to 60 feet from its outer railing. Here, we can discuss some surviving ones, which are known through numbering. Stupa 4 dates to the 1st century BCE, while Stupa 5, with an image of the Buddha in dhyan mudra, belongs to the 6th century CE. Stupa 6 was originally constructed in the 2nd century BCE, but it was repaired in the 7th–8th centuries CE. Stupas 12 to 16 are arranged in two rows near Temple 17, and most of them contain small relic chambers. Stupa 12 has a Mathura red sandstone image of Bodhisattva Maitreya, belonging to the 1st–2nd centuries CE, gifted by the daughter of one Vishakula. Stupa 14 also has a Mathura red sandstone image belonging to the 5th century, but it is of the Buddha styled in the Gupta tradition. Stupas 28 and 29 are located near Temple 31 and are assigned to the 5th century, or the Gupta period. Interestingly, many Buddha statues have been found buried in the stupas at Sanchi.

Temples belonging to different periods, starting with the 2nd century BCE, are also found on the main terrace at Sanchi. The earlier structural temples, belonging to the Shunga period, were mostly apsidal in plan. Squarish temples began to be built at Sanchi during the Gupta period. In the early centuries of the Christian era, images of the Buddha began to be enshrined in Buddhist temples. Temples had started making an appearance. The worshipping of the bodhisattvas in the form of images in shrines also reflected the impact of Mahayana Buddhism and the devotional cults at Sanchi. Of the temples, Temple 18 and Temple 17 are particularly important. Temple 18 is built on a raised platform and is apsidal in plan, like the Buddhist rock-cut temples of Bhaja and Karle (Fig 7.7). It consists of a central nave, which is a rectangular hall in the front, an apse in the rear and side aisles. The pillars are very high (5.18 m) with a square shaft and octagonal necking. The inner doorway has figures of river goddesses Ganga (identified by her vehicle and crocodile) and Yamuna. These once-Brahmanical goddesses begin to appear on the doorways of Buddhist temples from the Gupta period. The three different floors of the temple belong to the Maurya, Shunga and later Gupta periods. Temple 17, built around the 5th century CE, is a flat-roofed structure with a front portico supported by four pillars. The entrance doorway has floral patterns, and the door jams have images of Ganga and Yamuna. The shrine has no image now, but Lieutenant Frederick C. Maisey, who excavated the site in the 19th century, had reported the presence of an early medieval-style Buddha image seated on a lotus throne, supported by lions and inscribed with Buddhist mantras.

Some monuments are located on a slightly higher plateau, opposite the eastern gateway of Stupa 1. These include Monastery 46 (built in the 11th century CE, over the foundations of the 6th century CE), Monastery 47 (which has cells on three sides and Gupta-period sculptures) and Temple and Monastery 45, alongside many other structures simply known as 'buildings'. Temple and Monastery 45 (Fig 7.8) has charred remains of a temple belonging to the 7th–8th centuries CE, over which another temple with a double-storeyed shikhara was built in the 10th century CE. The sanctum of the later temple has yielded an image of the Buddha in bhumisparsha mudra, seated on a double lotus, dating to the 10th century CE. Images of the Buddha in dhyan mudra; Bodhisattva Manjushri seated on a lotus with his peacock; and Vajrasattva, a rare deity belonging to the Vajrayana school, have also been found in the temple with a host of other deities. The presence of Ganga and Yamuna on the doorway of the shrine alongside the image of Kubera (the god of wealth) reflects the Brahmanical influences. The monastery attached to this temple follows the regular plan of an open courtyard with cells around it.

The plateau area south of Stupa 1 also has some important buildings like Temple 40 and Monasteries 36, 37 and 38. Temple 40 is the earliest temple at Sanchi, perhaps contemporaneous with the Ashokan pillar. Originally an apsidal structure, it has two entrances and shows three phases of construction – Mauryan period, or the 3rd century BCE; 2nd century BCE, or the Shunga period; and the

7th–8th centuries CE, or the early medieval times. Monasteries 36, 37 and 38 were also built during the early medieval period and follow the regular plan of cells arranged around an open, central courtyard.

Finally, two important structures are located in the other part of the stupa complex, the western slope. These include Stupa 2, which we discussed earlier, and Monastery 51. Monastery 51 follows the regular plan of an open courtyard surrounded by cells (Fig 7.9). Twenty-two cells were discovered here along with a giant monolithic stone bowl.

DECLINE, REDISCOVERY AND MODERN AFTERLIVES

The post-Gupta period is considered one of gradual decline of Buddhism in India.[27] Several monasteries and temples were, however, erected at Sanchi till the 12th century CE. For example, Monastery 46 was built as late as the 11th century. Likewise, temples (such as Temple 45) continued to be built here as late as the 10th century; images of the Buddha were also being installed. The presence of the images of Vajrasattva, Tara and Marichi in the stupa complex, belonging to the 12th century CE, point to the influence of Vajrayana tradition at Sanchi during this time. However, no Buddhist monuments have been found at the site, which could be dated to the 13th century or later. We are uncertain about how the decline came about, but various explanations have been offered. Possibly, the site was abandoned by the Buddhists. Possibly, a Brahmanical revival pushed the Buddhists aside. Several Brahmanical plaques, which include representations of Vishnu, Ganga and Mahishasura Mardini, belonging to the 13th century CE, can be seen at the site museum. Some even ascribe the decline to Muslim invasions.

After the 13th century, we don't hear anything substantive about Sanchi till the beginning of the 19th century. In 1818, British officer General Taylor rediscovered the site and brought it back into visibility. Soon, the rich sculptures and carvings of the Sanchi complex started attracting amateur archaeologists and treasure hunters, some of whom ravaged the site. In 1822, Captain Johnson (assistant political agent in the Bhopal Durbar) opened Stupa 1 from top to bottom on one side, causing a great breach resulting in the collapse of the western gateway and a part of the enclosing balustrade. Some years later, in 1851, Alexander Cunningham, together with Captain Maisey, excavated the stupa complex. They sank a shaft down the centre of Stupa 1 but failed to retrieve any relics. However, they found the relic caskets of Sariputra and Maudgalyayana in Stupa 3, which eventually found their way to British museums. We will return to the story of these relics in the last section. For now, we will confine our discussion to the modern afterlives of the Sanchi stupa.

That the Great Stupa had become an architectural prototype in South, Southeast and East Asia is well-known. What is relatively less known is how the stupa continued to be reproduced in several representations of India's and Buddhism's past in modern times. It has had multiple sacred and secular afterlives. The monument repeatedly lent itself to copying and reproduction, which served a variety of functions including display, commemoration, nation-building, identity politics, etc.[28] The story of the stupa's modern afterlife probably began with Lieutenant Frederick Maisey's drawings of the gateway bas-reliefs in 1860s. These later appeared as tinted lithographs in a book in 1892. This first visual imaging was followed up by a richly illustrated volume on the Sanchi and Amravati stupas, called *Tree and Serpent Worship* (1868) by architecture scholar James Fergusson. In the 1870s, a full-sized plaster cast of the eastern gateway of the Great Stupa was displayed in the architectural courts of South Kensington Museum in United Kingdom (which was renamed as the Victoria and Albert Museum in 1899), alongside similar reproductions of the carved pillars of the Qutb mosque in Delhi and the Ibadat Khana of Fatehpur Sikri. There was also a plan to physically remove two of the actual gateways to London. In the 1850s, Alexander Cunningham had recommended the transfer of two of Stupa 1's standing gateways to the British Museum, where they were to form the 'most striking objects in the Hall of Indian Antiquities'. The political agent to the Bhopal Durbar even tried to persuade the Begum of Bhopal to send one of the gateways as a gift to Queen Victoria. And in the 1860s, there was a demand from the French Consul General in India to gift one of these gateways to Emperor Napoleon for installation at the Paris International Exhibition in 1867. Thankfully, none of these plans materialized.

From the 1880s, photographic images began to take the legacy of Sanchi forward. Two names worth mentioning here are those of Lieutenant Henry Hardy Cole, son of Henry Cole, who was the superintendent of the South Kensington Museum, and Indian photographer Lala Deen Dayal of Indore. Their photographs of Sanchi were reproduced on several forums. Later, a collection of photographs was published in James Burgess's monumental volume *The Ancient Monuments, Temples and Sculptures of India* published in London in 1897. John Marshall's three-volume monograph, *The Monuments of Sanchi* (which he authored along with Alfred Foucher and N. G. Majumdar), published in 1940, was another ambitious exercise. In the later colonial period, when New Delhi, the new capital of the British, was being planned, the Sanchi grille – the dome and balustrade railing of Sanchi – was deployed as a symbol of India's architectural past on the terrace of the Viceroy's House, which was designed on neo-classical lines. After India's independence, the Viceroy's House became the Rashtrapati Bhawan (the office and residence of the President of India).

The Great Stupa, particularly its hemispherical mound with its balustrade railing, also became a favoured classical architectural form for many official and non-official public buildings in the post-Independence period. Such reproductions are seen in the M. P. Birla Planetarium building in Calcutta (Fig 7.10), constructed in the 1960s, and the monuments built by former Uttar Pradesh chief minister Mayawati in the 1990s and 2000s in Lucknow.[29] Named Ambedkar Udyan (later Ambedkar Samajik Parivartan Sthal), the latter group of monuments are directly linked to the identity politics of the Dalits, a phenomenon discussed in detail in chapter 6. Imageries of Sanchi can be seen in several buildings associated with the Dalits, including the dome of Deekshabhoomi at Nagpur and carved gateways erected at Dr Ambedkar National Memorial in Delhi (the site of Ambedkar's death) (Fig 11.3 and Fig 11.4, Chapter 11).

The architectural form of Sanchi also travelled to the distant Buddhist monastic site of Luoyang in central China's Henan province, where a full-scale replica of the Great Stupa has become a symbol of official cultural exchange between the Indian and

Chinese governments. The site chosen for this new replica was the now-extinct Baima Si (White Horse temple), the oldest Buddhist monastery of China (and the cradle of Buddhism in China), dating to the 1st century BCE. The replica was installed to commemorate the arrival of Buddhism in China. According to a legend, two Indian Buddhist monks, carrying sacred texts, had arrived at this site on white horses.[30] More recently, the Sanchi stupa has become a prominent icon for tourism campaigns by both the state (Madhya Pradesh) and central governments, especially those aimed at attracting international tourists, reiterating, as such campaigns often do, India's status as the homeland of Buddhism.

HOW THE SANCHI RELICS WERE BROUGHT BACK FROM ENGLAND

In 1849, Lieutenant Fred C. Maisey was deputed by the colonial government to prepare illustrated reports on the stupas of Sanchi, their sculptures and inscriptions. He was soon joined by Alexander Cunningham, a known name in archaeology in India, who was keen on excavating the stupas with the idea of reconstructing an account of the historical Buddha. In 1851, they found relic caskets inscribed with the names Sariputra and Maudgalyayana in Stupa 3, located right next to Stupa 1. The relic caskets of the saints were found in two stone boxes. Sariputra's relic box contained the steatite casket; a small bone fragment; beads of garnet, lapis lazuli, crystal and pale amethyst; along with a flat pearl and two small seed pearls. It also had two pieces of sandalwood, presumably from his funeral pyre. The steatite casket of Maudgalyayana only held two small bone fragments. A similar set of relics of the two saints was found enshrined in Stupa 2 in nearby Satdhara as well.

Who were these two Buddhist saints? How did their relics reach Sanchi? Sariputra and Maudgalyayana were Brahmans who were close disciples of the Buddha. Both had reportedly died near Rajagriha during the lifetime of the Buddha. Their remains had been interned in the stupas built in the region. Based on his reading of the accounts of Chinese pilgrims Faxian (399–411 CE) and Xuanzang (629–41 CE), who had visited sites related to the Buddha, Cunningham concluded that the relics of these two saints were also enshrined in a stupa in Mathura. According to him, the relics of the Buddha's close disciples were as widely scattered as those of the Buddha himself; they were enshrined in several stupas and worshipped. What is not clear is how the relics in question reached Sanchi. In Cunningham's understanding, Mauryan emperor Ashoka was responsible for this.

What did Cunningham and Maisey do with the relics and caskets of Sariputra and Maudgalyayana? Well, it is held that they divided the finds according to their tastes –Cunningham preferred the relics with inscriptions, which were of archaeological interest; Maisey took the pieces that were of greater artistic value. Soon after, Cunningham transported his caskets to England on two ships, one of which reportedly sank near Jaffna. Maisey made separate arrangements for the caskets in his possession to be shipped to England.[31]

There is a debate among scholars about whether the caskets of the two Buddhist saints, which were returned to the Maha Bodhi Society for re-enshrinement in the purpose-built Chetiyagiri Vihara, had been discovered at Sanchi or Satdhara. We do not have any after-account of the relics and caskets found by Cunningham at Sanchi. Some scholars hold that they drowned with the ship. On this basis, they say that the only relics of Sariputra and Maudgalyayana that were left with Cunningham were those found in Stupa 2 at Satdhara. These were later re-enshrined at Sanchi.[32]

Letters and records related to the filing and documentation of the relics of Sariputra and Maudgalyayana at London's Victoria and Albert Museum, which eventually returned the relics to the Maha Bodhi Society in February 1947, tell a different story.[33] According to these records, the returned relics were a part of Maisey's collection from Sanchi, initially lent to the South Kensington Museum in 1866. They remained there on loan till 1921, when Dorothy Saward, the then inheritor of Maisey's collection, sold the relics and caskets to the Victoria and Albert Museum for a peppercorn amount of £250. According to the museum's records, this collection consisted of eight objects, including relics caskets of the two saints, obtained by Maisey from Buddhist stupas in Bhilsa district in 1851.

Given this, it is held that the relics eventually brought back to India in 1947 were neither a part of Cunningham's collection nor were they found at Satdhara. Instead, they were a part of Maisey's collection from Sanchi. But these could be obtained only after a protracted battle lasting several years, one that involved museum authorities, British Buddhists, the Maha Bodhi Society, the British and Indian governments and the Bhopal Durbar.[34] In this battle, the 'historical' and 'sacred' value of the relics were pitted against each other, just like discourses on 'museum custodianship' and 'devotional rights'.[35]

One of the first ones to demand the relics was the Bhopal Durbar, which initiated moves with the colonial government for the return of the Sanchi relics as early as 1919–20. The Begum of Bhopal had forcefully asserted her right to conserve and protect Sanchi, which lay within the dominions of the Bhopal Durbar. Incidentally, the durbar had also patronized and supported British surveys and excavations at Sanchi and the setting-up of Marshall's site museum. Soon, other candidates jumped into the fray. On 17 April 1932, one G. A. Dempster, acting on behalf of the Buddhist Mission (the British Maha Bodhi Society), wrote to the authorities of the Indian Museum at Kensington. The Indian section of the South Kensington Museum was officially opened in 1880 and was popularly referred to as Indian Museum till 1945. Dempster requested them to hand over the ashes of the Buddha's most famous disciples to the Mulagandhakuti Vihara in Sarnath, near Varanasi. In Britain, there had been recent news about the return of some of the Buddha's relics to India, which had been re-enshrined in a purpose-built edifice in Sarnath. Dempster's letter stated that the British Buddhists had also contacted the British Museum regarding other relics. When the Indian Museum authorities contacted their counterparts at the British Museum, they were told that the latter was 'precluded by law' to return any such object, and that such relics were kept with 'due care and respect'. Both museums remained opposed to the demand of repatriation of the objects, even the sacred ones, as they feared that 'once the trickle started, it may well become a flood', that the return of the relics would encourage more such claims. Dempster's request was declined.[36]

By October 1932, the story of the relics had taken a new turn. On 18 October, E. W. Adikaram, the honorary secretary of the Buddhist Mission, approached the Indian section of the Victoria and Albert Museum with a request to allow the Buddhists to worship the relics on 13 November, which happened to be the 2,476th death anniversary of Sariputra. He asked for the relics to be sent to the Buddhist Mission headquarters for a few hours on the designated day. The museum authorities acceded to the request on some conditions, which included that the relics could only be venerated at the Indian Museum.

After a seven-year gap, in 1938, the Indian Section of the Victoria and Albert Museum received a letter from a British Buddhist named Frank R. Mellor, requesting the museum to set up seats in front of the relics to enable the Buddhists to worship them. Mellor's request was denied. He followed it up with a flurry of letters demanding that the relics be returned to the Buddhists. Interestingly, in March 1939, the trustees of the Shwedagon Pagoda in Burma also lodged a strong protest with the British government for allowing the relics to be exhibited in a museum rather than enshrining them in a pagoda. Soon, there were similar representations from other British Buddhists. British journalists were attracted to the agitation that was building up.

In 1939, the Victoria and Albert Museum received a letter from the India Office (a British government department in London established to oversee administration of the provinces of India, through a viceroy and other officials) that, in turn, had received a letter from the Government of India, inquiring about the possession of such relics and the possibility of their return to the Maha Bodhi Society. This letter also enclosed a resolution unanimously passed by the Buddha Society of Bombay, appealing for the return of the relics to the Maha Bodhi Society of Calcutta. With this letter, the case assumed a new level of significance, as the Government of India had spoken on behalf of the Indian Buddhist organizations. The British Buddhists were sidelined. The museum authorities eventually, though reluctantly, agreed to hand over the relics to the India Office for transfer to the Maha Bodhi Society and to withdraw the relics from exhibition till the handover was executed. However, the process of handover was interrupted by the onset of the Second World War (1939–45), during which the hold of the British over India seemed to become untenable. During this period, the Bhopal Durbar continued to assert its ownership over Sanchi, demanding that the relics be housed in the Sanchi site museum, while the Maha Bodhi Society campaigned for the relics to be brought to a new vihara specially built at Sanchi.[37]

The relic handover process gained momentum again after the war. On 20 February 1947, the relics and caskets were handed over to Daya Hewavitarne, the representative of the Maha Bodhi Society appointed by the secretary of state for India. They were first carried to Ceylon, where they received a regal reception and were put on public display for two years. Soon, it was discovered that the caskets returned by the Victoria and Albert Museum were plaster copies of the originals. In June 1948, India's high commissioner to Britain wrote to the under-secretary of state of the Commonwealth Relations Office, asking for the return of the original caskets. On 8 October 1948, Sir D. N. Mitra, the Indian high commissioner's legal adviser, received the original caskets on behalf of the Government of India.

The prime minister of Ceylon handed over the relics to India's high commissioner in Colombo on 6 January 1949.[38] In a week, on 13 January, they were received on the naval vessel HMIS *Tir* by the then governor of Bengal, K. N. Katju. The occasion was marked by a state ceremony, which included a procession, guard of honour, cultural performances and a nineteen-gun salute. The return of the relics was treated as an occasion as important as the homecoming of the remains of the Buddha himself. They were installed in a temporary altar at the Government House (now called Raj Bhavan) in Calcutta, with Prime Minister Jawaharlal Nehru unveiling them before a gathering of diplomats, Buddhist monks and senior politicians. The following day, on 14 January, a grand reception ceremony was held at the Calcutta Maidan, during which Nehru handed over the sacred relics to Shyama Prasad Mukherjee, the president of the Maha Bodhi Society. In an evocative speech, Nehru highlighted the message of peace, goodwill and non-violence, which the Buddha and Gandhi also preached. After Calcutta, the relics were taken on a tour of South and Southeast Asia – Ladakh, Orissa, Bihar, Assam, Sikkim, Tibet, Nepal, Burma and Cambodia. They were brought back to Calcutta on 22 March

1951, from where they were taken by a special train for a tour across the country. In November 1952, the relics were finally re-enshrined at the Chetiyagiri Vihara (Fig 11.2, Chapter 11). The vihara was partly funded by the nawab of Bhopal, who also gave a piece of land for the construction of the vihara. Every year in November, a special fair is held at the spot where the relics are displayed in Sanchi.

As the journey of the relics of Sariputra and Maudgalyayana is relived, it offers us yet another opportunity to understand the larger connection of Buddhist sites with issues related to power politics, nationalism and religious revivalism. The story of the relics also signifies a power struggle between the politics of colonial archaeology and the museums and campaigns for international revival of Buddhism in Asia, led by the Maha Bodhi Society. Parallelly, the story also shows how the governments of Sri Lanka and India used the battle of relics to legitimize and consolidate the power of their state. For Nehru, the relics also suited his politics of projecting India as a secular, multireligious nation, especially after a communal partition.

Like Bodh Gaya, Sanchi also played a role in the building of diplomatic relations with the newly independent nations of Asia. In fact, parts of the returned relics were given to Sri Lanka and Burma, to be enshrined in Buddhist sites there.

8

AJANTA CAVES

This is the religious donation of the Sakyabhiksu Aparasaila ... for the attainment of Unexcelled Knowledge by [my] parents [and] all sentient beings.

This is what an English translation of an inscription in Cave 22 of the Ajanta complex reads like. Some scholars feel that it questions the ways in which the Ajanta caves and aspects of Buddhism have traditionally been understood. The caves excavated or carved out earlier are popularly known as the Hinayana caves, while those belonging to the later period are called Mahayana caves. We will discuss the details of this compartmentalization in the subsequent section, but for now let us confine ourselves to the three expressions in the translation: 'Aparasaila', 'Sakyabhikshu', and 'for the attainment of unexcelled knowledge by [my] parents [and] all sentient beings'. The term 'sakyabhikshu', scholars tell us, refers to a member of the Mahayana community who is also a monk. The expression about the attainment of unexcelled knowledge for the parents and all sentient beings is a formula, or tenet, related to the bodhisattva ideal of 'transfer of merit' and is popularly associated with the Mahayana tradition. Interestingly, the term 'aparasaila', used for the donor in this inscription, is unique to Ajanta. It refers to a member of one of the eighteen nikayas, or sects, typically associated with the Hinayana tradition.[1] So, this Ajanta inscription questions the rigidity of the use of the Hinayana–Mahayana divide in the study of Buddhism. Ajanta also questions several other assumptions and stereotypes regarding the way we conventionally understand the Buddhist faith and monks. Even the West struggled to accept that Buddhists, primarily devoted to spiritual pursuits, were also responsible for creating such exquisite paintings and sculptures.

Located 105 kms from Aurangabad, the city named after the controversial Mughal ruler Aurangzeb, are the famous Ajanta caves known worldwide for their iconic Buddhist murals. Aurangabad was recently renamed Chhatrapati Sambhaji Nagar, after a prominent Maratha leader executed by Aurangzeb, but the Buddhist caves in the city continue to be called the Aurangabad caves. Declared a World Heritage Site in 1983, the Ajanta caves present a unique coming together of sculpture, architecture and painting. Regarded as a masterpiece of Buddhist religious art, Ajanta throws light on the developments within Buddhism in the subcontinent, as well as everyday life, in early India.

The caves at Ajanta are carved out of an imposing vertical cliff above the left bank of the river Waghora, in the forests near Ajintha village, from which they get their name. They are aligned in a horseshoe form along the river (Fig 8.1). The numbering of the caves does not follow a chronological pattern but is based on the nomenclature used by the ASI (see site map). Out of the thirty caves at Ajanta, five are chaityagrihas, or prayer halls or shrines, with stupas (Caves 9, 10, 19, 26 and 29) and the remaining twenty-five are viharas, or monasteries, with cells meant to be the residence of the monks. Any cave that was discovered after the first thirty were identified by adding a suffix of a letter of the alphabet next to the number of the neighbouring cave, such as 15 A. Caves 3, 5, 14, 24, 28 and 29 were found in different stages of completion and provide insights into the architectural techniques employed for excavations. The floor levels of the caves vary – the one at the lowest level is Cave 8, while the one at the highest is Cave 29. A modern terraced path currently connects the caves, though remnants of ancient stairways can also be seen. Visitors to the site should know that the Ajanta caves are very dimly lit; they were originally meant to be experienced in the low light of lamps.

Site map of Ajanta Caves (after Percy Brown, *Indian Architecture, Buddhist and Hindu Period*, 1956)

HINAYANA OR MAHAYANA?

The Ajanta caves were excavated in two broad phases, spread over a period of 600–700 years, from around the 2nd century BCE to the 6th century CE. The first set of caves were excavated under the patronage of the Satavahanas (c. 2nd century BCE to 3rd century CE). Interestingly, the Satavahanas claimed descent from the Brahmans and culturally anchored themselves in the Brahmanical Vedic tradition. At the peak of their power, they exercised control over modern Andhra Pradesh, Maharashtra and parts of Karnataka, Madhya Pradesh and the Saurashtra region of Gujarat.[2] Caves excavated during the Satavahana period include 8, 9, 10 12, 13, 15 and 15A. They are located closer to the river Waghora. Of these, Caves 9 and 10 are prayers halls, while the rest are monasteries. It is popularly held that these early-period caves were executed by monks affiliated to the Hinayana school and are, therefore, called 'Hinayana' caves. The Hinayana monks are commonly believed to have represented and worshipped the Buddha in a symbolic form. They venerated relics and symbols associated with him, such as the Bodhi tree (symbolizing enlightenment), wheel (symbolizing first sermon), stupa (symbolizing death), etc. The Hinayana caves at Ajanta are known for their aniconic or symbolic representations of the Buddha in sculptures and paintings.

The second phase of excavations was carried out several centuries later, under the patronage of the Vakataka dynasty, particularly the Vakatakas of the Vatsagulma branch. The Vakatakas are said to have originated in the Vindhya region, north of the river Narmada, and gradually became a major political power in the Deccan region. Their rule lasted from around the mid-3rd century CE to the late 5th or early 6th centuries CE. The inscriptions describe the Vakatakas as Brahmans. They had matrimonial ties with several influential imperial dynasties, including the Guptas who patronized constructions at Nalanda. After the death of their second king, Pravarasena, the Vakataka empire split into at least two branches. Based on their political centres, these are known as the Padmapura-Nandivardhana-Pravarapura line and the Vatsagulma line. Vatsagulma has been identified with modern-day Washim in Akola district of Maharashtra, in the eastern Vidarbha region. Harishena was the last known king of the Vatsagulma line.³ Most caves at Ajanta were carved during his time. The inscriptions in Cave 16, and the nearby Ghatotkacha cave, were engraved at the behest of Harishena's minister Varahadeva, and the one in Cave 17 by one of his feudatories. Walter M. Spink, one of the foremost experts on Ajanta, argues that the caves belonging to the second phase were carved around the mid-5th century, over a brief period of twenty years, during the reign of King Harishena.

Under the Vakatakas, many of the earlier caves at Ajanta were expanded, refurbished, redecorated or repainted. Caves 9 and 10 have evidence of extensive repainting. Several new caves were excavated, too, including Caves 1 to 7, 11, 14, 16, 17, 18, 19, and 20 to 29. Of these, Caves 19, 26 and 29 are prayers halls, while the rest are monasteries.

The Vakataka period caves are popularly believed to be executed by monks affiliated to the later school of Buddhism (Mahayana), which is why they are known as the 'Mahayana' caves. The Mahayana school is commonly understood to have worshipped the Buddha and bodhisattvas in an anthropomorphic form, or as images.

The Hinayana–Mahayana distinction is not just limited to Ajanta. There has been a tendency in art and historical accounts to periodize and classify more than 1,000 Buddhist caves in western India into two distinct phases – the Hinayana phase, lasting from around the 2nd century BCE to the 3rd century CE; and the Mahayana phase, which began after a gap of 200 years. In the case of Ajanta, as we have seen, the gap between the two periods of excavations is more than 500 years. Some scholars even argue that the Ajanta caves occupy a unique position in Indian art and visually trace the development of Buddhist thought from the early, aniconic Hinayana phase through to the anthropomorphic Mahayana period.⁴ There is another layer of distinction inherent in the classification of the Buddhist faith in terms of yanas, or vehicles. It is held that after the death of the Buddha, the sangha split into eighteen nikayas on account of disputes over doctrine and monastic practices. Modern scholars see these nikayas such as Sthavira, Mahasanghikas, Sarvastivada, Sammatiya, Aparasaila, Chetika, etc., as a corporate group that emerged within the Hinayana tradition in contradistinction with the later Mahayana school. This watertight compartmentalization of the two schools sometimes limits our understanding of the development of Buddhist faith.

It must be clarified that the categories of Hinayana and Mahayana were more fluid and overlapping than has been made out to be. The assumption that the image cult was related to the Mahayana school is neither correct nor based on available evidence. Recent research indicates that, in general, almost all sects of the Hinayana school were actively interested in images and the cult of images, just like the Mahayanists. It has also been pointed out that the monks promoting the image cult from the 4th to the 5th centuries at Sarnath, Mathura and Ajanta were predominantly affiliated to the Mahayana school, while those connected with the same cult at Shravasti, Kaushambi, etc. for the same period, were not.[5] In the case of Ajanta, as we shall discuss later, the paintings and pictorial subjects in the so-called Mahayana caves relate to the form of stories that lie within the tradition of Hinayana Buddhism. Likewise, an inscription found with a Buddha image on a pillar in Cave 10 (assigned to the 5th–6th century period) or the 'Mahayana' phase mentions the word *chetika* (*cetika* in Pali). It is argued that the donor of the image belonged to the chetika nikaya, one of the sects of the Hinayana school. The cave's iconography is also held to reflect the chetika doctrine. Finally, as we saw at the start of this chapter, Cave 22 has an inscription that relates to both the Hinayana and the Mahayana schools.[6]

MONKS AS IMAGE DONORS AND OBLIGED SONS

Like Bodh Gaya and Sanchi, Buddhist monks played an important role in the development of Ajanta, too. The activities of the monks at Ajanta also help us understand the difference between the textual, or imagined, monks and the actual monks. Inscriptions from the site indicate that monks donated some of the caves. They also donated numerous images besides relics, stupas and paintings – items which were mostly religious in nature as opposed to those that had economic value such as land, housing, clothing or food. Religious gifts, therefore, were as much a part of the religious lives of the monks as it was for the laymen. All this could only be possible because the monks had access to resources. This leads us to an interesting conclusion: far from being universal renouncers of worldly goods, the monks were sometimes men of considerable wealth. And some, like Buddhabhadra, the monk who was the chief donor of the elaborate Cave 26 A, was a 'friend of [the] kings'.[7]

Of particular interest here is the association between the monks and the cult of images not just at Ajanta but at other caves in western India. In the case of Ajanta, Buddhist images were introduced in the second phase of the excavation of caves, i.e., in the 5th century CE. During this phase, new images were also erected in the caves excavated during the first phase. Of the thirty-six donative inscriptions connected with images at Ajanta, in which donor details are clear, thirty-three happen to be monks. This means that a sizeable majority of the images, more than 90 per cent, were donated by the monks. Inscriptions from sites like Kanheri and Kuda in western India also indicate a similar trend.[8] Interestingly, the images found in most of these sites also appear intrusive – they were not a part of the original plan but were introduced later by the monks. What is interesting to see in the list of the thirty-three monastic donors at Ajanta is that there is not a single nun. Of the thirty-three donor monks, at least twenty-five refer to themselves as sakyabhikshus, the Mahayana monks discussed at the beginning of this chapter. A similar pattern is noticed at Mathura and Sarnath. Women, or nuns, played an important role in monastic life till around the Kushana period. The Gupta period, or the beginning of the 4th–5th centuries CE, saw a decline in the involvement of nuns in monastic and religious activities. It is argued that this decline coincided with the rise of the Mahayana tradition, and the sakyabhikshus and Ajanta are reflective of this trend.

Some inscriptions also mention the intention behind such donations. Of the twenty-one such inscriptions, 19 (which is 90 per cent) of them declare that the intended beneficiaries of the gifts were the parents of the donors. A significant majority of these donors (more than thirteen of these nineteen) were monks. At least three of them belonged to a higher order of monkhood and are mentioned as teachers and transmitters of 'official' Buddhist literature. In eleven such inscriptions, or more than 50 per cent of such records, the donors express their intentions through a single basic formula with minor variations:[9]

> *What here is his merit, may that be for the obtaining of supreme knowledge*
> *by his mother and father and all living beings.*

Some others express similar intentions without repeating the basic formula:

> *This is the religious gift of ... Silabhadra (made) in the name of his father and mother*

The expression 'in the name of father and mother' comes out in at least four other inscriptions at Ajanta, where the parents had died. In the inscription of Buddhabhadra in Cave 26, he states that his gift was made 'in the name of Bhavvirāja and also his [Buddhabhadra's] mother and father'. Later in the inscription, he says:

> *... what merit is here, may that be for them [i.e., Bhavvirāja and his parents] and for the world, for the attainment of the fruit of great awakening and the accumulation of all pure qualities*

While there are some variations in the donative formula, its core remains the same and is connected primarily with the Mahayana school. It expresses an intention to catapult the self and others towards Buddhahood through the transfer or manipulation of merit. This was the dominant ideal of the bodhisattvas enroute to becoming Buddhas – they pursued spiritual welfare of both others and themselves.[10] From the point of view of questioning the stereotypes surrounding monkhood, these inscriptions reveal that the monks were concerned about the 'well-being' of both deceased and living parents. Religious giving for the benefit of donors' parents, living or dead, was an old practice widespread in India. Unlike textual or imagined monks, the actual monks come across as very human and vulnerable. They had a strong sense of obligation to their parents and were also concerned with the health of their companions and teachers.[11] Like the monks, another factor that played a crucial role in the development of rock-cut caves at Ajanta and of the spread of Buddhist faith in peninsular India was trade.

CAVES AND MONASTIC ESTABLISHMENTS ALONG THE TRADE ROUTES

Buddhist presence in the western Deccan can be dated even prior to the excavation of the rock-cut caves in the 2nd–1st centuries BCE. The prevalence of international trade enhanced its presence, making it more widespread.[12] Some texts, like *Dipavamsa* and *Mahavamsa*, refer to the presence of the Buddhists at Sopara, an ancient port located around 60 kms north of Mumbai. The Ashokan edict at the site also predates the caves. The discovery of around 200 inscriptional records in Prakrit, the language of the early Buddhists, from the western Deccan do not date earlier than the 2nd–1st centuries BCE. Some of them refer to early sects like Bhadrayaniya, Dharmottariya and Chetika, popularly bracketed as Hinayana Buddhism. Archaeological evidence from the subsequent Satavahana period and passages from the *Periplus of the Erythraean Sea*, the Greek navigational manual dating to the mid-1st century CE, provide details of a thriving socio-economic milieu, which was congenial for the growth of Buddhist caves. They allude to state formation and the development of urban settlements and diverse industries in the Deccan. These sources also affirm the existence of flourishing ports along the Arabian Sea (such as Sopara, Elephanta and Chaul), import of items from north India and shores of Indian Ocean, and overseas trade links with East Africa, the Red Sea region and the Mediterranean. There was a close relationship between the growth of economy and trade and the spread of monastic establishments. Most Buddhist caves in the region were located along the trade routes that facilitated movements of people and goods – from the Arabian Sea ports to trade centres in the Deccan plateau, especially the ancient city of Paithan, which was one of the powerful capitals of ancient Maharashtra. The location of Buddhist monastic sites on land routes, particularly at the heads of important passes connecting the inland centres with the ports – such as the Thalgat Pass, Naneghat Pass and Bhor Ghat Pass – suggests a causal link between trade and the new monasteries.[13] Merchants, pilgrims, traders and craftspeople, who travelled along these routes, often made donations to Buddhist establishments to earn prestige and spiritual and religious merit. The donors and patrons also got their names inscribed on the surfaces of the rock-cut caves. By the 5th and 6th centuries CE, when the second phase of excavations happened at Ajanta, the network of commercial activities had expanded further. It now linked the inland parts of the Deccan region, producing semi-precious stones and cotton textiles, with other trading and distribution centres, such as Ujjain to the north and the ports of Kalyan, Sopara and Baruch.

It has been suggested that cotton grown in the Deccan region, which was in international demand around the time, connected the Ajanta region with the expanded Indian Ocean trade network.[14] The regur soil, or black soil, of the upper parts of western Deccan was particularly suited for cotton. Even the *Periplus of the Erythraean Sea* mentions the town of Ter, located in the vicinity of the Ajanta region, as an important source point for cotton shipments. Interestingly, fragments of Indian cotton textiles have been unearthed during the excavations at the ancient Red Sea port of Berenike in Egypt. Some of these look identical to the ones represented in Ajanta paintings. Textiles of different designs and colour schemes can be seen in the paintings on the left wall of Cave 1, alongside depictions of women spinning cotton. A passage in *Bhikshunivinaya* of the Mahasanghikas, a sect that had settled in the western Deccan, mentions that nuns were involved in the spinning of cotton. Like cotton, wine was also in high demand during the reign of Vakataka king Harishena. Several representations of wine-drinking, mostly with foreigners, in the Ajanta paintings show how prevalent wine import was. A prominent example of this is the so-called 'Persian Embassy' depicted on the ceiling of Cave 1. Foreigners from different parts of Central Asia, Persia, the Middle East and possibly East Africa are represented in the painting of the Buddha's descent from trayastrimsa heaven in Cave 17. This one shows several non-Indic people in diverse clothing, hair styles and skin colours. In fact, the highest concentration of the remains of torpedo jars (often confused with Mediterranean amphorae shards), used for the transportation of wine, has been found on the west coast of India, particularly in Gujarat, Maharashtra and the Konkan region. Most of these are dated to the 5th and 6th centuries, originating from the Persian Gulf region, where they were in common use between the later Parthian and Sasanian periods (between the 1st and 7th centuries CE). Based on the discovery of residues of wine sedimentation in amphorae shards found at Devni Mori in Gujarat, and remains of liquor-distilling equipment from a monastery at Shaikhan Dheri (ancient Pushakalavati, now in modern-day Khyber Pakhtunkhwa province in the Peshawar valley), some scholars have suggested that monks collaborated with traders in the liquor trade. Findings of foreign coins around the Buddhist caves also corroborate the links between trade and commerce and monastic establishments.

Extended commercial activities and the Indian Ocean trade network expanded the scope of travel for merchants and traders. They were attracted to Buddhism because they believed that Bodhisattva Avalokiteshvara could save them from shipwrecks and protect their caravans from robbers. Such beliefs also acquired legitimacy through related textual references. Notably, the twenty-fourth chapter of the *Saddharmapundarika Sutra*, entitled 'The Exposition of the Miraculous Transformations of Avalokiteshvara, the One Who Faces in All Directions', describes Avalokiteshvara as one who can not only protect caravans and merchants against shipwrecks and robbers but also those thrown off mountains, those hit by rocks or swords, those attacked by frightful beasts and snakes, those victimized by witches or ghosts, or those who are about to be executed or imprisoned. The chapter also includes a rather long description of a shipwreck in the waters near Sri Lanka. It is this connection that explains the sculptural and painted depictions of Avalokiteshvara at Ajanta and its neighbouring sites. Here, he is shown as saving the world from the 'eight great perils' (astamahabhayas). Such depictions are also described as 'littany' and can be found at seven places in the Ajanta caves. Littany depictions of Avalokiteshvara can also be seen in a painting in Cave 3 in Pitalkhora; Caves 2, 41 and 90 at Kanheri; Cave 3 at Ellora and the most elaborate one in Cave 7 at Aurangabad (Fig 4.9, Chapter 4). The one in the Aurangabad caves also shows a boat and its occupants, two masts of a ship and a foreigner wearing a pointed cap and a caftan pointing to the Indian Ocean trade connection. Notably, the images of Avalokiteshvara performing the eight great miracles are conspicuously absent from north India. Their largest concentration can be found in the western Deccan caves and along the Silk Route at Dunhuang in China.[15] The factor that brought together trade, merchants, caravans and monks was the unique landscape and physiography of the Deccan region, which was congenial to the development of the caves.

GEOLOGY, LANDSCAPE AND PARADISIAL SYMBOLISM

The Western Ghats in Maharashtra, the geographical locale of the Ajanta caves and several other rock-cut caves, are punctuated by dramatic craggy peaks and tiers of cliffs. The landscape is described as the 'Deccan trap', after the Swedish word 'trap', or 'ghat', the Indian word that refers to a stepped formation. The comparative softness, optimum thickness and consistent superimposed layers of basalt rocks in the region, formed out of successive lava flows, were conducive to the excavations of the caves. Geology and physiography, therefore, played an important role in the rock-cut architecture of the Western Ghats. The cliffs also provided a beautiful scenic and spiritual landscape while exerting a critical influence on the movement of people, goods and monks.[16] Some scholars have even pointed out that there was a deeper religious and historical connection between the rock-cut caves and the surrounding landscape of the Ajanta, Ellora and Elephanta caves. The natural environment and the built, or carved, environment were interrelated. The natural environment was integral to the conception and architecture of these caves, and human excavations at such sites were shaped by nature and not superimposed onto them. Seen in this context, the rock-cut caves at Ajanta were not just conceived as simple Buddhist temples or monasteries. The caves and the surrounding natural landscape were metaphorically intended to evoke palatial abodes amidst heavenly gardens or mythical paradises.[17] An inscription of Varahadeva found in Cave 16, in fact, likens the architecture of Ajanta to Hindu god Indra's palace in paradise and the landscape to a heavenly garden.

[The dwelling] ornamented with windows, doors, splendid verandas, railings and images of the Devakanyas and delightfully arranged pillars with Chaitya Mandira ... A large reservoir of water and [adorned] by the abode of the chief of serpents and others .... Warmed in summer by the heat of the sun, and fit for enjoyment at all seasons ... [as] the dwelling of Indra and the bright caves of Mandara ... in the mountain to which none is equal in greatness... [he] made with love pleasure and expansive modesty ... a cave brilliant with the radiance of the crown of Indra.[18]

Similarly, the Buddhabadra inscription in the chaitya hall of Cave 26 at Ajanta describes the surrounding landscape as a celestial garden. Such metaphorical descriptions are not limited to Ajanta. Inscriptions from prayer halls in Bhaja and Karle also refer to such structures as divine palaces. They also compare such chaitya caves with Indra's palace in trayastrimsa heaven. By extension, the mountains on which such caves were excavated were symbolically believed to represent the mythical Mount Sumeru, on which the trayastrimsa heaven was located.[19] The symbolism was not just limited to the locational landscape but also extended to the appearance and architecture of the prayer halls and monasteries. This appearance and architecture evolves as one goes from the early to the later caves.

EVOLVING LAYOUT AND ARCHITECTURE OF PRAYER HALLS

Of the six early caves at Ajanta, only two – Caves 9 and 10 – are prayer halls. The remaining – Caves 8, 12, 13 15 and 15A – are monasteries.[20] Individual caves follow different architectural styles but, broadly speaking, the early prayer halls shared common elements. They were approached through a porch or a pillared veranda, which contained one to three doors to get to the hall inside. These doors were sometimes interspersed with windows to facilitate the entry of light. The entrance to the cave was surmounted by a tall, horseshoe-shaped window called the chaitya window (Fig 8.2). Further inside was the hall housing the stupa, which represented the most popular form in which the Buddha was worshipped in the early phase of Buddhism.

The monks had taken to the stupa cult very proactively and, as we have discussed earlier, they played an active role in the setting up of the stupas. Most such stupas were structural, or free-standing, and located in the open. However, in the case of the caves of the Western Ghats – such as Kondivite, Nadsur, Pitalkhora, Ajanta – the stupa was set up inside the cave as a part of the chaityagriha. It was integrated into the coenobitic life of the monastic community as one of its most central elements.[21] Since the stupa had to be circumnavigated inside the cave, the interior of the prayer halls had to be suitably designed (Fig 8.3). The chaitya caves contained a rectangular hall in front of the stupa (nave) and a round hall at the back (apse). Aisles or passages for circumambulation were created along the wall of the cave. These aisles were separated from the rectangular front by two rows of pillars, which met at the rounded back (Fig 3.6, Chapter 3). The hall had a vaulted ceiling adorned by a gallery of arches and cross-beams running along the arches (Fig 8.3). The chaityagrihas imitated wooden constructions in terms of architectural style and even used non-functional wooden beams and rafters. In the first set of excavations, such as Cave 10 (1st century BCE), the vault consists of a wooden ceiling. A little later, for instance in Cave 9, the architects use rock-cut stone ribs.[22]

Unlike Caves 9 and 10, Caves 19 and 26 represent the prayer halls of the later phase. Cave 29 was never completed. When one looks at Caves 19 and 26, one notices some conspicuous changes from the earlier phase.[23]

First, the prayer hall complex becomes bigger and the exterior includes a courtyard with mini shrines on the sides. One such mini shrine in the courtyard of Cave 19 carries the statue of the serpent king, Nagaraja, and his queen.

Second, the entrance and facade of the caves becomes more elaborate and ornate (Fig 8.5). They are approached by a pavilion-like porch with a balcony resting on pillars and pilasters, or columns, projecting from walls. The facade is dominated by a huge, arch-shaped chaitya window, which is flanked by sculptures, balconies and arcades at different levels.

Third, the interiors of the caves also undergo a change. Like the facade, the pillars, the triforium (arched gallery) and the walls in the interior are decorated with figures of Buddha and celestial beings.

Fourth, the stupa gets transformed with the superimposition of an image of the Buddha. It also gets a multi-tiered parasol supported by gods, angels and dwarfs. Its basal platform was modified to make it look like the base of a contemporary temple (Fig 8.4).

The changes in the appearance and architecture of the prayer halls (and the monasteries), from the earlier to the later phase, represented a shift in the conceptualization of the shrines or sanctuaries. Around the 3rd–4th centuries CE, the shrines came to be looked upon as *prasada*, a palace. In an earlier section, we discussed how inscriptions in some caves at Ajanta also liken them to the palace of the king of gods, Indra. In the case of Ajanta, the prayer halls (and the monasteries) came to symbolize a multi-storeyed royal palace with the Buddha as the king, or more precisely a spiritual sovereign. The Buddha is also shown seated on a royal lion throne surrounded by royal attendants. When Cave 9 was repainted during the later phase of excavations, bodhisattvas like Avalokiteshvara and Vajrapani were added as attendants of the Buddha. Like other palaces, 'Buddha's palace' was also guarded by royal guardians, the nagas.

ARCHITECTURAL EVOLUTION OF THE MONASTERIES

Like the prayer halls, the monasteries at Ajanta also underwent an architectural transformation from the earlier (Caves 12, 13 15 and 15 A) to the later phase (Caves 1, 2, 16 and 17). The basic initial plan of the monasteries consisted of an oblong, pillared veranda, an astylar hall, or a hall with no decorative columns or pilasters, meant for the congregation of monks, and cells on three sides for dwelling purposes. As one moves from the earlier to the later phase, some distinct architectural changes can be seen in the case of the viharas, or monasteries.[24]

First, unlike their earlier plain, austere and astylar counterparts, the later monastery caves are more spacious, have sculptural and painted decorations and narrative paintings and have more residential cells. They also include a courtyard and a porch.

Fig 8.1 View of a section of the Ajanta Caves, with the dry Waghora river stream in the foreground

Fig 8.2 The facade of Cave 9, an early-phase chaityagriha; the Buddha statue (on the right of entrance) was a later addition

Fig 8.3 An austere stupa inside the chaityagriha of Cave 9. This early-period cave contains no anthropomorphic images

Fig 8.4 A developed stupa with a Buddha statue in a chaityagriha from a later period, Cave 19

Fig 8.5 The ornately carved facade of Cave 19, a later-phase chaityagriha

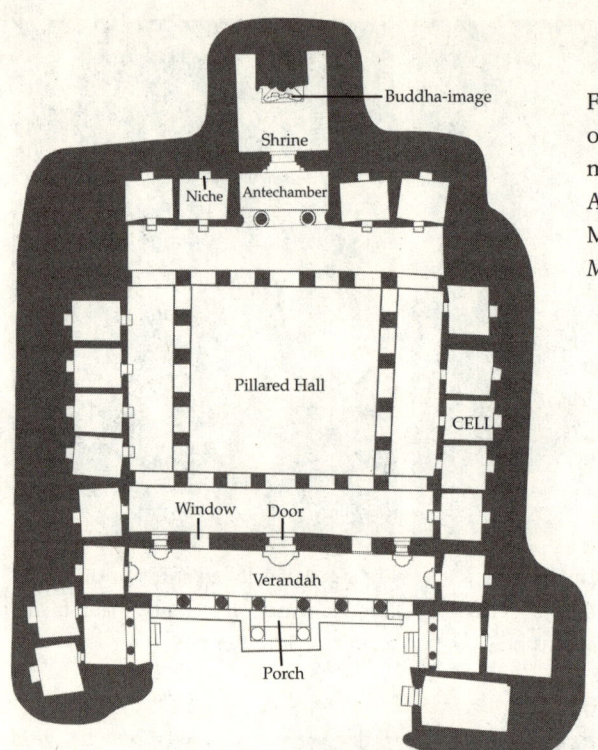

Fig 8.6 Layout of a developed monastery, Cave 1, Ajanta (after Debala Mitra, *Buddhist Monuments*, 1971)

Fig 8.7 Sculptural depiction of the Miracle at Shravasti, Cave 7

Fig 8.8 Detail from the story of the merchant Simhala, from *Simhalavadana*, Cave 17

Fig 8.9 Buddha seated like a king on a throne, flanked by two bodhisattvas as attendants, in Cave 16

Fig 8.10 Bodhisattva Padmapani (right) and a scene from the Mahajanaka Jataka (left), Cave 1

Second, the earlier monasteries contained twelve cells at the most, while the later ones (except for Cave 20) have between fourteen and twenty cells.

Third, like the later prayer halls, the later monasteries also symbolized a royal palace with Buddha as the spiritual sovereign. An inscription found in Cave 17 describes the Buddha as a 'king among ascetics'. Likewise, images of the Buddha are shown seated on a lion, or royal throne (Caves 15, 16 and 22). The Buddha is also depicted in several caves with royal insignia, such as parasols and fly-whisk bearers. Finally, in Cave 23, the naga doorkeepers wield axes (instead of flowers, as seen in the earlier caves) symbolizing royal doorkeepers guarding a palace.

Fourth, the most conspicuous change was the introduction of the shrine chamber in the back wall, containing a colossal image of the Buddha. We will discuss the idea of the shrine chamber in detail in the following section. With its introduction, the monasteries began to serve two purposes – monastic dwelling and sanctuary (Fig 8.6). The monasteries also included small rooms that functioned as regular, private shrines for the monks. Besides the main shrine chamber, there were subsidiary shrines not only at the back (sometimes occupied by yakshas) but also on the side walls. Such subsidiary shrines also appeared in the front veranda, just before the actual entrance to the caves.

THE RISE OF GANDHAKUTI: THE BUDDHA'S PRIVATE CHAMBER IN MONASTERIES

The introduction of shrine chamber(s) in the residential halls was the manifestation of a new conceptualization and imagination of the Buddha. In the early rock-cut Buddhist caves of the Deccan, the shrines (or chapels) and the residential quarters were spatially and architecturally distinct and separate. The Buddha was believed to reside in his own separate quarter in the stupa, which was housed in a separate cave used for public and congregational worship. Even in the case of the earliest monastic residential quarters at the Dharmarajika stupa in Taxila, the residential section faces the 'Great Stupa' but is separate from it. The residential quarters were typically quadrangular in shape and had an open courtyard surrounded by rows of residential cells, mostly on all four sides. In the later structures at Taxila, the stupa was sometimes placed in the middle of the residential section but distinct from the surrounding cells of the monks. Even in the case of the early rock-cut caves of western India (say, Ajanta), the shrine or the chaityagriha, meant for congregation, was separate from the vihara, which served as the residence of the monks. The standard plan of the vihara, right from the beginning, consisted of a squarish hall with cells on the side and back walls. By the 5th century, a new plan seemed to be fairly standardized at several Buddhist sites – the vihara had a shrine in the centre of the back wall, containing an image of the Buddha. This shrine-cum-vihara architecturally set apart a new, special room for a special resident, the Buddha, which was called the gandhakuti, the 'perfumed chamber'.[25]

An interesting episode is described in the *Sayanasanavastu*, which forms part of the larger corpus of the *Vinaya Pitaka*. Herein, a householder named Kalyanabhadra in Benares (modern-day Varanasi) asks the Buddha's permission to build a vihara for 'the disciples of the Blessed One'. Knowing that Kalyanbhadra was not familiar with the construction of such structures, the Buddha is believed to have given him specific instructions.

> [I]f you have three cells made, the Perfume Chamber is to be made in the middle, the two [other] cells on each side; likewise, if there are nine cells in three wings; in a quadrangular [vihara] the Perfume Chamber [is to be placed] in the middle [of the back wall] facing the main entrance, two cells on each side of the entrance.

This plan became a part of the vinaya rules followed by the monastic community.[26] We see the gandhakuti being created in the quarters of the monks at Ajanta, Bagh, Kanheri, Bodh Gaya, Kaushambi, Vallabhi, Sarnath, Nalanda and numerous other sites that developed between the 5th and the 14th centuries. Like Kalyanabhadra in Benares and Anathapindika in Shravasti, these monastic structures reserved special rooms where the Buddha was thought to live. In a sense, the implementation of this new shrine-cum-vihara plan,

5th century onwards, was like returning to an earlier tradition; only the Buddha seemed to have reoccupied his old quarters. In the next chapter on Nalanda, we will see how some inscriptions point out that, at some sites, these private chambers functioned as distinct and individual entities that either owned movable properties, or had official correspondence with other monasteries. They also had special monks, or groups of monks, attached to them. But it was not just the shrine chamber that made the monasteries vibrant. Their sculptures and paintings made the caves come alive too. This applied to the prayer halls as well.

SCULPTURES AND PAINTINGS: DEPICTING THE CHANGING BUDDHIST WORLD

What do the sculptures and paintings at Ajanta depict?[27] Carved images of the Buddha, in different attitudes and postures, feature prominently in the sculptural scheme. They appear everywhere – on the walls of the veranda, in associated sub-shrines, in the hall, on the pillars and pillar brackets and within the shrines and antechambers. Episodes from the life of the Buddha are also illustrated in both sculptures and paintings across several caves. These include the four major episodes – birth, enlightenment under the Bodhi tree, first sermon at Sarnath and death (or mahaparinirvana). Then there are stories connected with the life of the Buddha, for example, the 'Assault and Temptation of Mara' (Caves 1, 6 and 26) or the 'Miracle at Shravasti' (Caves 1, 2, 6, 7, 16 and 17, Fig 8.7).

Alongside the Buddha come the bodhisattvas. Examples of this include the iconic paintings of Padmapani Avalokiteshvara and Vajrapani in Cave 1, or the images of the bodhisattvas attending to the Buddha in Caves 2, 7 and 16 (Fig 8.9). In some caves, Avalokiteshvara is also depicted as the saviour of humankind against the 'eight great perils'.

The Jataka tales (birth stories, or stories of the previous births of Gautama Buddha) occupy a large part of the painted space in the Ajanta caves, particularly in the halls of the monasteries. Here, a bodhisattva in animal or human form was persistently striving for Buddhahood by acquiring all kinds of virtues. The Jatakas form a part of the canonical Buddhist text *Khuddaka Nikaya* (translated as 'minor/short collection') and were compiled between the 3rd century BCE and the 2nd century CE. Examples of this include *Mahakapi Jataka* in Cave 17, which narrates the story of a monkey king who rescues his entire troop by sacrificing his own life; or the *Sibi Jataka* in Cave 1, which tells the story Prince Sibi, who gives his own flesh to save a pigeon from a hawk. One can see an entire panorama of everyday life, inequalities and virtues, across sections of the human and animal worlds, in the Jataka paintings of Ajanta.

Unlike the Jataka tales, which deal with the previous births of the Buddha, the *avadanas* are mostly described as religious biographies or stories connected with the life of the human Buddha and other Buddhist figures. Painted on the walls of some caves, they offer moral instructions, or relate to Buddhist ethics like the Jatakas, and are meant for popular consumption. For example, the 'Story of Simhala' in Cave 17 is about a merchant who escapes from an island of witches and is crowned as the king after the ruling monarch of his homeland is killed by the pursuing witches.

The sculptural and painting scheme in the Ajanta caves also portrays a growing Buddhist pantheon. They depict Brahmanical gods like Indra or Sakra, the king of Gods, as well as demigods and goddesses, and deities connected with folk cults and popular devotional worship. The latter include the apsaras, gandharvas, kinnars, yakshas and yakshis, nagas and vidyadharas. It is held that between 200 BCE and 300 CE, many such popular deities were worshipped independently and appropriated by the dominant Brahmanical, Buddhist and Jaina traditions in various parts of India to increase their following. Later, these popular deities were subordinated and marginalized in the architectural schemes and sculptural (and textual) representations of these dominant religious traditions. Some of these once-powerful deities, such as the yakshas and yakshis, were even bracketed as 'demonic' and 'frightening creatures'. The independent worship of the nagas and yakshas, and their consorts, continued during the later centuries (c 300–600 CE). However, one does not come across colossal statues of them like the earlier times. These once-popular deities appear as subsidiary figures confined to secondary spaces in the shrines. In Ajanta, for instance, one comes across subsidiary shrines dedicated to yakshi Hariti and her consort, Panchika, (inside Cave 2, Fig 4.2, Chapter 4) and Nagaraja (in the external courtyard of Cave 19 and between the entrances of caves 15 and 16, Fig 4.3, Chapter 4). But, by and large, these popular deities largely appear at secondary places like entrances, facades, door jambs, pillars and pillar brackets.

The doors and ceilings of the Ajanta caves are decorated with auspicious motifs, including amorous couples, dryads, creepers, conches, scrolls, lotuses, flower garlands, griffins and geese. The paintings on the ceilings illustrate scenes from everyday life, including lovers, wine-drinking, cockfights, jesters and dwarfs, besides geometrical motifs and fauna and flora. Foreigners, shown with stitched clothes and caps, are believed to resemble traders from Central Asia. It is not just the illustrations and scenes that make the caves unique but also the painting techniques and the connecting themes.

FRESCOES VERSUS MURALS: PAINTINGS OF AJANTA

Most walls or ceilings of the Ajanta caves were once covered with paintings. The sculptures were painted, too. One of Ajanta's painted ceiling panels, a playful and galloping elephant surrounded by flowers (Cave 1), has in fact been adopted as the official logo of India's Ministry of Tourism. Over the years, these paintings have suffered under the impact of extreme temperatures, seepage, insect attacks and lack of (or improper) preservation. Now, only traces survive. These, nevertheless, constitute the earliest and the only comprehensive evidence of painting traditions in early India. Experts say they are as significant for the history of ancient Indian culture as the frescos of Pompeii for Graeco-Roman antiquity. The paintings are more discernible and visible around later afternoon/early evening when the sunlight penetrates the caves, but only for a short time. They can be appreciated the best in the dim, artificial light of oil lamps or candles as opposed to bright flashes or neon lights.

How were the rock surfaces of the caves prepared for painting? Two layers of organic mud plaster were used to prepare a coarse surface, over which a thin coat of lime wash was added as a third layer. Unlike the European frescoes, where colours were applied on wet lime plaster, a technique which gave the paintings durability, the painters at Ajanta waited for the lime wash to dry up before starting to paint. These paintings are therefore called murals – painted directly on a wall or a ceiling, as opposed to frescoes. On the surface so prepared, bold outlines, mostly in red, were first drawn. Limited colours, prepared mostly from local rocks, such as red and yellow ochre, malachite green, white and black, extracted respectively from lime or kaolin and lampblack, were used. Only lapis lazuli was imported from Afghanistan to add the colour blue to the palate. The colour pigments were held together with animal glue.[28]

The cave paintings at Ajanta, in general, are based on extensive narrative representations composed of numerous individual scenes embedded between landscapes related to the town and countryside. They showcase a panorama of contemporary life from hamlets, villages, forests, hermitages, towns, courts and places. They belong to different genres, including hunting and travel adventures, romances, stories concerning clever and ethical behaviour in general and comical tales.[29] From kings and slaves to the rich and beggars to saints and sinners, the paintings depict an entire gamut of human life from birth to death and include men, women and children from all stages of life. The costumes of the figures depicted, particularly the ornaments and headgears, are particularly striking and resemble those in the bas-reliefs of Bharhut and Sanchi. While they appear very wide-ranging and secular, these paintings served a deeper religious purpose – they supplemented the teachings of the Buddhist monks. They represented pictorial sermons, which were supposed to impart two fundamental teachings of Buddhism. First, they show that the Buddha was an exalted being, above all monks and lay people, and whose periodical appearance re-routed the course of world affairs. Second, before becoming the Buddha, he sacrificed himself for others in numerous existences as a bodhisattvas or a past Buddha.

Experts have also drawn attention to other characteristic features, which aid our understanding of the painting scheme at Ajanta.[30] First, the artists continued to use the technique of multiple perspectives, earlier seen in the sculptural panels at Sanchi, although there was a growing tendency to see foreground figures partially overlap with the background ones. Second, they made use of hierarchic scaling to emphasize the importance of the Buddha and the bodhisattvas. In Cave 1, for instance, the pictures of the bodhisattvas flanking the doorway of the shrine in the rear are painted much larger in size than the figures of princes, princesses and commoners surrounding them (Fig 8.10). Third, shading and highlighting are deployed in the paintings to add a sense of three-dimensionality.

Like the excavation, the paintings in the caves were executed in two phases: the first was in the 2nd–1st centuries BCE and the second was in the 5th century CE.[31] One can discern some distinct characteristics associated with the two phases. Traces of older paintings, superimposed by later ones, have survived on the walls of Caves 9 and 10. Dating around the 2nd–1st centuries BCE, these early caves are concerned mostly with the life of the historical Buddha and his previous lives as bodhisattvas. In these caves, the Buddha is represented in a symbolic form, not in flesh and blood. Cave 10 has traces of paintings that cover the entire life of the Buddha, from his birth in Lumbini to his death in Kushinagar. In both these early period caves, the Jataka verses or stories are painted as narrative scenes. The literary genre of the Jatakas borrowed from stories or folk tales transmitted orally from the pre-Buddhist times. The Buddhists retold the original stories and contexts by projecting the bodhisattvas, or the past Buddhas (in an animal or human form), as the protagonists. In such retold stories, the past Buddhas would put to test one of the cardinal virtues of Buddhism – generosity, morality, renunciation, steadfastness, goodness or composure. In the early caves, the events are composed horizontally in the paintings and appear like a continuous frieze-like band. In Cave 9, for instance, short stories are shown in only one or a few successive scenes, placed beside each other. In the case of Cave 10, large narrative events are broken into several individual scenes, arranged according to their place of occurrence and not chronologically.[32] By the time the later caves were built, after a gap of more than half a millennium, the painting techniques had not only become more elaborate but also more complex. Remains of the later phase of the paintings can still be seen in Caves 1, 2, 16 and 17.

The idea of breaking a painted narrative event into individual episodes or scenes, as seen in the older caves, continued in the later caves. The only difference was that now the scenes were spread across the walls, as opposed to following any chronological or linear sequence.[33] One could see this in the story of Simhala, which is painted across the right wall of the hall in Cave 17. In the later phase of paintings, individual episodes are embedded within the scene of action, such as cities, royal palaces, parks, forests, lakes and seas (Fig 8.8). The visitors are required to locate the episodes within the scenes of actions and visualize them in the larger sequence of events. The presence of various styles, even within the same cave, indicates that the compositions were produced by more than one artist, that painters from different regions were involved, that these paintings were not carried out in one continuous span. The later caves not just depict stories from the previous lives of the Buddha (or bodhisattvas) and important episodes in the life of the historical Buddha, they also include anthropomorphic depictions of the Buddha's biographical life and future Buddhas or bodhisattvas, particularly Avalokiteshvara. In the later caves, the paintings are not just limited to prayers halls or halls of worship (like in the early caves) but also executed on the walls and ceilings of the monasteries. This also became possible because of the emergence of the idea of gandhakutis, or the Buddha's private chamber in the monasteries. Located in the centre of the rear wall of the monasteries, such chambers, as discussed earlier, contained a statue of the Buddha and functioned as a shrine. In the later caves, the Buddha was not just seen as 'a monk among the monks' in the monasteries but also as someone enjoying an elevated status above all earthly and heavenly beings.

While the Jataka stories and episodes from the life of the Buddha continued to be represented in the later caves, they were given an extended Buddhist rendering. This was linked to the emergence of Sanskrit translations, the retelling of Buddhist texts, the transformation of earlier stories into works of poetry and their integration into scripts of monastic discipline and teachings. Therefore, the stories converted into pictures in the later caves at Ajanta had different origins, but they were held together by the common factor of Buddhist revision. So, besides painting secular themes and locations like royal palaces and houses of common citizens, the Buddhist revision of the stories also gave the painters a chance to play with the bodhisattva ideal. The depiction of the bodhisattvas working ceaselessly for the salvation of all beings, despite countless reincarnations, is a key theme of the paintings of the later period. In such paintings, the bodhisattvas, who were also mythical and celestial kings, appear conspicuously larger than other painted figures. However, the positioning of the bodhisattvas in the paintings serves to highlight the presence of the Buddha. The former are seen flanking the doorways of the veranda, the antechamber and the Buddha's private chamber – in a straight line from the entrance to the cave to the Buddha's statue in the chamber located in the centre of the rear wall – as if they are guards or attendants of the Buddha, the 'king of kings'.[34]

Finally, let us see how the Hinayana–Mahayana divide worked with regard to the paintings of the earlier and later caves. Such divides were, as discussed earlier, more fluid than have been made out to be. It needs to be borne in mind that all literary works and topics, which relate to or were represented in the paintings of the later period at Ajanta – such as the vinaya of the Mulasarvastivada school, or verses of Arya Sura and Ashvaghosha – are traditionally associated with the Hinayana school. With the possible exception of Bodhisattva Avalokiteshvara, themes that could be bracketed as being Mahayanistic were not portrayed in the later caves. The connotation of 'Mahayana' for the later caves originates from the time when the literary background to the paintings was still unknown. It can, therefore, only be used as a popular label and not to denote the ideology behind the later phase of paintings.[35]

Not much information is available about the decline of the caves. Scholars say they were abandoned after the reign of the Vakatakas, particularly Harishena. Some scholars have pointed out that Chinese pilgrim Xuanzang, who visited the Ajanta caves in the 7th century CE, described it as a flourishing Buddhist establishment. Further, a fragmentary inscription of uncertain purpose, belonging to the Rashtrakuta dynasty and found in Cave 26, signals that the caves were in use in the 8th–9th centuries CE.[36] For almost 1,000 years thereafter, the caves remained in obscurity. In 1819, they were accidentally discovered by Major John Smith, of the Madras regiment in the British Indian Army, who was on a hunting expedition in the forests nearby.

HOW THE CAVES WERE INTRODUCED TO THE WEST

In April 1819, Major John Smith and his party were chasing a tiger in the forests near the Ajintha village. They lost sight of the tiger somewhere near the river Waghora (which means 'tiger') but stumbled upon a cave that immortalized them in history. It was a cave adorned with ancient paintings. Major Smith decided to leave his mark on a beautiful mural in Cave 10. With his hunting knife, he etched the words 'John Smith, 28th Cavalry, 28th April, 1819', perhaps not realizing that he was vandalizing a portrait of a bodhisattva. The news of Smith's discovery spread fast and aroused tremendous interest in what was seen as one of the wonders of the ancient world. The Buddhist credentials of the paintings, sculpture and architecture of the Ajanta caves were soon established. The wild and exotic forest, which housed tigers, started attracting historians, archaeologists, epigraphists, Indologists and orientalists. They attracted treasure-hunters and smugglers, too, some of whom tried to scrape the paintings off the walls.

It is not well known that one of the few surviving paintings that left Ajanta can now be found in the Boston Museum of Fine Arts. It was sold by Sotheby's in London for £1000 in 1922.[37] Soon after Major Smith's discovery, Scottish historian William Erskine presented a paper on the Ajanta caves to the Bombay Literary Society in 1822. The Nizam of Hyderabad, in whose territories the caves lay, got an access road constructed. He even sent Ghulam Yazdani, a leading art historian, to conduct the first photographic survey of the murals in the late 1920s. These were later published in the form of four volumes, between 1930 and 1955. The Nizam also sought the help of two Italian conservationists to restore the paintings. By coating the pigments with a thick layer of shellac, these two conservationists, however, ended up doing more damage to the paintings.

Writings and publications by people like James Alexander, James Prinsep, Lieutenant Blake, James Fergusson and Gladstone Solomon offered good visibility to the caves in the first half of the 19th century. Indian antiquarian and art historian James Fergusson was involved in the numbering of the caves with the help of John Burgess. James Prinsep, an epigraphist, first reproduced some of the inscriptions in 1836, while Bhau Daji translated and added to this collection in 1863. Alongside publications, translations and presentations, efforts were made to create reproductions of the ancient wall paintings on canvases, for display in European museums, in the 19th and early 20th centuries. They exposed the chaityagrihas and viharas, and the unique and exceptional paintings to the outside world, further contributing to the rediscovery of the caves. Unfortunately, many such reproductions or copies were destroyed in fires or earthquakes. In the 1840s, Major Robert Gill, a painter and an army officer from the Madras Presidency, was commissioned by the Royal Asiatic Society and the East India Company to make copies of the murals and draw layouts of the caves. Gill made several copies of the wall paintings at Ajanta between 1844 and 1863. However, most copies, which were on display at the Indian Court of Crystal Palace in Sydenham, London, were destroyed in a fire in 1866. Gill returned to Ajanta again, this time armed with new cameras and brushes, and made several copies of wall paintings till his death in 1875. Meanwhile, the Royal Asiatic Society founded the Royal Cave Temple Commission in 1848 to clean, document and copy the murals. This commission became the nucleus for the formation of the ASI in 1861. With the formation of the ASI, the concern for the Ajanta caves grew further.

In 1872, John Griffiths, the principal of the Bombay School of Art, was commissioned by the Bombay Presidency to make copies of the Ajanta paintings. Griffiths and his students coated several paintings with varnish for easier viewing, but they ended up damaging them. Anyway, the team made some 300 canvases, which were sent to London and exhibited at the Imperial Institute on the Exhibition Road. Many such copies met the same fate as Gill's, and more than 100 such reproductions were destroyed when a fire engulfed the storage section of the institute in 1885. Interestingly, this institute later became the Victoria and Albert Museum that houses most of the surviving paintings.

Early in the 20th century, art patron Christiana Herringham (popularly known as Lady Herringham) worked in collaboration with students of the Calcutta School of Art, which included the likes of Nandlal Bose and Asit Kumar Haldar, to produce copies of Ajanta paintings. The copies so produced were published in full colour by the London Indian Society. Unlike the reproductions of Gill and Griffiths, which were more influenced by the Victorian style, Lady Herringham's project is regarded as belonging to the 'Indian Renaissance' style, pioneered and championed by the famous painter Abanindranath Tagore. This brings us to an important point. Most 19th-century characterizations of the Ajanta caves were orientalist and negative, shaped as they were by notions and preconceptions of the colonialists. In such characterizations, the cave paintings were seen as devoid of rationality and logic. Instead, they were stereotyped through the eyes of foreigners and infused with sensuality and spirituality.[38] It may be worthwhile to recollect here that this was also the period of discovery of Buddhism in the West. And for most early Buddhologists, the Buddha was primarily a social reformer. It took the West some time to realize that the Buddha was also connected to exquisite paintings, sculptural art and architecture. Paradoxically, the early colonial characterizations tried to link the paintings to the Hellenistic culture – whether it was the depiction of subjects, use of perspectives, the choice of pigments or the use of lime mortar. In some measure, this tendency prevails even today.

Within a decade of Herringham's project, another systematic attempt at producing copies of Ajanta paintings was undertaken by Japanese artist Kampo Arai. This project, not associated with the West but rooted within the larger Asian cultural tradition, speaks of a different reception of Ajanta. It was the famous poet and Nobel laureate Rabindranath Tagore who invited Kampo to teach Japanese paintings techniques to students at Santiniketan. Between 1916 and 1918, Kampo produced duplicates of the murals using tracings on Japanese paper. Kampo's copies were housed at Tokyo Imperial University, where they were destroyed in the Great Kanto earthquake of 1923.

The murals of Ajanta were not just copied or reproduced, but they also inspired cultural and literary compositions in the West. During one of her visits to India, Anna Pavlova, the famous Russian ballerina, was so impressed by the murals of Ajanta that she asked her staff choreographer, Ivan Clustine, to create a ballet on the theme. Titled *Ajanta Frescoes*, this 1923 composition received mixed reviews. While the *Daily Mail* stated that 'it was worked out with brilliance, with a colour of its own,' the *Saturday Review* saw it as 'a tedious spectacle copied with a wealth of superfluous accuracy from the dreary Buddhist art of India'.[39] Later, Jewish-American poet Muriel Rukeyser wrote a poem titled 'Ajanta', which formed a part of the collection *Beast in View*, originally published in 1944.[40] Rukeyser's composition was partly inspired by the writings of Mukul Dey, an Indian artist and photographer who made copies of the murals as early as 1919 and whose experiences and adventures are recollected in the book *My Pilgrimages to Ajanta and Bagh* (1925), and art historian Stella Kramrisch's essay on Ajanta, which was published in 1937.[41]

The tradition of discovery of Ajanta by the West perhaps reached its apogee in the writings of Walter M. Spink, an American art historian, who spent around five decades studying the site since 1950s. His multivolume magnum opus *Ajanta, History and Development* arguably remains the most authoritative resource on the site and is widely known for the chronology of the excavations, alongside sociological and political influences that shaped the history of the site. Another masterly work, particularly on the paintings, comes from Dieter Schlingloff, a German scholar, who is particularly known for the identification and interpretation of the Jataka tales depicted at Ajanta.

Together with publications and reproductions, efforts were also made to preserve and conserve the caves and restore the paintings. Particularly noteworthy in this regard have been the efforts of an ASI team led by Rajdeo Singh, chief of conservation and the head of science at Aurangabad. The team's use of infrared light, microemulsion and cutting-edge Japanese conservation technology has been very useful in restoring the paintings since 1999.

Some efforts have also been made to divert a part of the tourist traffic. In 2013, four replica caves, created by Mumbai-based designer Rakesh Rathod, were opened to the public. Located just 4 kms away from the site, this visitor centre has unfortunately not become very popular. And while we continue to spar over the renaming of Aurangabad, the Ajanta caves continue to make headlines globally. One of the digitally restored images of Ajanta, that of the bodhisattva king Mahajanaka, is now being preserved on an island called Svalbard in Norway, as part of a project called the Arctic World Archive (AWA).

9

NALANDA MAHAVIHARA

Nalanda has scholars well known for [their knowledge of] sacred texts ... She has rows of viharas [monasteries] whose spires lick the clouds. That [row of viharas] seem to have been built by the Creator himself like a garland hanging up high. Nalanda has temples which are brilliant with the network of rays from various jewels set in them and it is the pleasant abode of a learned and virtuous Sangha; and resembles [Mount]Sumeru, the charming residence of the noble Vidyadharas [wisdom holders].

This is how Malada, a minister of possibly 7th-century CE King Yashovarmadeva, about whom not much is known, describes Nalanda in his inscription.[1] Now there are only ruins. If we were to visit the site archaeologically described as the 'Ruins of Nalanda' now, we would come across an enclosed and excavated area containing remains of temples, monasteries, votive stupas and art works in stucco, bronze and stone. These artefacts and remains date from the 5th century CE to the 12th century CE and bear testimony to the lost glory of Nalanda. Some scholars even trace the beginnings of Nalanda to the 3rd century BCE, to the time of the legendary Mauryan emperor Ashoka, while mythological accounts link the origins of the site to the Buddha himself. Nalanda once lay on the route that connected Pataliputra, the capital of the Nandas and the Mauryas, to two of the most prominent Buddhist sites: Bodh Gaya, the site of the Buddha's enlightenment; and Rajgir (erstwhile Rajagriha), an important political centre during the time of the Buddha and one of his favourite haunts. Nalanda's ascendancy in the region, thus, marks the return of

Buddhism to Magadha, a core area of the original Buddhist heartland. Declared a World Heritage Site in 2016, Nalanda is dominantly seen as the world's most ancient university, flourishing much before Europe's University of Bologna came into being in the 12th century. The word 'university' is derived from the Latin word *universitas*, which denotes a 'whole' or a 'universe'. Broadly speaking, it represents a collective of students of diverse nationalities. Contemporary sources, however, describe the site as a mahavihara, a great monastery. Yet, the site was more than a vihara, a monastic dwelling, in the traditional sense – it functioned as a premier monastic-cum-scholastic establishment in ancient and early medieval India. The monument complex, popularly known as Nalanda, currently lies within a fenced enclosure, entry to which is allowed with a ticket. It is surrounded by features including settlements, fields, temples, tanks and excavated and unexcavated mounds, besides a site museum and some modern buildings that remind us of the once-flourishing Buddhist ecosystem. These surroundings have yielded a variety of artefacts and antiquities connected with multiple faiths, including Buddhism, Jainism and Hinduism.

THE ORIGINS OF THE MAHAVIHARA: BUDDHA, ASHOKA OR GUPTA?

There is a tendency in the Buddhist world to associate major sites connected with the faith with the Buddha himself, and/or Ashoka. Xuanzang had recorded two mythological traditions, which connect the origin of the name 'Nalanda' to the Buddha. According to the first, the place owed its name to a naga of the same name, who lived in a tank built on a mango grove (*amravana*) during the time of the Buddha.[2] As the legend goes, the site of the great monastery was originally a mango grove, which was purchased by 500 merchants for 100 million coins and gifted to the Buddha. Stories of land being gifted to Buddha are not rare. Even in nearby Rajgir, one finds instances of groves gifted to the sangha by the Magadha king Bimbisara (Veluvana/Venuvana), or the famous royal physician Jivaka. Anathapindika, the affluent merchant from Shravasti, is known to have gifted a mango grove to the Buddha, too. The second tradition connects the name of the place to the Buddha's compassion and kindness – Na-alam-da – which denotes abundance and perpetuity of gifts. It is said that in one his previous births as a bodhisattva, the Buddha ruled the region as a king, with his capital at Nalanda. Given his benevolence and kindness, the king and his capital came to be known as Nalanda.[3] Some traditions also trace the origin of the name to a stalk (*nalaka*) of local grass *kasa* (saccharum spontaneum). It is popularly held that cities like Pataliputra and Kushinagar were also named after plants like *patali* and *kusha* respectively.[4]

Like the Buddha, attempts have also been made to connect the origins of Nalanda mahavihara to Ashoka, who ruled the region during the 3rd century BCE. Xuanzang, the Chinese pilgrim, credits Ashoka with building a stupa to enshrine the remains of Sariputra, one of the Buddha's closest disciples. Taranatha, a Tibetan Buddhist monk and scholar, who wrote during the 16th–17th centuries, says Ashoka made offerings at the shrine of Sariputra and erected a temple dedicated to the Buddha there. Some archaeologists feel that Ashoka's structure represents the earliest phase of construction at Nalanda and that its remains could be located at Site 3/Temple 3, popularly known as Sariputra's stupa.[5] Interestingly, Buddhist texts are divided over the location of Sariputra's death. Taranatha says he was born in Nalanda and died there. Xuanzang says Sariputra died in Kalapinaka, around 15 kms from Nalanda. He even associates Maudgalyayana with being born in the vicinity of Nalanda, at a place called Kulika, which is less than 3 kms from the site. Other Buddhist texts mention Shravasti or Nalaka as the place of Sariputra's death. Taranatha associates many other luminaries with Nalanda. This includes Nagarjuna, the famous Mahayana philosopher of the 2nd century CE who made it a strong centre of Mahayana learning; Suvishnu, a Brahman contemporary of Nagarjuna who is said to have built 108 temples at the site; Aryadeva, a philosopher associated with the Madhyamika school of Buddhism in the 4th century CE; Asanga, the Buddhist philosopher of the Yogachara school in the 5th century CE and his famous brother, Vasubandhu, who succeeded the former as the head of the Nalanda mahavihara.[6]

It is only from the Gupta period, around the 5th century CE, that we begin to uncover systematic archaeological evidence from the site, particularly in the form of seals and inscriptions. While the Gupta dynasty (c. 300–600 CE) is typically known for supporting Brahmanical cults, some rulers also extended patronage to Buddhism, as mentioned in Chapter 4. Buddhist texts suggest that Gupta king Vikramaditya sent his queen and son, Baladitya, to study under the renowned Buddhist scholar Vasubandhu at Nalanda. Additionally, some sources mention that Gupta king Narasimhagupta became a Buddhist monk and ended his life through meditation. Xuanzang also reiterates the Gupta rulers' connection with Nalanda. He reports that shortly after the Buddha's demise, a king called Shakraditya built a monastery at the site. His son, Buddhagupta, built another monastery to the south of the one Shakraditya had built. Succeeding Gupta kings also built monasteries near Shakraditya's – Tathagata Gupta to its east and Baladitya to its north-east. An article by missionary and scholar H. Heras, published in 1928, tried to corelate the names of these kings with the actual rulers of the Gupta dynasty. His scheme finds acceptance with most historians. Heras identifies Shakraditya with Kumaragupta I, Buddhagupta with Skandagupta, Tathagatagupta with Puragupta and Baladitya with Narasimhagupta.[7] While it is historically not possible to imagine Gupta kings ruling soon after the Buddha's death, as Xuanzang would have us believe, seals of several Gupta kings, including those of Buddhagupta, Narasimhagupta, Kumaragupta III and Vainyagupta, have been excavated from Nalanda. These give us substantive evidence for Nalanda's royal patronage under the Guptas. It is, however, impossible to associate any of the existing dwellings or temples with any particular Gupta king.[8]

Nalanda continued to enjoy royal patronage in the post-Gupta period as well, during the reign of Harshavardhana (606–48 CE), the king of Kannauj (in Uttar Pradesh); and the Palas, who ruled over modern Bihar, West Bengal and present-day Bangladesh from the 8th to the 12th centuries.[9] Xuanzang visited Nalanda during Harshavardhana's reign. Seals and inscriptions belonging to this period at Nalanda record a gift from King Bhaskaravarman of Assam (during the 7th century CE) and an endowment from Malada, a minister of King Yashovarmadeva, who we mentioned at the outset of this chapter. Harshavardhana is said to have built a brass sheet-covered monastery, which was under construction when Xuanzang visited. He is credited with remitting the revenues of about 100 villages as an endowment to the mahavihara, so that its students did not have to beg for daily food and could concentrate on their studies instead. Around a 1,000 monks of Nalanda were believed to be present at the royal congregation at Kanauj convened by Harshavardhana.

The Palas were known to be Buddhists. The second Pala king, Dharmapala (c. 781–821 CE), is known to have supported the establishment of Somapura (better known as Paharpur, now in Bangladesh) and Vikramashila (in Bhagalpur in Bihar) monastries. An inscription from Nalanda also records his gift of a village for the upkeep of the great monastery. Another inscription from the site describes Dharmapala's successor, Devapala (c. 821–61 CE), as helping the ruler of Suvarnadvipa (Sumatra), Balaputra, build a monastery at Nalanda and acquire five villages to support its maintenance. This inscription, and the one recording the gift from a king of Assam, dated to Harshavardhana's reign, which points to a much wider royal patronage for Nalanda. The Pala period is associated with the widespread production of sculptures and images, though not under direct royal patronage. It is also known for several gifts being granted to the mahavihara, again independent of the Pala kings. It is widely held that Nalanda started declining during the late Pala period and that it was dealt a death blow by the attacks of Bakhtiyar Khalji around 1200 CE.

There are some significant gaps in our knowledge of Nalanda. These emerge primarily because of discrepancies between textual accounts and archaeological findings. As far as the texts are concerned, most information on the history, functioning and layout of the mahavihara comes to us from the accounts of Xuanzang (also known as Hiuen Tsang) and Yijing, but primarily the former. Both travelled to India and stayed in the great monastery complex during the 7th century CE, when it was in its prime. Xuanzang stayed here between 635 and 641 CE, while Yijing stayed between 671 and 693 CE. Were it not for the accounts of these travellers, Nalanda's very existence might have remained unknown to the posterity. Even the official plaque of the ASI at the entrance of the UNESCO World Heritage

Site is predominantly informed by Xuanzang's account. However, the layout of the structures excavated at the site does not exactly match Xuanzang's layout. Most studies trying to corelate the findings of the excavations conducted around the mahavihara in 1915–37 and 1974–82 with the descriptions given in the travel accounts encounter significant gaps. Notably, Xuanzang's account – available to us in the form of Samuel Beal's English translation (1884), which in turn borrows significantly from Stanislas Julien's French translation of the Chinese text published in 1853 – is based primarily on his memories and was recorded sometime after he returned to China. Besides, scholars point out, the purpose of his visit to India was to secure accurate translations of Buddhist texts from their places of origin. He was neither writing a travelogue, nor was he taking extensive notes during his stay.[10]

Another major gap stems from the fact that most visitors to Nalanda only get to experience the excavated and enclosed area, which contains the remains of the revealed structures. They never get to imagine, or experience, Nalanda in its entirety, or even as a significant part of the larger, extended complex. Recent excavations, surveys and satellite imageries have revealed that the mahavihara complex extended much beyond this excavated and enclosed area. Also, the mahavihara had an organic and symbiotic relationship with the surrounding agrarian countryside. In the next section, we will try and get an idea of the larger complex, but let us first have a look at the excavated and enclosed site.

BEYOND THE ENCLOSED ZONE

Before we explore the ruins, we need to bear in mind that the ASI follows a numeric scheme to denote the structures in the excavated and enclosed zone (see site map 1). The structures are known by their numbers rather than individual names. The most conspicuous part of the excavated and enclosed zone is Site 3, also known as Temple 3, Stupa 3, the Great Stupa, Sariputra's Stupa, or the 'Great Monument'. It is difficult to miss this structure as it features in most visual representations of Nalanda and Buddhist heritage of India. It also remains the focus of most tourist guides.

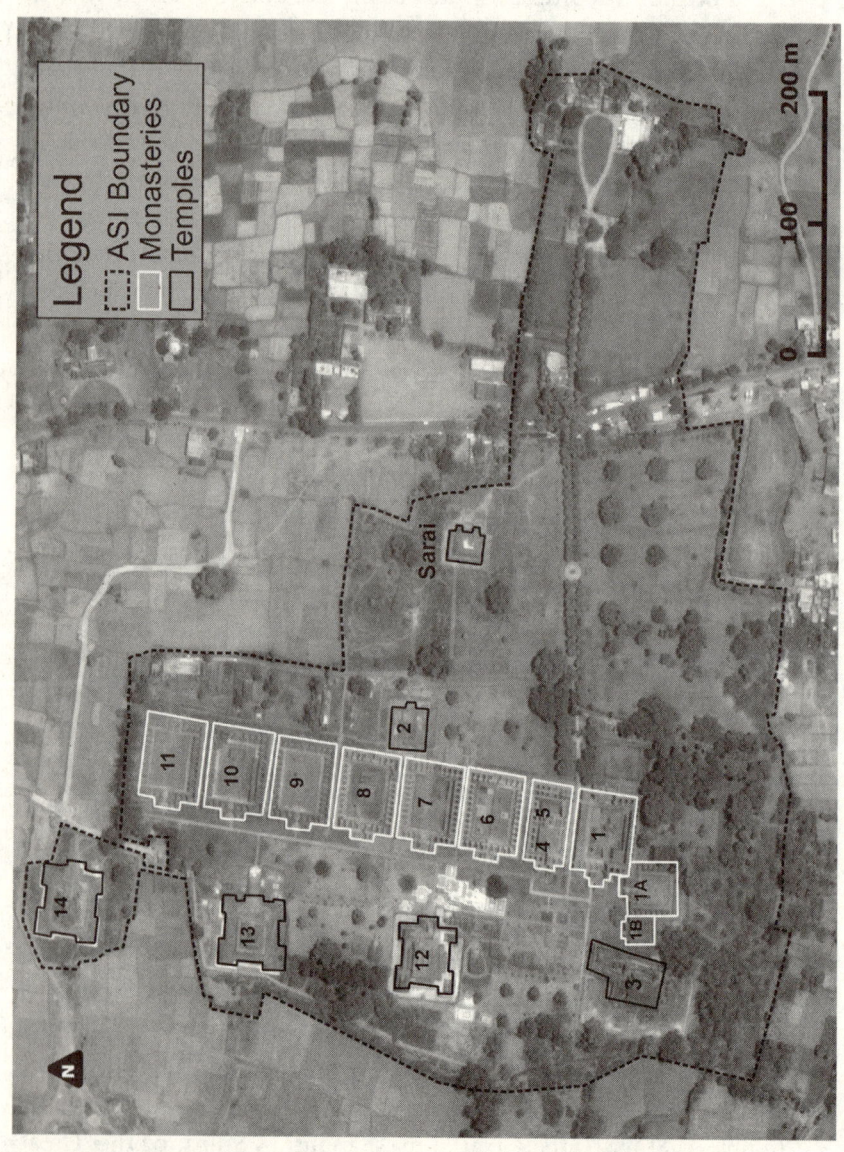

Layout of the enclosed-excavated area of the Nalanda mahavihara.
Courtesy M. B. Rajani

Site 3 represents the oldest part of the mahavihara, and its sacred core, too. Any visitor to Nalanda, familiar or unfamiliar with its history, can understand this from the clustering of structures around Site 3, which includes viharas, stupas and shrines. Like Taxila in the Gandhara region, this site reflects a clustered arrangement of structures around the sacred core. The later structures (6th–11th century CE) follow a prominent north–south, linear arrangement, with Site 3 as the focal point.[11] All monuments were originally built in brick and decorated with stucco. Some of them also carry stone structures that were added later during the Pala period.

The enclosed area, which is ticketed, broadly follows a rectangular plan with two parallel rows of monuments. It has rows of three temples and eleven viharas that flank the western and eastern sides of the principal north–south axis leading to Site 3. The temples appear to move south to north in the following order: Site 3 (Temple 3), Site 12 (Temple 12), Site 13 (Temple 13) and Site 14 (Temple 14). Running parallel to the temples is a row of eleven viharas, which run from the south to the north in the following order: 1, 4 (and 5), 6, 7, 8, 9, 10 and 11. Monastery 1A and 1B lie between Temple 3 and Monastery 1 in the south and are perpendicular to the two latter sites. Site 5 (Monastery 5) is regarded as an extension of Monastery 4. The temples face eastwards towards the monasteries, while the monasteries open westwards in the direction of the temples. Two structures, which somewhat disturb the linear arrangement in the enclosed and ticketed area, are Site 2/Temple 2, which has the remains of a temple till its plinth level; and the monument known as the 'shrine mound', located further east of Site 2. Both these structures are temples that lie behind the row of monasteries, further to the east.

For a very long time, it was believed that the enclosed and excavated area constituted the Nalanda mahavihara, which functioned between the 6th and 12th centuries. Later, deeper questions emerged around the site, which have led to a shift in the way we have traditionally understood Nalanda. How could such a small area accommodate so many resident monks? Xuanzang mentions 10,000 residents staying on the campus, while Yijing puts the figure at 3,000. Further, Nalanda must have grown even after the 7th century, once the Chinese travellers left, to become even more populous under the Palas. How did the mahavihara sustain itself? Were the monasteries multi-storeyed skyscrapers? Where did the residents get their food and water? What was the relationship of the university with the surrounding countryside? Do the antiquities found in the surroundings have any connection with the mahavihara?

Surely, the mahavihara complex must have been larger than the existing complex. Even historical eyewitness accounts of the mahavihara talk about areas and sites that currently lie outside of the excavated and enclosed zone. Scholars have tried to deploy new methods to locate and understand the extent of the complex, including satellite imagery and extended archaeological surveys. These have confirmed that Nalanda may have been around twice the size of the excavated-enclosed area, perhaps more (see site map 2). M. B. Rajani and others have underlined the following points regarding the extended boundaries of the complex.[12]

First, several water tanks (*pokhar*s) have been found around the enclosed and excavated Nalanda site, including Dighi, Pansokar, Indra, etc. This means that, like other Buddhist sites such as Sanchi, Thotlakonda or Anuradhapura in Sri Lanka, Nalanda had access to multiple water bodies to support agriculture and livelihood. Even the Chinese travellers, and later the British explorers, have mentioned the existence of such tanks in the vicinity. In a 1998 publication, names of twenty-nine tanks around the mahavihara were listed, even though local tradition speaks of fifty-two tanks. Some scholars have suggested that these tanks were not created to act as reservoirs but were dug up to procure earth to manufacture bricks used to build temples, monasteries and other structures. However, the location, layout and shapes of most of these tanks underscore careful planning. They are mostly geometrical, square or rectangular, with sides roughly parallel to the four cardinal directions of the complex. These carefully planned, human-made tanks once demarcated the physical boundaries of the monastery complex (Fig 9.1). There are also indications to suggest that the largest tank, Dighi Pokhar, was river-fed. It has been held that the Nalanda region once received water through a palaeochannel of the river Panchana, though archaeologists and geologists are yet to

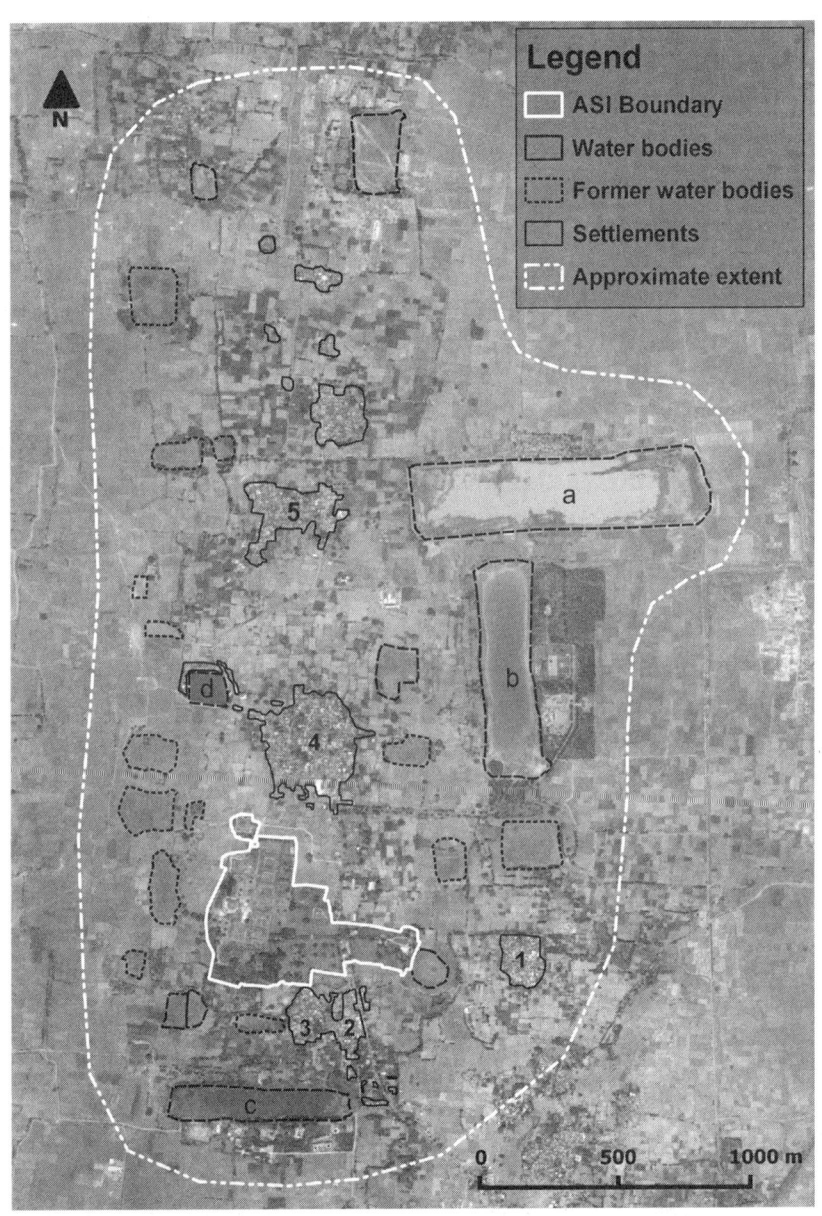

Extended layout of the Nalanda Mahavihara area. Courtesy M. B. Rajani

ascertain if this flow was contemporaneous with the period during which Nalanda was functional.

Second, surveys have revealed the existence of at least three more temples, which now lie outside the ticketed area. These fall in the same south–north linear layout as Temples 3, 12, 13 and 14. These temples are located at regular intervals. Two of them lie to the north of Temple 14 and one to the south of Site 3. The mound, on which two temples north of Temple 14 stood, is now used for agriculture. No ruins can be seen on the surface. These two temples once lay closest to the villages of Baragaon and Surajpur, the largest settlements in the region. It is, therefore, possible that bricks from these structures were mined and recycled for the construction of buildings and roads. Surveys have also revealed that there might have been three or four more monasteries further south of the existing monasteries, towards Kardigya, Muzaffarpur and Kapatia villages, and Indra and Rahela pokhars.

Third, the findings have brought to light two large and distinct mounds in and around the mahavihara complex. Separated by a gap of around 500 m, one is located in (or around) the south and the other to the north. The southern mound is larger and forms an elongated structure stretching 1.6 kms in a north–south direction. It includes the whole of the enclosed and excavated area – the temples (2, 3, 12, 13, 14 and Sarai) and the monasteries (1A, 1B, 1, 4 to 11) – and adjacent regions, including the villages of Muzaffarpur, Kapatia, Surajpur and Baragaon. The smaller, northern mound that lies outside of the enclosed and excavated area also falls within the cluster of water bodies that appear to surround the mahavihara complex. This mound is also referred to as the mud fort of Khamgar Khan. Some scholars feel this mound in Begumpur, 2 kms north of the enclosed and excavated site, formed the northern gate of the mahavihara. Others have suggested that it contains the hidden remains of a large four-pointed structure that was architecturally very similar (in size, shape and orientation) to two prominent Pala-period monasteries – Vikramashila and Somapura – both of which are large quadrangular structures consisting of a vihara with a cruciform stupa at the centre.

The idea of a much bigger mahavihara complex has, in turn, led historians and archaeologists to explore the larger networks and connections of the site, perhaps a larger Nalanda region too. It is now understood that the mahavihara enjoyed a dynamic relationship with the villages and habitations surrounding it to meet its food requirements and to source goods and services for the numerous resident monks who were exclusively consumers. Also, Nalanda had connections with the monasteries in the vicinity. These included the famous Odantapura (or Odantapuri) mahavihara reportedly located in modern-day Bihar Sharif, which is 16 kms north of Nalanda; where Atisha, the monk credited with spreading Buddhism in Tibet and Sumatra, reportedly taught; Yashovarmapura monastery at Ghosrawan, which is 22 kms to the east; and Telhara (earlier known as Tiladhaka), which is 33 kms north-west, from where the famous Black Buddha that is now housed in the Teliya Bhandar Bhairav Mandir at Baragaon, was found.

Nalanda's history was also connected with the images that were found in the surrounding villages and are currently housed in modern temples and worshipped locally. These include villages like Ghosrawan, Tetrawan (where a huge, seated image of the Buddha was found), Baragaon, Jagdishpur (known for the huge, seated stone image of the Buddha that is now housed in Rukmini-Harana-Sthana temple), Surajpur and Begumpur. These images once formed a part of Nalanda's artistic and sculptural achievements. To this list, one may add the stone and bronze sculptures excavated from Nalanda and now kept in the Nalanda Archaeological Museum, Patna Museum, Indian Museum in Kolkata and the National Museum in New Delhi. It has also been suggested that Nalanda possibly had an artistic exchange with nearby regions like Rajgir – whose urban and secular culture may have supported the needs of a growing monk population at the mahavihara – as well as important Jaina pilgrimage sites like Pawapuri (believed to be the site of Mahavira's death and nirvana) and Kundalpur (believed to be the birth place of Mahavira), though these connections need to be researched further.[13] Having discussed the larger geocultural boundaries and related networks, let us now explore the story of the mahavihara's enclosed zone – its buildings and structures, its functioning as a university, its sculptural wealth and its connections with the Buddha and other religious traditions. Among the buildings and structures, three are conspicuous by their presence: the temples, the monasteries and the stupas.[14]

TEMPLES, MONASTERIES AND STUPAS

Site 3 (Temple 3) is the most iconic of all the monuments in the excavated and enclosed zone. Excavations reveal that this structure went through seven phases of construction, through which a focal stupa was transformed into a five-fold temple complex called a panchayatana chaitya. The panchayatana architectural plan, which became common during the Gupta period, is normally seen in temples dedicated to Hindu god Vishnu. As mentioned earlier, this plan can be seen in the Mahabodhi temple complex. However, while the Mahabodhi temple was largely reconstructed in the 19th century by the colonial administration, the Nalanda temple retains the original brick-and-plaster construction built over centuries.[15] The present structure has several stories and remains of staircases, and a small shrine is visible on top. The subsidiary shrines, or towers, at Site 3 are square in shape, surmounted by octagonal constructions and carry beautifully carved stucco images in the lower portions, which belong to the 6th or 7th centuries CE (Fig 9.2). Over a period, numerous small and votive stupas were constructed around the site.

Next to Site 3, in the south–north direction, is Temple 12 (Fig 9.3). This comes across as the largest and most complex of all temples. Temple 12 was probably built in two stages. The earlier phase belongs to the 7th century CE and the latter one dates to the 11th century. The structure contains small shrines in the four corners and broadly follows the five-fold, or the panchayatana, plan seen in Stupa 3. The entrance to the shrine in the south-east corner has two carved stone pillars. One of the courtyards of the temple contains small stone and brick stupas. This temple has yielded inscriptions of Pala kings Dharmapala and Mahendrapala.

The other two temples, Temple 13 and Temple 14, have been found in very primary stages. Both were built on a plinth and carried stucco decorations. Both once contained images of the Buddha, details of which are difficult to describe now.

The monasteries facing the temples are of varying sizes. Now, one can only see the remains of the lower portions. Archaeologists tell us that they went through different phases of building or renovation, beginning during the Gupta period and seeing modifications during the Pala period. The monasteries possibly had a tower on the top, a Gupta-age speciality absent in traditional monasteries. Xuanzang talks about the Sarnath monasteries with 'lofty towers mingling with clouds'. Even Malada's inscription, mentioned at the beginning of the chapter, talks about cloud-licking towers or spires.[16] All of them follow a somewhat uniform plan – a row of monks' cells surrounding a large central courtyard; a single entrance from the west; a staircase in the south-west corner leading to the upper storeys; and a large cell (bigger than the others) in the centre of the eastern wall (opposite the entrance), which probably contained an image of the Buddha (Fig 9.4). These special cells came to be known as gandhakutis believed to be occupied by the Buddha himself. We shall discuss specifications of the gandhakutis at Nalanda in detail in the next section. For now, let us return to the monasteries.

The monasteries were probably several storeys high to accommodate even a part of the number of monks Xuanzang and Yijing talk about. They had facilities like a kitchen, a well and a granary, alongside a common place for meetings and prayers (Fig 9.5). Stucco images once adorned the entrances of the monasteries and the large cell in the eastern wall. Each monastery was perhaps headed by an abbot, or a chief instructor. Monastery 5, which is an extension of the eastern wall of Monastery 4, is sometimes referred to as a guest house. Monastery 1 has a somewhat special character – it is the largest of the monastic dwellings and went through at least nine phases of construction. It is here that the Pala inscription recording the gift of King Balaputra of Suvarnadvipa was found. Several copperplate inscriptions recording major donations to Nalanda have also been found here, along with bronze sculptures. The dwelling was entered through a portico supported by columns and flanked by stucco figures. Two rooms in the north, which come across as later additions, have corbelled entrances with true vaulted roofs, a feature rarely seen in pre-Islamic monuments. Two other dwellings, 1A and 1B, lie almost perpendicular to the rest of the dwellings and connect them to Site 3. Also, 1B is the smallest of all the monastic dwellings and was perhaps the earliest one to be constructed.

East of the row of monasteries lies Temple 2, of which only the large plinth and lower portions remain (Fig 9.6). From the fragments lying near the structure, one can make out that it once stood as a tall temple. The plinth carries carved stone panels of both Hindu and Buddhist deities and figures and probably dates to the 7th century. The panels also have depictions of scenes related to the 'great epics', like Ramayana and Mahabharata.

Further east of Temple 2 lies another temple called the Temple of Sarai Mound, which was excavated recently. Constructed around the 7th–8th centuries CE, this temple was built by a king called Purnavarman and once housed a colossal statue of the Buddha, about 80 feet long, as Xuanzang would have us believe. An inscription of Purnavarman, about whom not much is known, has also been found in the temple premises. Interestingly, the colossal statue's stucco-covered stone pedestal was found to contain paintings. So, the image was painted too, at some point. This multi-storeyed temple was once enclosed by a wall and contained miniature stupas and shrines.

The highest concentration of miniature stupas, both votive and commemorative, have been found around Site 3 and Site 12 (Fig 9.7). These stupas are principally of two types – those built of brick mostly between the 5th and 8th centuries CE, belonging to the Gupta and early Pala periods; and those constructed in stone between the 8th and 12th centuries CE, belonging to the mature and late Pala periods. The brick stupas were covered with stucco, painted or gilded, and adorned with stone images. Found in a dilapidated condition, they are mostly concentrated around Site 3. The stone stupas are comparatively better-preserved and are mostly found around Site 12. A few smaller bronze stupas have also been recovered from Nalanda.

Most stupas at Nalanda have a square base, over which stands a cylindrical drum. They are topped by a hemispherical dome. The drum had arched niches, which housed images of the Buddha and the bodhisattvas. These images show the Buddha in different mudras. Some niches depict four of the five dhyani buddhas, associated with the four cardinal directions. Few stupas also carried principal scenes from the life of the Buddha, a motif that became very conspicuous in Buddhist art 8th century CE onwards, a theme we will touch upon later in the chapter. The votive stupas probably had a funerary association and contained corporal remains of scholars and teachers associated with Nalanda. These structures were perhaps revered by the resident monks. The core of some later stupas at Nalanda also contain inscribed texts called dharanis – a practice also seen in stupas at Bodh Gaya, Paharpur, Odisha and some other sites. These texts, as discussed earlier, had a funerary association and were primarily concerned with the problems of death, avoidance of rebirths, other unfortunate destinies, or with the release of those already born.[17]

The temples, monasteries and stupas once formed an integral part of the socio-cultural and religious milieu of a complex, which has popularly been described as the world's most ancient university, a theme we will delve into now.

THE MAHAVIHARA AS A UNIVERSITY

We have already discussed that Nalanda has been mentioned as a mahavihara and not 'university' in contemporary sources. It was not a university in the modern sense, but it was not a traditional vihara either, devoted entirely to the cause of Buddhism. It served both as a centre for training monks and as a seat of higher learning and culture, especially of Mahayana scholastic philosophy. A closer reading of this institution helps us comprehend the evolving nature of the vihara and the lives of the resident monks therein.

The viharas, as we know by now, had commonly evolved as temporary retreats for the Buddhist monks during the monsoons. Later, more permanent structures were erected both within the caves (Ajanta) or as independent structures (Bodh Gaya or Sanchi). Under the Guptas, a new kind of monastic organization emerged. Known as a mahavihara, this was an aggregation, or confederation, of several monasteries. In these mahaviharas, old and traditional monastic learning outgrew its cloistered and inbred character of memorizing the canonical lore for the benefit and use of monks. Instead, it was progressively liberalized and made available to not only the monks but to all seekers of knowledge.[18] Instead of wandering from place to place to spread the teachings of the Buddha and the sangha, and refuting those of the other faiths, the monks at Nalanda led a settled life and were concerned more with scholasticism and Buddhist metaphysical and epistemological traditions.[19] Also, the viharas of Nalanda served as both residential and educational buildings.

Most information on the functioning of Nalanda as a university – its student strength, curriculum and buildings – comes from Chinese texts, that too in a very scattered form.[20] Xuanzang claims the mahavihara had 10,000 students, but Yijing puts that number at 3,000. The Chinese travellers claim that Nalanda received students from distant places. Also, monks from Nalanda travelled to places outside India, but we have no details available about the countries where the students came from. It is assumed that they came from China, Japan, Korea and other countries in Southeast Asia and Central Asia. Also, entry to the university was restricted. Outsiders were reportedly allowed to enter the premises only after an oral examination conducted by the gatekeeper, who appeared to be a person of substantive intellectual calibre. Hui Li, Xuanzang's biographer, wrote that during the time of Xuanzang's visit, there were 1,000 monks at Nalanda, who could explain twenty collections of sutras and shastras, 500 who could explicate thirty collections and only ten who could expound on fifty collections (including Xuanzang). He also mentions that, every day, around 100 pulpits were set within the temple for preaching, but he does not give any details. Possibly, there were multiple such pulpits within the courtyards of the monasteries.[21] Such pulpits, or the courtyards themselves, may have, at one point of time, buzzed with the lectures of illustrious figures like Gunamati, Sthiramati, Prabhamitra, Jinamitra, Jnanachandra, Sigrabuddha, Shantarakshita, Silabhadra, Dhammapala and Chandrapala, as Xuanzang would have us believe. They not only taught there but also composed treatises and commentaries. Taranatha, who wrote much later, points out that Nalanda was also the site for intellectual debates or disputations. He says Dignaga, the founder of the medieval school of logic, was a southerner who was invited to defeat a Brahmanist scholar in an intellectual dispute. Likewise, Dharmakirti is credited with having defeated Brahmanical philosopher Kumarila.[22] The teachers apparently were the focus of the monasteries, and the new students chose their residences based on the teachers they studied with. Xuanzang seems to have first met Buddhabhadra, one of the teachers at Nalanda, and settled in the latter's residence. The officials and the head of the mahavihara were likely elected by an assembly of monks who were formidable scholars in their own right.[23] Hui Li generally mentions that the subjects taught at Nalanda included logic, metaphysics, grammar and philology, philosophy, medicine and Buddhist scriptures. A recent book says around eighteen disciplines (and multiple sub-disciplines) were taught at Nalanda. It emphasizes the importance of the schools of medicine, metallurgy and astronomy. Its school of medicine in fact drew visitors from Central and East Asia.[24] Mahayanist philosophy may have been the forte of the mahavihara as all Nalanda luminaries listed by Xuanzang were known as its finest exponents. It is also held that the university had two categories of students – those who wore white robes and studied Buddhist scriptures and those who were interested in secular subjects. Yijing talks about the strict discipline that the monks observed and how their daily lives were regulated by a water clock. He mentions how the life led by the Nalanda monks was regarded as an ideal to be followed by Buddhists all over the world. From around the 9th to the 12th–13th centuries, as we shall deliberate later in this chapter, Nalanda functioned as an important centre of Vajrayana and was known for its tantric teachers and monk-scholars.

The Chinese travellers also talk about the richly carved eight halls and 300 apartments on the Nalanda premises. None of them, however, record the existence of a library, though they are known to have copied several manuscripts during their stay at the mahavihara. Xuanzang is said to have carried with himself 657 volumes of Sanskrit Buddhist texts on twenty horses. Scholars have pointed out that Nalanda had a huge number of manuscripts, which included original works composed at the mahavihara and copies of sutras and shastras. During the Pala times, three copies of the voluminous *Astasahasrika Prajnaparamita* were made. Further, Nalanda had an organized system in place for writing and copying manuscripts and keeping books. The book culture was promoted in a big way by the mahavihara which also arranged funds for it.[25] Information about a library is given in the later 17th-century Tibetan records. The library area was reportedly called dharmaganja. It apparently consisted of three buildings – Ratnasagar, Ratnadadhi and Ratnaranjak. Archaeological excavations conducted so far, however, have not revealed any evidence regarding a library.

The mahavihara complex was not just bustling with teachers, monks, scholars and philosophers, but it also reverberated with what was believed to be the personal presence of the Buddha.

For now, let us return to the special residential cell of the viharas.

THE BUDDHA'S LIVING PRESENCE IN THE MONASTERIES

Monasteries with cells created in the centre of the back wall, facing the main entrance, were also referred to as shrine-cum-viharas. Such special cells are called gandhakutis, or 'perfumed chambers' are also found in earlier monasteries like Kalyanabhadra in Benares and Anathapindika at Shravasti (along with supportive inscriptions). As we saw in the chapter on Ajanta, monasteries containing gandhakutis had become an established part of the Buddhist architecture 5th century CE onwards. They can be seen at several monastic structures, including those at Ajanta, Kanheri, Bagh, Bodh Gaya, Sarnath, Vallabhi, Kurkihar and Nalanda.

The idea of gandhakutis evolved over the years. In the earlier tradition, represented in Shravasti, the gandhakuti was 'the room occupied by the Buddha' but, in the later constructions like Nalanda, it was used to describe the 'Buddha's private chamber'. What did these structures symbolize?

The Buddha was believed to be a resident of such monasteries between the 5th and the 11th centuries. He is said to have lived in these monastic quarters. This is corroborated by contemporary inscriptions that describe the Buddha as residing in these specific structures.[26]

An inscription related to King Yashovarmadeva, found from Monastery 1 and dated to the 7th century, is a relevant case in point. The inscription records a series of benefactions made by the son of a royal minister. This includes a 'permanent endowment' meant specifically 'for the Blessed One, the Buddha'. It also carries a unique warning: 'Whoever would create an obstacle to this gift, which is to last as long as the created world [he should know that] the Conqueror in person, the Blessed One, dwells always here within on the "diamond throne".' It has been argued that the permanent endowment was given directly to the Buddha. Further, the place where the 'Blessed One' is always said to dwell was the *layana* (or *lena*), the residence given to the monks. The idea of the personal presence of the Buddha is also indicated in the passages where he is referred to as the *pramukha* (head) of the community of monks. Another inscription at Nalanda, an early 9th-century copperplate grant of Devapala, records the gift of five villages being made 'for the sake of providing an income to the Blessed One [residing] there.' While Yashovarmadeva's inscription describes the Buddha's personal presence through a permanent endowment given directly to him, the Devapala inscription refers to villages transferred directly to the Buddha, which he owned.

Some inscriptional references also clarify that these special cells were recognized as formal organizational components of the monasteries and had specific groups of monks attached to them.[27] References to the gandhakuti *varikas*, or 'monks in charge of the perfumed chamber', are found from monasteries in Nalanda, Kanheri and Andhra Pradesh. Interestingly, sealings recovered from Nalanda refer to two distinct groups of gandhakuti varikas: first, 'of/for/ belonging to the monks in charge of the perfumed chamber of Sri Baladitya at Sri Nalanda'; and second, 'of/for/belonging to the monks in charge of the perfumed chamber of Dharmapaladeva at Sri Nalanda'. These sealings and their language suggest a few things. First, individual monasteries, even at a single site, had their own gandhakutis. Second, these gandhakutis could be named individually after their chief donors or sponsors, like the monasteries themselves. Third, the gandhakutis functioned as distinct and individual entities that either owned their own movable property or had their own official correspondence with other monastic establishments in the region. The language of the sealings makes it clear that the Buddha was believed to have been a current resident, that he had an abiding presence in the medieval Buddhist monasteries.

Fig 9.1 Pushkarni, one of the water bodies located outside the excavated Nalanda site

Fig 9.2 Site 3, popularly believed to be Monk Sariputra's stupa

Fig 9.3 Ruins of Temple 12, the largest and most complex temple within the enclosed area

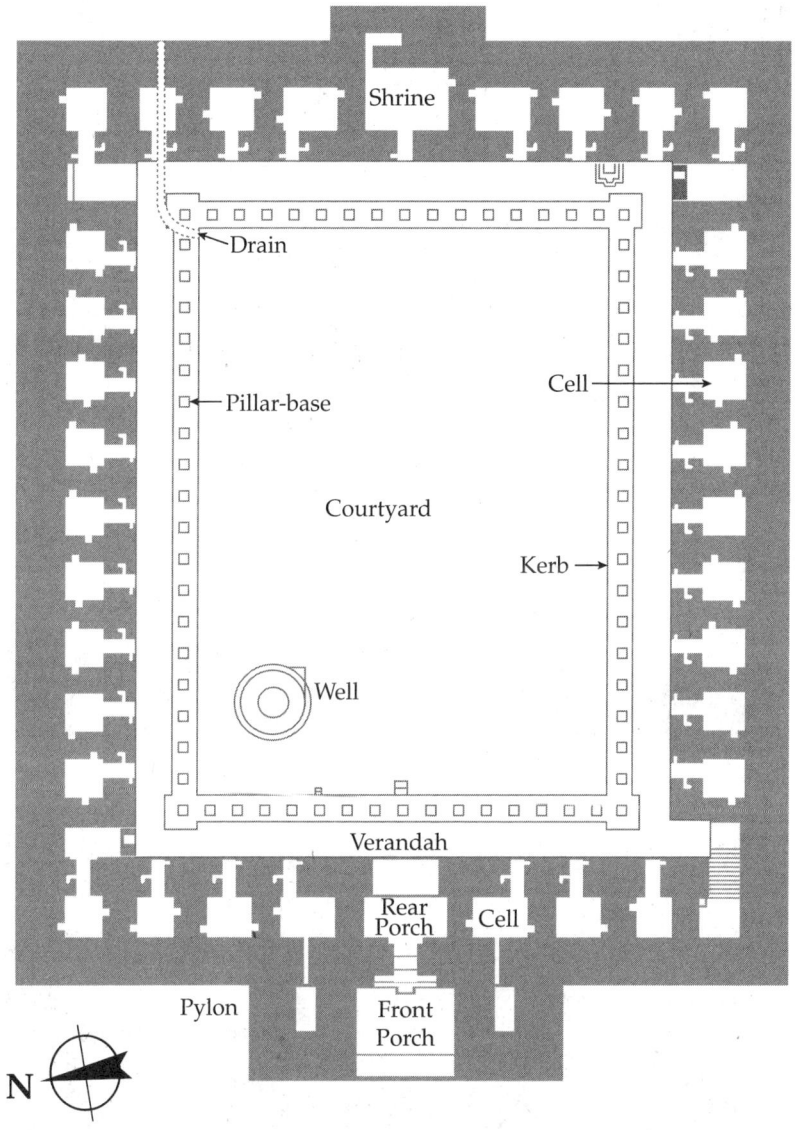

Fig 9.4 Layout of Monastery 8, Nalanda (after Debala Mitra, *Buddhist Monuments*, 1971)

Fig 9.5 Ruins of Monastery 6, displaying the arrangement of monk cells around a central courtyard

Fig 9.6 The plinth of Temple 2, which was once a large and imposing structure

Fig 9.7 Miniature shrines and votive stupas found in the Temple 12 complex

Fig 9.8 A black Buddha statue in bhumisparsha mudra, known as Teliya Baba, now enshrined in a temple in Baragaon

Fig 9.9 Nalanda Museum, established in 1917

Fig 9.10 A partial view of the Nalanda International University Campus, featuring architecture inspired by the ancient mahavihara

The presence of the Buddha manifested not only in the form of the gandhakutis, but also in the numerous stucco, stone and bronze sculptures found in the extended mahavihara complex. Unfortunately, the sculptures of Nalanda have not been studied adequately. They indicate that Nalanda was much more than a monastic-cum-educational establishment.

STUCCO, STONE AND BRONZE: UNDERSTUDIED ARTISTIC ACCOMPLISHMENTS

We discussed earlier how the Gandhara and Mathura regions emerged as cradles of Buddhist art in India. Gradually, with the spread of the Buddhist faith, new centres of art appeared in the Gangetic valley and in peninsular India (Amravati, Ajanta, Sarnath). On account of the volume and variety of art objects recovered from the site, some scholars have suggested that even Nalanda had its own school of art, which was centred around the mahavihara. Nalanda's long existence as a prominent centre of Buddhist learning and philosophy, it is held, offered it a pivotal position amongst other sites associated with pedagogical, religious and artistic development. Nalanda not only shaped Pala-period art but also influenced the development of art in the Malayan archipelago. The stucco, stone and metal/bronze sculptures of Nalanda showcase the expanding Buddhist pantheon of the Mahayana and Vajrayana traditions. They also show how the art traditions developed at Mathura and Sarnath, synthesized with local traditions and those developed under the Palas, to acquire beautiful forms.[28]

A wide variety of sculptures have been recovered from Nalanda.[29] These include stucco and stone images found at Site 3; images on the stone panels found at the plinth of Temple 2; and stone and metal images found in museums, including the Nalanda Site Museum, Patna Museum, Indian Museum in Kolkata and the National Museum in Delhi, besides a few in museums abroad. Some images have been found in the surrounding villages, too, enshrined in temples. These include the Jagdishpur Buddha image and the Teliya Buddha statue from Baragaon (Fig 9.8), which we will discuss later in the chapter. One of the most striking artistic achievements of Nalanda could be seen in the panels of stucco sculptures at Site 3. Most images, which have survived the onslaught of time and theft, are seen on the eastern facade of Stupa 3, or the Great Monument, and date to the first half of the 7th century. These include images of the Buddha in various postures, bodhisattva, Avalokiteshvara, Tara, Loknath, Manjushri, etc. Sadly, the heads of many stucco images at Site 3 were chiselled off in a case of night theft during the 1970s. Interestingly, stucco works from Nalanda are said to have influenced art in Thailand. Some stone images, mostly in black phyllite and a few in grey sandstone, have also been recovered from Site 3. These belong largely to the 8th century CE and include figures of an eight-armed Avalokiteshvara, Loknatha (or Samantabhadra) and Manjushri, besides some female deities. Miniature stone images of the Buddha and the bodhisattvas, which were used as objects of veneration by the resident monks, have also been recovered from the rooms in the monasteries.

Another prominent location of the stone sculptures at Nalanda is the plinth of Temple 2, lying further east of the monasteries. Around 220 stone sculptures have been recovered from here. Ascribed to the 7th–8th centuries, these are a continuous band of arched niches separated by pilasters. They include images which have been identified as Hindu gods Skanda, Shiva, Kubera and Krishna with his mother, Yashoda. The plinth is also adorned with scenes from the Ramayana and Mahabharata. The presence of such images has led some scholars to argue that this structure represented a Hindu temple, while others contend that the plinth depicted the outer circle of a Buddhist mandala that was inhabited by Hindu deities. Stone images of Hindu deities such as Vishnu, Durga, Shiva–Parvati, as well as those associated with popular cults (such as Kubera and Nagaraja) have also been found in the Nalanda and other museums. These belong to a later date, the 9th–11th centuries CE. Other images of this period, found in the site museum, include those of the Buddha, Avalokiteshvara, Manjushri, Vajrapani, Padmapani, Vajrasattva and Marichi. Of the various representations of the Buddha, those showing him in the bhumisparsha mudra, a posture which symbolizes him overpowering of the Buddhist demon Mara during the process of his enlightenment, are common in Nalanda.

Many stone images have been found in the surroundings of the enclosed and ticketed area of Nalanda, primarily in villages like Baragaon and Begumpur. These include the colossal statue called the Jagdishpur Buddha, which is now enshrined in a temple called Rukmini-Harana-Sthana. Dated to around the 10th–11th centuries CE, this image depicts the Buddha in the iconic bhumisparsha mudra. Interestingly, the Jagdishpur Buddha carries the eight scenes from the life of the Buddha. Representations of the Buddha in the bhumisparsha mudra and those carrying the eight scenes from his life around a central image of his are seen in some other images belonging to the same period at the Nalanda museum. Some scholars have argued how the eight scenes, depicted in different orders in different representations, became a noticeable feature of Buddhist art, particularly in eastern India, 8th century CE onwards. These indicated the growing cult of pilgrimage to the eight sites connected with the life of the Buddha (*ashthamahasthana*).[30] It should be noted that panels these eight events, or scenes, also feature in some miniature stone images recovered from the cells of the monks in the monasteries.

The 8th century is also known for the production of bronze images in eastern and southern India, as we talked about in Chapter 5. Excavations in Kurkihar, an ancient village in Gaya district located just 70 kms from Nalanda, brought to light a hoard of 226 bronze objects dateable to the 9th–12th centuries. Kurkihar was apparently known for the Apanaka monastery, which was said to be very popular among visitors from Kanchi in southern India. Images of the Buddha, bodhisattvas, votive stupas, bells and other ritual objects, alongside Hindu divinities, have been recovered from the excavations conducted here. These are currently on display in the Patna Museum. The inscriptions on the bronze objects found at Kurkihar connect them with the Pala kings. Many bronze images have been found in Nalanda as well, and they belong primarily to the 9th and 10th centuries CE. Some of these images were gilded, too. Was there some connection between these images and the presence of a brick-lined smelting furnace to the north of Site 13? Recovered mostly from the monasteries, the bronze images may have served as objects of worship for the resident monks. Now housed in museums at Nalanda, Patna,

Kolkata and Delhi, these include images of the Buddha, bodhisattva, Avalokiteshvara, Tara, Chunda, Prajnaparamita, Hariti and Panchika. Nalanda's metal art, meanwhile, is credited with influencing art and social life in the Malay Archipelago, Burma, Nepal and Tibet.

We don't have extensive evidence regarding the prevalence of an established painting tradition at Nalanda. Some stucco and bronze images, particularly those placed in the gandhakutis and the sanctum of the temples, were painted. One can see remnants of paintings from the pedestal of giant stucco images of the Buddha recovered from the Sarai Mound and the temple at Site 14. However, Nalanda was certainly known for painted manuscripts and some of them, primarily the colophons, were most likely prepared by the dharma preachers (*dharmabhanakas*). There was possibly a group of monks, which specialized in the preparation of such manuscripts, especially for foreigners. Many such manuscripts, with images, probably left the site in the distant past. The few that survive in museums belong mostly to the 11th century and are associated with the Pala period.

Sadly, like the construction of buildings, the production of sculptures and manuscripts also seems to have ended around the 12th–13th centuries. At least that is what the evidence seems to suggest. One sees a perceptible decline in Buddhist activities at Nalanda around this period. It is true that by the time mature Pala period set in, other Buddhist monasteries like Vikramashila (Bhagalpur district, Bihar), Somapura (Paharpur, Bangladesh) and Odantapuri (around Bihar Sharif) had become well-established and were competing for royal patronage. Their growing importance may have affected Nalanda's prominence in the region.[31] However, could this account for the sudden decline of an institution that had been flourishing for centuries? It is unlikely.

In Chapter 6, we discussed some structural factors responsible for the decline of Buddhism in major parts of India around this period. The absence of historical documentation certainly complicates our understanding of Nalanda after the 12th–13th centuries. Meanwhile, the sudden decline of Nalanda is a topic that continues to be debated vigorously in academic circles and the public domain. The most common factor cited is the 'Muslim destruction' of the site, a topic which we shall return to in the last section. What happened in Nalanda in the subsequent centuries? Did Buddhism disappear completely from the region? Part of the answers to these questions lie in the last years of Nalanda, a conversation we had in Chapter 5.

RECONFIGURATION OF THE SACRED SPACE, AND THE RISE OF TIBET

Between the 7th and 11th centuries, one sees a reconfiguration of the sacred landscape of Nalanda and eastern India, which continued during the 12th–13th centuries and after that as well. During this period, Nalanda revitalized and reinvented itself to attract newer followers by absorbing mythologies, tenets and images from other religious traditions. One notices three broader ramifications or manifestations.[32]

First was the emergence of tantric Buddhism. Between the 7th and 11th centuries, there was a decline in the Mahayana tradition at Nalanda, which moved towards the Vajrayana (or Mantrayana, or esoteric) Buddhism. This form of Buddhism had a close overlap with Shaivism (which worshipped Hindu god Shiva and related deities like Parvati, Ganesha, Kartikeya) and the Shakti cult (which worshipped the power and energy of goddesses such as Parvati, Durga, Lakshmi, Saraswati, etc). The tantric form of Buddhism was characterized, among other things, by the introduction of mandala drawings, female deities such as Tara as consorts of the Buddha and the bodhisattvas, sexual rites, initiation rituals like mantras and mudras, fire sacrifice and consecration rituals for kings, etc. This tantric phase is also known as the period of Pala Buddhism, named after the Pala kings who patronized it. Taranatha outlines the lives of several eminent siddhas or tantra gurus of Nalanda who led the Vajrayana tradition. One of them even became the head of Vikramashila and Mahabodhi monasteries, alongside Nalanda.

Second, there was a blurring of religious boundaries between Buddhism and Hinduism, and a mutual assimilation of rituals, icons, shrines and religious practices. In such a reconfiguration, the Buddha was not only assimilated within the Hindu traditions through epics and Puranas, as an incarnation of Lord Vishnu, but also through a close overlap with Bhairav, regarded as a tantric form of Shiva. Colossal statues of the Buddha, found at various places inside and outside of the mahavihara complex, came to be worshipped as protectors or guardians both by Buddhists and Hindus. This is how the large black Buddha image, enshrined in the temple at Baragaon, came to be worshipped as Bhairav and became popular as Teliya Baba. Likewise, the giant Buddha enshrined at the Rukmini-Harana-Sthana temple in Jagdishpur became associated with the Vaishnava tradition and came to be worshipped as Krishna, while the accompanying bodhisattva was regarded as Rukmini.

These two developments explain the presence of images of tantric Buddhist deities like Tara (in various forms like Mahashri Tara, Shyama Tara, Bhrikuti Tara, etc.), Vasundhara, Trilokavijaya, Heruka, Marichi, Jambhala, Aparajita, etc., in the later phase of Nalanda. It needs to be noted that all such images belong to the Pala period. Two other sub-points need to be mentioned here. First, tantric Buddhism also appropriated the Shaiva–Shakti concept of *pithas*, or holy sites inhabited by the gods. Second, it accommodated many other Hindu deities by the application of the mandala model, which was – simplistically speaking – a complex imagination of a Buddhist universe with multiple spaces and beings surrounding the central deity. The appropriation of Hindu gods sometimes brought a sense of tension, reflected in complex images like Trilokavijaya, where the Buddhist deity tramples Uma (a form of Parvati) and Maheshwara (a form of Shiva); Aparajita, a female Buddhist deity, is depicted trampling Ganesha; or Heruka and Vajrayogini are shown conquering Uma-Maheshwara (Shiva-Parvati). Such representations have been discovered at Nalanda. However, a greater number of images feature deities like Saraswati, Mahishasuramardini, Surya, Vishnu, Lakshmi, Ganesha, Kubera, Balarama and Kamadeva. Some of these deities were integrated as companions of Buddhist divinities or as minor figures within the tantric Buddhist mandala. Others, like Ganesha and Kartikeya, were included as guardians of the different directions and find a presence at monastic establishments like Nalanda and Vikramashila. The sharing of sacred space can also be seen in other places. At the Surya temple in Baragaon, one encounters images of Surya alongside a rare image of the crowned Buddha, a motif more common to Bodh Gaya.

Third, as far as centres of Buddhist learning and scholarship are concerned, one notices some geocultural shifts during the period under consideration. Countries in East and Southeast Asia, along with Sri Lanka and Tibet, emerged as new Buddhist hotspots while Nalanda progressively disappeared from the scene. However, Nalanda continued to maintain connections with these hotspots till around the 13th century. It also remained an important conduit of inter-Asian Buddhist links, while China emerged as a springboard.[33] The increased traffic between India and China during these years is attributed to two factors: the demand for Buddhist articles and artists, and the emergence of Nalanda as a premium centre of learning. We already know of Chinese pilgrims like Faxian, Xuanzang and Yijing, who visited and wrote about Nalanda and (or) its surroundings. Interestingly, Xuanzang had heard about Nalanda from Indian monk Prabhakaramitra who had visited China in the 7th century. Monks from Nalanda also visited China. A tantric monk–scholar from Nalanda, Subhakarasimha (d. 735), is believed to be one of the key figures behind the introduction of tantric Buddhism in China in the 8th century, alongside others like Vajrabodhi (671–741) and Amoghavajra (705–74).

Nalanda's connection with East and Southeast Asia was mostly routed through China. Yijing, for instance, had studied Sanskrit in Srivijaya (Sumatra) before travelling to Nalanda in the late 7th century. Srivijaya was the seat of a Buddhist empire, which dominated much of western maritime Southeast Asia between the 7th and 11th centuries. Yijing visited the place again during his return trip to consolidate his travel accounts. In fact, he even suggests that Srivijaya was a great place to learn Sanskrit for monks visiting India. He also mentions several Korean monks who made, or attempted to make, pilgrimages to India. These included Hyeryun, Hyeop, Hyonjo, Hyongak, Hyonyu and Hyontae. Some of them, in fact, lived and died at Nalanda, but the most famous Korean monk to visit Nalanda was Hyecho. He had studied under tantric monk Vajrabodhi in China and visited Nalanda in the early 8th century. Upon his return to China, he wrote a memoir, wherein he discussed the links between the Buddhist learning and pilgrimage centres in South and East Asia. Later, in the 13th century, a monk ordained at Nalanda, Dhyanabhadra (1225–1363) travelled to Beijing and the Korean peninsula. He is known as Chanxian in the Chinese accounts. However, by end of the 8th century, Tibet had largely replaced China as far as to-and-fro movements of the Buddhist monks are concerned.

In Chapter 5, we discussed the role of Tibet in the evolution of the Tabo monastery complex in the western Himalayas. Tibet also had strong connections with mahaviharas like Nalanda, Somapura (now in Bangladesh), Vikramashila, Odantapura and Jagaddala (in West Bengal), which were known for their Vajrayana preceptors. In fact, most of our knowledge of the functioning of these mahaviharas comes from Tibetan sources. Some Tibetan monks even became influential teachers at mahaviharas in eastern India. Thanks to flourishing pilgrim traffic between India and Tibet, many Vajrayana texts and practices were taken to Tibet, where they were translated and preserved. Many Buddhist sculptures and artefacts also found their way into Tibet. Monks from Nalanda were travelling to Tibet as well, and some of them are even credited with spreading Buddhism there. Shantarakshita, for instance, was invited by the king of Tibet and lived there for many years, till his death in 762. Dipankara (popularly known as Atisha) visited Tibet in the 11th century and contributed to the formation of what became known as Tibetan Buddhism.[34]

Nalanda starts becoming less visible in history 13th century onwards. It comes into the limelight once again during the 19th–20th centuries, when its ruins were discovered by colonial explorers and archaeologists. We have already seen in Chapter 6 how, on account of several developments in India and Europe, there was a renewed interest in the Buddha and his teachings in the 19th century. Consequently, the region of Magadha, which was closely associated with the historical Buddha, became a Buddhist hotspot again.

COLONIAL DISCOVERY AND RELOCATION OF MAHAVIHARA SCULPTURES TO MUSEUMS

During 1811–12, Scottish physician Francis Buchanan-Hamilton, during his exploration of Patna, Gaya, and Nalanda, visited Baragaon and came across an 'immense mass of ruins', which possibly constituted the modern excavated and enclosed site of Nalanda. He was followed by Markham Kittoe, a British military officer and an antiquarian who was guided by the 1836 French translation of Faxian's account of the region. However, systematic explorations began only with Alexander Cunningham, who was encouraged by French sinologist Stanislas Julien's French translation of Xuanzang's travels in India. To Cunningham, Xuanzang was an authentic source to discover the archaeological remains and geography associated with the historical Buddha. This led to more detailed explorations and excavations, including the 1915 ASI excavations funded by the Council of the Royal Asiatic Society of Great Britian and Ireland.

The dominant thrust of colonial archaeology during most of the 19th century was to establish the existence of the historical Buddha. The primary motive of most officials, explorers, excavators and archaeologists working in and around Nalanda was to unravel and establish the region's past identity as a prominent Buddhist university. In such a case, sculptures and artefacts belonging to other religious traditions – such as Hinduism or Jainism – tended to take a secondary place. And we know by now that several objects belonging to the Hindu or Jaina traditions were recovered from the mahavihara premises and the surrounding villages.[35] What also needs to be mentioned here is that, for the colonial officials or archaeologists, the sculptures and artefacts recovered from these sites mostly constituted art objects, as opposed to those being a part of a sacred tradition. To clarify their position on art pieces, the British came up with classifications that determined which art objects were valuable and worth preserving in museums, which could be bought and sold, and which could be taken away from India as mementoes or souvenirs. Soon, many sculptures and artefacts were removed from temples and religious sites. They were first kept in open-air sheds, or makeshift museums, and then transported to museums set up by the colonial administration. In the process of being shifted, many artefacts recovered from Nalanda were destroyed or damaged. Such sculptures were devoid of their original geographical, historical and sacred contexts and were simply showcased in museums and exhibitions as examples of Buddhist art. Many also ended up in private collections. An interesting case in point is the A. M. Broadley collection. As the district magistrate of Bihar

Sharif, Broadley (1847–1916) collected several sculptures and antiquities during his tours and explorations in Nalanda, Rajgir, Bihar Sharif, Patna and parts of Gaya. He kept these objects in a makeshift museum in Bihar Sharif in 1878. In 1891, these objects were transferred to the Indian Museum in Kolkata and displayed as the Broadley Collection. Later, when Patna Museum was set up in 1917, a large part of this collection was transferred there, and their provenance was mentioned as 'Bihar'. Some items from the Patna Museum were traded and can now be found in Varendra Research Museum (Bangladesh), Cleveland Museum of Art (Ohio, USA) and Museum fur Indische Kunst (Berlin, Germany). Likewise, many artefacts from the Nalanda site museum, set up in 1917 (Fig 9.9) to prevent the removal of antiquities from the site, were transferred to Patna Museum (in 1929) or the National Museum in Delhi (in 1949), particularly the Nalanda bronzes.

WAS NALANDA DESTROYED BY BAKHTIYAR KHALJI?

There are two major theories that explain the decline of Nalanda. Both talk about the destruction of the mahavihara and a somewhat sudden or cataclysmic decline. Interestingly, both theories are based on texts written in the aftermath of the reported destruction. The first is based on a Persian text written around sixty years later, and the second is based on Buddhist texts written 500 years later. There are conspicuous gaps in both explanations.

According to the most common theory, or explanation, offered for the decline of Nalanda, the site was ransacked in an attack by Bakhtiyar Khalji in 1193. He was one of the regional commanders of Turkish conqueror Muhammad Ghuri (and later his successor Qutbuddin Aibak) and is credited with laying the foundations of the Delhi Sultanate. The Khaljis were of Afghan origin and had come to India during the late 12th and early 13th century. Some, like Khalji, had established themselves militarily and politically in Bengal, but most of them had been employed by successive Delhi sultans to contain the Mongol invasions coming through north-west India.[36] The theory related to Khalji's destruction of Nalanda is frequently mentioned in school textbooks and deeply etched in public imagination. Interestingly, it is entirely based on *Tabaqat-i-Nasiri*, a

Persian work by Minhaj-i-Siraj Juzjani (1193–1260), which provides an elaborate history of the Islamic world during the reign of Delhi Sultan Nasiruddin Mahmud Shah (1246–66). In this work, Juzjani mentions that he learnt about the attack on the fortress of Bihar from two brothers who had participated in it. Juzjani had reportedly met these brothers at Lakhnauti (in Gauda, currently in Malda district of West Bengal) in 1243 CE. Based on the information provided by them, Juzjani writes that most of the inhabitants of the attacked site were Brahmans; that their heads were shaven and all of them were killed. The invading army discovered several books at the site. When they tried to identify the importance of these books, they discovered 'that the whole of that fortress and city was a college, and in the Hindui [Hindi] tongue, they call a college Bihar.'[37] Interestingly, the word 'Nalanda' does not appear in Juzjani's account – it simply talks about the ransacking of the Bihar fortress. Many later historians suggest that this fortress could have been the Odantapura vihara in present-day Bihar Sharif although its precise location has never been known. Others maintain that Nalanda 'escaped the main fury of the Muslim conquest because it lay not on the main route from Delhi to Bengal and needed a separate expedition.'[38] Some also argue that Bakhtiyar Khalji went from Bihar Sharif to Nadia in Bengal through the hills and jungles of Jharkhand.[39]

The second theory, which is less popular, relates the decline to the rivalry or animosity between the Brahmans and the Buddhists.[40] Unlike the first theory, which discusses the sacking of the fortress of Bihar, the second theory specifically talks about the destruction of Nalanda and Buddhist viharas by a fire produced by *tirthika* (a term used by some Buddhists for Hindus) beggars who had been humiliated by the resident monks. Two versions of this incident are in circulation. According to the version mentioned in Tibetan text *Pag Sam Jon Zang*, written by monk and scholar Sumpa Khan-po Yeçe Pal Jor (1704–88), the two angry beggars at whom the monks threw washing water, set ablaze the three buildings of Dharmaganja – Ratnasagara, Ratnaranjaka and the nine-storeyed Ratnodadhi, the library that contained the sacred books. According to the other version, recorded in the *History of Buddhism in India* by Tibetan monk and scholar Taranatha, one of the two angry tirthika beggars engaged in *'surya sadhana'* (spiritual practice dedicated to the sun) for twelve years. By the powers acquired from this exercise, he performed a sacrifice and scattered the charmed ashes around the site. This resulted in a miraculously produced fire, which destroyed eighty-four temples and scriptures. Some scriptures were, however, saved by water flowing from an upper floor of the Ratnodadhi temple.[41]

There is no doubt that the Turkish/Afghan attacks contributed to the decline of the Palas and the Buddhist establishments in the Bihar–Bengal region. Some scholars have argued that the monasteries were set on fire, perhaps repeatedly. Did the Turks set Nalanda on fire? There is no conclusive evidence to establish this proposition. Juzjani's account does not help us reach a definite conclusion. Further, none of the contemporary or near contemporary Buddhist sources (such as Dharmasvamin's account) refer to the Turks setting the mahavihara on fire. On the contrary, they hold the Brahmans responsible for the fire and destruction. Did this theory then take shape during the colonial rule? Wasn't such a formulation in sync with the communal politics of the colonial administration of which we have several evidences? We also don't come across any evidence related to a single, definitive attack that completely destroyed Nalanda. When Tibetan monk Dharmasvamin visited Nalanda in 1234, Odantapura had become a Turkish military headquarter. Nalanda was in a slightly better position, though it was damaged and deserted.[42] Dharmasvamin mentions that some buildings had remained unscathed, in which some pandits and monks resided and received instruction from Rahul Sri Bhadra. The number of resident monks had dipped considerably, to 100. The Tibetan monk also talks about small-scale resumption of scholarly activities at Nalanda, thanks largely to donations made by a wealthy Brahman named Jayadeva. One also hears of King Buddhasena of Magadha, who supported the Nalanda monks. Even if one were to go by Dharmasvamin's account, Nalanda's downfall was a part of a larger process of decline of Buddhist monasteries and establishments in the Magadha region, resulting from the raids of the Turkish and Afghan armies, the Turushkas. Bodh Gaya was also affected by these attacks. In what other ways did such attacks contribute to the overall decline of the Buddhist establishments? The political and economic instability resulting from such attacks might have deprived the Buddhist sites of royal patronage, as well as the availability of donations, funds and resources. This may have impacted the survival of the monastic establishments. Some scholars have even suggested that Nalanda had already passed its prime by the time of the Palas. During the Pala period, new universities such as Odantapura, Somapura, Vikramashila and Jagaddala became premier centres of the Vajrayana tradition and had started overshadowing the Mahayana tradition of Nalanda. Going by Tibetan legends and writings, Nalanda's prestige seems to have devolved to Vikramashila and that, at one point of time, the head of Vikramashila also controlled Nalanda.

Coming back to the point about the Turkish and Afghan attacks, what did the monks do after such attacks? A few probably stayed behind. They find a mention in Dharmasvamin's account. Some, possibly converted to Islam. Many, however, fled to Tibet and Nepal with texts and scriptures. Dharmasvamin records meeting Tibetan monks fleeing from Nalanda. The sacred geography of Nalanda, as we discussed in an earlier section, was also reconfigured. And the mahavihara became a crucial site for the transmission of Buddhist ideas in other Asian countries, primarily Tibet.

Tibet gained most from the decline of Nalanda – it emerged as the centre to study, copy and translate Buddhist manuscripts.[43] We discussed earlier how there was a reconfiguration of the sacred space in the larger Nalanda region. Viewed in the larger Indian context, it is important to remember that Buddhism also went through a period of decline in other parts of the country around the 12th–13th centuries. Not all these geographies were subjected to Turkish invasions. So clearly, there were other dynamics at work. We discussed some possible factors behind the decline of Buddhism in Chapter 5, but this topic needs to be researched in greater detail. We do not hear much about Nalanda after the 13th century. The institution and its legacy, however, remained ingrained in collective memory; and some efforts were made to plant the idea of Nalanda on foreign soils, too, though the forms varied. A Nalanda University was set up near Lhasa in Tibet by monk and scholar Rongston Sengge (1347–1449). Much later, in

1981, a Nalanda monastery was established near Toulouse in France by Lama Rinpoche and Lama Thubten Yeshe.

The idea of Nalanda experienced a revival in India in the decades following independence, beginning with the establishment of the Nava Nalanda Mahavihara. Originally founded in 1951 as the Magadh Institute of Post-graduate Studies and Research in Pali, Allied Languages and Buddhist Learning, it was later renamed. This institution was designed as an international centre for Buddhist studies and research, modelled after the ancient Nalanda. Its curriculum covers a range of disciplines, including Buddhist logic, philosophy, history, culture, and languages like Pali and Sanskrit, drawing students from various Buddhist countries.

Another important establishment, which seeks to reconnect with Nalanda's ancient past, is the Xuanzang Memorial Hall (Fig 11.8, Chapter 11). It was built as a tribute to Chinese traveller Xuanzang who visited and stayed at Nalanda during the 7th century and whose writings have predominantly shaped our knowledge of the site. The memorial hall is shaped like a Chinese temple, fronted by a statue of the Chinese traveller himself. It has a museum and visual documentation centre, which was inaugurated in 2007. The memorial hall is also a part of a diplomatic exercise to strengthen India–China ties. It was Nava Nalanda Mahavihara, which was put in charge of the creative development of the memorial hall that was completed in 1984. It received the relics of Xuanzang, some Chinese Buddhist texts and an endowment from the Chinese government. Finally, Nalanda University, an institution that has received a lot of public attention, also borrows on the idea of ancient Nalanda. Its architecture, facade and layout are reportedly inspired by ancient Nalanda. Since 2006, when former President of India A. P. J. Abdul Kalam mooted the idea of reviving the ancient university in the Bihar State Legislative Assembly, the plan has gone through several consultative stages, including the presentation of the 'Nalanda proposal' by the Singapore government and deliberations at two East Asia Summits (2007 and 2009). The university was finally established in 2010 after the Nalanda University Bill, 2010 was passed by the Indian Parliament. It comes under the Ministry of External Affairs and, unlike the Nava Nalanda Mahavihara that mostly concerns itself with traditional Buddhist learning, Nalanda university is intended to serve as a modern, world-class institution of higher learning. Its architecture, facade and layout are apparently inspired by ancient mahaviharas (Fig 9.10).

Most efforts to revive the idea of Nalanda in post-independence India have acquired an international dimension. In varying degrees, they also aim to strengthen inter-Asia Buddhist links, an area closely connected to India's soft power diplomacy. The award of a UNESCO World Heritage Site status only enhances the site's international and Buddhist positioning. While efforts to project Nalanda's international connections have always remained a dominant part of showcasing India's Buddhist legacy, attempts should be made to understand the site with regard to its immediate surroundings. What makes the region around Nalanda so special? How does one adequately understand the spatial and cultural overlapping of different religious affiliations and faiths? What were the mahavihara's connections with the surrounding agricultural and mercantile ecosystems? Was there a Greater Nalanda region that sustained cities, empires, religious traditions, establishments and urban and rural cultures? The answers to these questions perhaps lie in more comprehensive surveys, including remote sensing, Geographic Information System (GIS) and excavations around what is commonly understood to be the Nalanda ruins. After all, a lot of history remains buried here.

PART III

THE RETURN OF THE BUDDHA

10

THE BUDDHA MAKES A COMEBACK

> *It is little exaggeration to say of this great work [The Light of Asia] that it obtained for the Dhamma [teachings of the Buddha] a hearing, which half a century of scholarship could never have obtained.*

This is how Christmas Humphreys, a famous British Buddhist and the founder of the Buddhist Society of London, described the popularity of Sir Edwin Arnold's *The Light of Asia* in late Victorian England. First published in 1879, it went through at least a hundred editions in England and America and was translated into several foreign languages, including many Indian languages.[1] This publication is seen as a milestone in the development of an intellectual position, which argues that Buddhism was rediscovered in the West in the 19th century after its disappearance from India in the 13th century. This was to say that the West revived Buddhism or offered it a rebirth. In recent times, an alternate argument has developed, according to which India already had a tradition of conversations around Buddhism in the pre-colonial and early colonial India, that the modern 'revival' was led as much by Indians as other Asians and Europeans. The second argument cites the example of a Buddhist text in Sanskrit, called *Vajrasuchi* (diamond-cutter), attributed to 1st-century CE scholar Ashvaghosha. It is known for its contemptuous critique of the Brahmanical view of the caste system and was published in 1839, forty years before the publication of Sir Arnold's book, at a time when Buddhological or Indological studies were still in their embryonic stage in Europe. *Vajrasuchi*'s English translation was a big hit. It became widely known across India and Europe, among Hindu social reformers, Christian missionaries, Buddhist societies, and later, among anti-caste activists. It went through numerous reprints and was also translated into Hindi, Bengali, Tamil and Nepali. Interestingly, *Vajrasuchi* was published after much debate between a British diplomat in India, Lancelot Wilkinson (1805–41), and his hesitant Sanskrit tutor, Pandit Subaji Bapu, who eventually agreed to publish it only if the translated text also carried his rather long rebuttal.[2]

These arguments broadly represent the two positions in the debate regarding the recentering of the Buddha and Buddhism in the 19th and 20th centuries. Is it true that Buddhism become a forgotten creed in the land of its origin? Did the West rediscover the Buddha for India and help revive Buddhism? The answers to such questions can be sought in the relative trajectories of Buddhism in the West and in India after the 13th century, conventionally known as the period of 'disappearance' or 'extinction' of Buddhism.

THE WEST DISCOVERS THE BUDDHA

We have been talking about Buddhist ideas reaching the foreign shores – South, East and Southeast Asia – and acquiring roots there. We have taken note of the flourishing trade with the Byzantine empire in the early centuries of the Christian era. There have also been discussions about the trade routes connecting the north-west part of India with China, Central Asia and Europe, particularly the Silk Route. From the Gupta–Vakataka period, we also saw monks, scriptures and Buddhist artefacts travelling to East and Southeast Asia, alongside the rise of the Arabs who helped connect the ports of India with north Africa and the Persian Gulf region, and East and Southeast Asia. Where was the West in this scenario?

Ideas related to the Buddha and his legacy started reaching the West sporadically, in fragments, around the 13th and 14th centuries.[3] Marco Polo, the famous Venetian merchant and traveller who stayed in China between 1275 and 1291, produced a reasonably detailed account of the life of the Buddha. With greater movement of the merchants and missionaries of the West, ethnographic accounts about Buddhist beliefs and practices in different Asian nations began to be written

16th century onwards. This continued over the next two centuries, but India was still not the focus. This was despite the fact that some European travellers had visited sites like the rock-cut caves of Kanheri. These travellers were unable to discern the nature of the monuments, not to mention their Buddhist connections.

Most stupas and monasteries were dilapidated, abandoned, buried under subsequent habitations or appropriated by other religions and local faiths. Kanchipuram in Tamil Nadu, for instance, had been a flourishing Buddhist centre (as attested by the records of Xuanzang), but the presence of the Buddha's statues inside later Hindu temples suggests that the Buddha was assimilated into Hinduism. Similarly, parts of rock-cut Buddhist monasteries in the western Deccan, such as those at Junnar and Nashik, had begun to be used as shrines for local deities. In addition, Brahmans and pandits, the main informants of Indian culture for the early Europeans, were either antagonistic to the Buddha or understood religious practices associated with him as a part of Hindu worship, or the Vaishnavite tradition, where he was seen as an avatar of Lord Vishnu. However, Brahman intellectuals and other champions or practitioners of the Vedic and Puranic religion had continued to redefine and imagine themselves in relation to the Buddhist past.[4]

The early Europeans were unable to make the connection between the divergent forms of Buddhist practices and the dilapidated ruins in a largely 'Hindu' India. The documents, reports and ethnographic accounts prepared by missionaries, travellers, merchants and diplomats did not have any substantive impact on the understanding of Buddhism in the West.[5] A systematic engagement with Buddhism developed in the West only around the late 18th and early 19th centuries, which manifested in an obsessive engagement with the core Buddhist texts. This period also witnessed the emergence of greater European and colonial interest in India's ancient past. There was an added reason, too. Post the Industrial Revolution in the 18th century, there was a progressive demand in the United Kingdom and Europe for sources of raw material and a market for manufactured goods, since their own markets were saturating. Gradually, this resulted in a scramble for colonies. European trading companies, which made colonial forays into India, soon began to make political inroads. As India became more integrated with Europe, there was a growing curiosity about India's past. Initially, this interest was fuelled through the growing academic fascination for India's religions and classical texts, and the romantic charm of the ruins. Later, India became the focus of strategic colonial interests, which drew support from emerging ideas and disciplines like social Darwinism, archaeology and anthropology.

It was not as if there was an instant fascination for Buddhism in the late 18th and early 19th centuries. In fact, in the early encounters, there were more questions than answers.[6] Was the Buddha a mythical figure like the gods of Greece, Egypt or India? Or was he a human being? Were there two Buddhas – one, the founder of Buddhism (as referred to by the Hindus), the second, a later reformer? Was the Buddha born in Africa, Persia, Mongolia or India? Was Buddhism older than Brahmanism? It was also around this time that the word 'Buddhism' first began to be used in journals and publications in England.

Europe's engagement with the figure of the Buddha evolved over time.[7] In the first phase, Buddhism came to be seen more as a phenomenon geographically and culturally experienced in the East, or the 'Orient' – it was seen as the 'other'. Gradually, such curiosities and questions began to settle down. Around the mid-19th century, the idea of a historical Buddha began to gain ground. He began to be seen as a human being. He was as human as Jesus, Mohammad or Luther. Further, the Buddha's teachings or philosophy, it was held, could only be understood through the texts. Here, the Europeans deployed their traditional knowledge framework – classical texts were the only objects for studying ancient histories, religions and philosophies.

In the initial phase, there was an overt focus on Sanskrit texts as opposed to Pali, in which the bulk of the early Buddhist tradition was recorded. Sanskrit, as discussed earlier, became popular with the ascendancy of the Mahayana tradition. When such ancient texts were read together with the diverse ethnographic accounts of the beliefs of Futo, Hotoke (Japan), Sangay, Bodo, Booddhu, or Bauddha – as Buddhist practices were known in different parts of Asia – the seemingly divergent styles of worship started appearing as those belonging to the same religious tradition that had its origins in ancient

India.[8] The dust that had gathered over the Buddha's legacy and diverse Buddhist traditions was beginning to clear. The dots began to show a connect. It was in this context that Eugène Burnouf (1801–52) wrote the first comprehensive study of ancient Indian Buddhism in 1844, using the Sanskrit manuscripts procured from Nepal. The study was able to underscore that Buddhist texts from Tibet and China were translations of Sanskrit texts from India. By the middle of the 19th century, large collections of Buddhist texts and manuscripts had become available in libraries and institutions of the West. Buddhism, as P. C. Almond says, had become 'a textual object defined, classified and interpreted through its own textuality.' This process of textualization was also controlled and regulated by the West. Towards the end of the century, such collections grew bigger, especially with the addition of Pali texts. The study of Buddhist manuscripts in Pali began more systematically after the establishment of the Pali Text Society by T. W. Rhys Davids in 1881.

More textual studies meant more constructions of the Buddha and Buddhism. Gradually, the Buddha came to seen as a social reformer who challenged the authority of the Brahman priests and Vedic Hinduism based on rituals and sacrifices. The Christian missionaries started becoming more sympathetic to what came across as a humane and compassionate Buddha, whose teachings placed greater emphasis on the equality of human beings. Brahmanical Hinduism, on the other hand, came to be depicted as discriminatory and based on privileges and inequalities. A distinction began to be drawn between pure or authentic Buddhism, as taught by the Buddha and his close disciples, and the corrupt later Buddhist traditions and forms of worship.

Around the time the textualization of Buddhism was taking place, or classical religions of the East were being studied, Europe was experiencing the Romantic movement, one of the fascinations of which was the study of landscapes and ruins. This period saw some European artists travelling to India and documenting its ruins (Fig 10.1). William Daniel, for example, published his engravings in the 1830s, while Sir Charles D'Oyly's lithographs came out in 1838.

Gradually, British (and European) interests in India came to be studied within the larger framework of Orientalism. Orientalist constructions were informed by geopolitical concerns aimed at the consolidation of colonial power. It became important to know India better to rule it. Such constructions fuelled the British claims of conducting a scientific study of India's past and establishing the original and true history of Buddhism, Buddhist monuments and the Buddha himself. The establishment of archaeology as a modern discipline in the 19th century added a new dimension to such claims – now 'enlightened' European scholars would introduce India's glorious past to the colonial subjects. This exercise was carefully projected as part of a larger civilizing mission, whereby an 'enlightened' colonial administration would rescue India from ruin and decadence and help retrieve and restore its past.[9]

The first set of archaeological excavations, however, were neither conducted by trained professionals, nor were they executed professionally.[10] The first recorded study and survey of a Buddhist stupa was done in 1798, when Colin Mackenzie found the remains of the Amravati stupa. His extensive survey of the site between 1816 and 1817 was also motivated by the desire to locate sculptures for the ornamentation of another monument that had been built by a local British officer elsewhere. In 1800, a local doctor excavated the stupa at Vaishali. in 1905, during the course of an excavation at Sarnath, the Ashokan lion capital was discovered (Fig 10.2). The stupas at Sanchi were discovered by General Taylor in 1818 and subsequently explored by Captain Edward Fell in 1817. Captain Fell was unable to note the presence of the Buddha's images at Sanchi; he misidentified many Buddhist figures as Jaina or Hindu deities. In the north-west, Ranjit Singh got the stupa at Manikyala excavated in 1830 and, throughout the 1830s, Alexander Burnes and Charles Masson opened several stupas across the Gandhara region. On account of a large number of Greek coins and other precious objects being found in Gandhara, Burnes and Masson assumed that the stupas were tombs of Greek kings.

The early archaeological surveys, or excavations, can be best described as antiquarian endeavours. They were also an exercise of blatant treasure-hunting, largely done by government officials or private individuals with an interest in ancient ruins but with a considerably limited understanding of Buddhist sites. In many cases, they ended up making an inward dent or causing serious damage to the stupas. In addition, the objects yielded from such surveys were permanently removed from their original archaeological context, gradually reducing them to mere antiquities exhibited in colonial museums. Meanwhile, between 1834 and 1837, James Prinsep (an assay master of the East India Company) was able to decipher the Brahmi and Kharosthi scripts found on several coins and inscriptions retrieved from Buddhist sites throughout the Indian subcontinent. Consequently, a vast amount of numismatic and epigraphic evidence came to be translated rapidly. This, in turn, facilitated the first chronological understanding of many early Buddhist sites.

The nature of archaeological surveys began to change from around the mid-19th century, with the establishment of the ASI in 1861.[11] It was in this context that Alexander Cunningham (Fig 10.3), who became the first head of the ASI, stimulated the archaeological examination of Buddhist monuments. In doing so, he pushed Buddhist sites to the forefront of academic study for the first time. Cunningham's primary interest was the archaeological showcasing of the biography of the historical Buddha. Of related interest was Mauryan emperor Ashoka, who had monumentalized the Buddha's legacy by building stupas, shrines and pillars. Cunningham wanted to ascertain the locations of ancient Buddhist sites by aligning his archaeological excavations with the places visited by Chinese pilgrims Faxian (who visited India in the 4th–5th centuries) and Xuanzang (who travelled in the 7th century). The accounts of these pilgrims were first translated into French and published in the 1830s.

In the first four years, between 1861 and 1865, Cunningham identified more than 160 Buddhist sites in north India, a number that was set to increase. Reports, books and articles also began to be written by archaeologists and art historians, describing the Buddhist sites revealed. Soon, the giant Buddhas of Bamiyan, the illustrious cave paintings of Ajanta, the towering mahachaitya at Amravati, the monastic-cum-educational establishment at Nalanda and the magnificent stupa at Sarnath were firmly placed on the archaeological landscape of India. By 1884, even the Mahabodhi temple, considered the Buddhist navel of the earth, had been rebuilt and opened to the public. Unlike Cunningham, John Marshall, the director-general of the ASI between 1902 and 1928, was primarily concerned with tracing the archaeological correlates of the legend of Ashoka, as narrated in the 5th-century CE Buddhist text *Divyavadana*. His interest in identifying stupas built by Ashoka led him to the stupas at Taxila and Sanchi.

How did monuments and archaeological artefacts fit into a context where texts constituted the dominant way of looking at Buddhism? Stupa remains were correlated with episodes found in the texts, while sculptural representations helped to corroborate the popularity of certain stories in the texts, or to understand the related chronology, styles and geographies. The sculptures also served as visual evidence of Buddhist practices and of other social and economic realities described in the texts. Archaeology was deployed in the task of corroborating textual descriptions. The wider field of Buddhist scholarship continued to be dominated by the textual and philosophical study in the 20th century, but Cunningham's emphasis on archaeological remains created footprints and opened a world of dialogue between the texts and artefacts. The archaeological repertoire was further widened with the discovery of coins, inscriptions and artefacts.[12] Gradually, the idea of archaeological excavations began to gain currency among kings, officials and scholars in India, and surveys of Buddhist sites started finding new patrons and sponsors.

The discovery of Buddhism was also aided by two other related developments in the late 19th century.[13] The first was the emergence of a new intellectual discourse on 'world religions' and their 'holy lands' in the West. This discourse positioned Bodh Gaya as the Buddhist equivalent of the Muslims' Mecca and the Christians' Jerusalem. Foregrounded in European scholarly perspective, this discourse became popular among influential Asian Buddhist reformers.[14] One of the most powerful exponents of this discourse was Sir Edwin Arnold, the author of *Light of Asia*. A free adaptation of Buddhist text *Lalitavistara*, his book presents a narrative poem on the life, times and philosophy of Gautama Buddha.

The second development was the founding of the World Parliament of Religions in Chicago in 1893, which is known for Swami Vivekananda's famous address. However, there was another Asian in

Fig 10.1 Part of the Kanheri Caves in Maharashtra, depicted in a coloured aquatint by Thomas and William Daniell, 1800

Fig 10.2 Excavation of Ashoka's lion capital at Sarnath in 1905, on the right is an image of the Buddha delivering his first sermon

Fig 10.3 Alexander Cunningham, the first director general of the Archaeological Survey of India

Fig 10.4 Statue of Anagarika Dharmapala in the Mulagandhakuti Vihara premises, Sarnath

Fig 10.5 Mulagandhakuti Vihara, Sarnath

Fig 10.6 Buddha Vihara in New Delhi (left), is a part of the Laxminarayan Temple complex (right), constructed by the Birlas

this parliament who was instrumental in repositioning Buddhism both in the subcontinent and aboard, in a big way. He was Sri Lankan monk Dharmapala Anagarika (1863–1933). Anagarika (Fig 10.4) was inspired by Sir Edwin Arnold's *The Light of Asia*, and represented the cause of the Buddhists at the Chicago conference. His address, 'The World's Debt to Buddha', was instrumental in creating transnational awareness about Buddhism. Anagarika followed the lead of Sir Arnold and the West and internationalized the cause of Buddhism in Asia through the activities and branches of the Buddha Gaya Maha Bodhi Society (now called Maha Bodhi Society) he had originally founded in Colombo in 1891. He was also involved with the construction of the Dharmarajika Chaitya Vihara in Calcutta in 1920 and the Mulagandhakuti Vihara in Sarnath in 1931(Fig 10.5). Also, he took a branch of the Bodhi tree from Bodh Gaya and planted it in Sarnath. A statue of his was later erected in front of a temple at Sarnath, the place of Buddha's first sermon. However, much before Anagarika brought about an Asian revival, many Brahmic pandits and English-educated elites were already talking about Buddhism in India.

PRE- AND EARLY-COLONIAL CONVERSATIONS AROUND BUDDHISM

The Buddha and Buddhism remained ingrained in the collective memory of Indians even after the decline in the 13th century. They continued to encounter and imagine Buddhism in different forms, going beyond just buildings and iconography.[15] This included oral traditions, popular literary works, the Puranas (where the Buddha was assimilated as an incarnation of the Hindu god Vishnu), hagiographies such as Madhava's 17th–18th century Sanskrit work *Shankara Digvijaya*, the 16th–17th century Bengali writings of Gaudiya Vaishnavas that carried lively and antagonistic depictions of the Buddhists, Tamil devotional poetry and temple chronicles that were recited in public spaces, philosophical and scholastic manuals, and commentaries that engaged with Buddhist doctrines, alongside plays and performances. In short, there were conversations regarding Buddhism – across languages and regions – among philosophers, scholars and ascetics in India before the advent of European colonialism. And these continued well into the colonial period and beyond. It was this awareness of the Buddhist past, howsoever fragmented or biased it may have been, that the pandits or early informants of the East India Company were sharing with their officers and surveyors to help them locate manuscripts, artefacts and ruins. This is how Brian Hodgson, the British resident in Kathmandu between 1820 and 1843, located a rich cache of Buddhist manuscripts in Sanskrit. Even the reports and memoirs produced by the East India Company's surveyors and officials, and the early scholarly articles published in the journal, *Asiatick Researches*, the *Indian Antiquary* and *Journal of the Asiatic Society of Mumbai*, attested to the existence of a Buddhist past and a robust Buddhist present. It may be relevant to point out here that most influential Buddhological journals in the early 19th century were being produced at institutes based in India. These reports and writings were being produced at a time when armchair Buddhologists and Indologists in Europe were still debating the Buddha's identity and origins. The information base from India, in fact, helped them correct their understanding of the Buddha and Buddhism.

Conversations regarding Buddhism received a boost with the introduction of English education in India.[16] The Buddha became the centre of public conversations, especially among the English-educated Indian elites. These people had important and influential connections in the government and beyond. For instance, Sivaprasad, whose widely circulated book *Itihas Timir Nashak* (History as the Dispeller of Darkness) made the Buddha a modern icon in school textbooks, worked with the education department. Others, like Rajendralal Mitra and S. C. Das, were closely involved with the colonial archaeological excavations, together with several draftsmen and photographers. Some, like R. G. Bhandarkar and Dharmanand Kosambi (in Maharashtra) or Ashutosh Mukherjee (in Bengal), introduced Buddhism in the university curricula. Others were associated with the Census Commission of India and research societies. This group of English-educated Indian intelligentsia had wide academic networks both in the subcontinent and abroad. They led popular Buddhist campaigns and activities and were instrumental in constructing a robust discourse about Buddhism in the decades preceding the publication of

The Light of Asia (1879), or the founding of the Pali Text Society (1881) in the West, or even the establishment of the Maha Bodhi Society in Calcutta in 1891.

BUDDHA MOVES FROM THE MARGINS TO THE CENTRE

The intellectual context created by the English-educated intelligentsia, the long tradition of conversations around Buddhism, the development of print culture and the growth of Buddhist networks were among the major factors contributing to the widespread circulation of *The Light of Asia* in India. It is important to note that the first translations of this iconic book came about in Indian languages like Bengali, Marathi, Tamil, Telugu and Malayalam. *The Light of Asia*, in fact, captivated the imagination of many influential Indian leaders, intellectuals and thinkers – including Mahatma Gandhi, Jawaharlal Nehru, B. R. Ambedkar, Swami Vivekananda, Rabindranath Tagore and Abanindranath Tagore – some of whom played an important role in repositioning Buddhism in the 20th century.[17] We will discuss the role of some of these individuals later, but for now let us return to the English-educated elites.

The voice and reach of this English-educated group, constituted largely by upper-caste urban males based in the provincial capitals, was widely amplified by a diverse group of organizations and networks.[18] These included, among others, organizations like the Brahmo Samaj (1828), Prarthana Samaj (1867) and the Theosophical Society (1875), which were primarily concerned with social and religious reforms; the Maha Bodhi Society (1891), which gained global visibility under Dharmapala Anagarika; the Bengal Buddhist Association (1892) and the Sakya Buddhist Society (1898, later the Indian Buddhist Association), both of which had several branches but where Buddhism was intermeshed with issues of language, ethnicity and caste; societies propagating Buddhism like the Chittagong Buddhist Association (1887, now known as the Bangladesh Buddhist Association), the Buddhist Text Society (1892) and those based in places like Darjeeling (1907), Lucknow (1916), Agartala (1918), Bombay (1922) and Calicut (1925); and efforts of individuals like Bhikshu Mahavir who, along with his monastic network, played a significant role in the development of

Buddhism at Kushinagar. Most Buddhist organizations published journals, and some were even involved with organizing Buddhist events and installing images. These associations and networks, with diverse origins, constituencies and goals, and dissimilar or competing views, propelled Buddhism's popularity in the late 19th and early 20th centuries, giving it a mass, public character. Slightly different from these initiatives were the efforts of Nobel laureate Rabindranath Tagore (1861–1941) and his nephew Abanindranath Tagore (1871–1951), who used the Buddhist past to revitalize and redefine contemporary Indian art forms and Asian artistic cultures. The dynamic interactions and links between these individuals, associations and networks, and the vibrant context they created, brought the Buddha back to the centre stage. The process of recentering, however, went beyond these associations, networks and elites to include organizations and people of both the right and left leanings.

Several right-wing Hindu organizations, such as the All-India Hindu Mahasabha, and ideologues in the 20th century sympathized with, supported or patronized Buddhism while positioning the Buddha within the larger Hindu tradition.[19] For them, the Buddha was a Hindu and not the representative of a separate tradition. This contrasted with the early Brahman informants of the East India Company, who saw Buddhism in antagonistic terms. Some industrial groups, which supported the Mahasabha (such as the Birlas), became notable patrons of Buddhists as well. Jugal Kishore Birla (1883–1967), for example, financed the construction of fifteen major Buddhist temples, resthouses and academic institutions across India. The sites for these included those on the Buddhist pilgrimage circuit – such as Arya Dharma Dharamshala at Bodh Gaya, Arya Dharma Sangha Dharamshala at Sarnath, Mahabodhi Vidyalaya at Sarnath, Bhagwan Buddhdev ka Mandir and Arya Vihar at Kushinagar, Oshaji Vihara at Rajgir – as well those built in the new urban centres of Buddhist activities like the Shiva Buddhist temple and Saddharma vihara at Calcutta, the Mahabodhi Mission vihara in Kozhikode, Bahujan Vihar at Mumbai, the Buddha Vihara at New Delhi (Fig 10.6) and the Buddha Mandir at Ranchi. The Dharmarajika Vihara in Kolkata, constructed earlier, was also renovated and expanded. These constructions also reinforced the location of the Buddha within the larger Hindu tradition. Also, Birla resthouses at Buddhist pilgrimage sites carried a plaque explaining this dynamic. J. K. Birla also financed the printing of the Hindi translation of Pali scriptures. Interestingly, he supported left-leaning intellectuals like Rahul Sankrityayan and Dharmananda Kosambi, though their politics was completely different. The Buddhist ethos of Indian leftists, alongside those of the Dalit intellectuals, was based on the ideals of socio-economic equality and anti-caste politics. All of this helped to bring the Buddha back in circulation, although in a very different form.

So, where does this discussion lead us? There is no doubt that Buddhist practices and beliefs survived on the margins in the subcontinent. There is no doubt that public conversations regarding the Buddha and his doctrines continued in the subcontinent. There is no doubt that monks continued to move around Buddhist sites in the subcontinent. In that sense, Europe cannot be solely credited with its revival or rediscovery. Perhaps these are not even adequate expressions to describe what happened during the 19th and 20th centuries. In describing these developments, it would be advisable to shift the focus from geography and semantics to time and context. Here, the colonial context, with developments like better means of transport, communication, print culture and English education, played an important role. It brought to the fore the tangible foundations of Buddhist sites. In bringing together seemingly scattered sites, imageries, texts and practices related to the Buddha, and in connecting the live or semi-live margins with the hitherto dormant core of the Gangetic plains and the peninsular region, the colonial context certainly acted as a catalyst in recentering a faith and its founder in India. But it went beyond that. The colonial context brought together Buddhist sites, practices and beliefs across the East, connected them with the textual studies and archaeological practices originating in the West, and gave them a global platform and an identity of Buddhism. The parts could now relate to the larger whole of the Buddhist past, in more visible ways than ever. The Buddha had come to occupy the centre stage again.

The process of the Buddha's reemergence, which began in the 19th century, came full circle in India around the middle of the

20th century. Discussions on Buddhism had so far revolved around texts, archaeological sites, doctrines and practices. It was now set to play a different innings, with the Buddha's legacy being involved with issues like statecraft and the idea of a nation-state, and identity and refugee politics.

11

BUDDHISM 2.0

> *Buddhism was a revolution. It was as great a Revolution as the French Revolution. Though it began as a Religious revolution, it became more than Religious revolution. It became a Social and Political Revolution ... The first Social Reformer and the greatest of them all is Gautama Buddha.*

This is how iconic Dalit leader Dr B. R. Ambedkar, also known as Babasaheb, described Buddhism and the Buddha in one of his treatises.[1] In a speech, after converting to Buddhism in 1956, he said: 'I want the whole of India to be converted to Buddhism. It should not become only a Harijan religion. It is, after all, a universal faith.'[2] Ambedkar's conversion became a landmark moment in the history of Buddhism. Of course, there were other developments during the mid-20th century and beyond that gave new trajectories to an old faith. After India's independence, Buddhism was enmeshed with statecraft and the diplomacy of a nation-state, identity and caste politics of the Dalits and Tibetan refugee issues. During this phase, Buddhism became more visible in relation to then prime minister Jawaharlal Nehru's diplomatic relations with other newly independent Asian countries, the conversion and identity politics of Ambedkar and the neo-Buddhists, and the cause of the exiled Tibetan Buddhists led by the 14th Dalai Lama.

It is interesting to see how, in a changed context, the Buddha and his dharma acquire new meanings and purposes, some of which seek to redefine traditional Buddhism. In addition, enhanced cultural and diplomatic exchanges with other Asian nations, or transnational Buddhist networks, and the government's attempts to realize and/or maximize international Buddhist tourism potential have brought about new buildings, the installation of many new images and artefacts, and massive infrastructural development around select Buddhist sites – all of which have significantly transformed the traditional Buddhist landscape.

THE RISE OF A NATION-STATE

On 15 August 1947, India became an independent nation after almost two centuries of British domination. A Constituent Assembly was formed to debate the symbols that would represent India. The assembly finally chose two Ashokan symbols – the Sarnath Lion Capital, which became the national emblem; along with a legend from the *Mundaka Upanishad*, 'Satyameva Jayate' ('Truth alone Triumphs'); and the twenty-four-spoked wheel (dharmachakra) on the abacus of the Sarnath capital. It replaced the *charkha* (spinning wheel), the iconic symbol associated with Mahatma Gandhi's mass outreach programme, as the symbol on India's national flag. The wheel, Jawaharlal Nehru (independent India's first prime minister) explained to the Constituent Assembly, was 'a symbol of India's ancient culture. It's a symbol of the many things that India had stood for through the ages.' Likewise, the Ashokan period, he felt, was essentially an international phase in Indian history when many Indians went abroad 'as ambassadors of peace, culture and goodwill'.[3]

In short, Nehru was convinced that the legacy of the Buddha and Ashoka would not only represent and strengthen India's socio-cultural core but also make the country a strong force outside of its territorial borders. The dharmachakra flag represented, some scholars say, the double-edged nature of Nehru's universalist state, which was a strong and expansionist state securing its borders and maintaining a peaceful international order.[4]

The Constituent Assembly finally adopted the Constitution of India on 26 November 1949. It came into effect on 26 January 1950, signalling the birth of the Republic of India. An original lithographed copy of the Constitution was also prepared with twenty-two paintings by the iconic Nandalal Bose. The themes chosen for the paintings drew upon a larger national imagination and held pan-India appeal. These paintings included the Buddha's first sermon at Sarnath (Fig 11.1), with the famous Buddhist verse *'ye dhamma hetu pabhava'* ('ye dharma hetu prabhava' in Sanskrit) inscribed at the base; Mauryan king Ashoka spreading the Buddhist dharma in Sri Lanka, along with Mahendra (his son) and Sanghamitra (his daughter); a painting from the Ajanta Caves; and the monastic complex at Nalanda. Soon after the preparation of the lithographed copy of the Constitution, a government committee was appointed to commission murals that would represent India on the outer walls of the Lok Sabha (the lower house), as the new republic tried to Indianize its parliamentary building. In the process, fifty-eight murals were commissioned. Eleven of these panels brought to the fore the legacy of the Buddha. The Buddhist themes that appear on the outer walls of the original Parliament building (a new building has come up now) include the Buddha's first sermon, Ashoka sending out Buddhist missionaries, Indo-Greek king Menander in conversation with Buddhist monk Nagasena, the Buddhist council convened by Kushana king Kanishka, and so on.[5]

The Buddha's return to the limelight was not only accompanied by the adoption of Buddhist imagery and symbols but also through his deployment in the statecraft of a new nation. State-sponsored Buddhist institutes and educational centres were set up, and many public spaces were given Buddhist names. Substantive government funds were directed towards restoration and revitalization of sites like Bodh Gaya, Sanchi, Shravasti, Lumbini and Nalanda. The central government sponsored the publication of Buddhist texts in other Indian languages, including a forty-six-volume series of the *Tipitaka* (Words of the Buddha), originally written in Pali. The Ministry of Information and Broadcasting even produced a feature film called *Gotama, the Buddha*. Nehru's tenure has been described as a time when 'the Buddha spirit swept the nation'.[6] Buddhist principles of tolerance and non-violence, it was held, would promote harmony and a sense of secular and spiritual belonging in a nation-state torn by communal riots and the horrors of the Partition.

For an astute Nehru, however, Buddhism had the potential to play a bigger role – making India a soft power internationally. It would strengthen India's diplomatic relations with the newly independent Asian nations, especially those with substantive Buddhist following, and help project the country as a cultural superpower in a postcolonial world order.[7] His congratulatory message to Sri Lanka on its independence in 1948 contained elements of India's ambitious posturing. It described Buddhism as the 'great gift which India gave to Lanka and the world so long ago'. India's posturing as the axis mundi (the world axis) of the Buddhist world was reflected in many diplomatic missions, relic diplomacy and international cultural events. During Nehru's tenure, many long-standing Buddhists, such as Bhikshu Jagdish Kashyap, were employed as critical interlocutors or special envoys for initiatives abroad. Kashyap, a Pali monk and scholar from Bihar, accompanied India's then President, Rajendra Prasad, during his trip to Burma. Between 1951 and 1958, five friendship missions sent to China, which were led by Buddhist monks, scholars and officials. These informal missions discussed Buddhist links between the two countries. In the first official mission sent in 1955, Buddha relics and Bodhi tree saplings were gifted to the Chinese dignitaries. China, in return, got the Dalai Lama to present the relics of Xuanzang to India and pledged donation for the construction of a memorial hall dedicated to him at Nalanda. The Buddhist missions were supplemented by relic diplomacy.

In the chapter on Sanchi, we discussed how the 2,500-year-old relics of the Buddha's close disciples, Sariputra and Maudgalyayana, returned by the Victoria and Albert Museum in London, were received by the Governor of Bengal in 1949. They were subsequently unveiled by Nehru before an illustrious gathering of diplomats, Buddhist monks and senior politicians. The next day, a grand reception was held, which was attended by more than half a million people. After being displayed in Calcutta, the relics were taken on a tour of Buddhist sites across parts of India and countries like Tibet, Nepal, Burma, Thailand and Cambodia. The relics had already toured Sri Lanka before being brought to Calcutta. The subsequent permanent loan of a part of these Sanchi–Satdhara relics to Burma (1950–52) drew a lot of political and diplomatic attention. In 1952, when these relics were installed at Chetiyagiri Vihara at Sanchi (Fig 11.2), the event was attended by the who's who of the Asian Buddhist world – representatives of governments, Buddhist organizations, monks, ambassadors and royal households. In 1954, when the first peace pagoda (shanti stupa) was inaugurated at Kumamoto in Japan, Nehru and the Indian delegates presented ten reliquary urns to its founder, Nichidatsu Fujii (1885–1985). A delegation carrying relics to Burma was also organized in 1956. In the early 1950s, relic diplomacy was so intense that there was a fear in the Indian government circles that the country would run out of relics.[8] But the climax of Buddhist posturing came in 1956, when the Indian government decided to celebrate Buddha Jayanti, the occasion of the Buddha's 2,500th birth anniversary, in a grand way.

The celebration was a year-long-event consisting of festivals, gatherings, conferences and art exhibitions attended by other Asian countries with large Buddhist populations.[9] Thousands of international Buddhists, including Asian elites, converged in Bodh Gaya and reinforced the site's symbolic importance as the centre of the Buddhist world. The central government also constituted the Bodh Gaya Temple Advisory Board in 1956. Having representations from various Asian nations, the board allotted land for the construction of monasteries, temples and resthouses. The next couple of decades saw the establishment of transnational monasteries, temples and resthouses by organizations, communities and societies from countries including Tibet, Burma, China, Thailand, Vietnam, Japan, Korea and Sri Lanka. The proliferation of Buddhist establishments and images around the Mahabodhi temple complex has been described as the 'Buddhification' of Bodh Gaya's sacred space. These monastic establishments also developed transnational links, which further contributed to the spread of Buddhist ideas in the West.

The year 1956 was also seminal for the development of what is known as new Buddhism, or neo-Buddhism, which emerged from the writings and legacy of Dr B. R. Ambedkar.

AMBEDKAR AND THE NEO-BUDDHISTS

Ambedkar's public conversion to Buddhism, alongside around 400,000 other followers, on 14 October 1956 in Nagpur, Maharashtra, was one of the largest instances of mass conversions in the modern world. His followers hailed from the marginalized scheduled castes and shared a history of socio-political oppression, with some of them being stigmatized as 'untouchables'. They are commonly referred to as Dalits. Ambedkar's Buddhism evolved over a period of more than twenty years, featuring an anti-Brahmanical, anti-Hindu and an anti-caste tinge.[10] In 1935, he declared that he was born as a Hindu but would not die as one. Since then, his disillusionment with the state when it came to protecting Dalit interests; his growing conviction that the depressed classes constituted a political body separate from the Hindus, a proposition bitterly opposed by Congress leader Mahatma Gandhi; his bitterness against the caste system (espoused so well in his 1936 written but undelivered speech 'Annihilation of Caste') and Hinduism that rationalized and legitimized it; his dalliances with Islam, Sikhism and Christianity; his engagement with Marxism; his interactions with Buddhist societies and scholars; and his reading of the Buddha, who placed emphasis on equality and liberty, made him gravitate towards the indigenously grown Buddhism. His ideas on Buddhism found an expression in his book *The Buddha and His Dhamma*, which was published posthumously in 1957. Popularly described as Navayana (New Vehicle), Ambedkar's Buddhism was more humanistic and socially engaged. It was directed towards the marginalized and oppressed scheduled castes, comprising an element of political and social protest. On the day he converted, Ambedkar expressed his commitment to the usual Buddhist initiation rites, including the triratna and the 'five precepts'. However, he also took twenty-two vows that were unknown to the Buddhists and amounted to an emphatic repudiation of Hinduism and Hindu practices.

The conversion ceremony of 1956, in Nagpur, was chock-full of Buddhist paraphernalia. The occasion was the 2,500th anniversary of the Buddha's birth. A replica of the Sanchi stupa was prominently displayed on the dais, and the event was attended by D. Valisinha, the general secretary of the Maha Bodhi Society and U. Chandramani, apparently the oldest Burmese monk in India. After his conversion, Ambedkar was congratulated by prominent individuals from other Buddhist countries, including the prime minister of Burma. This mass conversion ceremony brought the Buddha and Buddhism into focus at a time when there were only a few practising Buddhists left. It positioned the Dalit, or Ambedkarite, Buddhists as the most visible component of Buddhist population in India, though a more political one. The number of neo-Buddhists soon grew to millions not only in states like Maharashtra and Uttar Pradesh, but also in poor villages and urban localities throughout the country, and among the Dalit diaspora abroad. There have been cases of more public conversions of Dalits to Buddhism in 2002, 2004 and 2007, but they could not create a similar impact nationwide.

How do neo-Buddhist, or Dalit Buddhists, impact our understanding of Buddhist monuments? Ambedkar's Dalit Buddhist movement reinterpreted ancient Buddhist symbols and motifs and gave them meanings in a new social context. The neo-Buddhists of Maharashtra asserted their new identity through visits to ancient sites like Ajanta, Ellora and Karle. Such visits amounted to pilgrimage and were privileged over visits to Hindu temples. Likewise, festivals like Buddha Jayanti (which marks the birth of the Buddha) were celebrated by Dalit Buddhists at rock-cut caves in Aurangabad, Junnar and Nashik. Even the homes of neo-Buddhists are decorated with replicas of Buddhas and photographs of Bodh Gaya, Sarnath and Sanchi, alongside Ambedkar.[11] The political campaigns of the Ambedkarite Buddhists, such as the demand for the control of the management of the Mahabodhi temple at Bodh Gaya also needs to be studied in this context. But perhaps the most tangible manifestation of this trend is the monumentalization of the sites associated with Ambedkar.[12]

The venue of Ambedkar's conversion in Nagpur is now known as Deekshabhoomi (literally, 'initiation ground'). A modern stupa, resembling the ones at Sanchi and Amravati, marks the site (Fig 11.3). Similarly, the site of his cremation in Dadar, Mumbai, is marked by a domed structure while his memorial in Delhi uses architectural elements from Sarnath Ashokan Pillar, Sanchi gateways, and Chaitya windows seen in Buddhist caves in the Deccan (Fig 11.4). The half-round dome of Ambedkar Memorial Shrine at Dadar represents the stupas of central India, while its square platform resembles those found in the stupas of the north-west region. Even the meeting halls of Dalit Buddhists are called viharas, after the ancient monastic establishments. Some, like the Triratna Buddha Vihara in Hanuman Nagar Government Colony (Mumbai), contain images of both the Buddha and Ambedkar. There are other ways in which Dalit Buddhists appropriate or associate with ancient Buddhist symbols. Statues of Ambedkar are found in the vicinity of, or on the way to, ancient Buddhist sites like Nagarjunakonda, Aurangabad and Ajanta. In a more modern context, images of the Buddha and Ambedkar can be found at crossroads, public squares or entrances to Buddhist neighbourhoods. Even modern parks connected with the Dalit identity have images of the Buddha (or Buddhism) and Ambedkar.

Like the Dalit Buddhists, the issue of the modern Tibetan diaspora is also linked to identity politics. However, unlike the Dalit Buddhists, it has a larger international context and is connected to issues related to refugees.

THE TIBETAN BUDDHISTS

One of the ways in which Buddhism has become visible in India's day-to-day life is through the presence and activities of Tibetan refugees – be it through Tibetan settlements at various locations, Tibetan Buddhist monasteries and temples, Tibetan markets, thangkhas and flags at various Buddhist sites, or the spiritual guru Dalai Lama himself. Such enhanced Tibetan presence has largely been a post-Independence phenomenon, though India has had historic and organic Buddhist links with Tibet. The spread of the Mahayana and Vajrayana traditions in Tibet was in many ways related to Nalanda and the other Buddhist mahaviharas in eastern India during the Pala period, but also because of long and sustained contact with Buddhist monastic establishments in the Himalayan region, primarily in Ladakh and Lahaul-Spiti. Monks like Padmasambhava, Shantarakshita and Atisha played an important role in the spread of Buddhism to Tibet, from where it reached Mongolia, Nepal, Central Asia and Bhutan. An institution that is unique to Tibetan Buddhism is the *tulku* (incarnate lama) – a compassionate teacher who is believed to be reborn, again and again. The most famous of lamas is the Dalai Lama.

India's relationship with Tibet changed substantively after the Chinese occupation of Tibet in 1951 and the subsequent crackdown on Buddhist establishments. In 1959, the 14th Dalai Lama, Tenzin Gyatso (born 1935), fled Tibet with 85,000 followers and sought refuge in India. The Tibetan refugees also set up a government-in-exile, with headquarters in McLeodganj, in Dharamshala district of Himachal Pradesh. Several Tibetan buildings were set up in Dharamshala, including government offices, monasteries, temples (Fig 11.5) and the Dalai Lama's residence. Over a period, parts of McLeodganj have come to acquire a very Tibetan look, contributing to the city becoming one of the top tourist destinations of India. In the 1960s and 1970s, the Indian government partnered with the office of the United Nations High Commissioner for Refugees (UNHCR) and some foreign donors to set up fifty-two Tibetan settlements across ten Indian states. The largest concentration of such settlement remains in Karnataka.

The tremendous international sympathy for the cause of the exiled Tibetans in India has majorly been possible because of the current Dalai Lama's global stature and high-profile international followers, friends and sympathizers. A Nobel laureate, his tireless and sustained espousal of the Buddhist cause, and his travel to various countries, has not only created international goodwill for the Tibetan Buddhists but also made them visible globally. Tibetan Buddhism is no longer looked down upon as 'corrupt' Buddhism in the West – as experienced in 19th-century Europe – but as an 'authentic' one. The Tibetan diaspora, spread across various countries, has only added to the globalization of Tibetan Buddhism. The presence of Tibetan Buddhists in India has also impacted the trajectory of Buddhism in the country. First, it has led to a revitalization and deepening of the traditional ties the Tibetans had with Buddhist establishments in Ladakh and Lahaul-Spiti. This has given a renewed life to the Buddhist sites in these regions, a phenomenon strengthened by Tibetan pilgrimage and the organization of large-scale Buddhist ceremonies at these and other Buddhist sites. Of particular importance here is the Dukor Wangchen, or Kalachakra tantra, initiation. This initiation has tremendous religious and political importance, and serves to unite the otherwise scattered Tibetan diaspora. Kalachakra initiations, therefore, invite Buddhists from several parts of the world.[13]

Over a period, the present Dalai Lama has conducted more Kalachakra initiations than any of his predecessors, and in different parts of the world. In India, these initiations have been held in Dharamshala and Karnataka, alongside ancient Buddhist sites like Bodh Gaya and Sarnath (which are closely connected to the principal events of the Buddha's life), Leh and Ladakh (with which Tibetan Buddhism has had historic connections) and Amravati, an extinct Buddhist site. How do such ceremonies impact Buddhist monuments?

Let us take the example of Amravati.[14] In 2006, the Dalai Lama performed a ten-day Kalachakra initiation at the Buddhist stupa complex there, which is in ruins. It was an active Buddhist site between the 3rd and 13th centuries CE, after which it fell into disuse. Later, during the colonial period, it was destroyed and a part of its railing was taken to the British Museum. The initiation ceremony not only infused the stupa with a new sacred authority (comparable to a relic-like quality) but also brought about physical changes to the stupa and the surrounding landscape. To prepare the ruined stupa for the ceremony, the ASI laid a second level of bricks to raise the drum of the damaged mound. Some limestone sculptural fragments, brought in from the site museum, were put on the raised drum to remind the visitors of the stupa's past glory. Finally, to create a circumambulatory path, metal railings were installed around the stupa. Some ancient devotional objects were also used in the initiation ceremony, albeit for a new purpose. Finally, some new constructions were erected in the surrounding landscape to serve as a permanent reminder of the Kalachakra initiation. These included a colossal, 125-foot statue of a seated dhyana Buddha and a smaller, gilded sculpture of Mahayana philosopher Nagarjuna who arguably hailed from the nearby Buddhist site of Nagarjunakonda. Incidentally, the Amravati Buddha (125 feet) is taller than the 80 foot tall Buddha statue (also in seated dhyana mudra) erected in Bodh Gaya in 1989. Finally, a new site museum was constructed and populated with objects brought in from the existing museum at Karimnagar. The Kalachakra initiation and the accompanying transformation of the stupa complex was aimed at giving a new image to an ancient site and to promote Andhra Pradesh as a Buddhist holy land, to construct a global identity for the site.

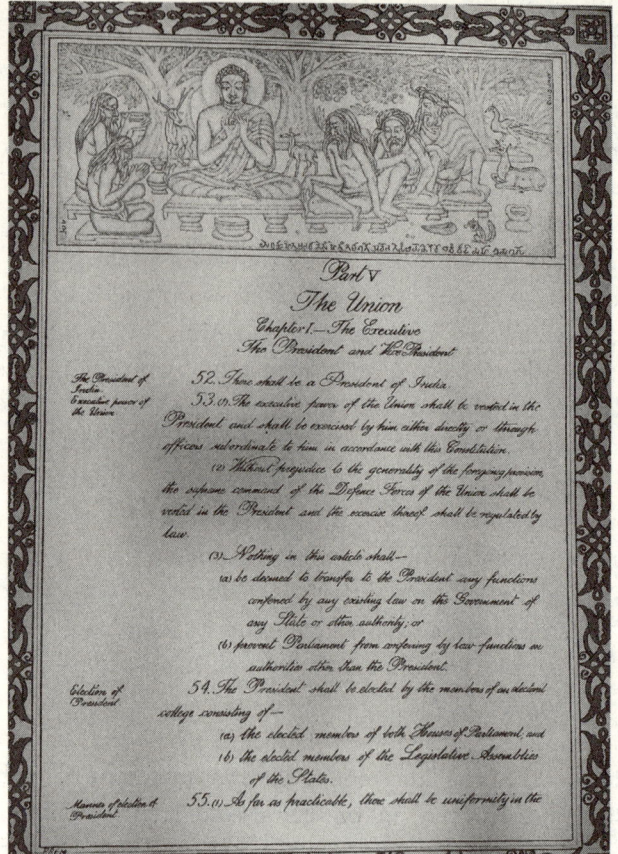

Fig 11.1 A visual replica of the Buddha's first sermon, depicted in the lithographed copy of the Indian Constitution, on display at the Dr B. R. Ambedkar National Memorial in Delhi

Fig 11.2 Chetiyagiri Vihara at Sanchi

Fig 11.3 Deekshabhoomi, Nagpur, the site of Ambedkar's conversion

Fig 11.4 Architecture of Dr Ambedkar National Memorial, Delhi

Fig 11.5 Kalachakra temple, a major Tibetan Buddhist shrine, located in the main market of McLeodganj

Fig 11.6 View of a section of the Indosan Nippon temple complex, Bodh Gaya

Fig 11.7 Shanti Stupa, New Delhi, inspired by Sanchi mahastupa

Fig 11.8 Xuanzang Memorial Hall, with a statue of the Chinese pilgrim at the front, located in Nalanda

Fig 11.9 The giant Buddha statue at Bodh Gaya, sponsored by Japan's Daijokyo sect

Fig 11.10 India's largest reclining Buddha, built in Bodh Gaya in 2023

EAST ASIAN BUDDHIST LINKS AND THE RISE OF JAPAN

Buddhist interactions with countries in East Asia, as discussed earlier, began in the Gupta–Vakataka age (c. 3rd–6th centuries CE) with the movement of monks, scriptures and artefacts. The earlier period, particularly the early centuries of the Christian era, are known for emerging ties with Central Asia, Greece and Bactria, though China had come into the picture via the Silk Route trade network under the Kushanas. Ties with East Asian countries strengthened during the Pala period (8th to 12th centuries CE), when Buddhist sites in India played a seminal role in the transmission of teachings and texts, architectural and sculptural styles and artefacts. Some sites, like Bodh Gaya, even received missions, particularly from Burma (and Sri Lanka), which were involved with constructions, repairs and renovations. The 14th and 15th centuries also saw replicas of the Mahabodhi temple being built in China, Thailand, Japan, Nepal, etc. Now, Bodh Gaya looks like a mini Asia, dotted with Buddhist viharas and temples from different countries, each following their respective architectural styles and designs. Even resthouses and culinary traditions from these countries are becoming common, not to mention monks, pilgrims and tourists. However, what is distinctive about the involvement of the East Asian nations and communities in the recent decades is their presence in regions beyond Bodh Gaya.

Of the East Asian countries active in the Indian Buddhist landscape – Myanmar, Thailand, China, Vietnam, South Korea and Japan – Japan has, in recent times, played the most important role in the conservation, promotion and showcasing of the country's heritage.[15] It has been the only country to offer systematic assistance for the conservation of Buddhist sites in India. This, of course, forms a part of a larger diplomatic exercise to improve bilateral relations between the two countries and is routed through the Overseas Development Assistance (ODA) programme of Japan. In this context, the Japan Bank for International Cooperation (JBIC) has been offering loans to the Indian government for infrastructural development of Buddhist sites for a long time. While the earlier loans were for sites like Ajanta and Ellora in peninsular India, the focus of the JBIC in the recent decades has been on modern Bihar and Uttar Pradesh – the Gangetic heartland of the Buddha's dhamma. These include Buddhist hotspots like Sarnath (associated with the Buddha's first sermon), Kushinagar (where the Buddha died), Kapilavastu (the Buddha's homeland), Shravasti (known for the Buddha's rainy retreats and miracles) and Sankissa (where the Buddha is said to have descended from heaven). In addition, the UNESCO/Japan Funds-in-Trusts for the Preservation of World Cultural Heritage have been utilized for the restoration of stupas in Sanchi and Satdhara regions of Madhya Pradesh.

Japan's presence has been very visible in Bodh Gaya, thanks to the construction of structures like the Indosan Nippon temple (Fig 11.6) and the Daijokyo Buddhist Temple. Likewise, Japanese influence on the sacred landscape of Sarnath is seen in the form of the Nichigai Suzan Horinji temple (also known as Japanese temple) and the frescoes on the walls of the Mulagandhakuti Vihara built by the Maha Bodhi Society of India between 1926 and 1931. The frescoes, depicting scenes from the life of the Buddha, were painted by famous Japanese artist Kosetsu Nōsu (1885–1973) and his assistant. Even the World Peace Bell in Sarnath was gifted by the Japanese Buddhist community. Another conspicuous component of Japanese Buddhist presence in India can be seen in the building of modern stupas known as peace pagodas, or shanti stupas. Such stupas form a part of a project started by Nichidatsu Fujii in Japan, as a larger pacifist movement in the aftermath of World War II. Fujii, who began his career as a monk with the famous Nichiren sect of Japan, is also the founder of a religious group called Nipponzan Myohoji. Over a period of time, more than forty peace pagodas have been built in different parts of the world. The first such stupa was built in Rajgir in 1969. Located near the Gridhakuta (Vulture Peak), where the Buddha is said to have meditated and taught the *Lotus Sutra*, this exercise is seen as a strategic effort on the part of the Nipponzan Myohoji group to locate themselves within the larger Mahayana tradition. Soon, such shanti stupas came up at various places, including Dhauli in Odisha (1972), Ladakh (1991), Darjeeling in West Bengal (1992), Wardha in Maharashtra (1993), Vaishali in Bihar (1996) and New Delhi (2007, Fig 11.7). Since 1988, Japan's growing emphasis on cultural diplomacy, along with its contributions to UNESCO, has made the Japanese

Funds-in-Trust a promising tool for preserving cultural heritage. Notably, part of this fund was used for the restoration of the Buddhas of Bamiyan, destroyed by the Taliban, as well as the preservation of Lumbini in Nepal.

China, on the other hand, has been involved with fewer constructions in the Buddhist landscape of India. In fact, in recent decades, it has been rivalling with India in terms of showcasing Buddhist heritage. The famous Xuanzang Memorial Hall at Nalanda was a product of India–China collaboration. Jawaharlal Nehru and his Chinese counterpart, Zhou Enlai, had laid the foundations of the structure in 1957. As part of the arrangement, the Indian government received an endowment, relics of Xuanzang and some Chinese Buddhist texts from the Chinese government. The hall opened in 1984, followed by the inauguration of the Xuanzang Memorial Museum in 2007 (Fig. 11.8). Modern monasteries and temples built by East Asian communities can also be found at key sites such as Kushinagar, Bodh Gaya, Rajgir and Sarnath. In Bodh Gaya, many of these communities have established schools and health centres for the less privileged or support local NGOs working in the area. Other Asian countries are also actively involved in India's Buddhist landscape.

Though Sri Lanka is not included in the list of East Asian countries, it has played a crucial role in shaping the Buddhist sacred landscape in India. In Sri Lanka, a strong popular tradition claims that the Buddha visited the island at least three times. Historic ties date back to the Mauryan emperor Ashoka, who sent a mission to Anuradhapura led by his son, Mahendra. In the 19th and 20th centuries, these connections were further reinforced by the efforts of Dharmapala Anagarika, the Maha Bodhi Society and various Buddhist missions that constructed temples and erected statues at key sites across India.

Among other Asian Buddhist communities, Tibetan Buddhists, as already discussed, have played a seminal role in the development of the Buddhist landscape and have been involved with several constructions. A recent manifestation of this has been the five-storeyed Padmasambhava Mahavihara in Gajapati district of Odisha. Inaugurated by the Dalai Lama in 2010, it is held to be the largest monastery of its kind in South Asia. Named after Padmasambhava, who spread Buddhism in Tibet and is popularly believed to be born in Odisha, the mahavihara is part of the Rigon Thubten Mindolling monastery near Chandragiri. The monastery is known for its Tibetan paintings and the 1,000-armed, 1,000-eyed image of Avalokiteshvara. The area surrounding the mahavihara has a strong Tibetan refugee settlement, popularly known as Mini Tibet.[16]

The Asian Buddhist communities have not only built monasteries and temples, but they have also been donating images of the Buddha. Images donated by Tibetan, Thai, Japanese, Burmese and Sri Lankan communities can be seen in various temples and public spaces. For instance, the Japanese made available images and priests for the Buddhist temple built by the Birla family in Mumbai in the 1950s.[17] Another famous image with a Japanese connection is the giant Buddha statue in Bodh Gaya (Fig 11.9). Inaugurated by the Dalai Lama in 1989, the statue was provided by the Daijokyo sect of Japan and is located next to the Daijokyo Buddhist temple built in 1983. More recently, a life-sized fibre glass image of a seated Buddha, donated by a trust from Sri Lanka, was installed at Shanti Vihara in Nagpur. Sri Lanka also donated the Avukana Buddha statue at Buddhavanam, a theme park inaugurated in Telangana in 2022, about which we shall talk later.

BUDDHA-CENTRIC TOURISM

The conjunction of several forces in India's post-Independence period, such as the greater involvement of East and Southeast Asian nations and communities; massive international response to the Indian government's celebration of commemorative events like the 2,500th and 2,550th anniversaries of the Buddha's birth; the increasing presence of Tibetan Buddhists and their establishments in the country, and their revitalization of ancient sites; noticeable growth in pilgrim traffic to Buddhist sites; and international tourism arising from Bodh Gaya, Sanchi, Ajanta, Ellora and Nalanda (all World Heritage Sites) have placed the Buddha at the centre of tourism planning as well. The growing tourism potential of Buddhism made the government realize that Buddhist sites not only require a greater focus but also a dedicated one. This was how the idea of the Buddhist Circuit was born. The action plan for the development of the circuit was launched in 1986, but it gained momentum only in the last couple of decades. In the initial phase, the focus of the Buddhist Circuit was on sites in Bihar and Uttar Pradesh, which constituted the heartland of early Buddhism. Later, it was expanded to include twenty-two sites in Bihar, Uttar Pradesh, Andhra Pradesh (especially Nagarjunakonda and Amravati), Madhya Pradesh (Sanchi) and Jammu and Kashmir (Leh). Spread over north, north-west and central India, and the eastern Deccan, besides the Gangetic heartland, many of these sites house important Buddhist monuments, temples and artefacts. Discussions are on to include more sites in the circuit. A major infrastructural push is being given to these sites, which are estimated to draw around 450 million practicing Buddhists, alongside non-Buddhist tourists interested in religion, history and culture. To attract pilgrims and tourists from Southeast Asia, a special campaign called 'Come to India, Walk with the Buddha' was also launched. There is also a growing focus on developing spiritual tourism. It is interesting to see how various states are now vying with each other to become preferred Buddhist destinations. And these happen to be outside of the dominant Bihar–Uttar Pradesh region. The case of Andhra Pradesh is particularly interesting in this regard.

We have already discussed how Amravati got a facelift in the wake of the Dalai Lama's Kalachakra initiation ceremony in 2006. Back then, the Dalai Lama not just revived the ancient stupa of Amravati but also consecrated a modern structure in the undivided Andhra Pradesh. This was the 58 feet tall monolithic granite statue, erected atop the Rock of Gibraltar in the Hussain Sagar Lake in Hyderabad. Placed in 1994, it remains one of the world's tallest monolithic statues of the Buddha. This statue was commissioned by the then chief minister of the state, N. T. Ramarao, who had been impressed by the Statue of Liberty during his visit to New York in 1984 and wanted something similar, though rooted in the indigenous tradition, to be set up in Hyderabad. Interestingly, during his 2006 visit to Andhra Pradesh, the Dalai Lama also planted some trees in Nagarjunakonda, another ancient Buddhist site. Located close to Amravati, the site has experienced a visible transformation in the recent decades. Nagarjunakonda, known as Vijayapuri in the ancient times, was the capital of the Ikshvakus, whose kings and queens supported both Brahmanical and Buddhist establishments. When the Nagarjuna Sagar Dam was being built in the 1950s, at the site where the Ikshvakus once lived, many structures were shifted on top of a hill that has become a heritage island of sorts. In the last couple of decades, Nagarjunakonda has been reinvented with the addition of symbols and imagery associated with Buddhism.[18] The entrance to the Nagarjuna Sagar Power Station is decorated with a gigantic plaster stupa. A bust of the Buddha has been installed in front of the recreation club in Vijayapuri (South). Likewise, images of monk Nagarjuna have been put up at various places in the city. In fact, Vijayapuri was renamed Nagarjunakonda (literally, the hill of Nagarjuna. 'Konda' means hill in Telugu) after the monk. This is despite the monk's connection with Vijayapuri being historically debatable. The projection of a predominantly Buddhist imagery of Nagarjunakonda is also not congruent with the site's multireligious past. It privileges Vijayapuri's Buddhist history over its Hindu past. Within this dominant Buddhist imagery, the site's connection with Ambedkar and Dalit Buddhism is particularly striking. A statue of Ambedkar has been installed at a crossroads in Vijayapuri (South). The canopy over Ambedkar carries a small, seated and gilded image of the Buddha. Interestingly, Amravati also has a statue of Ambedkar near the ruined stupa and, during the Kalachakra ceremony in 2006, a statue of the seated Buddha was erected in the same area.

While Andhra Pradesh has been reinventing Nagarjunakonda; Telangana, which once shared the same Buddhist heritage as Andhra but was carved out as a separate state in 2014, has come up with a modern mega theme park-cum-Buddhist spiritual centre, which is reportedly the largest of its kind in Asia. In 2022, the sprawling Buddhavanam (the forest of the Buddha) was inaugurated at Nagarjunasagar by the Telangana State Tourist Development Corporation (TSDTC).[19] Spread over 279 acres, Buddhavanam is aimed at creating awareness about Telangana's Buddhist past and attracting tourists, especially those from Southeast Asian countries. The two big attractions of the park include a replica of the 27-foot Avukana Buddha statue, found near Kekirawa in North Central Sri Lanka, and the mahastupa that depicts the Amravati Stupa. The Avukana Buddha was apparently inspired by both the Gandhara and Amravati schools of art and presents one of the best examples of standing Buddha status in Sri Lanka. It forms the tallest statue of the Buddha in the state of Telangana and was gifted by the Sri Lankan government, along with a 'dhamma bell', under the Indo-Sri Lankan Cultural Exchange programme. Other tourist attractions in the park include the Jataka Park, which depicts the Buddha's previous birth stories; a stupa park with miniature stupas from South and Southeast Asia; a Buddhist education centre, and a meditation park alongside hospitality and wellness centres. The complex also has a dedicated website.

The desire to attract international tourists has other takers, too. The Maharashtra government, for instance, recently announced plans to build an international Buddhist cultural centre near the Ajanta caves. To be built over 115 acres of land, the proposed 'Buddha Theme Park' will showcase Buddhist heritage from ten different countries, each of which will be allotted at least five acres. Venuvana, the bamboo grove gifted to the Buddha by the Magadhan king Bimbisara has come in for a massive modern facelift too as a Buddhist theme park in Bihar. A major infrastructural up-gradation and heritage restoration exercise is also in the works in the Buddhist circuit of Bodh Gaya-Rajgir-Nalanda. The governments of Uttar Pradesh and Odisha have also announced plans to develop their own Buddhist circuits. Festivals and events, both annual and occasional, celebrating the Buddha are also proliferating in the Buddhist landscape. In addition to the traditional ones like Hemis Festival at Leh, several others (including ultra-modern ones) have kicked in. These include the Lahaul Festival in Himachal Pradesh and the Global Buddhist Peace Festival at Amravati (touted for its largest online global chant for world peace). Buddha Mahotsav, which was once celebrated at the sites associated with the principal events in the life of the Buddha, is now celebrated at multiple locations. In early 2023, in a walking pilgrimage organized by Sangwol Society of South Korea, 108 Buddhist pilgrims from the country walked over 1,100 kms in forty-three days. The event was meant to commemorate fifty years of diplomatic ties between India and South Korea and coincided with India's G20 presidency.[20] Buddhism features prominently in India's 'Look East, Act East' policy. In recent times, many high-profile conferences have come up, in addition to multiple academic seminars. In August 2018, the President of India inaugurated the International Buddhist Conclave (IBC) at New Delhi and Ajanta, which was attended by representatives of twenty-nine countries. The conclave was jointly organized by the Union Ministry of Tourism and the state governments of Bihar, Uttar Pradesh and Maharashtra. Visits to Rajgir, Nalanda, Bodh Gaya and Sarnath were also organized as a part of the event. The IBC, organized biennially, saw earlier editions in New Delhi and Bodh Gaya (February 2004), Nalanda and Bodh Gaya (February 2010), Varanasi and Bodh Gaya (September 2012), Bodh Gaya and Varanasi (September 2014), and Sarnath/Varanasi and Bodh Gaya (October 2016).[21] In July 2022, the Union Ministry of Tourism collaborated with the Association of Buddhist Tour Operators to organize a webinar on cross-border tourism. The online event had representatives from the UN Peacekeeping Forces Council and travel and hospitality associations of Bhutan, Bangladesh, Afghanistan, Myanmar, Vietnam, Thailand, Cambodia, Indonesia, Myanmar, Nepal and Sri Lanka. The webinar saw a decision being taken to install signage in international languages at important Buddhist sites in India. In April 2023, the Union Ministry of Culture and the International Buddhist Confederation organized the first Global Buddhist Summit in Delhi to discuss contemporary global issues through a Buddhist perspective. It saw the participation of 170 delegates from foreign countries including Cambodia, Laos, Thailand, Japan, South Korea, Vietnam, Sri Lanka and Mexico, and 150 from India.[22] Inaugurating the summit, the prime minister of India, Narendra Modi, underlined how the Buddha's teachings could offer solutions to the greatest challenges confronting the modern world, including war, economic instability, terrorism and climate change.[23] And finally, the idea of a dedicated Buddhist Circuit made concrete progress in 2023, with the Buddhist Circuit train starting. The special tourist train visits nine places in India and Nepal. It starts at Delhi and stops at Bodhgaya, Rajgir, Nalanda, Varanasi, Lumbini (Nepal), Kushinagar, Shravasti and Agra.[24] The Buddhist circuit is not only aimed at improving tourism and related infrastructure, it also forms an important pillar of Act East policy – an important diplomatic framework to improve India's relations with other countries in the immediate eastern neighbourhood, and Far East too. Buddhist outreach has also become an important element of Narendra Modi's foreign policy.

Around the mid-20th century, significant shifts took place in the context of recentering the Buddha. Engagements with the Buddha and Buddhism expanded beyond texts, archaeological sites, doctrines and practices. It included issues and aspects related to statecraft, identity and caste politics, Tibetan refugees, enhanced diplomatic and cultural exchanges with Asian countries, and modern and organized tourism. From Nehru deploying Buddhism in nation-building and international relations, to Ambedkar and his fellow Dalits' converting, to the congregations and rituals of Tibetan Buddhists, to the construction of monasteries and temples by Asian countries and transnational Buddhist networks, and the setting up of modern constructions and theme parks equipped with all modern facilities, the Buddha's legacy and landscape have experienced dramatic widening and transformation. The Buddha is being recast and reinvented in the land where he preached his dharma, established the sangha and found his first followers. The reinvention was perhaps always a part of Buddhism, but the scale, constituency and positioning have become significantly different. The Buddha's dharma no longer remains confined to matters of doctrine and monastic discipline. The sangha is being replaced by zealous Buddhist governments and organizations working in a more globalized set-up. The austere viharas and mahaviharas have given way to well-endowed modern buildings. Amidst all these changes, the Buddha's iconographic presence has become more pervasive than ever before. His images proliferate streets, parks, temples, monasteries and recreational spots. They are also becoming larger, taller and more monumental. Whether it is Hussain Sagar Lake, Amravati or the Buddhavanam, the race to put in place a more dominating Buddha continues. In 2023, India's largest statue of the reclining Buddha – 100 feet long and 30 feet high – built by the Buddha International Welfare Mission, was unveiled at the site where he gained enlightenment (Fig 11.10).

Together, these developments have not only globalized the Buddha's appeal but also created a lucrative international market for his images and other Buddhist merchandise like never before. They have also made his figure omnipresent in India. The Buddha has also become an icon for wellness and meditation programs. Meditational techniques inspired by the Buddha have become an integral part of spiritual tourism initiatives, and Buddhist chants are now recited in many modern households. Today, he can be seen everywhere – in politics and vote banks, diplomacy and statecraft, art markets and souvenir shops, sects and religious affiliations, mantras and chants, tourism and infrastructural development, spiritual centres, names and university curricula, management guides, museums and government offices, parks and streets, and as a decorative piece in the houses of non-Buddhist citizens.

AUTHOR'S NOTE

How does one write the history of a subject where the intangible keeps taking on tangible forms? This was the first question I posed to myself when I started working on this book. As veteran art historian Frederick M. Asher would ask, how does one reconstruct the past between the 'truth of the devout' and the 'truth of the historian'? In most historical accounts, this line tends to get blurred. Some of my early readings raised further questions. The first set of Buddhist monuments, as we now understand them, appeared on the scene around the 3rd century BCE, while the earliest texts – the Pali Canon – were committed to writing around the 1st century BCE. How can we reconcile these timelines? Could an oral tradition have guided the construction of monuments before the texts appeared? How can we read monuments (practice) without a corresponding set of texts (theory)? How do Buddhist texts, especially the early ones – which are primarily concerned with the Buddha's teachings, working of the sangha or monastic discipline – help our understandings of early structures and artefacts? With few exceptions, the later texts primarily deal with matters of doctrine, monastic order, discourse or philosophy. These texts also bring up sects, traditions and an evolving mythology. More questions were in the offing.

The evolution of structures and artefacts across various periods demonstrated a clear intersection between art, architecture and the development of Buddhist doctrine and mythology. The emergence of the boddhisattva images, in the early centuries of the Christian era, and later the Taras and associated deities during the Gupta period, exemplified this connection. At the same time, the difference in the appearance of the buildings – such as stupas and viharas – and the related structures, artefacts and ornamental motifs highlighted the role of regional and temporal contexts. Through my readings and visits to various sites, it also became evident that the Buddhists co-existed alongside multiple religious and popular traditions, and that many of their constructions emerged from a matrix of multi-religious pasts. How did the interactions and tensions between such traditions manifest in the architecture of 'Buddhist' structures and artefacts? Equally striking is how various monuments and sites continue to be appropriated, modified – whether through additions of later structures or artefacts or by being reinvented. The existing sacred geographies are continually redefined with the appearance of new agents, for example, the Ambedkarite or Tibetan Buddhists.

The list of questions kept growing, with no easy answers. Nonetheless, they clearly indicated there were multiple layers and multiple dimensions to this subject. Monuments and artefacts are not entities frozen in time and space. They are also not just static, physical structures. They resonate with changes in surroundings and contexts and acquire different meanings over time. Often, artefacts and structures tell stories differently from the texts. A more dynamic and inclusive conceptual framework is necessary to better comprehend such complexities. This series attempts to fill that gap. Each volume studies monuments in wider geographical, sociocultural and historical contexts using a dynamic, multi-pronged approach.

The first book, *Delhi, Agra, Fatehpur Sikri: Monuments, Cities and Connected Histories*, presented an interdisciplinary, layered and multi-dimensional account of the monuments and cities tied to the Delhi Sultanate and Mughal empire. These structures were commissioned mostly by Muslims – a heterogenous group of people whose identities kept evolving – and their architecture was inspired by not just by readings of Islam and the Quran but also by cross-cultural borrowing from regional traditions in the subcontinent. This volume focused on imperial cities and monuments, and structures like forts, palaces, tombs and mausoleums, mosque complexes, gardens, domes, arches, pavilions, etc.

While monuments and cities remain important in this volume, it turns to the structures associated with the evolution of Buddhism from a heterodox sect to a full-fledged religion and beyond. Naturally, it centers around structures like stupas, viharas, mahaviharas and temples, examining their development and the ecosystems around them. But this book also delves into the role of artefacts – images, steles, tablets, votive stupas and donative inscriptions – that have largely remained understudied yet form a vital part of the Buddhist monumental legacy. Additionally, it discusses modern buildings and artefacts connected with the revival of Buddhism in the 19th and 20th centuries and brings it up right to the present day. In sum, it covers over 2,500 years of Buddhist heritage and history. This ambitious work was made possible through the contributions of numerous people and organizations.

I have benefited from discussions at various stages with Himanshu Prabha Ray, Amareswar Galla, Srikumar Menon, Shreedhar Lohani, Bijoy Kumar Choudhary, Nilanjan Sarkar, Suchandra Ghosh, Swadhin Sen, Sudhir Chandra, Amar Farooqui, Raziuddin Aquil, Jayanta Sengupta, S. A. Nadeem Rezavi, Janhwij Sharma, Chandan Ray, B. M. Pande, Arvind Sharma, Mugdha Sinha, A. Raghuramaraju, Sundar Sarukkai, Ashok Vohra, Biswamoy Pati, Kaiser Haq, Arun Gupto, Amit Prasad, Ranbir Singh, Pankaj Jha, Sanjeev Shankar, Prasun Chatterjee and Rajat Kain – some about monuments and history in general, and others about matters specific to this book. Himanshu Prabha Ray (one section of this volume is also named after her book *The Return of the Buddha*), Suchandra Ghosh, Amareshwar Galla and Nilanjan Sarkar also helped me with the readings – much gratitude, all of you!

I am obliged to my many old friends and well-wishers who have enthusiastically supported the 'monumental' turn in my research, writings – and the related pursuit of public history – and have offered valuable suggestions and feedback: My heartfelt thanks to Tanvir Aeijaz, Jayabrata Sarkar, Krishnan Unni, S. P. Verma, Ishrat Alam, Surinder Jodhka, Sangeetha Menon, Akshay Mukul, Parimala Rao, Amit Prakash, Arthur Needham, Tapti Roy, Indrani Sen, Amarendra Kumar, Chandan Sinha, Pranav Kumar Chaudhary, Tusar Upadhyay, Sanjay Kumar, Maneesh Prasad, Rajiv Kumar, Amitabh Shukla, Saniv Kumar Sinha, Monika Saxena, Sanjeev Roy, Rajesh Kumar, Tuktuk Ghosh, Tarika Uberoi, Nandini-Bhattacharyya Panda, Lata Singh, Amrit Abhijat, Haimanti Dey, Sekhar Dey, Sujata Roy, Amit Prasad, Vikas Kumar, Hitendra Anupam and Rakesh Kant Prasad. *Aabhar*!

I would like to specifically acknowledge the role of my teammates at my current workplace. Our lunchtime conversations have continually expanded the horizons of my thoughts, and their contribution goes far beyond the writing of this book – a big thank you, everyone. For me, you are much bigger rockstars than the BTS guys.

Anand and Nayana have been tremendous supports throughout this book project in so many ways. As have Mayank, Raj, Ruchika, Saket, OP, Abha, Meenakshi, Mona, Manish, Manju, Ojas, Shilpa, Khushal and Sarika. I am truly beholden! Neeraj – I always remember the excitement and seriousness with which you used to discuss my forays into the world of monuments and heritage. Your perspective continues to influence my writings and visual compositions. Miss you dearly, my friend!

I was fortunate to receive a lot of support even during my field visits. Bena Sengar: your tips, suggestions and warm hospitality during my visit to Aurangabad were of great help. Even my mother and sisters pitched in. Didi and Bhaisaab (Jyotsna Sinha and Ravi Sinha) organized my trips to Nalanda, Bodh Gaya and Rajgir multiple times. Muni-di and Satish Bhaisaab (Arpana Sinha and Satish Chandra) along with Rashmi and Sanjay accompanied me to Bodh Gaya. My mother and brother (Amit) came along on another trip. There was serious daytime work and relaxed family time by evenings. I can't thank you all enough.

My gratitude also goes to the organizations and individuals who gave me permission to use photos from their collections. The Metropolitan Museum of Art and Cleveland Museum of Art deserve a special mention here for making high-resolution photos so accessible and easy to download for all users. I am grateful to the American Institute of Indian Studies (AIIS), particularly Vandana Sinha and Sushil Sharma, for their prompt help with some photos featured in this book. Umakanta Mishra, Om Prakash Singh, Swadhin Sen, Alok Kumar (Alok Bhaiya – also for his insights from time to time) and Amit Kumar also opened up their personal collections for me. M. B. Rajani not only permitted me to use some of her maps, but also shared some relevant articles.

I also want to record my appreciation for permissions related to the text. Parts of my chapter on Bodh Gaya, Sanchi and Nalanda were previously published in a different form in *Frontline* magazine, while a different version of the story about Sanchi relics appeared in the *Wire*. These pieces have since been substantially revised, reworked and expanded to fit the scope of this book. I am grateful to R. Vijayasankar of the *Frontline* and Chitra Padmanabhan of the *Wire* for publishing those articles and allowing me to adapt them. Thanks are also due to the Bodh Gaya Global Dialogues team, especially Sanjay Kumar and Deshkal, for offering a platform to present my research to an audience engaged with Buddhism and Buddhist heritage. I made some good friends over the last three editions of the Dialogues, including Sudhirendar Sharma, Uday Sahay, Arvind Mohan, Manish Sinha, Arvind Mishra and Aviram Sharma; our continuing conversations have been intellectually fulfilling.

There are some friends who have stood by me through all my book projects. To Amitabh and Nupur, Atish and Anupama, Rajiv and Vasundhara, Amit and Rekha, Sumit and Tanuj, Rajiv and Aarti, Ravindra and Swati, Rajan and Archana, Rajat and Geetanjali, Anupam and Kattie, Atul and Ritu, Sandeep and Shaily, Madhukar and Ruby, Chandan and Neera, Rajeev and Rashmi, Shashi and Anisha and Nilendu and Reema – thank you for your unwavering warmth. I always look forward to our addas and evenings together. Kamal Bhai, Kumud Bhabhi, Priyanka, Renujee, Rohit, Hema and Reena – I value your friendship and affection. And HOXA 1985, you always rock and your presence is so special!

I am indebted to my emotional anchors through life and work within the family – Vishy, Vartika, Mittan, Mayank, Nishtha, Shubhangi, Mohnish, Amrit, Reyan, Prishu, Aryan and Veer. Reyan accompanied me on various field trips. I feel very privileged and confident to have you by my side, young man. And thank you Manisha, my friend and companion, for bearing with my obsessions, absent-mindedness and long hours of work, but also for asking the very question that sparked my journey on this series: 'Why is it so difficult for a common person to get a good historical essence of monuments?' Your insights continue to structure my thoughts and writings. Zara, you were such a beautiful distraction, and I realized only later how deep an imprint you had left behind. In perennial debt to your ever-loving spirit!

I am grateful to my publisher, Pan Macmillan India, for agreeing to publish this project with enthusiasm. Thank you, Isha Banerji, for steering this project with care and compassion, and Rajdeep Mukherjee, for his overall support. Also thank you to Pratap-ji (Pratap Narayan of Vertex Designs) for redrawing certain maps and images, Aslesha Kadian for line editing, Udyotna Kumar for proofreading, Haitenlo Semy for the cover design, Ajith Kumar for typesetting and Christu John for the index.

Finally, I wish to state that I have written this book purely in my capacity as an independent researcher. The content and views expressed in this book do not, in any way, relate to or represent the perspectives of any organization I have worked for in the past, or my current employers. It is a wholly personal exercise.

IMAGE CREDITS

All photographs are taken by the author,
other than those credited otherwise

1. THE BUDDHA COMES INTO BEING

Fig 1.1 A depiction of the Buddha's birth from Bengal, dating to the Pala period (800s). Courtesy: The Cleveland Museum of Art, John L. Severance Fund, 1959.349

Fig 1.2 An emaciated Siddhartha being offered pudding by Sujata. A painting from Mulagandhakuti Vihara, Sarnath

Fig 1.3 The mahabhinishkramana: the upper architrave shows 'The Great Departure', while the lower one depicts Ashoka's visit to the Bodhi Tree

Fig 1.4 Mara's Attack and Temptation, Kashmir (8th century CE). Courtesy The Cleveland Museum of Art, Purchase from the J. H. Wade Fund, 1971.18

Fig 1.5 Buddha calling on the earth to witness (bhumisparsha mudra), 9th century, Tetravan, Bihar. Courtesy Cleveland Museum of Art, Dudley P. Allen Fund, 1935.146

Fig 1.6 A descendant of the Bodhi tree with the enclosure containing the Vajrasana.

Fig 1.7 Gandhakuti in Jetavana Monastery, Shravasti. Courtesy Wikimedia Commons (CC BY-SA 2.5)

Fig 1.8 A sculpture depicting the Buddha's mahaparinirvana in the side aisle of Cave 26 at Ajanta.

2. EMERGENCE OF RELIC CULT, STUPAS AND PILLARS

Fig 2.1 War of Relics: Siege of Kushinagar, a relief from the Sanchi gateway.

326 IMAGE CREDITS

Fig 2.2 Vajrasana and the Bodhi tree on a panel of the Bharhut Stupa. From Alexander Cunningham, Mahābodhi, or the great Buddhist temple under the Bodhi tree at Buddha-Gaya, 1892.

Fig 2.3 Mayadevi temple and the Ashokan pillar at Lumbini. Courtesy Wikimedia Commons, Bibek Raj Pandeya (CC BY-SA 4.0, image cropped)

Fig 2.4 Ashokan Pillar in the Allahabad Fort. From Thomas A. Rust, *Album of Miscellaneous views in India* (c. 1870). Capt. Edward Smith surmounted it with a lion capital in 1838, later removed (Public Domain).

Fig 2.5 Drum panel depicting a stupa with the Buddha's descent from Trayastrimsa Heaven, Nagarjunakonda, Stupa Site 6, Ikshvaku period, late 3rd century CE. Courtesy Metropolitan Museum of Art, Rogers Fund, 1928.

Fig 2.6 Vaishali Stupa with the Ashokan pillar. Courtesy Om Prakash Singh

Fig 2.7 Remains of Dharmarajika Stupa, Taxila (Pakistan). Courtesy Creative Commons, Sasha Isachenko (CC BY-SA 3.0).

Fig 2.8 Kanaganahalli inscribed panel portraying Ashoka. Courtesy Indian Archaeology, 1997–98, Annual Report, Archaeological Survey of India, Government of India (GODL-India).

3. THE RISE OF IMAGES, MONASTIC COMPLEXES AND POPULAR CULTS

Fig 3.1 3rd-century schist image of the Buddha, Gandhara (Pakistan). Courtesy Metropolitan Museum of Art, Purchase, Denise and Andrew Saul Gift, 2014.

Fig 3.2 5th-century CE image of Mathura Buddha, now at Rashtrapati Bhawan, New Delhi. Courtesy The President's Secretariat, 2017, Rashtrapati Bhawan (GODL-India)

Fig 3.3 Satavahana period relief showing stupa worship by followers, including foreigners, Sanchi (99–1 BCE). Courtesy American Institute of Indian Studies (AIIS)

Fig 3.4 A drum slab from Amravati Stupa (100–299 CE). Courtesy American Institute of Indian Studies

IMAGE CREDITS 327

Fig 3.5 Various forms of stupas (after Percy Brown, *Indian Architecture*, 1956)

Fig 3.6 Evolution of rock-cut chaitya griha or shrine architecture (after Upinder Singh, *A History of Ancient and Early Medieval India*, 2009)

Fig 3.7 Plan of a typical monastic complex, Nagarjunakonda (after Debala Mitra, *Buddhist Monuments*, 1971)

Fig 3.8 Naga Muchalinda guarding the Buddha's throne, Pauni (railing pillar, Jagannath Tekri), 2nd–1st century BCE, National Museum. Courtesy Creative Commons, Gary Todd (CC0 1.0)

4. EFFLORESCENCE AND SPREAD AMIDST BRAHMANICAL REVIVAL

Fig 4.1 Temple 17, an early independent structural Buddhist temple from the Gupta period, Sanchi

Fig 4.2 Subsidiary shrine with Yakshi Hariti and her consort, Cave 2, Ajanta

Fig 4.3 Serpent King Nagaraja and his queen in the external courtyard of Cave 19, Ajanta

Fig 4.4 Dhamekh Stupa at Sarnath

Fig 4.5 Mahaparinirvana stupa and temple at Kushinagar. Courtesy Wikimedia Creative Commons, Mahendra 3006 (CC BY-SA 3.0)

Fig 4.6 A 1939–40 photo of the Big Buddha at Bamiyan, Afghanistan, by Annemarie Schwarzenbach (1908–42). Courtesy Wikimedia Commons, Swiss National Library Collection

Fig 4.7 A Gupta-period (5th century CE) chunar sandstone image of the Buddha seated in the 'Wheel of Dharma' gesture. Courtesy American Institute of Indian Studies

Fig 4.8 Tara flanked by female figures and dwarfs, Cave 7, Aurangabad Caves

Fig 4.9 Cave 7, Aurangabad. Left: Bodhisattva as the saviour from Eight Great Dangers. Right: Female Buddhist deities with attendants and celestial beings

328 IMAGE CREDITS

5. TANTRIC INFUSION, REGIONALIZATION AND DECLINE

Fig 5.1 The triple-storeyed Cave 12 at Ellora
Fig 5.2 Eight scenes from the Buddha's life, Pala period (10th century), black schist stele from Bihar. Courtesy Metropolitan Museum of Art, Gift of Raymond G. and Marsha Vargas Handley, 2009
Fig 5.3 Carvings on the facade of Cave 10 at Ellora
Fig 5.4 Cave 5 at Ellora, commonly known as the 'Dining Hall'
Fig 5.5 Cluster of Buddhist goddesses in Cave 12 at Ellora
Fig 5.6 Monastery 1 at Ratnagiri (Odisha). Courtesy Umakanta Mishra
Fig 5.7 Tara as the saviour from Eight Great Dangers, from Ratnagiri (Odisha). Courtesy Umakanta Mishra
Fig 5.8 The Somapura and Vikramashila monasteries follow a similar layout, with a cruciform stupa-shrine in the centre and rectangular cells along the square boundary
Fig 5.9 Remains of Somapura Monastery (Bangladesh). Courtesy Swadhin Sen
Fig 5.10 Kesariya Stupa, Kesariya (Bihar). Courtesy American Institute of Indian Studies
Fig 5.11 A Pala period (late 800s) bronze image of Akshobhya, the Buddha of the East, Kurkihar, Bihar. Courtesy The Cleveland Museum of Art, Purchase from the J. H. Wade Fund, 1970.10
Fig 5.12 Tabo Buddhist Monastery Complex. Courtesy Wikimedia Commons, Vikramsolan, 2008 (CC BY-SA 3.0, image cropped)

6. MAHABODHI TEMPLE AND BODH GAYA

Fig 6.1 The Mahabodhi temple complex, viewed from the southeast corner. The Tara temple is to the far right
Fig 6.2 Uninscribed pillar shaft, believed to have been erected by Mauryan king Ashoka
Fig 6.3 A gilded black stone statue of the Buddha in bhumisparsha mudra from the Pala period, located in the sanctum of the Mahabodhi Temple
Fig 6.4 Buddhapada: Representation of the Buddha's footprints
Fig 6.5 The Jewel Walk, where the Buddha is believed to have spent his third week after enlightenment. The raised flowers on the left represent his paces.

Fig 6.6 Muchilinda Lake, where the Buddha is believed to have spent his sixth week, protected from a rainstorm by a mythical serpent
Fig 6.7 Smaller votive stupas throughout the temple complex
Fig 6.8 A section of a collage stupa at the Mahabodhi temple complex, Bodh Gaya
Fig 6.9 Model (miniature replica) of the Mahabodhi temple, Bihar (12th century). Courtesy Metropolitan Museum of Art, Gift of John and Fausta Eskenazi, 2006
Fig 6.10 The Royal Thai Monastery, Wat Thai, Bodh Gaya

7. SANCHI AND THE HILLTOP STUPA COMPLEX

Fig 7.1 Remains of the Ashokan Pillar
Fig 7.2 Plan of Stupa 1 at Sanchi (after Debala Mitra, *Buddhist Monuments*, 1971)
Fig 7.3 Stupa 3, which contained the relics of Sariputra and Maudgalyayana
Fig 7.4 Buddha statue in dhyanmudra on the berm facing the eastern entrance
Fig 7.5 Eastern Gateway, one of the four toranas located at the cardinal directions
Fig 7.6 Southern Gateway with the staircase to the terrace for circumambulation. The in-situ remains of the Ashokan Pillar are visible to the right of the gateway
Fig 7.7 Temple 18, built on an apsidal plan
Fig 7.8 Remains of Temple and Monastery 45
Fig 7.9 Remains of Monastery 51 in the background
Fig 7.10 Birla Planetarium, Kolkata. Its dome is inspired by Sanchi

8. AJANTA CAVES

Fig 8.1 View of a section of the Ajanta Caves with the dry Waghora river stream in the foreground
Fig 8.2 Facade of an early-phase chaitya griha, Cave 9. The Buddha statue on the right of entrance is a later addition
Fig 8.3 An austere stupa within a chaitya griha in Cave 9. This early-period cave has no anthropomorphic images

330 IMAGE CREDITS

Fig 8.4 A developed stupa with a Buddha image in a later-period chaitya griha, Cave 1

Fig 8.5 Ornately carved facade of Cave 19, a later-phase chaitya griha

Fig 8.6 Layout of a developed monastery, Cave 1, Ajanta (after Debala Mitra, *Buddhist Monuments*, 1971)

Fig 8.7 Sculptural depiction of the Miracle at Shravasti, Cave 7

Fig 8.8 Detail from the story of the merchant Simhala, from Simhalavadana, Cave 17

Fig 8.9 Buddha seated like a king on a throne with two bodhisattvas as attendants, Cave 16

Fig 8.10 Bodhisattva Padmapani and a scene from the Mahajanaka Jataka, Cave 1

9. NALANDA MAHAVIHARA

Fig 9.1 Pushkarni, one of the water bodies outside the excavated Nalanda site

Fig 9.2 Site 3, popularly believed to be Monk Sariputra's stupa

Fig 9.3 Ruins of Temple 12, the largest and most complex temple in the enclosed area

Fig 9.4 Layout of Monastery 8, Nalanda (after Debala Mitra, *Buddhist Monuments*, 1971)

Fig 9.5 Ruins of Monastery 6, showing the arrangement of monk cells around a central courtyard

Fig 9.6 Plinth of Temple 2, once a huge and imposing structure

Fig 9.7 Miniature shrines and votive stupas found in the Temple 12 complex

Fig 9.8 A black-coloured Buddha statue in bhumisparsha mudra, known as Teliya Baba, now enshrined at a temple in Bargaon

Fig 9.9 Nalanda Museum, established in 1917

Fig 9.10 A partial view of the Nalanda International University Campus, featuring architecture inspired by the ancient mahavihara

10. THE BUDDHA MAKES A COMEBACK

Fig 10.1 Kanheri Caves on the island of Salsette, near Bombay, Maharashtra, coloured aquatint by Thomas and William Daniell, 1800 (Public Domain). Courtesy Wellcome Collection

Fig 10.2 Excavation of Ashoka's lion capital at Sarnath in 1905, alongside an image of Buddha delivering his first sermon (Public Domain)

Fig 10.3 Alexander Cunningham, the first director general of the Archaeological Survey of India

Fig 10.4 Statue of Anagarika Dharmapala in the Mulagandhakuti Vihara premises, Sarnath

Fig 10.5 Mulagandhakuti Vihara, Sarnath

Fig 10.6 Buddha Vihara in New Delhi (left), is a part of the Laxminarayan Temple complex (right), constructed by the Birlas

11. BUDDHISM 2.0

Fig 11.1 Visual replica of the Buddha's first sermon, depicted in the lithographed copy of the Indian Constitution. Displayed at the Dr B. R. Ambedkar National Memorial, Delhi

Fig 11.2 Chetiyagiri Vihara at Sanchi

Fig 11.3 Deekshabhoomi, Nagpur, the site of Ambedkar's conversion. Courtesy Alok Kumar

Fig 11.4 Architecture of Ambedkar National Memorial, Delhi

Fig 11.5 Kalachakra temple, a major Tibetan Buddhist shrine, located in the main market of McLeodganj

Fig 11.6 View of part of the Indosan Nippon temple complex, Bodh Gaya

Fig 11.7 Shanti Stupa, New Delhi, inspired by Sanchi mahastupa

Fig 11.8 Xuanzang Memorial Hall, fronted by a statue of the Chinese pilgrim, Nalanda

Fig 11.9 The giant Buddha statue at Bodh Gaya, sponsored by the Daijokyo sect of Japan

Fig 11.10 India's largest reclining Buddha, constructed in Bodh Gaya in 2023. Courtesy Amit Kumar

NOTES

INTRODUCTION

1. Percy Brown, *Indian Architecture: Buddhist and Hindu Periods* (third edition), D. B. Taraporevala Sons, Bombay, 1956; Sukumar Dutt, *Buddhist Monks and Monasteries of India: Their History and Their Contribution to Indian Culture*, George Allen and Unwin, London, 1962.
2. Debala Mitra, *Buddhist Monuments*, Sahitya Samsad, Calcutta (present-day Kolkata), 1971.
3. Vidya Dehejia, *Discourses in Early Buddhist Art: Visual Narratives of India*, Munshiram Manoharlal, New Delhi, 1997. One could add here the works of Susan and John Huntington, Pia Brancaccio and Dieter Schlingloff, which are cited later in this book, among others.
4. Gregory Schopen, *Bones, Stones and Buddhist Monks: Collected Paper on Archaeology, Epigraphy and Texts of Monastic Buddhism in India*, University of Hawaii Press, Honolulu, 1997; Himanshu Prabha Ray, *Archaeology and Buddhism in South Asia*, Routledge, Abingdon and New York, 2017; Robin Coningham, 'Buddhism', in Timothy Insoll (ed.), *The Oxford Handbook of the Archaeology of Ritual and Religion*, Oxford University Press, Oxford, 2011, 934–47. Also see, 'Archaeology of Early Buddhism', Oxford Bibliographies, https://www.oxfordbibliographies.com/display/document/obo-9780195393521/obo-9780195393521-0031.xml, accessed on 10 June 2024.

    I am thankful to Julia Shaw for alerting me to the shift from site-based analysis to landscape surveys. For details, see Julia Shaw, 'The Sacred Landscape', in Michael Willis (eds, with contributions by J. Cribb and J. Shaw), *Buddhist Reliquaries from Ancient India*, British Museum Press, London, 2000, 27-38; Julia Shaw, *Buddhist Landscapes in Central India: Sanchi Hill and Archaeologies of Religion and Social Change, c. 3rd century BC to 5th century AD*, British Academy, London, 2007 (later published by Routledge Abingdon and New York, 2016); Julia Shaw, 'A "reflexive" multi-stage survey methodology for historical landscape research in Central India: Fieldwalking, local knowledge, and satellite imagery as archaeological site prospection and mapping tools in the Sanchi Survey Project', *Current Science* (Special

Section on Geospatial Techniques in Archaeology), Vol. 113, No. 10, 2017, 1918-1933. On the application of remote sensing and GIS, see M. B. Rajani, 'The Expanse of Archaeological Remains at Nalanda: A Study Using Remote Sensing and GIS', *Archives of Asian Art*, Vol. 66, No. 1, 2016, 1–23 and Shaw's works cited above.

5. Vidya Dehejia, 'On Modes of Visual Narration in Early Buddhist Art', *The Art Bulletin*, Vol. 72, No. 3, 1990 (September), 376.
6. Ibid.; SuttaCentral, 'A Reader's Guide to the Pali Suttas', https://suttacentral.net/general-guide-sujato?lang=en, accessed on 14 February 2024.
7. Dehejia, 'On Modes of Visual Narration in Early Buddhist Art', 377.
8. Jan Willen de Jong, 'The Study of Buddhism: Problems and Perspectives', in Perala Ratnam (ed.), *Studies in Indo-Asian Art and Culture*, Vol. 4, International Academy of Indian Culture, New Delhi, 1975, 7–30.
9. For details related to these observations, see Schopen, *Bones, Stones and Buddhist Monks*, 1–9.
10. These mostly build on examples cited in Schopen, *Bones, Stones and Buddhist Monks*; Julia Shaw, 'Landscape, Water and Religion in Ancient India', *Archaeology International*, Vol. 9, No. 1, 2007, 43–48; Julia Shaw, 'Archaeologies of Buddhist Propagation in Ancient India: "Ritual" and "Practical" Models of Religious Change', *World Archaeology*, Vol. 5, No. 1, 2013, 83–108.
11. Schopen, *Bones, Stones and Buddhist Monks*, 258–89; Richard S. Cohen, 'Discontented Categories: Hinayana and Mahayana in Indian Buddhist History', *Journal of American Academy of Religion*, Vol. 63, No. 1, 1995, 10–13.

1. THE BUDDHA COMES INTO BEING

1. Uma Chakravarti, *The Social Dimensions of Early Buddhism*, Munshiram Manoharlal, New Delhi, 1996, 58–59. The story is narrated in *Cullavagga*, which is a part of the *Vinaya Pitaka* or Pali scriptures that deal with the disciplinary rules for the monks and nuns.
2. Upinder Singh, *A History of Ancient and Early Medieval India: From the Stone Age to the 12th Century*, Pearson Education, New Delhi, 2008, 265.
3. For socio-economic conditions at the time of the Buddha, see Chakravarti, *The Social Dimensions of Early Buddhism*, 7–35.
4. S. Gupta, 'Two Urbanizations in India', *Puratattva*, Vol. 7, 1974, 55; D. K. Chakrabarti, 'Beginning of Iron and Social Change in India', *Indian Studies: Past and Present*, Vol. 14, No. 4, 1973, 336–38.
5. Romila Thapar, *The Penguin History of Early India: From the Origins to AD 1300*, Penguin Books, New Delhi, 2002, 144–45.
6. Singh, *A History of Ancient and Early Medieval India*, 289–91.
7. For emergence of new elites alongside socio-economic disparities, see Chakravarti, *The Social Dimensions of Early Buddhism*, 7–121; Singh, *A History of Ancient and Early Medieval India*, 286–303.

8. Singh, *A History of Ancient and Early Medieval India*, 288.
9. It has been argued that Sudhodhana cannot be called a king because Kapilavastu was a gana-sangha and not a rajya. Also, it was ruled by a governor, or an elected chief, as opposed to a king. See John Keay, *India: A History*, Grove Press, New York, 2010, 64.
10. There are differences between scholars regarding the lifespan of the Buddha. Most agree on the broader time frame of 6th–5th centuries BCE. Up until the 20th century CE, Buddha's dates were regarded as c. 624–544 BCE, based on the Ceylonese Long Chronology. This was subsequently revised to c. 567–487 BCE on the basis of the edicts of the Mauryan king Ashoka. These dates, however, differed majorly from the Short Chronology of Indian tradition, according to which the Buddha lived between c. 448–368 BCE. The Indian tradition was based on the idea that Buddha died exactly 100 years before the coronation of Ashoka. Many modern scholars hold c. 563–483 BCE as the dates of the Buddha. For details, see 'The Dates of the Buddha – World History Encyclopedia', https://www.worldhistory.org/article/493/the-dates-of-the-buddha/, accessed on 08 September, 2024.
11. A. L. Basham, *The Wonder That Was India* (third revised edition), Picador, London, 2004, 259.
12. Ibid., 261.
13. Thapar, *The Penguin History of Early India*, 171.
14. For Buddha's teachings, see Singh, *A History of Ancient and Early Medieval India*, 304–06; Thapar, *The Penguin History of Early India*, 168–72.
15. Basham, *The Wonder That Was India*, 261.
16. Ibid., 261–62.
17. The following discussion on cities, based on their occurrence in Pali texts, largely borrows on B. G. Gokhale, 'Early Buddhism and the Urban Revolution', *Journal of International Association of the Buddhist Studies*, Vol. 5, No. 2, 1982, 7–22.
18. Singh, *A History of Ancient and Early Medieval India*, 266.
19. Ibid., 271.
20. Nayanjot Lahiri, *Ashoka in Ancient India*, Permanent Black, Ranikhet, 2015, 246.
21. Chakravarti, *The Social Dimensions of Early Buddhism*, 93.
22. Gokhale, 'Early Buddhism and the Urban Revolution', 16.
23. Ibid., 15.
24. Ibid., 16–17.
25. Ibid., 15–16.
26. Singh, *A History of Ancient and Early Medieval India*, 289.
27. K. Jayaswal, *Hindu Polity: A Constitutional History of India in Hindu Times*, Bangalore Press, Bangalore, 1967, 86.

28. Dutt, *Buddhist Monks and Monasteries of India*, 92.
29. Basham, *The Wonder That Was India*, 262.
30. Thapar, *The Penguin History of Early India*, 164.
31. Chakravarti, *The Social Dimensions of Early Buddhism*, 56.
32. Dutt, *Buddhist Monks and* Monasteries, 58–59.
33. Chakravarti, *The Social Dimensions of Early Buddhism*, 56–57.
34. For details, see Dutt, *Buddhist Monks and Monasteries*, 60–61.
35. Gokhale, 'Early Buddhism and the Urban Revolution', 16.
36. Chakravarti, *The Social Dimensions of Early Buddhism*, 57 and 139.
37. Dutt, *Buddhist Monks and Monasteries*, 93–94.
38. Ibid., 24.
39. Mohan Wijayaratne, *Buddhist Monastic Life According to the Texts of the Theravada Tradition* (Translated by Claude Grangier and Steven Collins), Cambridge University Press, Cambridge, 1990.
40. E. Lamotte cited in Himanshu Prabha Ray, 'The Archaeology of the Stupas', in Jason Hawkes and Akira Shimada (eds), *Buddhist Stupas in South Asia*, Oxford University Press, New Delhi, 2009, 14. Literary references record as many as 29 sites and buildings that were donated to the Buddha – 18 in Rajagriha (or Rajgir), four each in Vaishali and Kaushambi, and three in Kosala.
41. This is the declaration of faith found in the opening lines of an early Buddhist text called *Khuddakapatha*, which is preserved in Sri Lanka.
42. For details regarding the lives of monks and lay followers, see Thapar, *The Penguin History of Early India*, 172–3; Singh, *A History of Ancient and Early Medieval India*, 306–07.
43. For the following discussion on the social background of monks and nuns and lay followers, see Chakravarti, *The Social Dimensions of Early Buddhism*, 124–42.
44. Ibid., 142–48.
45. For details, see Thapar, *The Penguin History of Early India*, 172–73; Basham, *The Wonder That Was India*, 264; Gokhale, 'Early Buddhism and the Urban Revolution', 14.
46. Basham, *The Wonder That Was India*, 262–63.

CHAPTER 2: EMERGENCE OF RELIC CULT, STUPAS AND PILLARS

1. Schopen, *Bones, Stones and Buddhist Monks*, 133.
2. Michael Willis, 'Relics of the Buddha: Body, Essence and Text', in Hawkes and Shimada (eds), *Buddhist Stupas in South Asia*, 43.
3. A. L. Basham, *The Wonder That Was India*, 263.
4. For more details on how the sects emerged, see 'Eighteen Schools', Encyclopedia Britannica, https://www.britannica.com/topic/eighteen-

schools, accessed on 19 May 2024; 'A Short History of the Buddhist Schools – World History', https://www.worldhistory.org/article/492/a-short-history-of-the-buddhist-schools/, accessed on 19 May 2024.
5. Willis, 'Relics of the Buddha', 42–44.
6. Mitra, *Buddhist Monuments*, 21.
7. For categories of relics and related details, see Willis, 'Relics of the Buddha', 44–47.
8. Susan L. Huntington, 'Early Buddhist Art and the Theory of Aniconism', *Art Journal*, Vol. 49, No. 4, 1990, 402.
9. Willis, 'Relics of the Buddha', 47.
10. Ibid., 44.
11. Schopen, *Bones, Stones and Buddhist Monks*, 133.
12. Singh, *A History of Ancient and Early Medieval India*, 362.
13. H. Hartel, 'Archaeological Research on Ancient Buddhist Sites', in H. Bechert (ed), *When Did the Buddha Live*, Satguru Publications, New Delhi, 1995, 141–59.
14. Thapar, *The Penguin History of Early India*, 178–79.
15. Patrick Olivelle, *Ashoka: Portrait of a Philosopher King*, HarperCollins, New Delhi, 2023, 102.
16. Ibid., 113–15.
17. Ibid., 125. For variations in the language of schism edicts, see Ibid., 126.
18. Ibid., 127.
19. Olivelle, *Ashoka*, Prologue, 2.
20. Tanka Prasad Pokharel, 'Buddhist Councils: Means and Ends for Clarity and Revitalization', *Journal of Philosophy, Culture and Religion*, Vol. 39, 2018, 43.
21. Thapar, *The Penguin History of Early India*, 181–82.
22. Pokharel, 'Buddhist Councils', 43.
23. Mitra, *Buddhist Monuments*, 9; Singh, *A History of Ancient and Early Medieval India*, 351.
24. Thapar, *The Penguin History of Early India*, 184.
25. Ibid., 181.
26. Fredrick Asher, *Bodh Gaya: Monumental Legacy*, Oxford University Press, New Delhi, 2008, 3, 42–43.
27. Lahiri, *Ashoka in Ancient India*, 236–37.
28. Ibid., 237–38, for details of his visits and constructions.
29. Ibid., 239–41.
30. Schopen, *Bones, Stones and Buddhist Monks*, 115.
31. Ibid., 116.
32. Ibid.
33. Lahiri, *Ashoka in Ancient India*, 243.
34. Ray, *Archaeology and Buddhism in South Asia*, 24.

35. For details, see Ray, *Archaeology and Buddhism*, 65.
36. Willis, 'Relics of the Buddha', 44.
37. Lahiri, *Ashoka in Ancient India*, 243, 247–49.
38. Singh, *A History of Ancient and Early Medieval India*, 362–64.
39. Lahiri, *Ashoka in Ancient India*, 235.

CHAPTER 3: THE RISE OF IMAGES, MONASTIC COMPLEXES AND POPULAR CULTS

1. H. Luders' translation of an inscription dated to the year 51 of Huvishka from Mathura. For details, see Gregory Schopen, *Bones, Stones and Buddhist Monks*, 35.
2. Thapar, *The Penguin History of Early India*, 215–16.
3. R. S. Sharma, *Ancient India*, National Council of Educational Research and Training, New Delhi, 1982, 104–06.
4. For a detailed treatment of maritime trade and related networks and communities, see Himanshu Prabha Ray, *The Winds of Change: Buddhism and the Maritime Links of Early South Asia*, Oxford University Press, New Delhi, 1994.
5. For details, see Singh, *A History of Ancient and Early Medieval India*, 408–17.
6. Thapar, *The Penguin History of Early India*, 255–56; for details of trade with China, see Xinru Liu, *Ancient India and Ancient China: Trade and Religious Exchanges*, Oxford University Press, Delhi, 1988.
7. For details, see Himanshu Prabha Ray, *Monastery and Guild Commerce Under the Satavahanas*, Oxford University Press, New Delhi, 1986.
8. Basham, *The Wonder That Was India*, 275.
9. Anukul Chandra Banerjee, Hinayana and Mahayana: A Broad Outline, https://himalaya.socanth.cam.ac.uk/collections/journals/bot/pdf/bot_1990_01-03_03.pdf, accessed on 18 May 2023.
10. Schopen, *Bones, Stones and Buddhist Monks*, 5–7.
11. Singh, *A History of Ancient and Early Medieval India*, 441.
12. Basham, *The Wonder That Was India*, 280.
13. Ibid., 280–81.
14. Singh, *A History of Ancient and Early Medieval India*, 441–42.
15. H. Bechert (ed.), 'Notes on the Formation of Buddhist Sects and the Origins of Mahayana', in the Cultural Department of the Embassy of the Federal Republic of Germany, *German Scholars on India* (Vol. 1), Chowkhamba Sanskrit Series Office, Varanasi, 1973, 6–18; Mario D'Amato, 'Mapping the Mahayana: Some Historical and Doctrinal Issues', *Religion Compass*, Vol. 2, No. 4, 2008, 536–55; Singh, *A History of Ancient and Early Medieval India*, 442.
16. For details, see Huntington, 'Early Buddhist Art and the Theory of Aniconism', 401–02.

17. Alfred Foucher, *The Beginnings of Buddhist Art and Other Essays in Indian and Central-Asian Archeology*, Paul Geuthner, Paris, 1917, 7.
18. Okakura Kakuzo, *Ideals of the East with Special Reference to the Art of Japan*, E. Dutton and Company, New York, 1905.
19. Ananda K. Coomaraswamy, 'The India Origin of the Buddha Image', *Journal of the American Oriental Society*, Vol. 46, 1926, 165–70.
20. Huntington, 'Early Buddhist Art and the Theory of Aniconism', 407 (note 8), 402; Susan L. Huntington, *The Art of Ancient India: Buddhist, Hindu, Jain*, Weather Hill, New York and Tokyo, 1985, 120–21.
21. Kurt Behrendt, 'Narrative Sequence in the Buddhist Relief from Gandhara', in Hawkes and Shimada (eds), *Buddhist Stupas in South Asia*, 88; Singh, *A History of Ancient and Early Medieval India*, 454–57.
22. For characteristics, sculptures and other details of Gandhara art, see Singh, *A History of Ancient and Early Medieval India*, 462–63.
23. For sculptures, characteristics, and evolution of Mathura art, see Arathi Menon, 'A Buddha from Mathura', SmartHistory, available at https://smarthistory.org/buddha-mathura/, accessed on 19 May 2023; Mitra, *Buddhist Monuments*, 13.
24. Mitra, *Buddhist Monuments*, 13–14; Singh, *A History of Ancient and Early Medieval India*, 463–64.
25. For details, see Ray, *Archaeology and Buddhism in South Asia*, 82–83.
26. For connections between the stupa cult and Buddha biographies, see Jonathan S. Walters, 'Stupa, Story and Empire: Constructions of the Buddha Biography in Early Post-Ashokan India', in Hawkes and Shimada (eds), *Buddhist Stupas in South Asia*, 246–59.
27. Singh, *A History of Ancient and Early Medieval India*, 448.
28. For details, see Ray, *Archaeology and Buddhism*, 22–43; Julia Shaw and John Sutcliffe, 'Water Management, Patronage Networks and Religious Change: New Evidence from the Sanchi Dam Complex and Counterparts in Gujarat and Sri Lanka', *South Asian Studies*, Vol. 19, No. 1, 2003, 73–104.
29. For details, see Ray, *The Winds of Change*; Liu, *Ancient India and Ancient China: Trade and Religious Exchanges*; Ray, *Monastery and the Guild*.
30. For details, see Upinder Singh, 'Sanchi: The History of the Patronage of an Ancient Buddhist Temple', *Indian Economic and Social History Review*, Vol. 33, No. 1, 1996, 1–35; Schopen, *Bones, Stones and Buddhist Monks*.
31. Ray, *The Archaeology of Buddhism*, 30–31.
32. Dutt, *Buddhist Monks and Monasteries of India*, 220.
33. Juhyung Rhi, 'Images, Relics, and Jewels: The Assimilation of Images in the Buddhist Relic Cult of Gandhara: Or Vice Versa', *Artibus Asiae*, Vol. 65, No. 2, 2005, 203.
34. Himanshu Prabha Ray, *The Return of the Buddha: Ancient Symbols for a New Nation*, Routledge, Abingdon and New York, 2014, 90–93.

35. Ray, *The Archaeology of Buddhism*, 65.
36. Dutt, *Buddhist Monks and Monasteries*, 213–14.
37. Jason Hawkes, 'The Wider Archaeological Contexts of the Buddhist Stupa Site of Bharhut', in Hawkes and Shimada (eds), *Buddhist Stupas in South Asia*, 146–74.
38. Shaw, 'Landscape, Water and Religion in Ancient India', 43–48; for a comprehensive treatment, see Shaw, *Buddhist Landscapes in Central India*.
39. Schopen, *Bones, Stones and Buddhist Monks*, 186. Archaeological manifestations of these arguments are discussed in detail in Shaw, 'The Sacred Landscape'; Julia Shaw, 'Buddhist and Non-Buddhist Mortuary Traditions in Ancient India: Stupas, Relics, and the Archaeological Landscape', in Colin Renfrew, Michael J. Boyd, Iain Morley (eds), *Death Rituals, Social Order and the Archaeology of Immortality in the Ancient World: 'Death Shall Have No Dominion'*, Cambridge University Press, Cambridge, 2015, 382–403; Julia Shaw, 'Breathing Life into Monuments of Death: The stupa and the "Buddha body" in Sanchi's socio-ecological landscape', in Shonaleeka Kaul (ed.), *Eloquent Spaces: Meaning and Community in Early Indian Architecture*, Routledge, Abingdon and New York, 2019, 34–68.
40. Ray, *Archaeology of Buddhism*, 66–67. For a comprehensive discussion, see Shaw, 'The Sacred Landscape'; Shaw, *Buddhist Landscapes in Central India*; Shaw, 'Buddhist and Non-Buddhist Mortuary Traditions in Ancient India: Stupas, Relics, and the Archaeological Landscape'.
41. Schopen, *Bones, Stones and Buddhist Monks*, 193.
42. Jennifer Howes, 'The Colonial History of Sculptures from the Amaravati Stupa', in Hawkes and Shimada (eds), *Buddhist Stupas in South Asia*, 20–37.
43. For details, see 'India: Amravati', The British Museum, https://www.britishmuseum.org/collection/galleries/india-amaravati, accessed on 23 May 2023.
44. Upinder Singh, 'Exile and Return: The Reinvention of Buddhism and Buddhist Sites in Modern India', in *South Asian Studies*, Vol. 26, No. 2, 2010, 207–08.
45. Mitra, *Buddhist Monuments*, 15.
46. Ray, 'The Archaeology of the Stupas', 18; Peter Skilling, 'New Discoveries from South India: The Life of the Buddha at Phanigiri, Andhra Pradesh', *Arts Asiatiques*, Vol. 63, 2008, 96–118; Naman Ahuja (ed.), *Phanigiri: Interpreting an Ancient Buddhist Site of Telangana*, The Marg Foundation and the Department of Heritage Telangana, Mumbai, 2021.
47. For details, see Singh, *A History of Ancient and Early Medieval India*, 452–54; 'Nagarjunakonda Sculptures', *Marg* (special issue), Vol. 18, No. 2 (March), 1965; Ray, 'The Archaeology of the Stupas', 16.
48. Akira Shimada, 'Amravati and Dhanyakataka: Topology of Monastic Spaces in

Ancient Indian Cities', in Hawkes and Shimada (eds), *Buddhist Stupas in South Asia*, 229–33; Amareswar Galla, 'Society against the State: Perspectives on the History of Early Andhra Pradesh', PhD Thesis, Australian National University, 1982. See Chapter 4 in particular, 'Religious Undercurrents', 142–67.
49. Ray, 'The Archaeology of the Stupas' 15–16.
50. Himanshu Prabha Ray, 'Early Buddhist Caves of the Western Deccan: Indian Long-Distance Trade in The Early Centuries A.D.', https://www.penn.museum/sites/expedition/early-buddhist-caves-of-the-western-deccan/, accessed on 25 May 2023.
51. Ibid.
52. Mitra, *Buddhist Monuments*, 12.
53. For details of the cave shrines in Western Deccan, see George Michell and Gethin Rees, *Buddhist Rock-Cut Monasteries of the Western Ghats*, Deccan Heritage Foundation and Jaico Books, Mumbai, 2017, 28–43.
54. Ibid., 32–35.
55. Ibid., 35–42.
56. S. Nagaraju, *Buddhist Architecture of Western India, C. 250 BC–AD 300*, Agam Kala Prakashan, Delhi, 1981, 66.
57. For details, see Singh, *A History of Ancient and Early Medieval India*, 454–55; Dehejia, 'On Modes of Visual Narration in Early Buddhist Art', 374–92.
58. Huntington, 'Early Buddhist Art and the Theory of Aniconism', 401–08.
59. For details, see Shaw, 'Archaeologies of Buddhist Propagation in Ancient India', 95–96.
60. 'Yakshi, Eastern Gateway, Sanchi Stupa I', MAP Academy, 29 September 2023, https://mapacademy.io/article/yakshi-eastern-gateway-sanchi-stupa-i/, accessed on 1 September 2024. For details of yakshis and other related female figures from Sanghol, see Ardhendu Ray, 'Embodiment of Beauty in Stone: A Survey of Stone Sculptures from Sanghol', *Chitrolekha International Magazine on Art and Design*, Vol. 6, No. 1, 2016, 52-64.
61. Shaw, 'Archaeologies of Buddhist Propagation in Ancient India', 97.
62. For details, see Robert DeCaroli, Shedding Skins, in Hawkes and Shimada (eds), *Buddhist Stupas in South Asia*, 94–113; J. Strong, *Relics of the Buddha*, Princeton University Press, Princeton, 2004.
63. DeCaroli, 'Shedding Skins: Naga Imagery and Layers of Meaning in South Asian Buddhist Contexts', 94–113. For details on central India, see Julia Shaw, 'Naga sculptures in Sanchi's archaeological landscape: Buddhism, Vaisnavism and local agricultural cults in central India, first century BCE to fifth century CE', *Artibus Asiae*, Vol. 64, No. 1, 2004, 5–59; Shaw, *Buddhist Landscapes in Central India*.
64. For details, see Shaw, 'Landscape, Water and Religion in Ancient India', 47; and DeCaroli, 'Shedding Skins', 111. Also, see Shaw, 'Naga sculptures in Sanchi's archaeological landscape'; Shaw, *Buddhist Landscapes in Central India*.

65. For an analysis of donative inscriptions connected with monks and nuns, see Schopen, *Bones, Stones and Buddhist Monks*, 30–34.
66. Ibid.
67. For details, see Singh, 'Sanchi: The History of the Patronage of an Ancient Buddhist Temple', 1–35; Singh, *A History of Ancient and Early Medieval India*, 469.
68. Ray, 'Early Buddhist Caves of the Western Deccan'.

CHAPTER 4: EFFLORESCENCE AND SPREAD AMIDST BRAHMANICAL REVIVAL

1. For details, see Dutt, *Buddhist Monks and Monasteries of India*, 200–01.
2. Tansen Sen, 'The Spread of Buddhism', in Benjamin Z. Kedar and Merry Wiesner-Hanks (eds), *The Cambridge World History, Volume 5: Expanding Webs of Exchange and Conflict, 500 CE–1500 CE*, Cambridge University Press, Cambridge, 2015, 452.
3. Xinru Liu, 'Buddhist Ideology and the Commercial Ethos in Kushan India', in Hawkes and Shimada (eds), *Buddhist Stupas in South Asia*, 188–90.
4. Basham, *The Wonder That Was India*, 278–79.
5. Mitra, *Buddhist Monuments*, 15–16.
6. Debala Mitra, *Ajanta*, Archaeological Survey of India, New Delhi, 2004, 38.
7. Singh, *A History of Ancient and Early Medieval India*, 510.
8. Ibid., 511.
9. Basham, *The Wonder That Was India*, 281–83.
10. For different perspectives, see Joshua K. Mark, 'Tara', *World History Encyclopedia*, 9 August 2021 (online), https://www.worldhistory.org/Tara_(Goddess)/, accessed on 1 June 2023.
11. Dutt, *Buddhist Monks and Monasteries*, 215.
12. Ibid., 216–17. For details and changes in structure, see B. R. Mani, *Sarnath: Archaeology, Art and Architecture*, Archaeological Survey of India, New Delhi, 2006.
13. For details of findings, see https://www.asisarnathcircle.org/mulagandhakuti.php#:~:text=Mulagandhakuti%20Vihara%20is%20mostly%20addressed%20as%20the%20%E2%80%98main,in%20this%20part%20appear%20to%20be%20of%20wood. (asisarnathcircle.org), accessed on 22 March 2024.
14. Mani, *Sarnath*, 40–42.
15. Ibid., 45–47.
16. For details surrounding the site, see D. R. Patil, *Kusinagara*, Archaeological Survey of India, New Delhi, 2006, 10–11.
17. Kurt Behrendt, 'Gandhara', *Heilbrunn Timeline of Art History*, The Metropolitan Museum of Art, New York, http://www.metmuseum.org/toah/hd/gand/hd_gand.htm (April 2012), accessed on 1 September 2024.

18. Melody Rod-ari, 'Bamiyan Buddhas', SmartHistory, 21 November 2015, https://smarthistory.org/bamiyan-buddhas/, accessed on 8 April 2024.
19. Dutt, *Buddhist Monks and Monasteries*, 221–22.
20. Singh, *A History of Ancient and Early Medieval India*, 355.
21. Mitra, *Buddhist Monuments*, 13.
22. Ray, *Archaeology and Buddhism in South Asia*, 32.
23. 'Devni Mori Sculptures', MAP Academy, 21 April 2022, https://mapacademy.io/article/devni-mori-sculptures/, accessed on 6 June 2023.
24. For details surrounding the site, see Yadubir Singh Rawat, 'Vadnagar Excavations: Discovery of Ancient Buddhist Monastery', *Asian Renaissance*, Vol. 1, No. 3, 2017, 43–54.
25. Dutt, *Buddhist Monks and Monasteries of India*, 319; Fredrick M. Asher, *Nalanda: Situating the Great Monastery*, The Marg Foundation, Mumbai, 2015, 35.
26. Schopen, *Bones, Stones and Buddhist Monks*, 269.
27. For details of architecture and structures, see 'Excavated Remains of the Nalanda Mahavihara', Archaeological Survey of India (UNESCO World Heritage Site Nomination Dossier), New Delhi, 2015, 21–28.
28. Rajani, 'The Expanse of Archaeological Remains at Nalanda'.
29. Asher, *Nalanda*, 104–20.
30. Ray, *Archaeology and Buddhism*, 33–34.
31. For details, see R. Mahalakshmi, 'Placing Buddhism in Tamil Religious History: Institutions and Growth (c. Fifth–Tenth Centuries)', in Anand Singh (ed), *Rethinking Buddhism: Text, Context, Contestation*, Primus Books, 2023, 109–28.
32. For details, see Anne E. Monius, *Imagining a Place for Buddhism: Literary Culture and Religious Community in Tamil-Speaking South India*, Oxford University Press, New York, 2002.
33. Mahalakshmi, 'Placing Buddhism in Tamil Religious History', 116
34. R. Champakalakshmi, *Religion, Tradition and Ideology: Pre-colonial South India*, Oxford University Press, New Delhi, 2011, 344. Also see, Ray, *Archaeology and Buddhism*, 35.
35. Mitra, *Buddhist Monuments*, 14.
36. *Sarnath*, Archaeological Survey of India, New Delhi, 2006, 60–67.
37. John C. Huntington, 'The Buddhas of Sarnath', *Orientations*, Vol. 40, No. 2, 2009, 86.
38. Ibid.
39. Arvind Jamkhedkar, *Ajanta*, Oxford University Press, New Delhi, 2009, 16–17.
40. For details see Ray, *Archaeology and Buddhism*, 35–36.
41. Sen, 'The Spread of Buddhism', 452.
42. Singh, *A History of Ancient and Early Medieval India*, 522; Romila Thapar, *The Penguin History of Early India*, 321.

43. Singh, *A History of Ancient and Early Medieval India*, 522.
44. Ibid., 522–23.
45. Thapar, *The Penguin History of Early India*, 321–23.

CHAPTER 5: TANTRIC INFUSION, REGIONALIZATION AND DECLINE

1. Cited in Sukumar Dutt, *Buddhist Monks and Monasteries of India*, 379. Dutt refers to the edition by S. C. Das.
2. Thapar, *The Penguin History of Early India*, 318, 349, 482–84.
3. Singh, *A History of Ancient and Early Medieval India*, 584–87.
4. Suchandra Ghosh, 'Buddhist Cultural Linkages between Bengal and Southeast Asia', in Abdul Momin Chowdhury and Ranabir Chakravarti (eds), *History of Bangladesh, Early Bengal in Regional Perspectives (up to c. 1200 CE)*, Vol. II, Society, Economy and Culture, Asiatic Society of Bangladesh, Dhaka, 647–50.
5. Thapar, *The Penguin History of Early India*, 409, 487. For a detailed treatment of Buddhist connections with Southeast Asia, see Upinder Singh and Parul Pandya Dhar (eds), *Asian Encounters: Exploring Connected Histories*, Oxford University Press, Delhi, 2014.
6. Tansen Sen, *Buddhism, Diplomacy and Trade: The Realignment of Sino-Indian Relations, 600–1400*, Association of Asian Studies and University of Hawaii Press, Honolulu, 2003.
7. Dutt, *Buddhist Monks and Monasteries of India*, 196.
8. Singh, *A History of Ancient and Early Medieval India*, 606.
9. For details, see 'Dhyani Buddha', Encyclopedia Britannica, https://www.britannica.com/topic/Dhyani-Buddha, accessed on 11 June 2023.
10. Ray, *Archaeology and Buddhism in South Asia*, 79, 88–89.
11. For emergence of Vajrayana, Tara, and related divinities, rituals and mantras, see Basham, *The Wonder That Was India*, 281–83. For details about Tara, see Singh, *A History of Ancient and Early Medieval India*, 606–07.
12. Basham, *The Wonder That Was India*, 281–83.
13. For details related to stupa worship and ritual texts, see Ray, *Archaeology and Buddhism*, 79–81.
14. Mitra, *Buddhist Monuments*, 17.
15. Mani, *Sarnath: Archaeology, Art and Architecture*, 67–70; For details regarding the evolution of the cult, John C. Huntington, 'Pilgrimage as Image: The Cult of Astamahapratiharya', *Orientations*, Vol. 18, No. 4 and 8, 1987, 55–63.
16. Huntington, 'Pilgrimage as Image, 63.
17. For details related to architecture and sculptures of the various caves, see M. K. Dhavalikar, *Ellora: Monumental Legacy*, Oxford University Press, New Delhi, 2003, 9–31.

18. Ray, *Archaeology and Buddhism*, 88–89.
19. Dhavalikar, *Ellora*, 9–31.
20. Ray, *Archaeology and Buddhism*, 87–88, 113–14.
21. For details related to development of Buddhism at the site, see Ray, *Archaeology and Buddhism*, 84–87; 97; Vidya Dehejia, 'The Persistence of Buddhism in Tamil Nadu', *Marg*, Vol. 39, No. 4, 1988, 53–74.
22. Ray, *Archaeology and Buddhism*, 114–15.
23. Ibid., 114–16.
24. For details related to the site, see Dutt, *Buddhist Monks and Monasteries*, 224–32.
25. For Arab-Buddhist interactions, see Karam Tej Sarao, 'Buddhist-Muslim Encounter in Sind during the Eighth Century', conference paper, October 2015.
26. For details, see Sonam Spalzin, 'Chronological History of Emergence of Buddhism in Kashmir', *Voice of History*, No. 2 (New Issue), *Journal of Central Department of History*, Tribhuvan University, Kirtipur (Kathmandu), 2015, 33–46.
27. Advaitavadini Kaul, 'Buddhism in Kashmir', *Indologica Taurinensia*, Vol. 31, 2005, 159–71
28. Upinder Singh, 'How Hinduism incorporated Buddha and then distanced the religion', The Print, 6 November 2021, https://theprint.in/pageturner/excerpt/how-hinduism-incorporated-buddha-and-then-distanced-the-religion/761987/, accessed on 5 April 2024.
29. For details, see Spalzin, 'Chronological History of Emergence of Buddhism in Kashmir', 33–46.
30. The following discussion on the two sites builds on Umakanta Mishra, 'Continuity and Change in the Sacred Landscape of the Buddhist Site of Udayagiri, Odisha', in Himanshu Prabha Ray (ed), *Negotiating Cultural Identity: Landscapes in early Medieval South Asian History* (second edition), Routledge, Abingdon and New York, 2020, 230–56.
31. Ibid., 245–47.
32. Ibid., 230–56. Also see, Ray, *Archaeology of Buddhism*, 54–55, 73.
33. Debala Mitra, *Ratnagiri (1958–61)*, Vol. I, Archaeological Survey of India, New Delhi, 1981.
34. Mishra, 'Continuity and Change in the Sacred Landscape', 241–44.
35. For details related to mandala and Tara images in Odisha, see Ray, *Archaeology and Buddhism*, 36, 89–90.
36. Susan L. Huntington and John C. Huntington, 'Leaves from the *Bodhi Tree*: The Art of Pala India (8th–12th Centuries) and Its International Legacy', *Orientations*, Vol. 20, No. 10 (October), 1989, 3–4.
37. Dutt, *Buddhist Monks and Monasteries*, 201–02.

38. For details related to the two phases, see Ibid., 350–51.
39. Ibid., 354–55.
40. For details related to the site, see Ibid., 371–74.
41. For details related to the site, see Pranava K. Chaudhary, 'ASI to develop ancient site of Vikramshila Mahavihara', 10 October 2009, https://timesofindia.indiatimes.com/city/patna/ASI-to-develop-ancient-site-of-Vikramshila-Mahavihara/articleshow/5107966.cms, accessed on 13 June 2023; Hitendra Anupam, 'Significance of Tibetan Sources in the Study of Odantapuri and Vikaramsila Mahavihars', *Proceedings of the Indian History Congress*, Vol. 61, Part 1, 2000–01, 424–28.
42. Monalisa Lamba, 'Some Selected Buddhist Monasteries As Centres of Learning of the Pala Period', *Proceedings of the Indian History Congress*, Vol. 76, 2015, 146.
43. Suchandra Ghosh, 'Patronage of Buddhist Monasteries in Eastern India (600–1300 CE)', *Oxford Research Encyclopedias, Religion* (online), 15 August 2022, 1–29.
44. Dutt, *Buddhist Monks and Monasteries*, 352–53.
45. Lamba, 'Some Selected Buddhist Monasteries', 1146–48; also see Ghosh, 'Patronage of Buddhist Monasteries in Eastern India'.
46. Reena Sopam, 'First hilltop Buddhist monastery found in Bihar's Lakhisarai', *Hindustan Times*, 4 January 2021. https://www.hindustantimes.com/india-news/first-hilltop-buddhist-monastery-found-in-bihar-s-lakhisarai/story-mbgH6ZPvDvDV76H27Ho6rI.html, accessed on 17 June 2023.
47. Sanjoy Dey, '10th Century Buddha Vihar Discovered in Jharkhand's Hazaribag', *Hindustan Times*, 23 February 2021, https://www.hindustantimes.com/cities/ranchi-news/10th-century-buddha-vihar-discovered-in-jharkhands-hazaribag-101614072362306.html, accessed on 29 March 2024.
48. Swati Chemburkar, 'Visualising the Buddhist Mandala: Kesariya, Borobudur, and Tabo', in Anna L. Dallapiccola and Anila Verghese (eds), *India and Southeast Asia: Cultural Discourses*, K. R. Cama Oriental Institute, Mumbai, 2018, 197–222.
49. This following discussion on Buddhist finds and networks in the trans-Meghna region builds on Ghosh, 'Buddhist Cultural Linkages between Bengal and Southeast Asia', 647–64.
50. For details, see Huntington and Huntington, 'Leaves from the *Bodhi Tree*', 2–22.
51. For trade linkages, phases of Buddhism in the region and related details, see Laxman S. Thakur, *Buddhism in the Western Himalayas: A Study of the Tabo Monastery*, Oxford University Press, New Delhi, 2001, 5, 35–40.
52. Ibid., 20–58.
53. For details related to the Tabo monastery complex, see https://www.tabomonastery.org/, accessed on 10 June 2023.

54. Thakur, *Buddhism in the Western Himalayas*, 50.
55. K. R. Hall, 'Indonesia's Evolving International Relationships in the Ninth to Early Eleventh Centuries: Evidence from Contemporary Shipwrecks and Epigraphy', *Indonesia*, No. 90 (October), 2010, 6; Sen, *Buddhism, Diplomacy and Trade*, 467.
56. Jan Nattier, *Once Upon A Future Time: Studies in a Buddhist Prophecy of Decline*, Asian Humanities Press, Berkeley, California, 1991, 119–132. This book talks about the different prophecies behind the demise or decline of Buddhism.
57. For a discussion on popular explanations of decline, see Singh, *A History of Ancient and Early Medieval India*, 606–07; Thapar, *The Penguin History of Early India*, 487–88.
58. Lars Fogelin, *An Archaeological History of Early Buddhism*, Oxford University Press, New York, 2015, 202–24.
59. Dutt, *Buddhist Monks and Monasteries*, 207–09.
60. For details, see Nagendra Nath Vasu, *Modern Buddhism and Its Followers in Orissa*; U. N. Bhattacharya Hare Press, Calcutta, 1911, 174–75; David Geary, *The Rebirth of Bodh Gaya: Buddhism and the Making of a World Heritage Site*, Dev Publishers and Distributors, New Delhi, 2018, 22, 48–49; Arthur McKeown, *Guarding of a Dying Flame: Shariputra (c. 1335–1426) and the End of Late Indian Buddhism*, Havard University Press, Cambridge, 2019; Douglas Ober, *Dust on the Throne: The Search for Buddhism in Modern India*, Navayana, New Delhi, 2023, 26–29; Dehejia, 'The Persistence of Buddhism in Tamil Nadu', 53–74; Pratapaditya Pal, 'A New Document of Indian Painting', *The Journal of the Royal Society of Great Britain and Ireland*, Vols. 3 & 4, October 1965, 103–11.
61. Ober, *Dust on the Throne*, 26–27; McKeown, *Guarding of a Dying Flame*, 19.

CHAPTER 6: MAHABODHI TEMPLE AND BODH GAYA

1. Mathew R. Sayers, 'Gaya-Bodh Gaya: The Origins of a Pilgrimage Complex', in David Geary, Matthew R. Sayers and Abhishek Singh Amar (eds), *Cross-disciplinary Perspectives on a Contested Buddhist Site: Bodh Gaya Jataka*, Routledge, Abingdon and New York, 2012, 24.
2. Ibid.
3. For details about the bhumisprasha mudra images, see Janice Leoshko, 'Time and Time Again: Finding Perspective for Bodhgaya Buddha Imagery', *Ars Orientalis*, Vol. 50, 2021, 6–32.
4. Sayers, 'Gaya-Bodh Gaya', 13–28.
5. Robert DeCaroli, *Haunting the Buddha: Indian Popular Religions and the Formation of Buddhism*, Oxford University Press, Delhi, 2004, 117.
6. Fredrick Asher, *Bodh Gaya*, Oxford University Press, New Delhi, 2008, 20.
7. For details, see Rajat Sanyal, 'In the Name of Myself: Donors of Images at Bodh Gaya', *Seminar*, No. 745 (Bodh Gaya special issue), September 2021, 62.

8. For details, see Abhishek Singh Amar, 'Bodh Gaya: The Buddhaksetra of Gotama Buddha', in Geary, Sayers and Amar (eds), *Cross-disciplinary Perspectives on a Contested Buddhist Site*, 32–35.
9. K. K. Chakravarty, *Early Buddhist Art of Bodh-Gaya*, Munshiram Manoharlal, New Delhi, 1997, 53.
10. For the evolution of monuments see Asher, *Bodh Gaya*, 1–23; Shashank Shekhar Sinha, 'Mahabodhi Mahavihar in Bodh Gaya: Temple of Enlightenment', *Frontline*, Vol. 37, No. 21, 23 October 2020, 101–14.
11. Asher, *Bodh Gaya*, 80.
12. Ibid., 9–10.
13. Huntington and Huntington, 'Leaves from the *Bodhi Tree*', 2–22.
14. Asher, *Bodh Gaya*, 61–65.
15. For details, see Janice Leoshko (ed), *Bodh Gaya: The Site of Enlightenment*, Marg Publications, Mumbai, 1988, 45–60; Asher, *Bodh Gaya*, 61–71.
16. Asher, *Bodh Gaya*, 68–69.
17. For details, see Amar, 'Bodh Gaya', 38–39.
18. For a detailed discussion on Uma–Maheshwara images at Bodh Gaya, Nalanda and other regions of south Bihar, see Salila Kulshreshtha, *From Temple to Museum: Colonial Collections and Uma–Maheswara Icons in the Middle Ganga Valley*, Routledge, Abingdon and New York, 2018.
19. For details, see Asher, *Bodh Gaya*, 12–16
20. Dutt, *Buddhist Monks and Monasteries*, 203.
21. The following discussion on the monuments of the first seven weeks builds on Tara N. Doyle, '"Why Cause Unnecessary Confusion"?: Reinscribing the Mahabodhi Temple's Holy Places', in Geary, Sayers and Amar (eds), *Cross-disciplinary Perspectives on a Contested Buddhist Site*, 119–37.
22. Ibid., 127.
23. Ibid., 119, 131. These interviews were conducted by Tara N. Doyle, the author of the article being referred here.
24. For details, see Peter Skilling, 'Buddhist Sealings and the Ye Dharma Stanza', in Gautam Sengupta and Sharmi Chakraborty (eds), *Archaeology of Early Historic South Asia*, Pragati Publications, New Delhi, 2008, 503–25. For the inscriptions being discussed here, see Sanyal, 'In the Name of Myself', 59–64.
25. Daniel Boucher, 'The Pratityasamutpadagatha and Its Role in the Medieval Cult of the Relics', *Journal of International Association of Buddhist Studies*, Vol. 14, No. 1, 1991, 1–27.
26. For an analysis of these inscriptions, see Sanyal, 'In the Name of Myself', 59–64.
27. Fredrick Asher, 'Bodh Gaya: The Tangible Heritage', *Seminar*, No. 745 (Bodh Gaya special issue), September 2021, 14.

28. For details related to the two phases, see Max Deeg, 'The Centre of Centres: Bodh Gaya in Chinese Sources', *Seminar*, No. 745 (Bodh Gaya special issue), September 2021, 29–33.
29. Asher, 'Bodh Gaya', 17.
30. Cited in Schopen, *Bones, Stones and Buddhist Monks*, 118.
31. Jinah Kim, 'What Makes a Stupa? Quotations, Fragments and the Reinvention of Buddhist Stupas in Contemporary India', in Hawkes and Shimada (eds), *Buddhist Stupas in South Asia*, 289.
32. Schopen, *Bones, Stones and Buddhist Monks*, 134–35.
33. Ibid., 121–24.
34. For details, see Kim, 'What Makes a Stupa?', 297.
35. John Guy, 'The Mahabodhi Temple: Pilgrim Souvenirs of Buddhist India', *The Burlington Magazine*, Vol. 133, No. 1059, 1991 (June), 356–67.
36. Claudine Bautze-Picron, 'Moving and Resettling the Sacred Centre', *Seminar*, No. 745 (Bodh Gaya special issue), September 2021, 38.
37. For details, see Janice Leoshko, 'Seeing Mahabodhi', *Seminar*, No. 745 (Bodh Gaya special issue), September 2021, 21–26.
38. Ibid., 21, 25.
39. Asher, 'Bodh Gaya', 17, 31.
40. Bautze-Picron, 'Moving and Resettling the Sacred Centre', 37.
41. Asher, 'Bodh Gaya', 17.
42. For a short history of the afterlife of the Mahabodhi temple complex, from its disintegration in the 12th–13th centuries to the colonial restoration, see Shashank Shekhar Sinha, 'Why and How the Afterlife of a Heritage Site Matters', *Seminar*, No. 745 (Bodh Gaya special issue), 2021, 47–52.
43. Asher, 'Bodh Gaya', 19.
44. Geary, *The Rebirth of Bodh Gaya*, 20–21.
45. Tara N. Doyle cited in Geary, *The Rebirth of Bodh Gaya*, 22.
46. Bautze-Picron, 'Moving and Resettling the Sacred Centre', 34.
47. Asher, 'Bodh Gaya', 47.
48. Tapati Guha-Thakurta, *Monuments, Objects, Histories: Institutions of Art in Colonial and Postcolonial India*, Columbia University Press, New York, 2004, 288–89.
49. Janice Leoshko, 'The Changing Landscape at Bodh Gaya', in Geary, Sayers and Amar (eds), *Cross-disciplinary Perspectives on a Contested Buddhist Site*, 46.
50. Asher, 'Bodh Gaya', 21.
51. Geary, *The Rebirth of Bodh Gaya*, 28–29.
52. Edwin Arnold, *East and West: Being Papers Reprinted from the Daily Telegraph and other Sources*, Longmans, Green, 1896, 314.
53. Geary, *The Rebirth of Bodh Gaya*, 42–43.
54. For a detailed account, see Geary, *The Rebirth of Bodh Gaya*, 44–82.

55. For details regarding transformation in physical and cultural landscape, see Geary, *The Rebirth of Bodh Gaya*, 44–82.
56. Abhishek S. Amar and Sanjay Kumar, 'The Problem', *Seminar*, No. 745, September 2021 (Bodh Gaya Special issue), 12.
57. Cited in Geary, *The Rebirth of Bodh Gaya*, 3.
58. C. Robert Pryor, 'Bodh Gaya in the 1950s: Jawaharlal Nehru, Mahant Giri and Anagarika Munindra', in Geary, Sayers and Amar (eds), *Cross-disciplinary Perspectives on a Contested Buddhist Site*, 114–18.
59. PTI, 'Bihar government constitutes advisory board of Bodh Gaya temple', *Hindustan Times*, 30 July 2023, https://www.hindustantimes.com/cities/patna-news/bihar-government-constitutes-advisory-board-of-bodh-gaya-temple-101690715882982.html, accessed on 19 August 2023.

CHAPTER 7: SANCHI AND THE HILLTOP STUPA COMPLEX

1. Schopen, *Bones, Stones and Buddhist Monks*, 129–30.
2. Debala Mitra, *Sanchi*, Archaeological Survey of India, New Delhi, 2003, 11.
3. Shaw, 'Landscape, Water and Religion in Ancient India', 43–48; Shaw, 'Archaeologies of Buddhist Propagation in Ancient India: "Ritual" and "Practical" Models of Religious Change', 83–108. Shaw and the team surveyed 145 habitational settlements, 17 ancient dams and 1,000 temple and sculptural fragments across Brahmanical, Jaina and Buddhist traditions. For the purposes of this book, we will refer to the larger excavated area as the wider Sanchi area. This survey included 35 Buddhist monastic sites (especially Mawasa) of which Sanchi, and the other four Bhilsa tope sites form a part. For a detailed coverage, see Julia Shaw, 'Monasteries, Monasticism, and Patronage in Ancient India: Mawasa, a Recently Documented Hilltop Buddhist Complex in the Sanchi Area of Madhya Pradesh', *South Asian Studies*, Vol. 27, No. 2, 2011, 111–130; Julia Shaw, 'Sanchi as an Archaeological Area', in D.K. Chakrabarti and M. Lal (eds.), *History of Ancient India*, Vol. 4, Vivekananda International Foundation and Aryan Books, New Delhi, 2013, 388–427.
4. Schopen, *Bones, Stones and Buddhist Monks*, 64, 189. Also, see Shaw, *Buddhist Landscapes in Central India*.
5. Shaw, 'Archaeologies of Buddhist Propagation in Ancient India', 97. For a comprehensive discussion, see Shaw, *Buddhist Landscapes in Central India*.
6. Shaw, 'Landscape, Water and Religion in Ancient India', 47. For a comprehensive discussion, see Shaw, *Buddhist Landscapes in Central India*.
7. M. K. Dhavalikar, *Sanchi: Monumental Legacy*, Oxford University Press, New Delhi, 2003, 109–10.
8. Julia Shaw, 'Stupas, Monasteries, and Relics in the Landscape: Typological, Spatial, and Temporal Patterns in the Sanchi Area', in Hawkes and Shimada (eds), *Buddhist Stupas in South Asia*, 115.

9. Mitra, *Sanchi*, 8–9.
10. Shaw, 'Stupas, Monasteries, and Relics in the Landscape', 127–38. For a detailed treatment, see Shaw, 'The Sacred Landscape'; Shaw, *Buddhist Landscapes in Central India*; Shaw, 'Breathing Life into Monuments of Death'.
11. Schopen, *Bones, Stones and Buddhist Monks*, 129–30.
12. Shaw, 'Stupas, Monasteries, and Relics in the Landscape', 124–38.
13. For an accessible and illustrated account of these monuments, see Shashank Shekhar Sinha, 'Buddhism in Stone', *Frontline*, 19 August 2016, 67–82. For details of monuments on the main terrace, see Dhavalikar, *Sanchi*, 12–97; Mitra, *Sanchi*, 32–67.
14. Dhavalikar, *Sanchi*, 2–3.
15. Mitra, *Sanchi*, 85–86.
16. Schopen, *Bones, Stones and Buddhist Monks*, 179–80. For a detailed application of such theories to the archaeological landscape of Sanchi, see Shaw, *Buddhist Landscapes in Central India*; Shaw, 'The Sacred Landscape'.
17. Mitra, *Sanchi*, 15.
18. For details of the sculptural reliefs of the carved gateways, see Dhavalikar, *Sanchi*, 18–81; Mitra, *Sanchi*, 26–50.
19. Ibid.
20. Not all inscriptions at Sanchi carry details and purposes of donations. Scholars use different kinds of numbers for different types of analysis. For an overall analysis of such inscriptions, see Singh, 'Sanchi: The History of Patronage of an Ancient Buddhist Establishment', 1–35.
21. Vidya Dehejia, *Indian Art*, Phaidon Press, London and New York, 1997, 67–68.
22. For details of representation, see Dehejia, *Indian Art*, 51–68. Also see, Dehejia, 'On Modes of Visual Narration in Early Buddhist Art', 374–92.
23. Dehejia, *Indian Art*, 54; Dehejia, 'On Modes of Visual Narration in Early Buddhist Art', 380.
24. Huntington, 'Early Buddhist Art and the Theory of Aniconism', 401–08.
25. For details of these structures, see Dhavalikar, *Sanchi*, 85–106; Mitra, *Sanchi*, 56–80.
26. Schopen, *Bones, Stones and Buddhist Monks*, 119; Himanshu Prabha Ray, *Archaeology and Buddhism in South Asia*, 66–67.
27. For later years of Sanchi and decline, see Mitra, *Sanchi*, 14–17.
28. For details of modern lives of Sanchi, see Tapati Guha-Thakurta, 'The Production and Reproduction of a Monument: The Many Lives of Sanchi Stupa', *South Asian Studies*, Vol. 29, No. 1, 2013, 77–109.
29. Ibid., 85.
30. Ibid., 77–109.
31. Michael Willis, *Buddhist Reliquaries from Ancient India*, British Museum Press, London, 2000.

32. For details, see Willis, *Buddhist Reliquaries from Ancient India*; John S. Strong, *Relics of the Buddha*, Princeton University Press, Princeton NJ, 2004; Gary M. Tartakov, 'New Paths to Sanchi', in Vidya Dehejia (ed), *Unseen Presence: The Buddha and Sanchi*, Marg Publications, Mumbai, 1996, 110–30.
33. Torkel Brekke, 'Bones of Contention: Buddhist Relics, Nationalism and Politics of Archaeology', *Numen*, Vol. 54, 2007, 270–33. The journey of the relics discussed in this section largely builds on this article.
34. For an accessible account, see Shashank Shekhar Sinha, 'The Lesser Known Journey of Buddhist Relics – From India to UK and Back', *The Wire*, 1 April 2018 https://thewire.in/history/the-lesser-known-journey-of-buddhist-relics-from-india-to-uk-and-back, accessed on 10 July 2023.
35. Saloni Mathur, *India by Design: Colonial History and Cultural Display*, University of California Press, 2007.
36. Guha-Thakurta, 'The Production and Reproduction of a Monument', 93–94.
37. Ibid., 94.
38. For the journeys of the Sanchi relics in India, see Himanshu Prabha Ray, *The Return of the Buddha: Ancient Symbols for a New Nation*, Routledge, New Delhi and Abingdon, 2014, 119–22.

CHAPTER 8: AJANTA CAVES

1. For details, see Richard S. Cohen, 'Discontented Categories: Hinayana and Mahayana in Indian Buddhist History', 10–13.
2. Upinder Singh, *A History of Ancient and Early Medieval India*, 381–83.
3. Ibid., 481–84.
4. For a discussion on such dichotomies, and also the nikayas, see 6. Cohen, 'Discontented Categories', 1–24.
5. Gregory Schopen, 'Mahayana in Indian Inscriptions', *Indo-Iranian Journal*, Vol. 21, No. 1 (January), 1979, 16, also see note 7.
6. Cohen, 'Discontented Categories', 1–24.
7. Schopen, *Bones, Stones and Buddhist Monks*, 4, 71.
8. Ibid., 241–42, 250, for details related to monks and image cults.
9. Ibid., 61–65, also for variations in the donative formulas.
10. Cohen, 'Discontented Categories', 14.
11. Schopen, *Bones, Stones and Buddhist Monks*, 61–62, 252.
12. For connections between growth of trade and the spread of monastic establishments, see Michell and Rees, *Buddhist Rock-Cut Monasteries of the Western Ghats*, 17–25.
13. Ray, 'Early Buddhist Caves of the Western Deccan'.
14. For connections between Indian Ocean trade and Buddhist establishments, see Pia Brancaccio, 'The Buddhist Caves in Western Deccan, India, between the Fifth and Sixth Centuries', *Hualin International Journal of Buddhist Studies*, Vol. 1, No. 2, 2018, 1–13; Liu, *Ancient India and Ancient China*, 122–23.

15. For details, see Brancaccio, 'The Buddhist Caves in Western Deccan', 1–13.
16. Michell and Rees, *Buddhist Rock-Cut Monasteries of the Western Ghats*, 14.
17. Pia Brancaccio, 'Monumentality, Nature and World Heritage Monuments: The Rock-cut sites of Ajanta, Ellora and Elephanta in Maharashtra', in Himanshu Prabha Ray (ed), *Decolonising Heritage in South Asia: The Global, the National and the Transnational*, Routledge, Abingdon and New York, 2019, 111–28.
18. Translation by James Burgess and Indraji Bhagwanlal, cited in Brancaccio, 'Monumentality, Nature and World Heritage Monuments', 121.
19. Brancaccio, 'Monumentality, Nature and World Heritage Monuments', 117–19.
20. For a detailed description of the Ajanta caves, both prayer halls and monasteries, as well their individual attributes, see Arvind Jamkhedkar, *Ajanta*, Oxford University Press, New Delhi, 2009, 13–17; Mitra, *Ajanta*, Archaeological Survey of India, New Delhi, 2004, 6–19; and Walter M. Spink, *Ajanta: A Brief History and Guide*, Asian Art Archives, University of Michigan, Ann Arbor, 1990. For a general account of paintings, see A. Ghosh (ed), *Ajanta Murals: An Album of Eighty-five Reproductions in Colour*, Archaeological Survey of India, New Delhi, 1996. The section on sculptures and paintings in this chapter also builds on this resource base.
21. Schopen, *Bones, Stones and Buddhist Monks*, 33.
22. Jamkhedkar, *Ajanta*, 14–15.
23. For details, see Jamkhedkar, *Ajanta*, 15–17.
24. Ibid.
25. For details see, Vidya Dehejia, *Early Buddhist Rock Temples: A Chronology*, Cornell University Press, Ithaca (NY), 1972, 71; John Marshall, *Taxila. An Illustrated Account of Archaeological Excavations Carried Out at Taxila Under the Orders of the Government of India between the Years 1913 and 1934*, Vol. I, Cambridge University Press, Cambridge, 1951, 275; M. K. Dhavalikar, *Late Hinayana Caves of Western India*, Deccan College Postgraduate and Research Institute, Pune, 1984, 3, 79; Schopen, *Bones, Stones and Buddhist Monks*, 268–69.
26. For details related to Kalyanabhadra's story and the evolution of the gandhakutis, see Schopen, *Bones, Stones and Buddhist Monks*, 268–69, 275–76.
27. For details, see Jamkhedkar, *Ajanta*, 18-26. For sculptures of popular cults in particular, see Singh, *A History of Ancient and Early Medieval India*, 430, 510.
28. Mitra, *Ajanta*, 18–19.
29. For details, see Ibid., 14–17; Dieter Schlingloff, 'Narrative Ajanta Paintings', *Sahapedia*, 28 July 2016, see https://www.sahapedia.org/narrative-ajanta-paintings, accessed on 17 September 2023.
30. For details, see Vidya Dehejia, *Indian Art*, 118–19.

31. For details related to two phases, see Schlingloff, 'Narrative Ajanta Paintings'.
32. Mitra, *Ajanta*, 53–54.
33. For a discussion on paintings, see Schlingloff, 'Narrative Ajanta Paintings'; Dehejia, *Indian Art*, 118-23.
34. Ibid.
35. Ibid.
36. Mitra, *Ajanta*, 11–12.
37. For events and episodes in the discovery of Ajanta in the West, see Jonathan Glancey, The Ajanta Caves: Discovering Lost Treasure', BBC, 23 February 2015, https://www.bbc.com/culture/article/20150223-uncovering-caves-full-of-treasure, accessed on 3 May 2024.
38. Justin van Huyssteen, 'Ajanta Caves – A Look at the Paintings in the Caves of Ajanta', *Art in Context*, 23 June 2023 (published online), https://artincontext.org/ajanta-caves/, accessed on 1 October 2023.
39. Ashish Mohan Khokar, 'Anna Pavlova', *Sahapedia*, https://www.sahapedia.org/anna-pavlova, accessed on 2 October 2023.
40. The complete poem can be read at https://murielrukeyser.emuenglish.org/2018/12/07/ajanta/, accessed on 2 October 2023.
41. For details, see David Bergman, 'Ajanta and the Rukeyser Imbroglio', *American Literary History*, Vol. 22, No. 3 (Fall 2010), 553–83.

CHAPTER 9: NALANDA MAHAVIHARA

1. A translation of Malada's inscription is given in Hirananda Shastri, 'Nalanda Stone Inscription in the Reign of Yashovarmadeva' in *Epigraphia Indica*, Vol. 20, 1929–30, 45. Scholars ascribe it to the 7th century CE based on the style of the script used in the inscription.
2. Some traditions also trace the name 'Nalanda' to the cult of the nagas. Even the 5th-century CE Chinese traveller Faxian traces the name to 'Na lo' as it was situated around a Naga tank while Yijing says it was named after a serpent king called Naga Nanda.
3. T. Watters, *On Yuan Chwang's Travels in India (AD 629–645)*, Vol. 2, Low Price Publications (reprint), Delhi, 2004, 164.
4. Anand Singh, 'Origin of Nalanda Mahavihara: Structure as Evidence and Seal as Symbol', *Ancient Asia*, Vol. 13, No. 5, 2022, 1–11.
5. B. R. Mani, 'Excavations of Stupa Site No. 3 at Nalanda and Early Chronological Evidence', in C. Mani (ed), *The Heritage of Nalanda*, Aryan Books International, New Delhi, 2008, 13–22. Mani dates artefacts excavated from three mounds near Jagdishpur village to the 3rd century BCE, or the Mauryan period.
6. For details see O. P. Jaiswal, 'Nalanda Mahavihara – Victim of a Myth Regarding Its Decline and Destruction', *Mainstream*, Vol. 56, No. 26, 16 June

2018, https://www.mainstreamweekly.net/article8012.html, accessed on 7 January 2024.
7. H. Heras, 'The Royal Patrons of the University of Nalanda', *Journal of the Bihar and Orissa Research Society*, Part I, Vol. 14, 1928, 1–23.
8. Asher, *Nalanda*, 24.
9. For details, see Jaiswal, 'Nalanda Mahavihara'; Asher, *Nalanda*, 24–26.
10. Asher, *Nalanda*, 32, 103.
11. 'Excavated Remains of the Nalanda Mahavihara', Archaeological Survey of India (UNESCO World Heritage Site Nomination Dossier), New Delhi, 2015, 21–28.
12. The following three points build on Rajani, 'The Expanse of Archaeological Remains at Nalanda' while the suggestion about larger linkages borrows on Asher, *Nalanda*, 104–20.
13. Asher, *Nalanda*, 104–20; also see Ray, *The Return of the Buddha*, 252.
14. For details, see A. Ghosh, *A Guide to Nalanda*, Manager of Publication, New Delhi, 1950; Asher, *Nalanda*. For a short and accessible account, see Shashank Shekhar Sinha, 'Revisiting Nalanda', *Frontline*, Vol. 38, No. 20 (September), 25 October 2021, 99–114. For a virtual tour of the ruins, buildings and sculptures, see 'Nalanda: From Mound to Monument', https://artsandculture.google.com/story/cQWhgvVSyhQA8A, accessed on 13 May 2024.
15. 'Excavated Remains of the Nalanda Mahavihara', 30.
16. Dutt, *Buddhist Monks and Monasteries of India*, 203–04.
17. Schopen, *Bones, Stones and Buddhist Monks*, 30–31.
18. Dutt, *Buddhist Monks and Monasteries*, 319; Asher, *Nalanda*, 35.
19. Singh, 'Origin of Nalanda Mahavihara', 2.
20. For a dedicated discussion on Nalanda as a university, see H. D. Sankalia, *The University of Nalanda*, B. G. Paul and Co., Madras (Chennai), 1932; Dutt, *Buddhist Monks and Monasteries*, 331–40. A revised edition of Sankalia's book was published by Oriental Publishers in 1972.
21. Asher, *Nalanda*, 16, 63.
22. For details, see Jaiswal, 'Nalanda Mahavihara'.
23. Asher, *Nalanda*, 63.
24. For details, see Anand Singh, *Nalanda: A Glorious Past*, Primus Books, Delhi, 2024.
25. Dutt, *Buddhist Monks and Monasteries*, 344; Singh, *Nalanda*.
26. For details, see Schopen, *Bones, Stones and Buddhist Monks*, 264, 267–68. Schopen puts Yashovarmadeva inscription between 6th to 8th centuries CE.
27. Ibid., 269.
28. For details, see Debjani Paul, *The Art of Nalanda: Development of Buddhist Sculpture AD 600–1200*, Munshiram Manoharlal, Delhi, 1995.

29. The following discussion on Nalanda sculptures builds on 'Excavated Remains of the Nalanda Mahavihara', 54–61; Asher, *Nalanda*, 70–101.
30. For details, see John C. Huntington, 'Pilgrimage as Image: The Cult of Astamahapratiharya', *Orientations*, Vol. 18, No. 4 and 8, 1987, 55–63.
31. Rajani, 'The Expanse of Archaeological Remains at Nalanda, 1.
32. For details, see Dutt, *Buddhist Monks and Monasteries*, 350–52; Salila Kulshreshtha, *From Temple to Museum: Colonial Collections and Uma–Mahesvara Icons in the Middle Gangetic Valley*, 310–23; Sankalia, *The University of Nalanda*; Asher, *Nalanda*, 119.
33. For details, see Sen, 'The Spread of Buddhism', 437, 462–64, 467.
34. Kulshreshtha, *From Temple to Museum*, 310–23; Dutt, *Buddhist Monks and Monasteries*, 350–51.
35. Ibid., 58–94, for details regarding the relocation of artefacts.
36. Shashank Shekhar Sinha, *Delhi, Agra, Fatehpur Sikri: Monuments, Cities and Connected Histories*, Pan Macmillan India, 2021, 18.
37. For details, see D. N. Jha, 'How History was Unmade at Nalanda', Kafila Online, 2014, https://kafila.online/2014/07/09/how-history-was-unmade-at-nalanda-d-n-jha/, accessed on 12 January 2024. That the fortress of Bihar was Odantapura in Bihar Sharif is even supported by historians like Jadunath Sarkar.
38. Ibid.
39. Ibid.
40. This theory finds expression in the writings of historians like D. N. Jha, B. N. S. Yadava, R. K. Mookerji and Sukumar Dutt.
41. For details, see Jha, 'How History Was Unmade at Nalanda'.
42. For later years of Nalanda, see Dutt, *Buddhist Monks and Monasteries*, 347–48, 349–53, 358–59; Asher, *Nalanda*, 130–31; Sinha, *Delhi, Agra, Fatehpur Sikri* discusses several cases to show how the British deployed communal politics to the study of monuments.
43. Dutt, *Buddhist Monks and Monasteries*, 362–66.

CHAPTER 10: THE BUDDHA MAKES A COMEBACK

1. Philip C. Almond, *The British Discovery of Buddhism*, Cambridge University Press, Cambridge, 1988, 1.
2. Ober, *Dust on the Throne*, 38–40.
3. For details, see Hawkes and Shimada (eds), *Buddhist Stupas in South Asia*, xiv, xli, endnote 4.
4. Ibid., xiv-xv, for details.
5. Ibid.
6. See, Almond, *The British Discovery of Buddhism*, 15–24.
7. Ibid., 12, 56, 20–24.

8. For details, see Hawkes and Shimada (eds), *Buddhist Stupas in South Asia*, xv–xvi; Ray, *Archaeology and Buddhism in South Asia*, 5–6; Almond, *The British Discovery of Buddhism*, 12–13.
9. Geary, *The Rebirth of Bodh Gaya*, 20–21; Sinha, 'Why and How the Afterlife of a Heritage Site Matters', 47–52.
10. See Hawkes and Shimada (eds), *Buddhist Stupas in South Asia*, xvi–xvii.
11. For details, Ray, *Archaeology and Buddhism*, 6–7; Ober, *Dust on the Throne*, 80.
12. Hawkes and Shimada (eds), *Buddhist Stupas in South Asia*, xxii–xxiii.
13. Geary, *The Rebirth of Bodh Gaya*, 25-26.
14. Arnold, The British Discovery of Buddhism, 3; Geary, *The Rebirth of Bodh Gaya*, 28–31.
15. Ober, *Dust on the Throne*, 38–64. This section on pre- and early-colonial conversations and the next section on margins to centre builds on Ober's book.
16. Ibid., 65–105.
17. Ibid., 104; for details, see Jairam Ramesh, *The Light of Asia: The Poem That Defined the Buddha*, India Viking, New Delhi, 2021.
18. Ober, *Dust on the Throne*, 106–50.
19. Ibid., 151–84, 227-51.

CHAPTER 11: BUDDHISM 2.0

1. B. R. Ambedkar, 'Revolution and Counter-Revolution in Ancient India', in *Dr Babasaheb Ambedkar: Writings and Speeches*, Vol. 3 (compiled by Vasant Moon), the Government of Maharashtra, Mumbai, 1987, 153, 165.
2. Cited in Ober, *Dust on the Throne*, 222.
3. Ray, *The Return of the Buddha*, 16.
4. Srirupa Roy, 'A Symbol of Freedom: The Indian Flag and the Transformations of Nationalism', *Journal of Asian Studies*, Vol. 65, No. 3, 2006, 495–527.
5. Ray, *The Return of the Buddha*, 208–46.
6. Ober, *Dust on the Throne*, 253–54.
7. Ibid., 257, 272–73, 277–79.
8. Ibid., 274–75.
9. For details, see Geary, *The Rebirth of Bodh Gaya*, 44–82; Sinha, 'Why and How the Afterlife of a Heritage Site Matters', 47–52.
10. For details, see Ober, *Dust on the Throne*, 214–23; Singh, 'Exile and Return: The Reinvention of Buddhism and Buddhist Sites in Modern India', 193–217; Gary Michael Tartakov, 'Art and Identity: The Rise of a New Buddhist Identity', *Art Journal*, Vol. 49, No. 4 (New Approaches to South Asian Art), Winter 1990, 410.
11. For details, see Singh, 'Exile and Return', 200.

12. For details, see Tartakov, 'Art and Identity', 411–14.
13. For more information, see Singh, 'Exile and Return', 193–217.
14. For details surrounding the Kalachakra ceremony at Amravati, see Catherine Becker, 'Remembering the Amravati Stupa: The Revival of a Ruin', in Hawkes and Shimada (eds), *Buddhist Stupas in South Asia*, 267–87.
15. For more information on Japan's role, see Singh, 'Exile and Return', 204–05; Sushila Narsimhan, 'Buddhism As a Soft Power Tool in India-Japan Cultural Relations', *Asian Studies International Journal*, Vol. 1, No. 1 (December), 2019, 64–70; Kim, 'What Makes a Stupa', 298–306; Madhu Bhalla (ed.), *Culture As Power: Buddhist Heritage and the Indo-Japanese Dialogue*, Routledge, Abingdon and New York, 2021, 15.
16. 'Padmasambhava Mahavihara Monastery', https://timesofindia.indiatimes.com/travel/destinations/padmasambhava-mahavihara-monastery/articleshow/47175574.cms, accessed on 23 June 2023.
17. Tartakov, 'Art and Identity', 410–11.
18. For details related to the reinvention of Nagarjunakonda, see Singh, 'Exile and Return', 207–14.
19. See Buddhavanam, https://www.buddhavanam.telangana.gov.in/index.php, accessed on 14 April 2024.
20. See '108 Buddhists from Republic of Korea to walk for over 1100 kms on a 43-day pilgrimage; Sangwol Society to organize walking pilgrimage to Buddhist sites in India and Nepal; Motto of India's G20 Presidency similar to Buddhist teachings: Mr Chang Jae-bok, Ambassador of South Korea to India', Ministry of Information and Broadcasting, 6 February 2023, pib.gov.in/PressReleaseIframePage.aspx?PRID=1896682, accessed on 15 April 2024.
21. 'President Inaugurates "International Buddhist Conclave 2018"', Ministry of Tourism, https://pib.gov.in/PressReleaseIframePage.aspx?PRID=1543687, accessed on 15 April 2024.
22. 'The two day Global Buddhist Summit 2023 concludes with New Delhi Declaration; The Summit concludes that peace is the foundation for human happiness and well being', Ministry of Culture, 21 February 2023, pib.gov.in/PressReleaseIframePage.aspx?PRID=1918640, accessed on 15 April 2024.
23. 'Buddha's teachings offer solution to global problems: PM Modi at Buddhist summit', *Hindustan Times*, 20 April 2023, https://www.hindustantimes.com/india-news/pm-modi-addresses-global-buddhist-summit-says-lord-buddha-s-teachings-hold-solution-to-world-s-greatest-challenges-including-war-terrorism-and-climate-change-101681997059302.html, accessed on 6 September 2024.
24. Buddhist Circuit Tourist Train, https://www.irctcbuddhisttrain.com, accessed on 15 April 2024.

INDEX

Abdul Kalam, A. P. J. 280
Abhayagiri monastery in Sri Lanka 139
abhay mudra 72, 116, 168, 171
Abhidhamma Pitaka 51
Abhyakaragupta 142
Adikaram, E. W. 214
Afghans 23, 47, 62, 64, 70, 75, 104, 121, 123, 196, 203; attacks by 152, 278–79
afterlife 3, 6, 10, 13
Agnimitra 200
Agnivarma 106
agricultural practices 21–23, 74, 77–78, 83, 89, 93, 111, 154, 193, 195–96, 255, 257, 281
Ahichhatra, Panchala (present day Bareilly) 22
Aibak, Qutbuddin 170, 276
Ajanta, History and Development, Spink 245
Ajanta caves 10, 12–17, 95, 98, 107–10, 116, 131–32, 218–19, 221–26, 228, 234–41, 245–46, 265, 305–6, 315; architectural evolution 232–33; architecture of prayer halls 108, 219, 221–22, 230–33, 235, 240; *gandhakutis*, rise of 233–35; inscription 218; murals vs frescoes 237–42; outline of 220; paintings 227, 235–37, 243–44; sculptures 235–37; shrines in 171
Ajapala Nigrodha tree 174–75
Ajatashatru 32, 40, 47, 89

Ajivikas 58
Akara mahajanapada 191
Akshayavata, banyan tree 163
Akshobhya 125, 127, 139, 151
Alam II, Shah, Mughal emperor 182
Alexander, James 61, 242; invasion 23
Allahabad: edict 50–51; museum 77
Allakappa 57
All-India Hindu Mahasabha 296
Ambedkar, B. R. 295, 299, 303–6, 314, 317; Buddhism of 304; conversion 6, 299, 305; statues of 306
Ambedkarite Buddhists (followers of Navayana) 186, 305
Ambedkar Udyan (later Ambedkar Samajik Parivartan Sthal) 211
Amoghasiddhi 126–27, 139
Amoghavajra 142, 273
Amrapali/Ambapali 32, 35, 40, 89
Amravati 5, 72, 74, 78–79, 81–82, 85–86, 88, 197, 201, 305, 308, 313–14, 317; Global Buddhist Peace Festival 315; schools of art 315; stupas 85
Anagarika, Dharmapala 173, 184, 293, 295, 311
Ananda 7, 39–40, 44, 202
Anandapur 107
Anathapindika 35, 39–40, 89, 234, 248, 265
Andher 76, 78, 191, 196–97, 201, 207
Andhra 63, 71, 314; art centres in 72, *see also* Amravati

Angkor Wat, Cambodia 119
Angulimala 30
aniconism 87
Aniruddh, Bhante 174–75
anthropomorphic: depictions 65, 69–73, 86, 108, 206, 222, 240; Mahayana period 222; stone sculptures 87
Anuradhapura, Ceylon 111, 117, 255, 311
Apadana 73
Apanaka *mahavihara*, Kurkihar 146
Aparajita 272
Aparamahavinaseliya sect 80
Aparasaila 218, 222
apsaras 97, 236
Arabs 64, 123–24, 135, 149, 286
Arai, Kampo 244
Arakanese monks 156
Arakans 121, 125
aramas 19, 35–37, 39; 'pleasure gardens' 35; Veluvana 35
Aravana Adigal 113
architecture 2–3, 80–81, 98, 104, 107, 142, 144, 146, 229–30, 232, 242, 244, 280; Gupta-style 142; landscape 89, 129; Mandala 12; Palas 142; styles 74, 98, 148, 159, 187, 230–31
Arctic World Archive (AWA) 246
Arikamedu 64
Arnold, Edwin, Sir 68, 185, 285, 292–93
art, wood carvers 85
artefacts 1–2, 4–7, 10, 21, 136, 138, 147, 149, 159–60, 195–96, 247–48, 274–76, 292, 294, 309
Aryadeva 68
Arya Dharma Sangha Dharamshala, Sarnath 296
Arya Sura 241
Arya Vihar, Kushinagar 296
Asanga 68, 95, 249

asceticism 2, 26, 29, 160
Ashmaka / Ashvaka / Assaka 20, 34
Ashoka, Mauryan emperor 47–51, 53–56, 57–58, 73, 75, 88–90, 101–3, 112–13, 136–37, 165, 191–92, 195–96, 247–49, 291–92, 300–301; conversion of 48; as devanampiya piyadassi/ priyadarsi 47; Devi as wife of 77; as Dharmaraja 56, 76, 183; edicts 33, 47, 52, 195, 226; epigraph 54; inscriptions 48, 52–53, 79; patronized by 65; Piyadassi 48; royal patronage of 47–52; symbols as national emblem 300
Ashoka pillars 55–56, 78, 146, 195–96, 203, 208; inscription 47; in Rampurva 53; remains as Phuteshwar Mahadev 54; Sanchi 53, 195
Ashokavadana 56
Ashvaghosha 62, 241
Asian Civilizations Museum in Singapore 181
Asian nations 286, 300, 303
Asitanjana 112
Assaji 140, 176
astamahapratiharya, 'eight great events' 129
Astasahasrika Prajnaparamita Sutra (spiritual perfections of bodhisattvas) 67–68, 129, 264
atman (souls) 29, 100
Aurangabad caves 95, 107, 117, 126, 132, 202, 219, 228, 245–46, 305–6; renamed Chhatrapati Sambhaji Nagar 219
Aurangzeb, Mughal ruler 219
Avalokiteshvara (Padmapani, with lotus/ lord who looks down), eight great miracles 67, 71–72, 116, 128, 131–33, 139, 141, 228, 232, 235, 240, 268, 270; Bodhisattva 97, 116, 173, 228, 241

Avanti 20, 33
avasas 19, 33, 35–36, 49
avatars 100, 134, 287
Ayaka pillars 81

Baberu (Babylon) 64
Bactria (in modern-day Afghanistan) 62, 309
Badarikarama, monastery 35
Bagh 110, 234, 245, 265
Bahujan Vihar, Mumbai 296
Bahalika/Bhallika 111
Bahushrutiya sect 80
Bairat inscription 49–50
Bala 115
Baladitya 95, 250
Baladitya temple 98
Balaputra 4, 125, 251
Balarama 272
balustrades (*vedika*) 194, 200–203
Bamiyan 105, 114, 291, 311; Taliban destruction of Buddha, 104
Banaras 102
Bangladesh 141–43, 147, 156, 168–69, 177, 179–80, 187, 196, 270, 274, 276
Bangladesh Buddhist Association 295
bankers 19, 40, 91, 204
Bappapadiya Vihara (Monastery of Father) 135
Bapu, Pandit Subaji 286
Baroda Museum and Picture Gallery 106
Basavanna 124
Bava Pyara, cave at 106
Bavikonda 80
Bayon temples, Cambodia 119
Bedsa 79, 82–83, 201; cave 82
begging bowl 45
Beglar, J. D. 184
Begumpur 257–58, 269
Bengal 12–13, 23, 118, 122, 124–25, 127, 138–39, 141–42, 146–48, 155, 276–77
Bengal Buddhist Association 295

Berachampa 115
Besnagar 87
Bhadra, Rahul Sri 154
Bhagalpur, Bihar 251; Antichak in 142
Bhagavata cult 192
Bhagwan Buddhdev ka Mandir, Kushinagar 296
Bhairav 271–72
Bhaja 79, 82–83, 201, 207, 230; caves 82, 85
bhakti 94, 97–99, 120, 123
bhanakas (reciters) 7–8
Bhandarkar, R. G. 294
Bharhut, Pauni 46, 66, 73–74, 76, 85–86, 88, 90–91, 194, 197, 200, 205; monastic complex 77; stupa 8, 53, 77, 165, 200
Bharukaccha (Bharuch) 22, 31, 106
Bhaskaravarman 4, 122
Bhasu Vihara 146
Bhaumakara dynasty 122
Bhavaviveka 68, 95
bhikshu 24, 34, 37, 295, 302, *see also* monks
Bhikshunivinaya 227
The Bhilsa Topes, Cunningham 77
Bhir mound 75
Bhojpur 76, 78, 207
Bhopal Durbar 209–10, 214–15
Bhrikuti 127, 132–33, 139
bhumisparsha mudra 27, 130, 140, 146, 161, 169, 171, 181, 208, 268–69
Bhutan 159, 188, 306, 316
Bihar 141–48; Bihar Sharif 143, 258, 270, 275–76
Bihar Heritage Development Society (BHDS) 189
Bimaran 70
Bimbisara 32–33, 35, 40, 47, 89, 248
Birla, Jugal Kishore 296–97
Al-Biruni 136
Black Buddha 272; Teliya Bhandar Bhairav Mandir 258

Blake, Lt. 242
Bodh Gaya or Gaya 3–6, 12–14,
    52–53, 98, 100, 109–10, 141–42,
    154–55, 160, 162, 165, 167–68,
    176–89, 262, 292–93, 303, 305,
    308–12, 316; Ashoka constructions
    in 53; Buddha statue in 312; as
    'Buddhist Jerusalem' 185; Burmese
    delegation for repair 170; decline
    of 3; enlightenment in 30; temple
    complex 179
Bodh Gaya Temple Act (Bihar Act
    XVII of 1949) 185
Bodh Gaya Temple Advisory Board
    186, 303
Bodhgaya Temple Management
    Committee (BTMC) 175, 185, 188
Bodhicharyavatara, Shantideva 125
Bodhidharma 118
bodhighara (house for the Bodhi tree/
    tree shrine) 45, 54, 165
Bodhimanda /Bodhi Pallanka 167,
    172–73, 179
Bodhisattva Maitreya 207
Bodhisattva Manjushri 173, 208
bodhisattvas 12, 60–61, 65–69,
    71–72, 95–96, 100, 113–17, 125–27,
    130–33, 141, 147, 149–50, 155, 235,
    238–41, 268–69; conceptualizations
    66; female attendants 117; in
    mandala formation 147; in metal
    and terracotta 117; multiple 67
Bodhi tree 27–28, 45–46, 53, 162–63,
    165–67, 172–73, 175, 178–79, 184,
    204, 206; as 'tree of knowledge'
    160; as Vajrasana 52
Bon cults 143, 151
Borobudur stupa, Java 8
Bose, Nandalal 244, 301
Boston Museum of Fine Arts 242
Bota-Sriparvata 191
Brahma 28, 70, 72, 90, 162
Brahmanical 8, 71, 90, 97–98, 130, 148,
    162, 168, 208, 285, 314; cults 95,
    250; deities 165, 169, 173; divinities
    148; goddesses 99, 208; Hinduism
    120, 289; images 148; institutions
    90; *karma* in 29; learning 123;
    plaques 209; revival 93, 152, 209;
    sacrifices 200; shraddha 162;
    shrines 80; traditions 87, 97–98;
    Vedic tradition 221
Brahmanism 97, 100, 113, 120, 288;
    and assimilation 124
Brahmanization, of royal courts 123,
    154
Brahmans 23–25, 38–40, 95, 123, 154,
    174, 197, 212, 221, 277, 287, (*see
    also* caste system); Drona 46
Brahmo Samaj 295
Brihadeeswara temple, Tanjore 134
British Buddhists 214–15
British Maha Bodhi Society 214
British Museum, London 79, 90, 133,
    169, 210, 214, 308
Brom-ston temple 150
bronze 109, 148, 247, 267–71; images
    14, 106, 117, 133–34, 147, 155,
    269–70; at Nagapattinam 134
Brown, Percy 2
Buchanan-Hamilton, Francis 183, 274
Buddha, Gautama/Goutama (*see also*
    Siddharth): 96–97, 235, 292, 299;
    as Amitabha 67, 96–97, 126, 139,
    151; 'Assault and Temptation of
    Mara' 116; bodies of 96; Brahma's
    advice 28; chakravartin 116, 169;
    cremation of 46, 103; death 28,
    43–45, 56, 66, 86, 176, 197, 250;
    followers 30, 37–42; images 60,
    69–70, 72, 120, 126, 168, 187, 206,
    290; images, installation of 60; life
    2, 8, 30, 72, 77, 81, 86–87, 93, 120,
    180, 191; meditation 27, 165, 174,
    (*see also* Bodhi tree) 'Miracle at
    Shravasti' 116, 235; names of 25;

seated 71–72, 107, 129, 132, 134, 144, 168, 171, 312, 314; statue 75, 207; West discovers 286–93
The Buddha and His Dhamma, Ambedkar 180, 299, 304
Buddhabhadra 224–25, 264
Buddhagaya, *see* Bodh Gaya
Buddha Gaya Maha Bodhi Society (now called the Maha Bodhi Society), Colombo 184–85, 293
Buddha Gaya Temple Act, 1935 185
Buddhaghosa 113, 117
Buddhagupta 119, 155, 250
Buddhahood 5, 66, 225, 235
Buddha International Welfare Mission 317
Buddha Jayanti celebrations 186
Buddha Konakamana/Kanakmuni 53
Buddhakshetras 67
Buddha Mahotsav 315
Buddha Mandir, Ranchi 296
Buddham saranam gacchami... 38
buddhapadas 46, 81, 113–14, 171–72
Buddhapalita 68, 95
Buddha Society of Bombay 215
Buddhavamsa 73
Buddha Vihara, New Delhi 296
Buddhayashas 118
Buddhification 6, 187, 303
Buddhism 9–11, 13, 19, 55–56, 91–92, 94, 97–99, 103–6, 111–13, 119–20, 122–24, 130–31, 136, 151–53, 160, 176, 184–86, 209, 214–15, 287–88, 292–93, 297, 304–5, 307; cardinal virtues of 239; colonial conversations 293–95; decline of 3, 9, 11–13, 121–56, 170, 177–78, 209, 224, 250–51, 270–71, 277, 279; evolution of 1; as Kshatriya reaction to Brahmanical dominance 40; oral teachings of 7; revival 185–86; textualization of 289

Buddhist: art 3–4, 8–9, 67, 69–71, 75, 77, 85–88, 103–4, 114–15, 148, 244–45, 267, 269–70, 275–76; canon 7–8, 28; caves 65, 84, 95, 98, 117, 130, 219, 226, 228, 233; caves in Ajanta 107; circuit 52, 126, 312–13, 316; deities 98, 126, 132, 139, 149, 168–69, 261; establishments 9, 12–13, 59, 63–65, 80, 109, 112, 122, 135, 137–38, 153, 278, 303, 307; faith 2, 40, 45, 58, 89, 110, 163, 167, 219, 223, 226; ideas 13, 41, 64, 89, 112, 118, 140, 147, 187, 286, 303; missions 117, 196, 214–15, 302, 311; monasteries 82, 98, 107, 186–87, 270, 278, 287; monuments 1–2, 10, 13, 59, 92, 101, 183, 209, 290–91, 305, 308; pantheons 65, 87–89, 96, 100, 120, 125–26, 128; poetry 156; scrolls 64; shrines 12, 98; texts 6, 21, 61, 64, 118, 161–62, 249–50, 252, 276, 285, 289; traditions 26–28, 48, 71, 89, 166, 175, 289; transnational networks 300; upasaka 37, 40, 48–50
Buddhist sites 106, 132, 134, 140–41, 153, 155, 191, 193, 217, 290–92, 297, 300, 302, 306–9, 312–13; Assam 4, 122, 216, 250–51; Chittagong 147; Devni Mori 106; Kannauj (now UP) 4, 102, 122, 124, 154, 250; map of viii; Suvarnadvipa 4, 64, 251, 260; Talaja 106; in Tons Valley 57; Turkish destruction of 121; Vadnagar 107
Buddhist structures 60, 75, 82, 149; at Harwan 136; Huna attack on 137; at Uskara 136
Buddhist Text Society 295
Burgess, James 211
Burgess, John 243
burial mounds 41, 45, 197

Burma (Myanmar) 68, 121, 144, 151, 174, 178, 180–82, 187, 215–17, 302–4, 309; monasteries 175; monks 133, 155; Theravada monks 175
Burnes, Alexander 290
Burnouf, Eugène 289

Cambodia 68, 119, 121, 144, 188, 216, 302, 316
canon, Pali 7, 25, 30, 44, 46, 51, 56, 66, 96, 159–60, 195–96
caravans 23, 63, 228–29
Cariyapitaka 73
carvings 83, 91, 102, 166, 203–4, 209
castes 24, 40–41, 124, 295; norms 123; politics 299, 317; system 285, 304
caves 10, 13, 82–85, 104, 106–9, 114, 116–17, 126, 130–32, 218, 221, 223–37, 239–46; at Ajanta 98, 116, 219, 221–22, 226, 229–30, 232, 240; Aurangabad 95, 107, 117, 126, 132, 202, 219, 228, 245–46, 305–6; chaitya 74, 108; Deccan 12, 85; Ellora 12, 98, 117, 123, 126, 130–32, 228, 305, 309, 312; excavation 221; of Girnar hills–Junagarh 106; Hindu 12; Indrashala 83; inscription 218; at Kanheri 95; narrative figures in 85; sculptural themes of 85; Vakataka period 222; wall painting 85, 239; of Western Ghats 231
Central Asia 23, 61, 63, 75, 94, 104, 118, 227, 237, 306, 309
Central India 13, 71, 74, 76, 78, 88, 91–92, 94, 105, 107, 123, 126, 132
Chaddanta Jataka 205
Chaitya. *See* shrines
chaityagrihas 219, 231, 234, 243; complexes 80, 138–39, *see also* shrines
Chalukyas 114, 123

Champa 20, 22, 31, 33, 123
Champaran 56, 146
Chanakramana, or Ratnachankrama ('jewel walk') 173
Chandrakirti 68, 95
Chandramani, U 304
Chandrapala 263
Channa 25
Chan/Zen 118
charkha (spinning wheel) 300
charya, tantra 139
Chavannes, Édouard 178
Chetika 222
Chetiyagiri Vihara 213, 217, 302
Chetru 149
China 63–64, 89–90, 94, 96, 117–19, 124–25, 135–37, 142–43, 180–82, 212, 273, 286, 302–3, 309, 311; Baima Si (White Horse temple) monestry 212; Buddhism in 118, 143, 212, 273; Five-Pagoda Temple in Beijing 181; Han-ruled 118
Chinese pilgrims/ travellers (see also under *separate entries*) 53, 69, 135, 177, 212, 249, 255, 264, 273, 280, 291
Chittagong 125, 147, 155–56
Cholas 112, 123
Christianity 68
Chunda 40–41, 132, 270
clay: seals 103, 143, 146; tablets 140–41, 147–48, 155
Cleveland Museum of Art (Ohio, USA) 276
Clustine, Ivan 245
coins 9, 76–77, 106, 134, 150, 248, 291–92
Cole, Henry Hardy, Lt. 211
collage stupas/sahasrabuddha stupas/'Thousand Buddha stupas' 180
colonial administration 183, 259, 275; discovery of 274–76

Comilla 147, 156
commerce 63–65, 228, see also trade
confederation of monasteries 262
conversions 30, 52, 87, 167, 299, 303–5, 317
Coomaraswamy, Ananda 70
councils 7, 44, 196, 201, 275
Crockatt, James 183
crypto-Buddhists 155
cudamani, crest jewel 73
cults 2, 5, 12, 14, 87, 92, 93–94, 97–99, 119–20, 192, 194, 204, 207; Bhagavata 192; of bodhisattvas 95, 98; Bon 143, 151; of chaityas 13, 32, 41, 74, 80, 83–84, 91, 107–8, 113, 130–31, 137; devotional 61, 92, 207; fertility spirits (*yakshas* and *yakshis*) 5; of images 69, 91, 223–24; Mahima 155; of monastic dead 78; of *naga* 14, 88; popular 2, 5, 10, 12, 14, 78, 87, 97–98, 120, 192, 268; practice 194; of relics 61; at Sanchi 10, 207; serpents (nagas and *nagis*) 5, 99, 162, 204, 230; of stupa 58, 61, 73–74, 90–91; temple based sectarian 93; yakshas 14; *yakshas* and *yakshis* 5, 71, 87, 97, 163, 166, 194, 204, 236
Cunningham, Alexander 77, 172, 178–79, 184, 210, 212–13, 275, 291–92: excavation of stupa complex 210; identification scheme 172–73

Daijokyo Buddhist Temple 310
Daijokyo sect, of Nagoya 312
Daji, Bhau 243
Dakshinapatha 22–23, 63
Dalit Buddhism 305–6, 314, see also under Ambedkar, B.R.
Dalits 211, 299, 304–5, see also caste system
dana (giving) 19, 39, 204
Daniell, Thomas 183

Daniel, William 183, 289
Darjeeling 295, 310
Das, S. C. 294
Dayal, Lala Deen 211
death, of enlightened, see parinirvana/Parinibbana; rites 82, 153, see also rebirth
Deccan 12–13, 82, 85, 88, 92, 94–95, 100, 105, 107, 114, 117, 221, 227, 129–30, 132, 134, 226; caves 85, 229
Deekshabhoomi, Nagpur 6, 211
Dehejia, Vidya 3
deities 87–88, 93, 124, 126, 128, 131, 148, 151, 155, 161–62, 194, 198, 271–72; pantheon of 120; tantric Buddhist 272; worship of 28
Delhi Sultanate 122, 170, 276
demigods 87, 98, 131, 201, 236
Dempster G. A. 214
destructions 38, 56, 104, 121, 167, 170, 270, 276–77
Deva, Pratapanirudra 155
Devadatta 25, 27, 30
Devapala 251, 266
Devikota Vihara 146
Devni Mori, in Gujarat 105–6, 117, 134, 228
Dey, Mukul 245
dhamma. See dharma
Dhammaceti 133, 155
Dhammapada 7
Dhammapala 263
Dhanyakataka/Dharanikota 79
Dharamshala 186, 307–8
dharanis 5, 134, 138–40, 176, 179, 262; stupas 138, 140
Dharapalem 80
Dharma/dhamma (doctrine/teachings of Buddha) 7, 10, 33–34, 37–39, 42, 44, 50, 61, 65, 112, 140, 151–53, 176, 180, 197, 285, 299, 304, 310, 317
dharmabhanakas/dharma preachers 270

dharmachakra 81, 101, 115, 300; flag 300; mudra (teaching pose) 71, 115
dharmachakrapravartana: first sermon as 28, 115; 'Turning of the Wheel of the Law' 28
Dharmaganja 265, 277
Dharmakirti 68, 143, 264
Dharmapala, Pala kings 113, 143–44, 184–86, 251, 259
Dharmapaladeva 266
Dharmapala Vihara 143
Dharmarajika Chaitya Vihara in Calcutta 293, 296
Dharmasvamin 169–70, 278–79
Dhauli 112, 310
Dhundibissara 51
Dhyanabhadra/Chanxian 273
dhyana mudra/dhyan mudra (meditative pose) 71, 130, 168, 207–8
dhyani buddhas 125–27, 138–39, 141, 151
diamond throne. *See* Vajrasana
Dignaga 113, 263
Digvijaya, Shankara 293
Dipankara/Atisha 119, 143, 145, 274
Dipavamsa 43, 51, 196, 226
dissensions 49–51
divine beings 67, 73–74; see also under *separate entries*
Divyavadana 53, 88, 292
donations 73, 77, 83, 133, 142, 145, 147, 176–77, 201, 204, 224, 227, 278; by Kurangi 166, *see also* patronage
donors 8, 35, 73–74, 90–92, 139, 176, 200, 204–5, 218, 223–25, 227, (*see also* gifts); along trade routes 226–29
downfall 151–56; Ajanta 218, 223–24, 225, 227; Bodh Gaya 176; Nalanda 266; Sanchi 194, 200, 204–05
D'Oyly, Charles 183

Dudda-vihara mandala 135
Dunhuang 64, 229
Durga 132, 268, 271
Dutt, Sukumar 2
dwarfs 98, 108, 117, 131, 232, 237

earthen mounds 73, *see also* burial mounds
East Asia 13, 119, 124, 151, 210, 264, 273, 309; Buddhist links 309–12
Eastern Deccan 74, 82, 95, 133, 313
edicts 47–50, 58; Allahabad 50–51; Ashokan schism 51; at Dhauli and Jaguada 112; in Kharosthi script 75; minor rock 48, 50; schism 49–50, 55, 78, 196
eight bodhisattvas 132, 141, 147, 155
Eightfold Path 28–29, 41
eight Sacred Locations (*astamahachaityas*) 129
Elliot, Walter 79
Ellora caves 12, 98, 117, 123, 126, 130–32, 228, 305, 309, 312
embellishments 91, 194, 204
Enlai, Zhou 311
Enlightened One 1, 27, 160
enlightenment 27–30, 46, 52, 81, 88, 111, 116–17, 159–61, 167, 169–70, 172–75, 178, 181; tree representation of 86; site of 101
Erskine, William 242
Esoteric Buddhism 100, 138, 271
excavation 10, 57–58, 81, 106–8, 110–12, 126, 129–30, 146–47, 207–8, 218–19, 221–22, 227, 229–32, 247–48, 252, 254–55, 257–59, 269, 274–75, 290–92; in Ajanta 107; along river Waghora 107; at Begram 203; of Buddhist caves 82–83, 130, 224; of Buddhist sites 106; complex of Nalanda 109; Deccan region 107; Dharmarajika stupa 102; Jaipurgarh 181; rock-

cut caves 82–83; in Sanchi region 78; stupa complex 210; Taradih mound 163; Vankia hills 106

families 24, 39, 41, 55, 103, 151
Fatehpur Sikri, Ibadat Khana of 210
Faxian, Chinese pilgrims 89, 93, 102–3, 167, 177, 195, 212, 273–74, 291
Fell, Captain 290
feminine divinities, *see* goddesses
Fergusson, James 210, 242
fertility 87, 194
festivals 56, 73–74, 303, 305, 315, *see also under* stupas; *see also* Hemis Festival; Lahaul Festival
fire-spewing serpent 30, 162, *see also naga* cults; *nagas*
fire worshippers 163
First Buddhist Council 7
first sermon: at Sarnath 28, 30, 46, 52, 55, 81, 103, 115, 293, 301, 310; site of 101
five Ms (panchatattva) – mamsa (meat), matsya (fish), madya (alcohol), maithuna (sexual intercourse) and mudra (parched grain) 99
Foucher, Alfred 69, 211
four great events 30
four Noble Truths 28–29, 41
Fourth Buddhist Council 62
frescoes 237–38, 310
Fujii, Nichidatsu 303, 310
funerary 79; association 4, 14, 140, 178–79, 262; deposits 179, *see also* burial mounds

Gahadavala dynasty 154
Gampo, King Songtsen 119
gana-sanghas (*ganas*) 20–21, 34, 39–40
gandhakutis (perfumed/private chamber/shrine chamber) 10, 110, 128, 139, 233–35, 240–41, 260, 265–67, 270

gandhakuti *varikas* 110, 266
Gandhara 12–13, 46, 51, 64, 70–72, 74, 78, 80, 85, 90, 92, 100, 103–4, 109; artists 71; bodhisattva figures in 71; depictions 116; monastic complexes 76; region 64, 69–70, 75, 103–5, 118, 254, 290; school of art 64, 71, 75, 90, 107, 114, 136, 315; sculptures 71; stupa-monastery complexes 75–76
gandharvas 97, 236
Gandhi, Mahatma 185, 295, 300, 304
Ganesha 132, 163, 169, 173, 271–72
Ganga 33, 144, 208–9
Gangetic: heartland 12–13, 58, 73–74, 92, 100, 117, 153, 192, 310, 313; plains 20–23, 41, 77, 103, 122, 151, 154, 191–92, 297; valley 21, 30, 146, 154, 192, 267;
Ganwaria region, Uttar Pradesh 21
Gaudas 122, 141, 167, 277
Gaudiya Vaishnavas 293
Gautama Buddha. *See* Buddha, Gautama
Gaya Mahatmya 162
Gaya Museum 181
geese (hamsa) 52, 171, 237
general council 44
Geographic Information System (GIS) 281
Ghatotkacha cave 222
Ghositarama, monastery 35
Ghosrawan 111, 258
Ghuri, Muhammad 170, 276
gifts (*see also* donations, of *aramas*; donations, of aramas, danam) 36, 39, 107, 110, 194, 202, 210, 224–25, 249–51, 260, 266
Gill, Robert, Maj, copying Ajanta paintings 243–44
Giri, Gossain Ghamanda 182
Girnar hills 105–6
Global Buddhist Summit, Delhi 316

goddesses 93, 99, 125–26, 132, 236, 271; Bhrikuti 131; Brahmanical 99; Buddhist 132; Kali 127; Mahayana and Vajrayana 151; Mayamayuri 131; worship of 93
Gopala, Pala ruler 143
Gopala III 177
Gotama, the Buddha 301
Gotihawa 53–54
Government Museum, Chennai 79, 113, 133–34; Mathura 115
Govindachandra, King 154
Graeco-Bactrians (Hellenistic) 71
Graeco-Roman 64, 70–71, 104, 237
grants 95, 123, 145, 154, *see also* donations; gifts
'Greater Gandhara' 75
Great Monkey Jataka 205
Griffiths, John 243–44
Guhyadhatu 139
guilds (corporate bodies) 1, 3, 5, 22, 92
Gujarat 105–7, 129; Buddhism in 136
Gulf of Cambay 63
Gunamati 263
Gunavarman 118
Gupta dynasty 12–13, 94, 97–107, 110–11, 113, 115–16, 119–20, 122, 142, 166–68, 202, 207–8, 248–50, 259–60, 262; *panchayatana* plan 110; patronization 109
Gupta-style: architectural 142; *shikharas* 110
Gupta–Vakataka Age 92–93, 98, 100, 106, 109, 120, 153, 156, 286, 309; temples 98; tradition 135, 207

Hadda, Afghanistan 104
Haldar, Asit Kumar 244
Haribala 103
Harikela 125, 147
Harishena, King 108, 222, 227
Harisvamini 203
Hariti 30, 98, 270

Harshavardhana (Harsha) 4, 122, 146, 250–51
Hazaribag monastery 146
health 87, 225; *see also* fertility
Heliodorus 192
Hemavata: monks 196; school 78, 196
Hemis Festival at Leh 315
Heras, H. 250
heretics 51, 124
hermitages 34, 238
Herringham, Christiana 243–44
Hewavitarne, Daya 216
Himalayas (Hemavata) 25, 78, 148, 150, 196
Hinayana Buddhism 10, 44, 68–69, 126, 135, 218, 221–23, 241; caves 108, 218, 221; sects 69
Hindu: deities 72, 268, 272, 290; caves 130; goddesses 105; mahants 182–85, 188; temples 200
Hinduism 2, 248, 271, 275, 287, 304
Hisar 56
Huike, Dazu 118
Hui Li 263–64
Humphreys, Christmas 285
Hunas 152; invasions by 153
Hussain Sagar Lake in Hyderabad 313
Huvishka, Kushana king 165

iconography 27, 88, 116, 119, 126, 128, 147, 151, 161, 184, 194
Ikshvakus 80, 90, 95, 313–14
Illankilli 113
imageries 65, 89, 121, 134, 180, 297, 314
images 3–6, 46, 60–61, 86–88, 90–92, 25–26, 132–33, 138–42, 176–77, 222–24, 232–35, 258–61; Hindu gods 268; Marichi 209; Tara 209; images of Buddha 12, 69–72, 74–75, 102, 104–6 114–16, 129–31, 134, 146–48, 155, 168–69, 181, 202, 206–9, 223, 268–70, 306; installation of

61; Jagdishpur 267; metal 148, 267; miniature of Buddha 147; Pala times 148; seated cross-legged, 115; of Vajrasattva 209 image worship 12, 120, 123, 135; Brahmanical 125; Mahayanists of 69
India–China Trade 65, 125
Indian Court of Crystal Palace in Sydenham, London 243
Indian Museum, Kensington 214; Kolkata 77, 79, 104, 168–69, 214–15, 258, 267, 276
Indian National Congress (INC) 185
Indian Ocean trade network 227–28
Indian traders 64, 94, 119
Indic Buddhism 156, 295
Indo-Bactrian Greeks or Indo-Greeks/ yavanas 62
Indo-Greeks 62–63
Indonesia 119, 146, 148, 316
Indo-Parthians 71, 136
Indosan Nippon Temple 310
Indo–Sri Lankan Cultural Exchange programme 315
Indra 28, 70, 90, 166, 230, 232, 236, 255, 257; as Sakra 83
Indrashala cave 83
initiation *(diksha/deeksha)* 44, 99, 121, 129, 307–8
inscriptions 7–10, 48–49, 52–54, 60–61, 90–91, 95, 105–7, 116–17, 133–35, 167, 169–70, 173–78, 190–92, 194, 196, 200–205, 221–25, 250–51, 259–61, 265–66; in cave 218, 222; Devapala 266; donative 66, 73, 90–91, 125, 177, 194, 204–5, 224; Gupta-period 112; Kesava Prasasti 162; Kushana and Gupta 102; Malada 260; Pali 119; on pillar 54; Sanchi 91; Sanskrit 119; schism edicts 49
institutions 9, 19, 36, 89, 94, 103, 112, 270, 279–80, 289, 296; monastic 103
International Buddhist Conclave (IBC) 315–16
iron pillar in Qutb Minar complex 4, *see also* Qutb mosque, Delhi
iron technology 21–22
irrigational dams 78, *see also* agricultural practices
Islam 105, 170, 279, 304
Itihas Timir Nashak, Sivaprasad 294

Jagaddala 145, 274, 278; monastery 121
Jagdishpur Buddha 258, 267, 269, 272
Jaggayyapeta/Jaggaiahpet 78–79
Jainas 19, 71, 87, 97, 99, 106, 123–24, 290; caves 12, 130; deities 98; pilgrimage 258; scriptures 8; temple 143; traditions 98, 236, 275
Jainism 2, 113, 120, 248, 275
Jamal Garhi 104
Jambhala 131, 272
Janguli 132
Japan 68, 118–19, 151, 159, 178, 187–88, 263, 303, 309–10, 312, 316; Buddhism in 309–12; Daijokyo sect 187
Japan Bank for International Cooperation (JBIC) 309
Jatakas 63–64, 67, 71, 77, 81, 84, 86, 92, 204, 235–36, 239–40, 245
jatis. *See* caste system
Jaulian 104
Java 8, 118–19, 144, 147
Jayachandra 154
Jayadeva 278
Jayendra 137
Jayendra Vihara, Srinagar 137
Jesuits 133, 155
Jetavana 31, 35, 37
Jhewari (or Jhiuri) 147
Jinamitra 263
Jinattha Pakasani, Sayadaw 175

Jivaka 35, 40
Jnanachandra 263
Johnson, Captain 209
Jor, Sumpa Khan-po Yeçe Pal 121, 277
Julien, Stanislas 252
Junagarh 84, 105–6; monastic complexes in 106
Junagarh–Devni Mori–Vadnagar region, Gujarat 105
Junnar 82, 84, 92, 287, 305
Juzjani 277

Kabul valley, Afghanistan 104
Kadphises, Kujula 62
Kakanadabota 191
Kakanava/ /Kakanaya (Stupa at Sanchi] 190–91
Kakandaputta, Yasa 33
Kakuzo, Okakura 70
Kalabhras 114
Kalachakra ('Wheel of Time') 5, 140, 187, 307–8, 313–14; *tantra* 155
Kalama, Alara 26, 160
Kalinga (present-day Odisha) 48, 61; war of 48, 112
kalpavriksha wish-fulfilling tree 204
Kalyanabhadra 234, 265
Kamadeva 272
Kamalasila 143
Kampilya 135
Kanaganahalli stupa 89
Kanchipuram 113, 123, 287
Kangra 149
Kanheri 79, 82, 84, 116–17, 131–32, 134, 201, 224, 228, 234, 265; cave 85
Kanihara 149
Kanishka 5, 62, 89–90, 136, 154, 301; casket 90; headless statue of 72
Kannauj (present-day Uttar Pradesh) 4
Kanthaka 26
Kapilavastu 21, 24–25, 30–32, 36, 47, 53, 57, 124, 129, 310

Karad 84
Karandavyuha 67
Karkota dynasty 123, 137
Karle caves 82–85, 92, 116–17, 207, 230, 305
karma 26, 29
Kartikeya 271–72
Kashgar 62, 64, 118
Kashmir 12, 71, 75, 80, 118, 121, 123, 129, 136–38, 150, 153; Buddhism in 136; Buddhist learning 137; Shaivism in 137
Kashyap, Jagdish 302
Kashyapa brothers 30, 161–62, 204
Kassapagota 51, 196
Kathavattu 51
Katju, K. N. 216
Kaushambi/Kosambi 20, 22, 31–35, 47, 50–51, 55–56, 61, 100, 115, 152, 200; edict 50, 55
Kaveripoompattinam (Puhar) 113–14, 133
Kayarohanaswami temple 133
Kesariya Stupa 146; as 'devalaya' 146
Khadiravani Tara 127, 132
Khalji, Bakhtiyar 14, 170, 251, 276–81
Khan, Khamgar 257
Khapra Kodiya cave 106
Kharavela 61
Kharosthi, silver scroll inscription in 76
Khotan 64, 137
Killivalavan 113
kinnars 97, 201, 236
Kinnaur 149
kinship 24, 40, 92
Kitab-ul-Hind, al-Biruni 136
Kittoe, Markham 183, 274
Koliyas 39
Konakamana 53–54
Kondana 83–84
Kondivite 83, 231
Korea 118–19, 151, 159, 178, 187, 263, 303; monks from 273

Kosala 20, 22, 31–33, 40, 192
Kosambi, Dharmanand 294, 297
Kosetsu Nōsu 310
Krakuchhanda, twenty-second Buddha 54
Kramrisch, Stella 245
Krishnacharya 155
Kshatriyas 20, 24, 38–40, *see also* caste system
Kubera 208, 268, 272
Kucha 64, 118
Kuda 84, 116, 224
Kukkutarama, monastery 35
kulas 24, 38–40, 179
Kullu 123, 149
Kuluta 149
Kumamoto peace pagoda (shanti stupa) 303
Kumaradevi, Queen 5, 102, 154
Kumaragupta I 250
Kumaragupta III 250
Kumarajiva 118
Kumarila 264
Kumrahar 166
kundalini 99
Kunti Har 77
Kurangi 166
Kurkihar 146, 148, 265, 269
Kushanas 62–63, 69–72, 76, 90–91, 101–2, 104, 112, 115, 118, 129, 136, 202
Kushinagar/Kasia 41–42, 46–47, 52–53, 57, 100, 103, 141, 146, 296, 310–11, 316; death in 30, 239
Kutikanna, Sona 33
kutuhalashalas 34

Ladakh 127–28, 137, 149–50, 216, 306–8, 310
Lahaul 126, 132, 149–50, 155; festival 315
Lahaul-Spiti valley 151, 306–7; Buddhism in 138, 149

laity or lay followers 1, 9–10, 34, 37–44, 61, 65, 82, 87, 91–92, 112–13, 129, 153, 145, 148, 194, 203–4, 206–7, 238, 303–4, 307; constituencies of 40; *grihapatis* 23, 38–40;
Lakshmi 100, 271–72
Lalitagiri 112, 138–41
Lalitavistara (narrative of life of Buddha) 67–68
Lama, Dalai 5, 186–88, 299, 302, 306–8, 311–13; fourteenth 5
Langudi hills 112
Laos 188, 316
Lauriya Nandangarh in northern Bihar 41
legends 4–5, 25, 31, 51, 56, 58, 98, 103, 112, 195–96, 292; of Devi 196; of Mahendra 43
Liang dynasty 118
Lichhavis 32, 34–35, 39
The Light of Asia: Arnold 68, 185, 285, 292–93, 295; translations of 295
Loknatha (or Samantabhadra) 268
Lomas Rishi 58; cave 83
'Look East', 'Act East' policy 315
Lord of Pratishthana (present-day Paithan) 63
Lotus Pond 172, 174
Lotus Sutra 310
Lumbini 47, 52–55, 57, 115, 128, 176, 239, 301, 311, 316; birth in 30; tree 25

Macedonians 71
Mackenzie, Colin 290
Madhava 293
Madhvacharya 124
Madhyamaka 95
Madurai 113, 123
Magadha 20, 22–23, 32–33, 40, 47, 49, 93–94, 120, 121, 142, 274, 278; *mahajanapada* 47

INDEX 371

Magadh Institute of Post-Graduate Studies and Research in Pali 279
magical formulae (*mantras*) 97, 99, 127
Mahabharata 261, 268
mahabhinishkramana ('Great Departure') 26, 86, 205
Mahabodhi 142, 148, 185; monasteries 142, 271; *taru* (Great Bodhi tree) 162
Mahabodhi Mission vihara in Kozhikode 296
Maha Bodhi Society (MBS) 173, 184–86, 188, 213–17, 293, 295, 304, 310–11
Mahabodhi temple 3, 6, 53, 98, 101, 159–61, 163–70, 171–86, 188–89, 259, 303, 305, 309; Bodh Gaya 3, 110; in Burma 181; Burmese repairing 183; colonial restoration 182–84; Central Walkway and 171–72; outline of 164; restoration of 172
Mahabodhi Tree 122, 162–63
Mahabodhi Vidyalaya, Sarnath 296
mahachaitya (great shrine): Amravati 79, 95; at Nagarjunakonda 80
Mahachina Tara 127
Mahad 84
Mahadeva 51
Mahadharmarakshita 51
Mahajanaka 246
mahajanapadas 20, 70
Mahakasyapa 39, 103
Mahakatyayana 33
mahamatras 50
Mahamayuri 131–32
Mahanaman 142, 167, 169, 177
mahants 163, 168–69, 182–83, 185
Mahaparinirvana Sutra/Mahaparinibbana Sutta 42, 45–46, 52, 55, 86, 103, 235
Mahaparinirvana Temple 103
Mahaprajapati Gautami 30

Mahasanghikas 44, 51, 96, 222, 227
Mahastupa (Great Stupa), Sanchi 77–78, 80, 138–39, 165, 190–92, 197–98, 200, 202–3, 206, 210, 211, 233, 314; war of relics 46, 197
Mahavamsa 51, 56, 196, 226
Mahavastu 128
mahavidyas 100
mahaviharas 12–14, 100, 102, 109–11, 122, 140, 142–46, 251, 254–55, 257–58, 262, 263–65, 274, 274–76, 312; of Kakanadabhota 105; in Murshidabad 146; Nalanda 12; Odantapura (or Odantapuri) 258; origins of 248–52; at Vikramashila 144
Mahaviharavasin sect 80
Mahayana (Great Vehicle) 14, 60, 65–69, 72, 92, 122, 126, 131, 138, 169, 207, 218, 221–23, 241; caves 108, 218, 222–23; deities 98, 140; doctrines 122, 141; monasteries 146, 149; monks 169, 224; mythology of 95–97; ritualization and expansion in 125–29; scheme 97; school 10, 44, 68–69, 80, 95–96, 222–23, 225; sutras 116, 139; texts 67, 95, 190; tradition 12, 60, 66–67, 100, 142, 151, 155–56, 218, 224, 267, 271; worship 125;
Mahayanists 69, 102, 223
Mahendra 43, 51, 196; to Sri Lanka 52
Mahendrapala 259
Maheshwara 163, 169–70, 272
Mahima cult 155
Mahindra 43, 301, 311
Mahipala I 177
Mahishamandala (probably Mysore) 51
Mahishasaka sect 80
Mahishasura Mardini 209, 272
Mainamati 141, 147
Maisey, Fred C. Capt. 208, 210, 212–13
Maitrakas 106, 125, 135

Maitreya 66, 71–72, 149–50
Maitreyanatha 68
Madhyantika/Majjhantika 51, 136
Majjhima 51, 196
Majumdar, N. G. 211
Malada 247, 250
Malay Peninsula/Suvarnabhumi 4, 33, 51, 119, 140, 147
Mallas 21, 39, 46, 197
mandala 126, 128, 130, 132, 138, 140–41, 144, 151, 268, 271–72; architecture 12; design 147; stupa 139–40; temple 150
Manimekalai 112–13
Manjushri ('gentle, or sweet, glory') 67, 133, 147, 155, 268
Manjushri-mulakalpa 95, 100, 127, 132
Mantrayana. *See* Vajrayana
manuscripts 7, 121, 148, 150, 264, 270, 289, 294
Mara, Buddhist devil 27, 116, 161, 235
Marichi 133, 169, 209, 268, 272
maritime networks 61, 63–64, 74, 82, 118, 124, 136, 273
Marshall, John 191, 211, 292
Masson, Charles 290
Masulipatnam, Robertson's Mound 79
Mathura 62, 70, 72, 79, 81, 87–88, 93, 95, 103, 105, 114–15, 201–2, 207, 223–24, 267; artists 72; images 115; Museum 90; sandstone images 202; school of art 70–72, 90, 107, 114–15
Maudgalyayana 38, 78, 140, 176, 198, 210, 212–13, 217, 249, 302; relics and caskets 213
Mauryans/ Mauryas 43–59, 61, 63, 71, 73, 75–77, 79, 83, 86, 89, 94, 101, 112, 190, 192, 200, 208; art 86; construction 54
Maya 24, 86; dream of 24–25
Maya Devi temple, Lumbini 54
Mayawati 211

meditation (*dhyana*) 27, 29, 68, 72, 95, 99, 111, 126, 130, 160–61, 165, 168, 173–74
Mediterranean Europe 63
Meerut 56
Mellor, Frank R. 215
Menander (Milinda) 7, 62, 301
merchants 3, 5, 33, 40, 82–83, 91–92, 94, 111, 113, 116, 174, 227–29, 286–87
metal plaques 140
Metropolitan Museum of Art and Rubin Museum of Art in New York 181
migrations 61–63
Mihirakula 137
Milindapanha 7
Minhaj-i-Siraj Juzjani 276
miniature: replicas 4, 181; shrines 76; stone images 268–69
miracles 30, 204, 310
Miran 64
Mirpur Khas, Sindh 136, 206
missionaries 51, 62, 64, 104, 150, 196, 250, 286–87, 289, 301
mithuna figures 85
Mitra, Debala 2
Mitra, D. N., Sir 216
Mitra, Rajendralal 183, 294
Modi, Narendra 316
monasteries 13–14, 35–36, 75–76, 80, 82–84, 101–5, 107–8, 110–11, 113–14, 135, 137–40, 142–46, 196–97, 208–9, 232–33, 240, 254–55, 257–62, 263–66, 268–69; Bamiyan valley 105; complexes, caves in 85; complexes, expansion of stupa 12; Intwa as Maharaja Rudrasena Vihara 106; in Lakhisarai 146; living presence in 265–67; at Nagapattinam 125; Pala-period 257; at Pandrethan 136; at Shaikhan Dheri 228;

INDEX 373

Shakraditya by 250; sites of 64; Yashovarmapura 111, 258
monastic: community/*sanghabheda* 49, 91–92, 145, 231, 234; complexes 60–61, 74, 78, 103, 106; dead 4, 10, 73, 78–79, 201, 207; dissensions 49; donors 91, 224; dwellings 109, 233, 248, 260–61; indiscipline 51; order 7, 34, 36–37, 50, 176; reliance on laity 39; sites 56, 73–74, 76–77, 80, 82, 86, 109, 126, 168, 201, 226; structures 110, 234, 265
Mongolia 159, 181, 188, 288, 306
monk–laity distinctions 9–10
monks 3–5, 9–10, 33–41, 48–51, 89–92, 93–95, 110, 134–37, 142–45, 152–55, 169–70, 176–80, 192–97, 201, 218–19, 221–25, 228–29, 231–35, 263–66, 273–74; as *bhikshus* 24, 37; as image donors 223, 223–26; Nalanda 251, 264, 278; Narasimhagupta 250; and nuns 6, 10, 37–38, 44, 46, 49, 75, 90–91, 194, 204; reciting pratimokha/*patimokka* 37; Sariputra 33, 140; ten vows of 38; Tibetan 145, 154, 169, 274, 277–78; on uposatha-day 50; versha-vasa/*vassa-vasa* of 34
monumentalization, Buddhist faith 52, 58
monuments: brick or stone 81; of First Seven Weeks 14, 27, 172, 172–75
Morel Khurd 191, 196–97
'mortuary stupas' or kulas 179–80
Mother Goddess Mahadevi or Adi Parashakti 100
motifs 12, 52, 84, 87, 130, 148, 201, 203–4, 206, 237, 305
M. P. Birla Planetarium, Calcutta 211
Muchilinda, *naga* king 88, 168, 174
Muchilinda Lake (Lotus Pond) 172
Mukherjee, Ashutosh 294
Mulagandhakuti 101; chamber of the Buddha 101; at Sarnath 98; Vihara 101–2, 214, 293, 310
Mulakadeva 51
Mulasarvastivada school 241
multiple Buddhas 60, 67
Mundaka Upanishad 300
murals 148, 150–51, 219, 237–38, 242–45, 301; of Ajanta 244–45
Museum fur Indische Kunst (Berlin) 276
museumization 4
Museum of Fine Arts in Boston 169, 181
museums at Sanchi 191
Muslim invasions 170, 209
Muzaffarpur 56, 257
Myanmar 119, 121, 148, 154, 159, 174, 177, 182, 188, 309, 316; Thatta Thattaha Maha Bawdi Pagoda 182
mythology 5, 66, 83, 92, 95–96; of Mahayana 95–97

Nadsur caves 231
naga cult 88, 163
Nagapattinam 125, 133–34, 155
Nagaraja 231, 237, 268
Nagarjunakonda 5, 70, 72, 78–82, 85, 95, 112, 153, 306, 308, 313–14; monastic complex 80; stupa 85
Nagarjuna/Nagasena 62, 68, 80, 88, 249, 314
Nagarjuna Sagar dam 79, 314
nagas 71, 74, 78, 85, 87–89, 97–98, 163, 191, 194–95, 201, 204, 232, 236; sculptures 88, 195
Nagasena 5, 7, 62, 301
nagis 5, 71, 87–88, 97–98
Nakaiyalakar 133
Nalagiri 30
nalaka 249
Nalanda 4–5, 12–14, 95, 109–12, 118–19, 122, 141–43, 145, 148, 154, 170, 247–58, 260–62, 263–69, 271–

73, 275–77, 279, 301–2, 311–12, 316; Baragaon 257–58, 267, 269, 272, 274; decline of 13–14, 270, 276, 279; destruction of 276–77; Mahavihara as University 109, 262–65; monasteries 259–62; royal patronage 250; Site Museum 267, 276; outline of monastery complex 256; stupas 259–62; Temple of Sarai Mound 261; temples 259–62; *vihara* 147
Nalanda Archaeological Museum 258
Nalanda Mahavihara 14, 249, 254; outline of 253
Nalanda University 109, 280; Lhasa 279
Nandadirghi Vihara 146
Nandangarh, Lauriya 141
Nandas 47, 247
Narasimhagupta 95, 250
narrative panels 206
Nashik 83, 91–92, 287, 305
nationalism 217
National Museum in New Delhi 79, 258
nation-state 186, 298, 299–303
Nava Nalanda Mahavihara 279–80
Navayana (New Vehicle) 186, 304
Nehru, Jawaharlal 186, 216–17, 295, 299–303, 311, 317
neo-Buddhism 299, 303, 303–6
Nepal 9, 13, 21, 24, 32, 148, 154–55, 180–81, 302, 306, 309, 311, 316; Sanskrit texts of 9
Newar Buddhists 154
New Delhi 4, 6, 79, 115, 211, 258, 296, 310
Nichigai Suzan Horinji temple 310
nidanas 29
Nigali Sagar (or Niglihawa) 47, 53–54
Nigrodharama 35–37
Nikaya, Majjhima 159
nikayas 44, 135, 218, 222

Nipponzan Myohoji 310
nirvana/nibbana 10, 29, 43–44, 60, 66, 69, 258; statue 103
Northern Black Polished Ware (NBPW) 22
nuns (*bhikshunis*) 6, 9–10, 30, 37–38, 40, 44, 46, 49–50, 89–91, 194–95, 224, 227; ten vows of 38

Odantapura 111, 121, 142, 145, 274, 277–78; mahavihara 143; vihara, Bihar Sharif 277
Odisha 12, 100, 109, 111–12, 122, 127, 132, 138–41, 310, 312, 315, (*see also* Kalinga); Diamond Triangle of 138, 141
oral tradition 6–8, 28, 56, 124
orthodox tradition 66–68
Oshaji Vihara at Rajgir 296
Overseas Development Assistance (ODA) 309

Padmapani 71, 130, 132, 140, 169, 268
Padmapura-Nandivardhana-Pravarapura 221
Padmasambhava 119, 143, 306, 311
Pag Sam Jon Zang 121, 277
Paharpur 4–5, 134, 139, 142, 145, 168, 177, 179, 206, 251, 262, 270
Pahlavas 62
paintings 12–14, 84–85, 107–8, 114, 116–17, 134, 180, 183, 219, 221, 223, 236–45, 300–301; at Ajanta 12, 235–38, 243; on cloth in Nalanda 148; of Padmapani Avalokiteshvara 116, 228, 235; phases of execution 239; three-dimensionality 239; Tibetan cloth 180; Vajrapani 116
Palas 111, 122, 125, 127, 141–42, 145–48, 167–69, 170–72, 177, 250–51, 254, 260, 267, 269–70, 271, 278, 306, 309; architecture 142; art

142, 169, 267; Buddhism 271; (*see also* tantric Buddhism) decline of 170, 278
Pali 6–9, 23, 28–31, 36, 45, 66, 117, 140, 176, 279, 288–89; canonical texts 90; texts 7–8, 23, 31–32, 39, 289; texts of Sri Lanka 9
Pali Vinaya 194
Pallavas 112, 114, 123
palm leaves 140, 148; Bengali script on 155; paintings 148
Palur 112
pan-Asian Buddhist revivalism 184–86
Panchapandava Annapurna temple 172
panchayatana chaitya 171, 259
Panchika 98, 237, 270
Pandara 132
Pandavleni 84; caves at 85
Pandrethan 136–37
Pandyas 112, 114, 123
Paramartha 118
Parantapa 32
paribhogika dhatu ('relics of use') 45
parinirvana/*parinibbana* 28–30, 38, 41–42, 46–47, 52–53, 81–82, 176, 179, 186–87, 221–22, 235, 238–39, 243
parivrajakas 24, 34–35, 38–39
Parthians 62, 152, 228
Parvati 163, 268, 271–72; trinity of 100
Pataliputra 7, 23, 28, 31, 47, 91, 149, 192, 249; Third Buddhist Council in 51
Pathiar-Lakhamandal triangle 149
Patna Museum 148, 169, 258, 267, 269, 276
patronage 65, 90, 92, 95, 97, 103–4, 106–8, 112, 135, 137, 145, 153–54, 168, 170, 192–93, 221, 250–51; art 243; female 92; Mauryan 192; by rulers 250
patrons 89–92, 93, 95, 154, 178, 227, 296; Ajatashatru 32; Prasenjit 31

Pauni 66, 86
Pava 41, 57
Pavarikambavana, monastery 35
Pavurallakonda 80
Pawaya 87
peace pagoda (shanti stupa) 303, 310
'perfumed chambers' 10, 110, 234, 265–66
Periplus of the Erythraean Sea 64, 226–27
Persian 71, 149, 156
Peshawar 62, 75, 81, 90, 228; Museum 90
Phanigarhi, hilltop stupa complex 80
pilgrimages (*dharma yatra*) 47, 52, 52–56, 58, 81, 175–76, 178, 181–82, 205–6, 269, 273; Buddha on 55; sites 80, 89, 106, 127, 162, 176–80, 188
pilgrims 95, 113, 141–42, 154, 159, 168, 175–78, 195, 227, 309, 313
pillars 49, 52–56, 83–84, 87, 89, 98, 101–2, 130–31, 165–66, 191–92, 195–96, 202–8, 231–32, 235, 237; colossal Mauryan 58; with elephant capital 55; memorial 81–82; memorialization 55; monolithic 54, 195; Nigali Sagar 54; railing 32, 79, 101, 166, 194; Sankissa 55
pipal tree (*ficus religiosa*) 26–27, 72, 160–61
Pippala monastery, Taxila 76
Pitalkhora 83, 89, 117, 228, 231
Pliny the Elder 64
Polo, Marco 286
ports 22–23, 33, 63–64, 82, 94, 119, 124–25, 226–27, 286; Baruch 227; Chaul 226; Elephanta 226; Kalyan 227; Sopara 226–27
Potana/Potali (modern Bodhan) 20, 34
Potaniha 77
Prabhakaramitra 273

Prabhamitra 263
pradakshinapatha 102, 200
prajnaparamitas 100, 128, 270
Prajnaparamita Sutra 88, 129
Prasad, Rajendra 302
Prasenjit 31, 89
Pratishthana (modern-day Paithan in Maharashtra) 23, 31, 34, 63
pratityasamutpada/paticca-samuppada 29, 176
Pratityasamutpada Sutra 138, 140–41, 176
Pravarasena 221
Pravarasena II 137
Prinsep, James 47, 242–43, 291
Priyadarsi, King 54
proselytization 52, 197
Pubbarama 31
Puhar 113
punya (merit) 19, 39
Punyatrata 118
Puragupta 250
Purang-Guge kingdom 150
Puranic Hinduism 152, 154
purificatory baths 161–62
Purnavarman 261
Purushapura 62
Pushpagiri 112, 140
Pushyabhutis 122
Pushyamitra 200

Qarashahr 64
Qutb mosque, Delhi 210

Rahula 30
Rajagriha. *See* Rajgir
Raja monastery, Parihaspur 137
Rajaraja I, Chola kings 133
Rajatarangini, Kalhana 137
Rajayatana tree 174
Rajgir (earlier Rajagriha) 7, 19, 22–23, 28, 30–32, 35–37, 40, 47, 57, 60, 83, 88, 247–48, 258, 275, 296, 310–11,
316; Magadha capital 44; *shresthin* of 19, 23, 35, 36, 39, 40, 60; Venuvana/Veluvana in 32, 248
Rakshita 51
Ramagrama 57
Ramanujacharya 124
Ramarao, N. T. 313
Ramayana 261, 268
Ranigat 104
Rashtrakutas 123, 135, 241
Rasmivimala 128, 139
Rathod, Rakesh 245
Ratnachankrama 173
Ratnaghar chaitya 174
Ratnagiri 4–5, 126, 132, 134, 138–41, 154, 179, 206
Ratnagupta monastery, Anupamapura 137
Ratnarashmi monastery, Anupamapura 137
Ratnasambhava 125, 139, 151
Ratnodadhi temple 278
rebirth 5, 29, 39, 176, 179, 262, 285, *see also* death; salvation
reformers 286, 292
regional identities 122–25
relics 10, 43–47, 56, 58, 61, 73, 75–76, 86, 88, 190–91, 196–97, 201, 210, 212–17, 302–3; caskets 51, 56, 76, 78, 81, 88, 210, 212–13; consecration 73; corporeal 45; cult 10, 61, 194, 197; from England 212; and hilltop stupas 197–98; of Sariputra 46, 212; 'war of relics' 46
reliefs: art 85–87; kinds of narration 84, 86, 114, 205; sculptural 70, 77, 85–88
religious: mutations 122–25; traditions 71, 90, 92, 151, 259, 271, 275, 281, 288; traditions, demigods in 87
replicas 6, 80, 166, 170, 180–82, 212, 304–5, 309, 314
representations 70, 76–77, 87, 89, 126,

130, 132, 138, 180–82, 204, 209–10, 268–69, 272; sculptural 114, 129, 131, 180–81, 292
revolution 287, 299
Rhys Davids, T. W. 289
Rigon Thubten Mindolling monastery, Chandragiri 312
Rinpoche, Lama 279
Rishi, Lomas 58
ritualization 197; in Mahayana 125–29; in Vajrayana Buddhism 125–29
rituals 2–5, 9, 24, 28, 38, 40–41, 123, 128–29, 135, 138, 140, 162, 271; Brahmanical 24, 40–41; Hindu funerary 160; tantric 99; Vedic sacrificial 123
rock carvings: Gondala 149; Kardang 149
rock-cut: activity 130; beds and pillows 84; elephant at Dhauli 112; excavations 79; monastic centres 82; shelters 106; shrines 14; stone ribs 231; stupas 74, 112
rock-cut caves 13, 82, 226–27, 229, 234, 287, 305; excavation of 83; in Koteshwar 106; Talaja 106
rock edicts 52, 56; Girnar hills 105
Roman Empire 63–64
Roman gold 64
Romanticism movement 183
Royal Asiatic Society 243, 275
Royal Cave Temple Commission 243
royals 55, 91, 145; patronage 90, 94–95, 113, 123, 135, 250–51, 270, 278, *see also* gifts; donations; patronage
Rudrasena, Saka Kshatrapa 106
Rudrasena III, King 106
ruins 252, 288–90, 294; Amravati site 79, 308; Basarh village 32; Deccan 130; Gangetic plains 151; Kushinagar 103; Bodh Gaya 183–84; Nalan 247, 257, 274, 281; of Samye 143; Sanchi 201; stupa-monasteries complexes 75
Rukeyser, Muriel 245
Rukmini-Harana-Sthana temple 258, 269, 272

Sacred: sites 53, 87, 101, 103, 160, 163, 172, 178, 187; space 187, 271–742, 279, 303; trees 87
sacrifices 24, 28, 40, 123, 271, 278, 289
Saddharmapundarika (The Lotus of the Good Law) 67
Saddharmapundarika Sutra 228
Sadhanamala 128, 132, 141
Sahadeva 51
Sahri-Bahlol 104
Sakala (modern-day Sialkot) 62
sakyabhikshus 218, 224
Sakya Buddhist Society 295
Sakyamuni Buddha 54, 60
Salban vihara 147; in Mainamati 147
sal trees 25, 42
salvation 29, 60, 66–68, 96, 126, 241; Brahmans for 40
Samatata 147
Sambodhi 52–53, 160
Sammatiya 102, 107, 222
Samye monastery 143
Sanchi 4–6, 13–14, 49, 51, 55–56, 73–74, 76–79, 85, 88–92, 105, 111, 165, 191–94, 196, 200, 202, 204–6, 209, 212, 214, 216, 290; architraves 202–6; Ashokan connection 195–96; Buddhist monuments in 193; chunar sandstone Pillar 206; edit 50; gateways 203–6; Great Stupa/ *mahastupa* complex 165, 8, 57, 191–92, 197, 210, 212, 304; hilltop complex 191, 193, 195–96, 198, 199; irrigation around 196; *Khamba Baba* (Pillar Saint) 192; monastic landscape 105; monuments at 198; motifs 203–6; narrative panels 203–6; relics 13, 214; temple at 208

Sanchi–Satdhara relics to Burma 302
sanctuaries 76, 102, 104, 233; conceptualization of 232
sanctum 132, 139, 171–73, 184, 208, 270
Sangam poems 64
sangha 30, 32–41, 48, 50–51, 57–58, 61, 65, 68–69, 74–75, 87, 89, 152, 154, 193–94, 317; donation to 35; unity of 49
Sanghamitra 301
sangharamas 35, 107
Sanghol (now Punjab) 76, 88, 149, 326n
Sankaram 80, 133
Sankissa (now Sankisa Basantapura, UP) 30, 55, 129, 310
Sankrityayan, Rahul 297
sapta ratna (seven treasures) 96
Saraswati 100, 271–72
Sariputra 38, 40, 46, 78, 155, 176, 210, 212–13, 215, 217, 249; death of 249; monk 33; relics and caskets 213
saririka dhatu (body parts of Buddha) 45
Sarnath 49, 51–53, 55–56, 93, 100–103, 114–16, 128–29, 141–42, 214, 223–24, 234–35, 267, 290–91, 293, 296, 310–11, 316; ascendancy of 114–17; Buddha standing images of 116; edit 50; first sermon in 30; Nichigai Suzan Horinji temple / Japanese temple 161; monasteries 260; museum 115, 129; names of 28; school of art 115
Sarnath Lion Capital 300
Sarvastivada Buddhism of Kashmir 102, 137, 222
Sarvastivada Vinaya 118, 137, 222, 241
Sasanians 228
Satadru 149
Satakarnis 202

Satavahanas 5, 13, 62–63, 74, 78–79, 84, 90, 94, 192, 107–8, 202–3, 221, 226
Satdhara 76, 78, 191, 196–97, 212–14
Satyameva Jayate (Truth alone Triumphs) 300
Saward, Dorothy 213
Sayadaw, Kyithe Layhtap 175
Sayanasanavastu 234
schisms 68, 195
Schlingloff, Dieter 245
sculptures 1–5, 10, 12–14, 71, 78–79, 83–85, 87–88, 104, 106–8, 114, 130–32, 180, 184, 191, 194–95, 205, 208–9, 219, 267–68, 274–75; at Ajanta 12, 235–37; Amravati 79; Amravati Marbles 79; at Bharhut 76; bronze 148, 258, 260, 267; clay 151; depiction 74, 86; efflorescence 12, 114–17, 167; of mahaviharas 274–76; Pala bronze 148; Pala-Sena 147; Pala times 148; panels 89, 92, 162, 197, 238; school of 147; trans-Meghna region 147; Vishnu 163
Scythians 62
sealings 181, 266
seated image of Buddha: in Rukmini-Harana-Sthana temple 258; Sarnath Museum 115
Second Buddhist Council 48
sects 3, 44, 51, 58, 65, 69, 124, 151–52, 218, 223, 227; Aparamahavinaseliya 80
Sengge, Rongston 279
sermon of enlightened, first 28–29
settlements 20–23, 31, 34–37, 43, 81, 185, 193, 226, 248, 257, 306–7; in Sannati 79
sexual: rites 99, 271; symbolism 127
Shah, Sultan Nasiruddin Mahmud 277
Shahi dynasties 123
Shahji-ki-Dheri stupa, Peshawar 90
Shaikan Dheri 115

Shaivism 14, 97, 271; in Kashmir 137
Shaivites 97, 99, 162–63
Shaka-Kshatrapas 62, 90, 202
Shakas 62–63, 71, 84, 152
Shakraditya 250
shakti 93, 97, 120, 127; cult 97, 99, 271
Shakyamuni 25, 103
Shakyas 21, 25, 31–32, 39, 160
shalabhanjikas (women holding tree branches) 88, 204
Shamlaji Museum 106
Shankaracharya 124, 152, 182
Shantarakshita 119, 143, 263, 274, 306
Shantideva 68, 125
shanti stupas (peace pagodas) 303, 310
Shashanka 122, 167
Shelarwadi cave 82, 84
Shiva/Shaiva 93, 99, 101, 133–34, 162–63, 166, 170, 268, 271–72; cults 99; lingas 155, 163, 172; mahants 166, 178, 182; his wife Uma 99; worshipping 134, 166, *see also* Shaivism
shraddha (ancestors ritual) 162
shramanas 24
Shravasti (present-day Saheth–Maheth) 22, 30–34, 40, 47, 63, 114, 248–49, 265, 301, 310, 316; monks settlements at 31
shresthins 23, 39; of Rajagriha 60
shrine chamber. *See gandhakutis*
shrines (chaityas) 13–14, 41, 55–56, 73–74, 76, 80–81, 83–85, 87, 97–98, 102, 104, 106–8, 130–31, 137–40, 144–45, 171–72, 174, 207–8, 230–36, 239–40; arches 76, 84; caves 74, 106, 230–31; conceptualization of 232; cross-shaped brick stupa 144; cum-viharas 234, 265; horseshoe-shaped 85; miniature 76
Shungas 8, 13, 61, 74, 78, 129, 165–66, 192, 200–1, 207–8
Shwedagon Pagoda, Yangon 174, 215

Shyama Tara 127
Siam (Thailand). *See* Thailand
Siddhartha/Siddhartha Gautama 4, 24, 159–62; birth of 25; as Buddha 24–27; enlightenment ('Great Departure') 86, 160–62; Gautama gotra 25; marrying Yashodhara 25; seeing signs of 25–26; wandering of 26
Sigrabuddha 263
Sikkim 127, 216
Silabhadra 225, 263
Silappadikaram 112
Silk Route 63, 90, 94, 104, 149, 229, 286, 309
Sindh 134–36, 206
Singh, Jagat 102
Singh, Rajdeo 245
Sinhalese monks 167, 175
Sirkap 75
Sirmour 149
Sirpur 107, 126, 132
Sirsukh 75
Skandagupta 250
Smith, John. Maj. 241–42
social: ethics 28–29; life 41, 144, 270
Solomon, Gladstone 242
Somapura Mahavihara Somapura Mahavihara/Paharpur 142–45, 168–69, 177, 251, 257, 270, 274, 278
Sona 51
Sonari 76, 78, 191, 196–97, 201, 207
Song dynasty 178
Sopara 134, 226–27
Southeast Asia 63–64, 68, 94, 117, 119–20, 121, 125, 142, 147–48, 151, 154–56, 180, 273, 286, 312–14, 315
South Kensington Museum 211, 213–14; United Kingdom 210
South Korea 188, 309, 315–16
Spink, Walter M. 108, 222, 245
spiritual: pursuits 9, 194, 219; tourism 313, 318

Spiti valley 126, 132, 150, 155
SPS Museum, Srinagar 137
Sribhadra, Sakya 121
Sri Lanka 43, 45–46, 51–52, 66–68, 111–12, 117–18, 187–88, 193, 196, 301–3, 309, 311–12, 315–16; monks 177; Pali texts 9; Ratnadvipa 64
Srimaddharma Vihara 146
Srivijaya dynasty 119, 125, 133, 146, 273
Stanislas 275
state formations 61–63, 74, 94, 226
statue 75, 133, 137, 163, 171, 174, 207, 231, 240, 280, 293, 312–14; Avukana Buddha 32, 314; black stone 169, 171; colossal 131, 140, 236, 261, 269, 271; of standing Buddha 70–71, 90, 102, 115–16, 171, 177, 184, 315; Taliban destruction of 104; reclining Buddha 317, 361
Teliya Buddha 267
Sthavira 222
Sthaviravadins 44, 137
Sthiramati 68, 263
stone 71, 74, 81, 85, 89, 109, 111, 179–81, 258, 261, 267–71; images 14, 70, 140, 168–69, 176, 261, 267–68; pillars 259
stories 3, 5, 7, 9, 27, 86, 152, 174–75, 196–97, 204–5, 210, 217, 235–36, 238–40, 258–59; of Bavari 33; of eight drona stupas 56; 'Great Monkey Jataka' 205; of relics 214; Simhala 236, 240; of voyages 64
Straits of Malacca 119
stucco 71, 104, 109, 111, 247, 254, 261, 267–71
stupa complex 55, 73–76, 80, 92, 105, 146, 190–92, 210, 308; Amravati 57; Central Indian Stupas 76–78; Chir Tope 76; Eastern Deccan Gandhara 78–82; Gandhara 75;

Sanchi 13; Western Deccan 82–85
stupas/'thupa,' 5–6, 45–47, 72–74, 77–78, 80, 83–91, 102–3, 105–8, 136–40, 149–53, 190–91, 194–98, 200–204, 206–10, 212–13, 230–34, 261–62, 290–92; Amravati 79, 81, 210, 290, 314; at Bharhut 32; brick 58, 73, 79, 111, 259, 261; of Central India 78; cult 73, 90, 140, 194, 231; as 'dagaba' in Sri Lanka 45; decorative sculptures on 114; Dhamekh 57, 101–2; *dharani* 138–40; Dharmarajikas 57, 76, 81, 101–2, 118, 206, 233; at Diamond Triangle 140; Drona 46; festivals 73–44, 88; funeral mounds 46; at Hukalitar 136; across Jambudvipa 56; in Kanaganahalli 58; of Konakamana 53–54; maha 105; mandala 139–40; Manikyala 290; in Mathura 213; of mud 57, 73; original eight 45, 57; parts of stupa 198–206; Ramagrama 57, 88; rock-cut 74, 112; at Sanchi 85; Sariputra's 'Great Monument' 252; in Sarnath 57; sites of 64; across subcontinent 56–59; symbol of Buddhist dhamma 58; in Taxila 57; two-level terraced 161; at Udayagiri 138; Vaishali 57; at Vethavutur 136; votive 1, 4, 14, 78, 139, 144, 179, 247, 259, 262, 269; worship 73–74, 128, 204; *Ye Dharma* verse in 140
Subhadra 103
Subhakarasimha 142, 273
Sudama caves 83
Sudarshana 106
Sudhodhana 24–26
Sujata 26–27, 161–62
Sukhavativyuha (glories of Amitabha and his paradise) 67
Sumatra 4, 119, 251, 258, 273

Sunga period 101
Surajpur 257–58
Surendra, King 136
Surya 163, 166, 272
Surya temple, Baragaon 272
Sutta Pitaka (collection of sermons) 44, 51, 67, 159
Suvarnadipa 125
Suvishnu 249
Swat Valley 70, 104, 143
symbols and emblems 12, 46, 58, 79, 81, 86–87, 108, 126, 205, 211, 221, 300–301, 314

Tabaqat-i Nasiri 276
Tabo Monastery/Golden Temple Ladakh 138, 148–51, 274
Tagore, Abanindranath 244, 295–96
Tagore, Rabindranath 244, 295–96
Takht-i-Bahi 75, 104
Tamil Nadu 12, 80, 100, 109, 112–14, 133–34, 155, 287
Tamralipti (present-day Tamluk in Midnapore district) 23, 119, 149
Tang dynasty 177
tantric or Vajrayana Buddhism 93–94, 98–99, 117, 126–28, 132, 142–43, 148, 271, 273; Shaiva–Shakti concept and 272; text 155
tantrism: mandalas or chakras 81, 99, 126, 141, 144, 271; and Shakti 99; *yantras* 12, 97–100, 120, 127–28
Tara 99–100, 114, 117, 126–28, 130–33, 138, 141, 145, 147, 150, 155–56, 268, 270–71; eight armed 155; forms of 272; names of 127; tantric deity 141, 146; temple 127, 164, 169, 173
Taranatha 142, 249, 263, 271, 277
Tarapith temple 127
Tarikh-ul-Hind, Al-Biruni 136
Tashkend 64
Tathagata Gupta 25, 250

Taxila 20, 22, 57, 75–76, 81, 103–4, 107, 118, 149, 206, 233–34; Ashoka as governor of 75
Taylor, General 209, 290
teachers 10, 24, 33, 80, 90, 187, 190, 224–25, 262, 264–65, 274
teachings of Buddha 6, 8, 28–29, 31, 35, 40–41, 43–44, 48–49, 112, 136, 288; 'doctrine of elders' 51
Telangana 81, 312, 314–15
Telhara/Tiladhaka 111, 142, 258
Teliya Baba 267, 272
Teliya Bhandar Bhairav Mandir, Baragaon 258
temples 98, 101–2, 105, 133–34, 155, 159–60, 165–67, 169–70, 171–73, 182–89, 202–4, 206–9, 247–50, 254–55, 257, 259–62, 267–70, 303, 306–7, 311–13; apsidal 76; by Ashoka 53, 165; at Baragaon 272; by Birlas 312; enshrinement 72; with Gana and Yamuna images 105; Horinji/Nihonji 161; Maitreya 150; Mahabodhi temple complex 6; with murals 150; at Nalanda 110; Sanskrit use in 123; Shaivite connection 162; of Tara 145; Tsuglakhang 151; Vishnu sculptures in 163
Tenasserim, Malaysia 119
terracotta: plaques 140–41, 144; sealings 181; tablets 176
Thailand 68, 119, 147, 151, 154, 159, 179, 181–82, 187–88, 302–3, 309, 316
Thareli 104
Theosophical Society 295
Theravada 51, 89, 113, 117, 119, 151, 172, 175–76, 183; 'doctrine of elders' 51
Third Buddhist Council 51, 137, 196
Thotlakonda monastery complex 79–80, 111, 255

three mudras 130
Tibet 119, 121, 125, 127, 143, 145, 148–51, 154–55, 177–78, 180–81, 270, 273, 279, 302–3, 306; Chinese occupation of 186; Kalachakra ceremonies 187; lama system in 143; rise of 271–74; Samye (Bsam-Yas) in 143
Tibetan: Buddhism 128, 149–50, 170, 178, 186, 249, 274, 278, 306–8, 311–12, 317; Buddhist pilgrimage map 178; Buddhist tradition 100, 128, 140, 181; cloth paintings 180; refugees 299, 306–7, 312, 317
Tilaurakot, in Nepal 24
Tilokarat, King 178
Tin, U Han 174
Tirtha Chintamani 162
tirthankaras, cult of 72, 98
Tissa, Devanampriya/Devanampiya 43, 52, 117
Tosali 112
tourism 186, 188, 312–18; international Buddhist 300
trade 5, 22–23, 33, 63–65, 74, 82, 94, 107, 119, 122–25, 226–29; links 65, 125, 226; routes 33, 65, 75, 106, 149–50, 226–29, 286, *see also* Silk Route
traders 1, 23–24, 40, 65, 89, 92, 116, 131, 154, 226–28, 237; Bahalika 40, 174; Trapusa 40
Traikutaka Vihara 146
Trang, Thailand 119
transnational Buddhist networks 300, 317
Trapusa/Tapussa 40, 174
travellers 176–80
trayastrimsa/tavatimsa Buddhist heaven 30, 56, 227, 230
tree 26–27, 41, 86–88, 160–61, 163, 166–67, 173, 313; worship 210
Trigarta 123, 149

trikaya 96, 113, 141
Trilokavijaya 272
Tripitaka/Tipitaka 7, 28, 37
Tripurantaka 134
triratna (Buddha, dharma and sangha/three jewels) 37–38, 43–44, 49, 106, 165, 200, 204, 304
Triratna Buddha Vihara, Mumbai 306
Tulja 83
Turfan 64
Turkish Shahiya 123
Turks/Turushkas 121–22, 152–54, 170, 278; attacks 137, 152, 154, 278; depredations in eastern India 170

Udayagiri Mahastupa 138–41
uddesika dhatu 46
Uddiyana (now in Swat Valley) 143
Ugra Tara 127
Ujjayini/ (present-day Ujjain) 20, 22, 31, 33–34, 55, 196, 202, 227
Uma-Maheshwara (Shiva-Parvati) 99, 163, 169, 173, 272
UNESCO/Japan Funds-in-Trusts for the Preservation of World Cultural Heritage 310
UNESCO World Heritage Sites: Ajanta 218–46; Anuradhapura 117; Bodh Gaya 187, 280; Nalanda 109, 251–52; Somapura 12, 143; Taxila 75; Sanchi 190–217
Upagupta 48
Upali 7, 32, 39, 44
Uparkot Fort, cave at 106
upasakas/upasikas (followers) 37, 48–50
upavasatha/uposatha 37–38
Uposatha-ceremony 50
Urasaka 76
urbanization 21–24, 74, 118
Uruvela village (present-day Bodh Gaya) 26, 30, 52, 160–62
Usnisavijaya 132
Utpala 123

Uttara 51
Uttarapatha 22–23, 63

Vadnagar 107; monastic complexes in 106
Vainyagupta 250
Vairochana 125, 151
Vaishali 7, 22–23, 26, 28, 30–35, 41, 44, 56, 57, 124, 129
Vaishnavism 14, 97, 124, 134, 162–63, 192
Vajjian monks 33
Vajrabodhi 142, 273
Vajrachedika (Diamond-cutter) 67
Vajradhatu-ishvari 132
Vajrapani 67, 72, 116, 131–33, 140, 149, 169, 206, 232, 235, 268
Vajrasana (diamond throne/Adamantine Seat), Bodh Gaya 13–14, 52, 58, 101, 163, 165, 167, 172, 266; gandhakuti 167; links with Shaivism 14
Vajrasattva 208–9, 268
Vajrasuchi 285–86
Vajra Varahi 169
Vajrayana (esoteric) 12, 14, 99–100, 122, 127, 131, 138–39, 142, 264, 271, 274; influence 117, 140, 146; pantheon 127; ritualization and expansion in 125–29; school 120, 129, 208; texts 274; traditions 13, 125, 142, 151, 155–56, 169, 209, 267, 271, 278, 306
Vakataka, caves 108
Vakataka dynasty 5, 12–13, 94–95, 108, 122, 221–22, 241
Valisinha, D 304
Vallabhi 125, 129, 135, 141, 234, 265
Vamgisa monk 33
Vanaratna 155
vanijjas 23, 40
Vanji 113
varada mudra 171

Varahadeva 222
Varanasi 28, 56, 62, 124, 214, 234, 316
Varendra Research Museum (Bangladesh) 276
varnas 24, 40. *See* caste system
Vastiputrika 102
Vasubandhu 68, 95, 249–50
Vasumitra 62
Vatsagulma 221–22
Vatsas or Vamsas 20, 22, 32
Vattagamini, King 7
Vedic: age 20; Brahmanism 100, 113; polities 20
veneration 47, 58, 73, 83, 167, 178, 187, 268
Venuvana/Veluvana 36, 37, 39, 41, 281, 358
Vethadipa 57
Victoria and Albert Museum in London 181, 210, 213, 215–16, 243, 302
Vidisa/Vidisha 34, 55, 77, 191–93, 196, 203
vidyadharas 97, 131, 236, 247
Vietnam 159, 187–88, 303, 309, 316
viharas (monasteries) 13, 36–37, 39, 80–81, 83–84, 93, 106–7, 109, 136–37, 217, 219, 234, 247–48, 254, 262; traditional 109, 262, *see also* mahaviharas
Vijayapuri 80, 313–14
Vikramaditya 95, 250
Vikramashila *mahavihara* 121, 142, 144–45, 168, 251, 257, 270–72, 274, 278–79
Vimalosnisa 128, 139
Vinaya Pitaka 'Rules of Monastic Order' 7, 34, 37, 44, 51, 176, 234, 241
Vindhya mountains 33, 77
Vipulashrimitra 145
virtual pilgrimage 4, 180–82
Viryendra 169

Vishakula 207
Vishnu 93, 98, 134, 209, 259, 268, 272, 287, 293
Vishnupad temple, Gaya 189
Vishnu–Surya–Lakulisa 163
vishvakarma 131
Visuddhimagga (Path of Purification) 117
Vivekananda, Swami 292
votive stupas 80
Vrijjis/Vajjis 20–21, 39
vyakhyana mudra 130

Wangchen, Dukor 307
Wardha 310
water 87, 89, 129, 193–95, 228, 230, 255
Wat Khuhaphimuk in Yala 147
Wat Thai 349
Wei dynasty 118
West Bengal 23, 115, 127, 141–48, 168, 250, 274, 277, 310
Western Deccan 74, 82–83, 92, 116, 130, 132, 226–27, 287
Western Ghats 82, 84, 229; caves of 84, 231
Western Himalayas 12, 126, 128–29, 132, 136, 148–51, 274
wheel 5, 28–29, 46, 55, 86–87, 101, 115, 205–6, 221, 300
White Horse Monastery at Luoyang 64
White Temple (Nuns' Temple) 150
Wilkinson, Lancelot 286
women 30, 41, 88, 152, 201, 204, 224, 227, 238
World Heritage Sites 151, 160, 188–89, 219, 312; Nalanda 248; Sanchi hilltop complex 191
worship 43, 46, 60, 65, 69, 93, 96–99, 125–28, 187, 192, 194, 215, 288–89; of gods in 123; of images 46; of multiple Buddhas 60; in sculptural reliefs 87; of serpent 210; of symbols 46; Tara 100; of tree 161, 210

Xuanzang/ Hiuen Tsang (Chinese pilgrim/traveler) 53, 56, 101–3, 105, 107, 109–11, 113, 122, 135, 137, 140, 167, 172, 241, 248–52, 260–61, 263–64, 273, 275, 280
Xuanzang Memorial Museum 311

yakshas 74, 78, 85, 87, 98, 161, 163, 191, 194, 201, 204, 233, 236
Yakshi Hariti 98
yakshis 5, 71, 85, 87, 97–98, 163, 166, 194, 201, 204, 236
Yamantaka 169
Yamuna 105, 208
Yarkand 64
Yashodhara 25–26
Yashovarmadeva, King 247, 250, 265
Yavana Dharmarakshita to Aparantaka 51
yavanas (Greek) 51, 62, 83, 92; Sangam poems on 64
ye dharma (ye dhamma) verse 157, 164, 201, 206, 340
Yeshe, Lama Thubten 279
Yijing/I-tsing 111, 177, 251, 254, 260, 263–64, 273
Yogachara (way of union) 68, 72, 95, 249
yoga tantra 139
Yuezhi (Yueh-chih) 62
Yunan 62

Zangpo, Rinchen 150
Zanskar 150

ALSO BY SHASHANK SHEKHAR SINHA